by Frances Mossiker

NAPOLEON AND JOSEPHINE

THE QUEEN'S NECKLACE

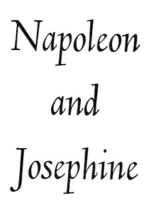

Napoleon
and
Josephine

THE BIOGRAPHY OF A MARRIAGE

BY

FRANCES MOSSIKER

SIMON AND SCHUSTER · NEW YORK · 1964

Second Printing

LIBRARY OF CONGRESS CATALOG CARD NUMBER: 64–12483
MANUFACTURED IN THE UNITED STATES OF AMERICA
BY H. WOLFF, INC., NEW YORK, N. Y.
DESIGNED BY EVE METZ

For Robert Gottlieb

ACKNOWLEDGMENTS

My first expression of gratitude is directed to Mr. Douglas Schneider, cultural attaché of the American Embassy in Paris, and to Madame Anne-Marie Degory, special assistant to the attaché, who have, in the course of recent years, facilitated and expedited my research in the libraries, archives and museums of France. I owe thanks to the staff of the Bibliothèque Nationale of Paris: to Madame Janine Roncato, archiviste paléographe and bibliothécaire; to Mademoiselle Nicole Villa, conservateur, Cabinet des Estampes; to Mademoiselle Chabrier of the Service Photographique. And at the Musée du Louvre, to Madame Guinet of the Service Documentation Photographique. At the Château de Malmaison M. Pierre Schommer, directeur en chef, and M. Yvan David, adjoint au directeur en chef, opened to me the treasury of the museum and of their own vast personal fund of knowledge. I am grateful to them for enlightening hours and days in Josephine's house. For entree to Josephine's pleasure pavilion on the site of Malmaison's storied hothouses, which is today a storehouse of Consulate and Empire memorabilia, I am indebted to M. and Madame Stefan Czarnecki, owners of La Petite Malmaison; as I am to the Bibliothèque Thiers for access to the precious Fonds Masson. In London, at the British Museum, facilities for research were courteously extended to me by the staffs of the Reading Room, the Department of Engravings and the Photograph Service. At the Dallas Public Library, Mrs. Lillian Bradshaw, the director, and Mr. George Mitchell, the reference librarian, gave me invaluable assistance in locating and procuring rare books requisite to the research on this one. I thank them for their time and services so generously expended in my behalf, as I thank those city and university libraries across the United States which co-operate so generously in the interlibrary loan system. Here, too, I express my gratitude to Dr. Martin S. Buehler of Dallas for his application of modern medical diagnostic techniques to the case history of the Empress Josephine and to the autopsy and medical reports issued by the attending physicians during her fatal illness and after her death in May of 1814. Nor am I unmindful of the specialized scholarly vigilance exercised over this manuscript by Mrs. Vera Schneider.

Contents

Illustrations

BOOK ONE

Napoleon in Love with Josephine

I

The Italian Letters

To live through Josephine—that is the story of my life.
LETTER FROM NAPOLEON TO JOSEPHINE, APRIL 3, 1796

He's funny . . . Bonaparte.
JOSEPHINE TO A FRIEND, SPRING OF 1796

1

To the Citizeness Beauharnais
No. 6 Rue Chantereine, Paris

> From Chanceaux*
> 24 Ventôse, An IV
> [March 14, 1796]

Every moment increases the distance between us, my dearest, and with every moment that passes I feel myself less able to endure the separation. You are the eternal object of my thoughts. My imagination exhausts itself wondering what you are doing. If I picture you as sad, my heart is racked and my distress acute. Yet if I picture you as gay and giddy among your friends, then I reproach

* A commune some 150 miles southeast of Paris, on Napoleon's route to Nice.

you for having so soon forgotten our cruel parting three days ago. In that case, you are frivolous, superficial, incapable of profound emotion. As you see, I am difficult to please, but on the other hand, my darling, it is altogether a different matter if the fear assails me that your health may be affected or that you may be troubled by causes I cannot divine. Then I resent the haste with which my orders tore me away from you who are my very heart. Then the realization is borne in upon me that I face an existence no longer imbued with your sweetness and dearness. Then, too, I realize that only in the certainty of your well-being can I know peace of mind.

If anyone asks me whether I have slept well, I find that I cannot answer the question until I have had a message assuring me that you have spent a restful night. I am impervious to all the ills, all the furies of humanity, save only to the extent that they might threaten you, my beloved. If only the star which has been my safeguard in the midst of direst perils would transfer its protection to you instead, then would I gladly confront fate vulnerable, unshielded. Ah, be not gay, but slightly melancholy; but, above all, may your spirit be as free of care as your beautiful body is free of malady. . . .

Write to me, my dearest, and at length. Here, for you, are a thousand and one kisses of truest, tenderest love.

BUONAPARTE

To Citizeness Bonaparte
In care of Citizeness Beauharnais
No. 6 Rue Chantereine, Paris

Nice
10 Germinal, An IV
[March 30, 1796]

Not one day has passed that I have not loved you, not one night that I have not clasped you in my arms. I have not drunk so much as a cup of tea without cursing the call of glory and ambition which have wrenched me from you who are my life, my soul. In the midst of military affairs, at the head of my troops, in my inspections of the camps, my adorable Josephine holds undisputed sway over my heart, possesses my mind, engrosses my thoughts. If

I travel away from you with the swiftness of the torrent of the River Rhone, it is only in order to see you again the sooner. If, in the middle of the night, I arise from my bed to work, it is only because I may thus advance by some few hours the moment of the arrival of my beloved.

And yet, in your letter dated 23-26 Ventôse [March 13-16], you address me formally as "you" [vous]. "You" thyself! Ah, wicked one, how could you have written that letter? How cold it is! And besides, begun on the thirteenth, not completed until the sixteenth: a lapse of four whole days. What were you doing all that time that you could not finish a letter to your husband? Oh, my darling, that formal "you" instead of the familiar "thou," those four lapsed days, make me rue my formerly indifferent heart. . . . "You"! "You"! Ah, what will it be two weeks from now?

My soul is saddened, my heart enslaved, my imagination frightens me: You love me less; you will find consolation elsewhere; someday you will cease loving me. Then tell me so. I should at least know how I have merited the misfortune . . .

I ask of you neither eternal love nor fidelity, but only truth, utter honesty. The day upon which you should say "I love you less" would be the last day of my love—or the last day of my life. Were my heart so base as to love unrequited, I would gnash it between my teeth . . .

Ah, Josephine! Remember what I have told you before: Nature created my soul strong and resolute, yours she wrought out of gossamer and lace.

Have you left off loving me? Forgive me, light of my life; my mind must encompass projects vast in scope, but my heart is given over utterly to you, and it is assailed by fears which make me wretched.

Adieu! Ah, if you love me less, it can only be that you have never loved me. Then I should become indeed an object of pity.

BONAPARTE

P.S. The war, this year, is no longer recognizable. I have ordered the issuance of meat, bread and forage to my troops. My armed cavalry will soon be on the move. My soldiers manifest an inexpressible confidence in me. You alone cause me anxiety. You

alone, the delight and the torment of my life. A kiss for your children—whom you do not even mention. But that, pardi! would cost
you the writing of a letter half as long again. And that would mean
that all those visitors arriving at ten o'clock to pay their morning
call would be deprived of the pleasure of your company! Woman!!!

To Citizeness Bonaparte
In care of Citizeness Beauharnais
No. 6 Rue Chantereine, Paris

> Porto Maurizio*
> 14 Germinal
> [April 3]

I have received all of your letters, but none has had such an effect upon me as the last. Do you have any idea, darling, what you
are doing, writing to me in those terms? Do you not think my situation cruel enough without intensifying my longing for you, overwhelming my soul? What a style! What emotions you evoke! Written in fire, they burn my poor heart!
   . . . You are the one thought of my life. When I am concerned
by the pressure of military affairs, when I am anxious as to the outcome of battle, when men disgust me, when I am ready to curse
life, then I put my hand to my heart, for it beats against your portrait . . .
   By what magic have you captivated all my faculties, concentrated in yourself all my conscious existence? It constitutes a kind
of death, my sweet, since there is no survival for me except in you.
To live through Josephine—that is the story of my life. My every
action is designed to the sole purpose of reunion with you. I am
driving myself to death to reach you again. Madman that I am, I
fail to perceive that I am constantly moving farther away from you.
   How many lands, how many frontiers, separate us! How long it
takes, how much time is required before you will even read these
words, these feeble expressions of the distraught heart over which
you reign! Ah, my adorable wife, I do not know what fate awaits

* A former commune on the Italian Riviera, between Nice and Genoa. Together with Oneglia, it is now part of the town of Imperia.

me, but if it detains me much longer far from you it will be unen-durable. My courage will not suffice.

There was a time when I prided myself on my courage; and sometimes, envisioning the evil men might do me or the fate des-tiny might hold in store for me, I could contemplate the most unheard-of misfortunes without lifting an eyebrow, without so much as a sense of astonishment. But today the thought that my Josephine might be languishing, might be ill—and, above all, the cruel, the fatal thought that she might love me less—blights my soul, congeals my blood, devastates me, strikes me down, deprives me of even the courage of fury or despair . . .

It is as if I were suffocating.

I bring my letter to a close, my sweet. My soul is sad. My body is weary. My mind is distraught. Men revolt me. I have reason to detest them: they separate me from my heart. I am at Porto Mau-rizio, near Oneglia. Tomorrow I will be at Albenga. The two armies are on the move. We are seeking to outwit each other. To the cleverest, the victory. I am well enough satisfied as to Beaulieu.*

If he maneuvers well, he will prove a more formidable adversary than his predecessor. I shall beat him, I hope, and with a flourish. Have no fear.

Love me as you love your eyes. But that is not enough. As you love your very self. More than yourself, your mind, your spirit, your life, your all. . . .

Sweetheart, forgive me, I am raving. Human nature is weak for him who feels as keenly as he whose soul you animate.

N.B.

P.S. Adieu, adieu, adieu. I go to my bed without you. I shall try to sleep without you. I entreat you, let me sleep. For several [nights] now, I have been enfolding you in my arms. Happy dream! And yet, and yet, it is not you.

* Baron Jean-Pierre de Beaulieu, commander of the Austrian forces in Italy.

2

These are the first of the Letters to Josephine, the Honeymoon Letters, the Letters of Delirium, the Letters from Italy, as they have been variously titled—the immortal love letters of the Italian campaign, that first crucial military exploit of the Napoleonic epic.

The letters, like the man himself, are extraordinary, startling, sometimes shocking; alternately savage and tender, suppliant and imperative, rapturous and tormented, philosophical and erotic; they are letters to transfix the heart. The sentiment is as original, as vivid, as incandescent as first love, yet this is not just any young man in love; this is the expression of a formidable intellect, of a personality so powerful as to dominate the century, of an imagination so vast as to sweep and awe the world. The letters are, moreover, lyrical, rich in imagery, stirring to the senses and the imagination. Almost one must stop and remind oneself that they are not from the pen of a poet, of a Byron, a Hugo, a Browning, but from that of a military scientist, a General of the Armies Bonaparte. Yet neither should that be considered too surprising. Did not the man live out a *chanson de geste*, compose his years into an epic poem of action, an *Eroica*, brilliant improvisations upon the classical themes of strategy and logistics?

If the substance of the letters is powerful and compelling, the grammar and the structure are original, unorthodox, sometimes to the point of incoherence: sentences disjointed, phrases fragmented, words isolated and marooned in space as if the pen could not keep pace with the tidal waves of emotion, with the lightning-flash trains of thought that drove it slashing and sputtering across the page—into blots and blobs of ink further to complicate the deciphering of the notoriously illegible Napoleonic script (the despair of secretaries and correspondents during his lifetime, as it is of researchers and historians more than a century after his death).

These messages from the commander in chief of the Army of Italy were scrawled at his camp table, upon his map box, by the light of bivouac fires along the Po, the Adda, the Adige, in the Alps, in the Ligurian hills, across the plains of Lombardy and the

Papal States, in the marshes of Venetia, or by candlelight in his tent pitched beside the bridge at Arcole or Lodi, before the walls of a Castiglione or a Rivoli (place names better known today by Paris street signs than by a map of Italy)—scrawled if not in the din of battle, then in the after stillness. And they were sent off on the gallop by courier, his "thousand and one kisses" traveling no less swiftly to Josephine than did his victory bulletins to the five Directors who governed France in that period following the Revolutionary Terror.

Daily or nightly or twice in every twenty-four hours the general wrote to his wife in Paris; or oftener still, to judge by those letters "too foolish to send" with which, he wrote her later, his pockets were stuffed. That he wrote at least twice a day we know from the reproach he made her for her negligence as a correspondent: "If you loved me, you would write me twice daily." Of all the letters written in those months of their separation during the Italian campaign, only forty-two have come to light; the rest were lost, misplaced or purloined, or sequestered and suppressed in accordance with the policy traditional to the Beauharnais and Bonaparte families and their descendants to this day. Josephine's daughter, Hortense de Beauharnais, in 1833 reluctantly published a collection of Napoleon's letters to her mother (releasing them at that time only because copies of the originals were beginning to appear in other publications), but she held back all those written prior to Josephine's arrival in Milan in July of 1796—as if thus could be held back all evidence of the bride's reluctance to join her husband on that Italian honeymoon.

The letters comprise a documentation unique (to use a favorite word of Napoleon's) in recorded history. No papyri, no parchments of such intimate revelation exist among the annals of an Alexander, a Caesar or a Charlemagne—Napoleon's triad of personal heroes. This documentation provides a glimpse of the man of genius, the enigma of modern European history, in what is perhaps the sole unguarded moment of his life. There is this one glimpse and no more; henceforward Napoleon will be, in his every deed and word, supremely conscious of the ages; he will deliberately assume and hold a pose for posterity. He will never again reveal himself, his secret inner self, as he will never again wholly open his heart, never again enter into unreserved, intimate communion with any other living creature.

The honeymoon letters are further significant in that they reveal the essence of the relationship between Napoleon and his inamorata-wife and chart the course of that tempestuous quasi-tragic love affair. If no other record of their romance had been preserved, these letters written in the months immediately after their marriage would serve as an outline from which the story might be reconstructed; all the seeds of doubt, of jealousy, of suspicion, of the basic conflict between them, are implicit. If no one of the scores of biographies of Josephine and no one of her hundreds of portraits and statues had survived, her image would here emerge, in these epistolary sonnets from her husband, her lover: the "incomparable Josephine," the "beautiful," "adorable," the "sweet and gentle," "tender and kind," the "beguiling," "enchanting" and yet also, ominously, the "giddy," "superficial and capricious," the "inconstant"—"ah, Josephine!" Here she is caught up, held, like a butterfly in resin, fossilized, eternalized in the amber of his words.

The wording of the datelines of these letters—"Ventôse," "Germinal," "An [Year] IV"—is a key to the story's background. Ventôse was the Month of the Wind, Germinal the Month of Germination, Floréal the Month of Flowers, Prairial the Month of Meadows. For this was the period of the fanciful Revolutionary calendar; the Gregorian had been scrapped in the Revolutionary fury, along with all the hated debris of the past and all its hated institutions, along with monarchy and Church. September 22, 1792, had been reckoned as the first day of the Year I of the French Republic, and new and arbitrary divisions of the year had been made.*

Titles had been scrapped, of course, along with the nobility

---

* The Revolutionary calendar had twelve months of thirty days each, plus five extra days for festivals and one more in every leap year. The months in turn were divided into three *décades* of ten days each, the tenth day—the *décadi*—being the day of rest. The months and their approximate Gregorian equivalents were: Vendémiaire (Sept.22-Oct.21); Brumaire (Oct.22-Nov.20); Frimaire (Nov.21-Dec.20); Nivôse (Dec.21-Jan.19); Pluviôse (Jan.20-Feb.18); Ventôse (Feb.19-Mar.20); Germinal (Mar.21-Apr.19); Floréal (Apr.20-May 19); Prairial (May20-June18); Messidor (June19-July18); Thermidor (July19-Aug.17); Fructidor (Aug.18-Sept.16).

which bore them. Not only such exalted titles as duke and duchess, count and countess, marquis and marquise, but even *monsieur* and *madame* were deemed too reminiscent of the despised caste system; a simple "Citizen" or "Citizeness" (in the nature of the Russian Revolution's "Comrade") was deemed more democratic, the great equalizer of a denomination.

So it is to "the Citizeness Beauharnais" that the first letter is addressed, though this is, in itself, an amusing feature. Here was so recent a bridegroom—the hasty, sketchy, casual civil marriage ceremony having been performed only five nights earlier on March 9 —that he was still addressing his bride by the name of her first husband, the Marquis de Beauharnais.

The newlywed Bonapartes could count only thirty-six hours of marital bliss before the newly appointed commander in chief of the Army of Italy was ordered south to headquarters on the Riviera. But this honeymoon was not a new one. The groom was no stranger to the delicately frescoed boudoir of the bride, nor to her oval bedroom with its floor-to-ceiling mirrors multiplying embraces into infinity, for the Citizeness Beauharnais and General Buonaparte had become lovers a few weeks, possibly a few months, before the wedding.

By March 30, the date of his second letter, from Nice, the groom has finally remembered that a lawfully wedded Josephine now bears his name, and the superscription reads: "To the Citizeness Bonaparte, *in care of the Citizeness Beauharnais.*" There is a second curious and amusing feature to be noted in the first and second letters: the first is signed "Buonaparte"; the second, "Bonaparte." During the two weeks of the journey south to Nice, the u of the Italian-Corsican family name has been dropped, in a Gallicization appropriate to a commander of French forces.

By April 3, General Bonaparte had led those forces out of Nice to Porto Maurizio: a straggling, tatterdemalion army of raw and mutinous recruits with which the struggling young French Republic would oppose the Austrian troops drawn up on France's Italian border—just as they had been obliged to oppose on every border, during the past two years, the superior forces of the combined powers of Europe. All the monarchs of the Continent had hoped, by swamping this presumptuous new republican regime, to stem the tide of eighteenth-century national revolutionary movements; but they were a concert of King Canutes—Austrian, Prussian, English, Spanish—all vainly commanding the Wave of the Future to recede.

By April 4, Napoleon and his Army of Italy had reached the midway point between Nice and Genoa on that crescent of Mediterranean littoral known today as the Riviera dei Fiori, the Riviera of Flowers. He headed this letter to Josephine on April 7, "18 Germinal, from Albenga:"

I have just received a letter which you had to interrupt, you say, to go to the country. And after that you assume a tone of jealousy —jealousy of me, here, burdened down with military affairs and fatigue. Oh, my darling! . . .

But I am being unreasonable. In the springtime the countryside is beautiful, and besides, your nineteen-year-old lover was there, no doubt? How should I expect you to waste an instant more than necessary on the chore of letter-writing to one who, separated from you by three hundred leagues, lives only, exists only, finds his only joy in, the memory of you, who reads your letters as ravenously as the hunter devours his favorite dishes after six hours in the saddle?

I am dissatisfied. Your last letter is as cold as friendship. I could find there no trace of that fire which can light up your eyes, and which I have thought sometimes to see shining there. But what inconsistency on my part! I complained that your last letter worked havoc in my soul, disturbed my sleep, aroused my senses. I said I wanted colder letters. But they bring me the chill of death. The fear of not being loved by Josephine, the thought of finding her inconstant, the idea of— But I am conjuring up troubles for myself. As if there were not real ones enough already! Must I add to my own misery?!! You could not have inspired in me so infinite a love unless you felt it, too. And with your soul, with thoughts and a mind like yours, it is impossible to believe that, in response to my total surrender and devotion, you could deal me a mortal blow. . . . A token from my unique wife and a victory from fate: these are my fondest wishes. . . .

A kiss below your breast, and lower—lower still.

The Italian Letters

                                 From headquarters at Carru
                                 5 Floréal [April 24]

TO MY SWEETHEART:

. . . *I have received your letters of the sixteenth and the twenty-first. You let many days go by without writing to me. What, then, are you doing? No, my dearest, I am not jealous, but sometimes anxious. Come quickly, come soon to join me. I warn you, if you delay longer, you will find me ill. These fatigues and your absence —the two together are more than I can bear. Your letters constitute the happiness of my days, but my happy days are few.*

Junot* is bringing twenty-two flags to Paris. You are to come back with him, do you understand? He is not to return without you. Inconsolable sorrow, irremediable misfortune, were I to see him return alone! My darling, he will see you and breathe the air within your shrine. Perhaps you will even accord him the unique, the inestimable favor of a kiss upon your cheek—while I am still alone, and far, far away. But you will return with him, will you not? You will be here at my side, against my heart, in my arms, close to my lips.

Take wings, and fly. Come, come! But travel carefully. The roads are bad, long, wearisome. Should your carriage overturn, should you be harmed or fatigued— Come carefully, my beloved, but keep in constant touch with me in thought. . . .

A kiss upon your heart, another a little lower, another lower still, far lower!

                                                  N.B.

I do not know whether you are in need of money, for you have never spoken to me of your business affairs. Should you have need of it, you are to go to my brother, who has two hundred louis belonging to me.

                                                  B——

If there is anyone for whom you want a position with the army, you may send him to me and I will place him.

* Colonel Andoche Junot, Napoleon's first aide-de-camp, later General Junot and Duke d'Abrantès.

ARMÉE D'ITALIE.

LIBERTÉ.   ÉGALITÉ.

Au Quartier Général de Carru   le 5 Floreal
l'an quatrième de la République Française, une et indivisible.

LE GÉNÉRAL EN CHEF
DE L'ARMÉE D'ITALIE,

"To my Sweetheart" Napoleon's letter to Josephine from his headquarters at Carru. The second and third paragraphs are translated on page 23. (The first paragraph concerns Napoleon's brother, who is to deliver the letter to Josephine.)

The Italian Letters

From Cherasco
10 Floréal [April 29]

"Murat,* who will be the bearer of this letter, will explain to you, my darling, what I have done, what I shall do next, and what I hope to do. I have concluded an armistice with the King of Sardinia. Three days ago I sent Junot, with my brother, to Paris. But they will arrive after Murat, who will go via Turin.

I wrote to you by Junot to set out with him upon his return and come here to join me. Today I beg you to set out instead with Murat, to come via Turin. That will shorten your travel time by two weeks. Thus it is possible that I shall see you before fifteen days have passed!

Lodgings have been prepared for you at Mondovi and at Tortona. From Mondovi you can go . . . to Nice and to Genoa, and from there throughout the rest of Italy, if that would give you pleasure. My happiness lies in seeing you happy, my joy in your joy, my pleasure in your pleasure. Never was a woman loved with more devotion, more fire or more tenderness. Never has a woman been in such complete mastery of another's heart, so to dictate all its tastes and penchants, so to influence all its desires. If it is otherwise with you, I deplore my blindness and leave you to the remorse of your soul. And if I should not die of the sorrow of it, then my heart—maimed for life—would never again wholly trust itself to respond to any sentiment of tenderness or rapture. Then my life would be lived solely on a physical plane. For in losing your love, your heart, your adorable person, I would have lost all that makes life sweet or precious.

Ah! Then I should have no regret in dying, and would perhaps succeed in seeking death upon the field of honor. My love, my life, how can you expect me to be anything but sad? No letters from you; only once every four days do I receive one, whereas if you loved me you would write me twice a day. But then, you must gossip with those little gentlemen who come calling on you at ten o'clock in the morning, and then you must listen to all the prattle and the tittle-tattle of a hundred fops and idlers until an hour past midnight. In those countries where some moral code is observed,

* General Joachim Murat, future King of Naples and future husband of Caroline Bonaparte, Napoleon's youngest sister.

everyone is at home by ten o'clock at night; in those lands, a wife writes to her husband, thinks of him, lives for him. Adieu, Josephine, you are a monster whom I cannot explain to myself—yet every day I love you more. Absence alleviates the minor infatuations, augments and intensifies the grand passions. A kiss upon your mouth, or upon your heart. There is no one else, no one but me, is there? And then another upon your breast. How lucky for Murat, [to touch? to kiss?] your little hand. Oh, should you fail to come!!!

Bring your maid with you, your cook, your coachman. I have carriage horses here for your use, and a splendid carriage. Bring only those things necessary to your personal use. I have silverware and china at your disposal here. Adieu, work calls me. Yet I cannot put down the pen. Oh! If by this evening I have not received a message from you, I shall be desperate. Think of me, or tell me outright that you do not love me, and then perhaps I shall find it in my soul to appear less an object of pity.

In the letter to be delivered to you by my brother, I wrote you that the two hundred louis of mine in his possession are at your disposal. By Murat, I am sending you two hundred louis which you are to use if you have need, or which you might apply to furnishing the room in the house which you will appropriate to my use. If only you could decorate it entirely with portraits of yourself! But no, it is so lovely, the image of you which I carry in my heart, that no matter how beautiful you are, no matter how skillful the artist, any other likeness could only suffer by comparison. That will be the great, the happy day—the one on which you cross the Alps! That will be the supreme reward for my pains and for the victories I have won.

B——

3

But victories for General Bonaparte were more easily wrested from the enemy—from the Austrians, the Sardinians and the Piedmontese—than "the supreme reward" from Josephine. No word of her crossing of the Alps; few words at all were forthcoming.

It may have been only coincidental that the prime military objectives of the campaign facilitated and ensured the commander's reunion with his beloved. The surrender of Piedmont opened the short cut to France through Turin and the Alpine passes, expediting passage for matériel, for reinforcements—and for Josephine; the conquest of Lombardy and the key city of Milan resolved the main issue of the war—and assured the consent of the Directory to Josephine's journey into a theater of war.

A prodigious feat of arms had accomplished it. The ill-equipped, ill-trained army of conscripts which General Bonaparte had joined at Nice a mere six weeks earlier had been galvanized under his command into a formidable, a fanatic fighting force. It may have been that some undercurrent of the passion which engulfed him, having been frustrated of its natural outlet, was diverted into that campaign. The same tone of fervor and the same lyric quality that sound in his letters to Josephine ring out in his proclamations to the army:

> My brothers-in-arms, you have rushed down like a torrent from the heights of the Apennines, sweeping aside every obstacle in your path. . . . You have in fifteen days piled up six victories, captured twenty-one enemy flags, numerous strongholds. You have conquered the richest portion of Piedmont, taken fifteen thousand prisoners, killed or wounded more than ten thousand. . . . Lacking everything, you have surmounted all. You have won battles without cannon, crossed rivers without bridges, made forced marches without shoes, bivouacked without liquor, often without bread. Only republican phalanxes, only soldiers of liberty, could have endured what you have endured.
>
> Yes, soldiers, your achievements have been magnificent . . . but do not yet others await you? . . . Yours is to be the immortal glory of having changed the face of the fairest land of Europe. . . .

Did he, under the compulsion of that burning eagerness for reunion with his wife, require his brothers-in-arms to change the face of that land too rashly, too precipitately? The waters of the torpid Adda, according to military textbooks, flowed unnecessarily red on

May 10 when the bridge was forced at Lodi—the speediest but the costliest approach to Milan. Or was it because, that very night in early May, the general was struck with his first conscious realization of being "an exceptional man, a man of destiny," as he phrased it? Because, that night on the Lodi bridge, he experienced a brush with the supernatural—"feeling," as he was afterward to say, "the earth move off in flight beneath me"?

However it was, in his letter of May 13 to Josephine from Lodi he could speak only of the news that had just reached him from Paris concerning her—though not by her own hand:

It is true, then, that you are pregnant! Murat writes to tell me so. But he says that you are not feeling well and that thus he does not deem it prudent for you to undertake so long a journey. So I am to be still longer deprived of the joy of clasping you in my arms! So I am to be months longer still, far from all that is dear to me. Is it possible that I shall be denied the joy of seeing you with your little pregnant belly? That should make you interesting indeed!

You write me that you have changed a great deal. Your letter is brief, sad, and written in a trembling hand. What is wrong with you, my darling? What can be troubling you? Ah, do not stay out in the country. Return to the city. Seek diversion. . . . I thought I was jealous, but I swear to you that it is not so. Rather than to see you melancholy, I believe that I myself would choose a lover for you! Be gay and happy, and remember that my happiness depends on yours. If Josephine is unhappy, given over to sadness and discouragement, then it can only be that she does not love me.

Soon you will give life to another being who will love you as much as I do. No, that's impossible—for any creature so to love. Your children and I, we will hover over you to assure you of our solicitude, our love. You'll not be perverse or petulant, will you? None of your naughty hmmms!!!—unless it be in one of your teasing moods. In that case, we'll be treated to some of those funny little faces that you make—and even those are pretty! And just so we end it up with a little kiss to make up on.

How sad your letter of the eighteenth makes me. A courier has just delivered it. What can be lacking to your happiness, Josephine?

I am impatiently awaiting Murat's return for a report on every-thing you do, every word you speak, every gown you wear, every person you see. My heart is hungry for every detail concerning my adorable wife.

Things go well here, but my heart is in an indescribable state of anxiety. . . .

Things there were going, actually, far better than well, were go-ing famously. When he wrote next, he was fresh from his triumphal entry into Milan, hailed as "the Liberator" by a populace that welcomed wildly the exhilarating new wave of freedom rolling in from across the Alps with the forces of the young French Republic and its youthful but imposing commander. (With his assurance to all the "Peoples of Italy": "The French Army comes to break your chains. The French people is the friend of all peoples. Come before us with confidence: your property, your religion, your tradi-tions are all to be respected . . .")

No echo of that wild acclaim in the capital of Lombardy sounded, however, in his letter of May 18 to Josephine; to her he represented Milan merely as a citadel of safety, a resort of pleas-ance he had prepared for her arrival:

You will come here to Milan, which cannot but please you, for this is a very beautiful land. As for me, I shall be wild with joy. . . .

I am dying of curiosity to see how you carry your child. It should give you a little air of majesty and dignity which cannot but be very becoming.

Above all, don't get sick. But you won't, my darling, you'll come here, you'll feel very well, you'll bear a baby as pretty as its mother, a child that will love you as does its father. And when you are old —very, very old, a hundred years old—that child will be your com-fort and your joy. But until then, until that far-off time, take care that you do not love him more than you love me. Already I am becoming jealous.

Adio, mio dolce amor. Adio, my well-beloved. Come quickly to hear the fine music and to see beautiful Italy. The only thing lack-

ing here is you. You will embellish the scene. In my eyes, surely.
As you well know, when my Josephine is in sight I have eyes only
for her. . . .

Milan
4 Prairial [May 29]
Josephine, no letter from you since the twenty-eighth [Floréal—
May 17]. I have received mail by the courier who left Paris on the
twenty-seventh, but no reply, no news from my beloved. Could
she have forgotten me, or could she be oblivious to the fact that
my greatest torment is in not hearing from my sweet love?

Here they have given me a great fete. Five or six hundred of the
prettiest and most elegant ladies in Italy vied to please me. But
none resembled you. None had that sweet and harmonious face
which is so deeply engraved upon my heart. I could see only you,
think only of you. Thus, all else was intolerable, and a half hour
after my arrival I went sadly off to bed, telling myself, There is
only an aching void, a great emptiness, where my adorable wife
should be. Are you coming?

Your pregnancy, how does it go? Ah, my beautiful one, take
good care of yourself, be gay, take exercise, let nothing dismay
you, worry about nothing, have no fear about your journey. Travel
by easy stages. All I can think about is seeing you with your little
swollen belly. You must look charming.

Adieu, my beloved. Think sometimes of him who thinks constantly of you.

Milan
20 Prairial [June 8]
Josephine, you were to have left Paris on the fifth. You were to
have left on the eleventh. You still had not left on the twelfth.
. . . My soul had yielded itself to delight; it is filled with sorrow.

All the couriers come in, but they bring no letters from you. . . .
When you do write, your few words, your style, give no indication
of profound sentiment. You loved me out of a caprice. Now you
realize how ridiculous it would be to allow a whim to set the
course of your life.

I have the feeling that you have made a choice and that you

know to whom you will turn to replace me. I wish you happiness —if inconstancy can ever bring happiness. The word perfidy I avoid. You have never loved me.

I have accelerated my military operations. I counted on your being at Milan by the thirteenth, but you are still in Paris. I withdraw into my own soul. I stifle a sentiment beneath my dignity. And if glory does not suffice to my happiness, it shall furnish the element of death and of immortality.

As for you, may my memory not be odious to you. My misfortune is to have known you so little; yours, to have judged me by the men whom you have known, who surround you. My heart knows no halfway sentiments. It had sealed itself off against love, but you inspired in it a limitless passion, an intoxication that is degrading. The thought of you took precedence over that of all nature. Your whim was my sacred law; to see you, my sovereign joy. You are beautiful and gracious. Your sweet, celestial soul finds reflection in your face. I adored everything about you. Had I been younger, more naïve, I might have loved you less. Everything about you pleased me, even to the memory of the error of your ways— even to the devastating scene that took place two weeks before our marriage. Virtue, for me, consisted of what you made it. Honor, whatever pleased you. Glory held no appeal for my heart save only as it might flatter your vanity.

Your portrait was always upon my heart. Never a thought without looking at it and covering it with kisses. While you—you have left my portrait for months without so much as a glance. Nothing, you see, escapes my notice. If I should go on loving you, I would be the only one of us who loved. And of all roles, that is the one I cannot play.

Josephine, you might have made the delight of a man less bizarre than I. You have made me wretched, I warn you. I sensed it even at the moment my heart was about to be involved, even at the moment you were taking possession of my soul and enslaving my senses. Cruel one!!! Why make me believe in a sentiment you were not experiencing? But these are reproaches beneath my dignity. I have never really believed in happiness. Every day, death brushes me with its wings. . . . Is life worth making such a fuss?

Adieu, Josephine, stay in Paris, write me no more letters, but at least respect my refuge. A thousand daggers rip my heart. Plunge them no deeper. Adieu, my happiness, my life, all that I hold dear on earth.

4

"He's funny . . . Bonaparte." ("*Il est drôle, Bonaparte.*")

Josephine said it with a little shrug of amusement; not disparagingly, not mockingly, for she was incapable of mockery or malice, but as if in apology for the extravagance of her husband's passion, as if to say that he must be humored, young as he was and a fiery, untamed Corsican to boot. She said it to playwright Antoine Arnault, her friend and frequent escort at Paris' victory celebrations that spring of 1796, her admirer and apparently a platonic one, since she did not hesitate to share with him that most intimate of correspondences.

> The letter she showed me, like all the rest the general had addressed to her since his departure [Academician Arnault wrote later], was characterized by the utmost violence of passion. Josephine was amused at this emotion, which was not exempt from jealousy. I can still hear her reading a passage in which her husband, trying to suppress the anxieties which obviously tormented him, had written: "If this should be true, however, then tremble before the dagger of Othello!" I can still see her smile, still hear her saying in that Creole drawl of hers, "He's funny . . . Bonaparte."
>
> The love she inspired in so extraordinary a man evidently flattered her, although she took the thing less seriously than he. She was proud to see that he loved her almost as much as he loved glory; she enjoyed that glory, which was enhanced by every day that passed, but it was in Paris that she preferred to enjoy it —in the midst of the acclamations which rang out about her at every fresh victory bulletin from the Army of Italy.

Not that Arnault was to be her only confidant. It was, to be sure, with unadulterated pride that Josephine later pointed to that

Josephine under fire from Austrian gunboats during the Italian Campaign in the summer of 1796; General Junot rescues her party from attack on the shore of Lake Garda. (Since Josephine's retinue in the flight from Verona is known to have included only her

Josephine in her thirties, in the years of the Consulate (1799–1804). Lithograph after the miniature by Jean-Baptiste Isabey. [BIBLIO-THÈQUE NATIONALE, PARIS]

friends Hamelin and Monglas and her maid, Louise Compoint, the
other female figures are probably the painter's romantic invention.)
Oil painting by Lecomte, from the Musée de Malmaison. See page
131. [PHOTOGRAPH BY LAVERTON]

Napoleon at the Battle of Arcola. The first formal portrait of Napoleon, painted by Gros in Milan in 1796. See page 140. [MUSÉE DU LOUVRE, PARIS]

The Empress Josephine at Malmaison. Detail from the portrait painted in 1805 by Prud'hon, from the Musée du Louvre. [PHOTO-GRAPH BY GIRAUDON]

Hortense de Beauharnais, Queen of Holland. Painting by Gérard.

Eugène de Beauharnais at the age of sixteen, in his uniform of aide-de-camp to General Bonaparte. Painted by Gros in 1797. See page 149. [PHOTOGRAPH BY L. BLAISE]

Napoléon-Charles, first-born son of Hortense de Beauharnais and Louis Bonaparte (who died in 1807, at the age of 4½). Painted by Gérard. See page 281. [FROM COLLECTION AND WITH PERMISSION OF S.A.I. PRINCE NAPOLEON. PHOTOGRAPH BY L. BLAISE]

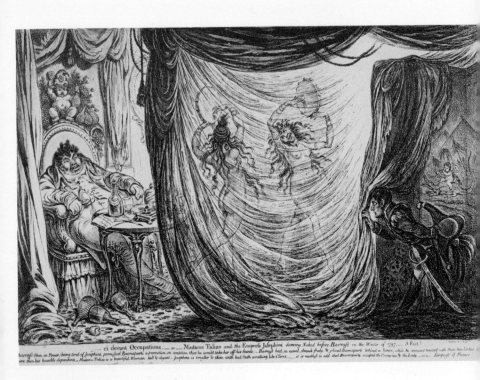

ci-devant Occupations — or — Madame Talian and the Empress Josephine dancing Naked before Barrass in the Winter of 1797. — A Fact!

Barrass (then in Power) being tired of Josephine, promised Buonaparte a promotion, on condition that he would take her off his hands; — Barrass had, as usual, drank freely, & placed Buonaparte behind a Screen, while he amused himself with these two Ladies, who were then his humble dependents. — Madame Talian is a beautiful Woman, tall & elegant; Josephine is smaller & thin, with bad Teeth, something like Cloves, — it is needless to add that Buonaparte accepted the Promotion & the Lady — now — Empress of France

Cartoon by the English caricaturist Gillray, published in 1805 and captioned: "ci-devant Occupations—or—Madame Talian and the Empress Josephine dancing Naked before Barrass in the Winter of 1797—A Fact! Barrass (then in Power) being tired of Josephine, promised Buonaparte a promotion, on condition that he would take her off his hands;—Barrass had, as usual, drank freely, & placed Buonaparte behind a Screen, while he amused himself with these two Ladies, who were then his humble dependents.—Madame Talian is a beautiful Woman, tall & elegant; Josephine is smaller & thin, with bad Teeth, something like Cloves,—it is needless to add that Buonaparte accepted the Promotion & the Lady—now—Empress of France!" See pages 73 to 77. [BRITISH MUSEUM, LONDON] correspondence as the proof, in black and white, of the great man's adoration, but it is still somehow shocking to consider how indiscriminately, how carelessly she would hand round those pages on which he had laid bare his heart—to her friends, to her honor attendants, even to her maids (who, in publishing their inevitable memoirs, included copies of the originals).

Lady-in-waiting Claire de Vergennes de Rémusat would be treated to an inspection of the famous packet, and, shrewd observer that she was, intimate member of the Bonaparte family as she came to be, her comments and conclusions are of exceptional interest:

They were extraordinary letters: the handwriting almost indecipherable, the orthography faulty, the style bizarre and confused, but marked by a tone so impassioned, by emotions so turbulent, by expressions so vibrant and at the same time so poetic, by a love so apart from all other loves, that no woman in the world could fail to take pride in having been their inspiration. And besides, what a circumstance for a woman in which to find herself—as one of the motivating influences for the triumphal march of an entire army! Even so, these letters from Napoleon revealed symptoms of jealousy, sometimes somber, sometimes menacing. On these occasions, a melancholy reflectiveness evidenced itself, a sort of disgust with the all too ephemeral illusions of life. Perhaps these were the disillusionments which bruised Bonaparte's heart in its original ardor; these, perhaps, the disappointments which took their toll, made their mark, and blighted, one by one, his capacity for love. Perhaps he would have been a better man had he been more and, above all, better loved.

Yet had Josephine's ardor matched his, had she been other than she was—bewitching, seductive, a coquette, a woman of the world and a belle of Paris' Directoire society—it is unlikely that she would have exerted upon Napoleon, at that particular period of his life, so irresistible an attraction. And had Napoleon been other than he was, had he been older or more experienced with women, he would have realized that Josephine, in all her glamour and enchantment, represented the ideal mistress rather than the ideal wife. Josephine herself may have sensed it, for though she embarked unhesitatingly upon their romantic liaison, she was reluctant to embark on matrimony.

How had he come to choose, to insist upon, this particular reluctant heroine? And in full knowledge of her frailties, of the tarnish to her reputation: "Everything about you pleased me, even to the memory of the error of your ways . . . Virtue, for me, consisted of what you made it." How explain Josephine's reluctance? What manner of woman was she, what experiences had formed her, what adventures, what disillusionments of her own had rendered her incapable of response to so ardent a wooing, to such love and passion from this most extraordinary man?

Some biographers attribute Josephine's reluctance to a subconscious impulse to avoid the tug of fame, but that theory is not supported by the facts of her life. It was not the limelight that she shunned; the publicity, the social prominence, the "acclamations," she thoroughly enjoyed, as Arnault has shown. Nor was it the remorseless glare of history from which she instinctively shied away; of that she was totally unsuspecting, as of the fact that Napoleon's offer of escort was to a vertiginous ascent. Josephine was slow, painfully slow—among the last—to perceive his genius, to recognize him as a man of destiny; their friend Claire de Rémusat, more imaginative, more perceptive, was among the first: "It was impossible not to feel the tremendous impact of the man, impossible not to be stirred by his presence." Josephine managed the "impossible" for an astonishing length of time. In any event, whether or not she would have preferred to linger in anonymity, whether or not she might have lived more happily and serenely there, Napoleon willfully plucked her out; "I have always been able to impose my will on destiny," as he warned her in one of his letters.

Willy-nilly, she was to be made over in the image he decreed: he would place the crown upon her head, assign her her titles, her role and her niche in history. Scarcely a shred of her original identity remains to her; at times, she almost seems merely another figment of his colossal imagination; the very name by which she is remembered was of his choosing: his "sweet and incomparable Josephine!"

When they met, she was not even that, not even Josephine.

II

Josephine Before Napoleon

Bring us whichever of your daughters you consider most likely to suit my son.

LETTER FROM THE MARQUIS DE BEAUHARNAIS
TO JOSEPHINE'S FATHER, 1779

I can assure you that her delightful manner and the sweetness of her nature exceed our fondest expectations.

LETTER FROM VISCOUNT ALEXANDRE DE BEAUHARNAIS
TO HIS FATHER, OCTOBER 28, 1779

1

HER NAME WAS ROSE; Marie-Josèphe-Rose, at her christening; called Rose, like her mother, for more than half her life. She was still signing herself "Rose" in 1796, at the time of her marriage to General Buonaparte: "Marie-Rose Detascher," as it can be clearly read on one line of the marriage document; "M.J.R. Tascher," on another.

Napoleon changed it to Josephine, an association, perhaps, with another person dear to him, his brother Joseph. Or it may have been out of a subconscious desire, as Director Paul Barras analyzed it, "to put out of his mind the Rose who had unfurled and blossomed for other men before him." Napoleon would be the first to possess her as Josephine, the first to whisper the name into her ear, against her lips—his own, his "divine Josephine."

It would have been impolitic in the extreme for Josephine, in the Year IV of the French Republic, to have signed a marriage document with her family name in its full, original form, de Tascher de la Pagerie: the *de*, the aristocratic particle, had been stripped from noble names along with the titles as despised reminders of the infuriating feudal system. As a noble name, de Tascher de la Pagerie dated back to the twelfth century in the Loire Valley region. Josephine's grandfather emigrated from Orléans in 1726 to the fertile French colony of Martinique, seeking, like so many younger sons of ancient but impecunious nobility, to make his fortune in the New World. But the fortune never materialized, neither for him nor for his son Joseph-Gaspard, Marie-Josèphe-Rose's feckless and philandering father, to whom she was born in 1763, the first of three daughters (though even such vital statistics as these have been at times contested in the many versions of her life story).

"The lovely Creole," "the ignorant Creole," "the languorous Creole," "the voluptuous Creole," "the wanton Creole": contemporary accounts make repeated reference to Josephine's Creole origins and characteristics, which evidently were as distinctive as the accent upon which her friend Arnault commented. The word "Creole" in the original French definition carries no connotation of an admixture of Negro blood, but refers to persons of pure French or Spanish descent, born and raised in remote or colonial regions, especially tropical ones, the environment and culture of which have entailed a characteristic adaptation of the national type. If the French language spoken in Martinique became less crisp, so did the Gallic character, which wilted in the tropic sun, or perhaps was subject to some piquant Caribbean sea change, as was the classic French cuisine under the influence of exotic island herbs and spices.

It was a pleasant enough, comfortable enough, lazy, leisurely way of life lived by the French colonial in Martinique; reminiscent of life in the antebellum South, but less affluent, especially in the case of the Taschers; with a plenty of natural produce and a dearth of cash. It was a well-bred, well-mannered, gentle and gracious society in which Marie-Josèphe-Rose reached girlhood; it was nevertheless a rustic, unsophisticated one, for Martinique was a backwater of the world, cut off from the mainstream of French political and cultural development by weeks or months, depending upon the winds in the sails of vessels crossing the Atlantic.

The Taschers' sugar plantation, at Les Trois-Îlets, lay twenty-two miles across the bay from Fort-Royal, today's Fort-de-France, then the seat of colonial government—an hour and a half by water, by swift light pirogue; hours longer by road, by horse and carriage. Marie-Josèphe-Rose was sent to Fort-Royal in 1772, at the age of nine, to the Convent of the Ladies of Providence, to acquire the accomplishments suitable to eighteenth-century colonial females: for instruction in the catechism, in deportment, in penmanship, in drawing and embroidery, in dancing and music—the most meager educational bill of fare. Beyond the fact of her five years' study with the nuns, there is little save oral tradition to fill in the outline of her girlhood, and so biographers have been tempted by their imaginations along the theme of the legendary beauty and languorous grace of Martinique women, the legends of sirens on the Antilles' shores, brought back by Columbus' sailors.

It is more than mere conjecture to say that the beaches in Marie-Josèphe-Rose's eighteenth century, as in our twentieth, extended their broad invitation to island children to build castles in the sand, to splash in the warm blue water—though not necessarily in the nude, as more fanciful biographers suggest, in the creation of an early ambiance of voluptuousness for their voluptuous subject. It is probable that she learned to ride horseback as a girl, with her two sisters, on the Spanish ponies known to the islanders as "Porto-Ricans"; that she watched in fascination, as tourists do today, the ritual dances of the Negroes performed by torchlight and to the rhythm of the native drums—and imitated them, as her daughter Hortense recalls having done in her childhood. A nostalgia for the flamboyant birds and flowers of Marie-Josèphe-Rose's Trois-Îlets gardens would inspire the Empress Josephine to import tropical birds for the aviaries, tropical blooms for the hothouses, of her Château of Malmaison. The island imprint was deep; the bonds of island kinship and island friendship never weakened across the years or seas. The name of Martinique on a passport always constituted a passport to the Empress's society and bounty; she sent to Martinique for her maids, for nurses for her children; an island "woman of color" was listed in her will among her many pensioners.

She never recovered from what she herself called "my Creole nonchalance" and which more objective contemporaries called her "Creole indolence"—Madame de Rémusat, for one, marveling that she "could idle away her days doing nothing and yet never be bored with it." Her blood was attuned to the tempo of her Islands-below-the-Winds, to the long afternoons of siesta and the long evenings of idle gossip on wind-cooled verandas with neighboring planters.

The monotony of island life was broken by the arrival of visitors from France—government officials, commercial agents, army and navy officers—providing the occasion for house parties at Les Trois-Ilets, for balls and receptions and galas at Fort-Royal, to which Marie-Josèphe-Rose was invited by her uncle, the Baron de Tascher, commander of the port. Any pleasure-loving girl on a remote plantation in Martinique would have kept her eyes fastened on Fort-Royal Bay, watching for the sails to loom up and head for harbor, waiting for the joyous summons there. As for any colonial debutante, these visits to Fort-Royal were Marie-Josèphe-Rose's chief delight, the red-letter days of her calendar. But it was the prospect of a journey to Paris upon which her fondest hopes were pinned.

Paris was the city of her dreams, her spiritual home before she ever saw it. She was homesick for Paris before she set foot inside its walls; she would be homesick for it every time she left it, and would never willingly leave it again. As a girl, the tale she never tired of hearing and one her father never tired of telling was that of his sojourn in the capital, the five years of his youth spent at the royal court as a page (an honorary service to which the Tascher patents of nobility entitled him) in the household of the Dauphine Marie-Josèphe, mother of the present King, Louis XVI.

The prospect of the journey to Paris hinged upon another more dazzling still: that of a betrothal. Betrothal to a viscount—Alexandre, Viscount de Beauharnais, handsome, wealthy and young.

Both prospects had long been dangled tantalizingly before her eyes, but with an agonizing doubt involved: while the identity of the fiancé was established, that of the fiancée hung in the balance. Would it be Marie-Josèphe-Rose or one of her two sisters? The question was to be debated by the families, by mail, over a period of months, of years.

The matchmaker was the Tascher girls' Aunt Edmée, Madame Renaudin, who occupied a position as influential as it was unique in the Beauharnais household, which she had joined during the Marquis de Beauharnais's term of office as governor of Martinique. She had joined it originally as *dame de compagnie* (companion) to the governor's lady; she stayed on as mistress to the governor and as godmother to the governor's younger son, Alexandre, born in Fort-Royal in 1760. Edmée Renaudin sailed with the family to France upon the governor's recall, and eventually she took over responsibility for both father and son when the Marquise obligingly retired from the field to a château of her own near Blois. It is a commentary upon the morals of the age that Madame Renaudin was criticized not for her romantic liaison with the Marquis but for her assumption of marital duties as head of his household and mother to his son.

When her godson, the Viscount Alexandre, reached a marriageable age, it was not surprising that Madame Renaudin should suggest one of her three nieces as his bride, nor that her suggestion should be accepted. It was only a question of which of the three Tascher sisters Alexandre might prefer, sight unseen. His first choice fell on Catherine, the second eldest, as most appropriate in age, but by the time the letter indicating his choice had arrived in Martinique, Catherine had died. Whereupon the seventeen-year-old prospective groom began to vacillate between the elder daughter, fifteen-year-old Marie-Josèphe-Rose ("too old") and the younger, eleven-year-old Marie-Françoise ("too young"). The bedeviled father could only say that the younger expressed reluctance to leave her mother, whereas the elder was "all eagerness to go," having frequently requested to be sent to France; and he could catalogue the latter's attractions as "an exceptionally sweet disposition, a fine complexion and beautiful eyes and arms." Aunt Renaudin stepped in with: "We leave you to be guided by

Providence. Bring either or both your daughters, but come, come, I conjure you!" (Lest the match fall through altogether and this highly eligible *parti* be lost to both of his dowryless daughters!)

The groom's father was likewise willing to leave the choice to the father of the bride. "Bring us whichever daughter you consider most likely to suit my son," he wrote, and he forwarded the marriage banns to Martinique with the name of the groom filled in and the space for the name of the bride left blank.

2

"Marie-Josèphe-Rose" was the name that would be written in, and it was Marie-Josèphe-Rose who disembarked at Brest, in the company of her father and her mulatto maid, Euphémie, on October 12, 1779. There, on October 27, her fiancé came to greet and to inspect her.

The marriage contract, according to the negotiations, had been subject to ratification by mutual approval of the parties concerned. "We are not expected to go through with the marriage, are we, if we find each other repulsive?" Alexandre de Beauharnais had inquired of his father earlier. Now, however, in a letter to the Marquis on October 28 from Brest, he signified approval if not unqualified enthusiasm. "Mademoiselle de la Pagerie may perhaps strike you as less pretty than might have been anticipated," Alexandre wrote, "but I can assure you that her delightful manner and the sweetness of her nature exceed our fondest expectations."

One finds oneself searching for the motive which prompted the young fop Beauharnais to accept this naïve, uneducated little Creole as a bride—shy and awkward in her ludicrous island finery, with no dowry, no lineal prestige, no social or physical distinction to recommend her to a connoisseur of female flesh, a social and intellectual snob such as Alexandre. The only reason that can logically be advanced is that marriage served him as a legal maneuver, technically removing his disabilities as a minor, permitting him to enter into control—four years earlier than would have otherwise been possible—of the estate which his mother had bequeathed him under the guardianship of his father until he should come of age.

For Marie-Josèphe-Rose, on the other hand, it may well have been a case of love at first sight of the handsome, dashing young Viscount. Women far more mature and sophisticated than this sixteen-year-old colonial were to be counted among his conquests. And Alexandre was a man who counted his conquests aloud and by name, just as he ticked off the list of his bastards and gloated over his campaigns of seduction to any fellow officer of his infantry regiment who cared to listen. One who did not was Louis-Amour de Bouillé, who complained in his memoirs that Captain de Beauharnais's philosophy of love, so cynical and profane, had warped his own. It is not beyond the realm of possibility that Alexandre served another comrade at arms, Choderlos de Laclos, as a model for the character of Valmont, the ruthless, loveless experimenter in love of *Les Liaisons dangereuses.*

He was nonetheless, in his flashy white-and-silver infantry uniform, "one of the most attractive gentlemen of his time." He also had the reputation of being the best dancer in France, a title which had won him the privilege of dancing in the Queen's quadrilles—while his title of viscount was insufficiently authenticated and the Beauharnais patents of nobility were insufficiently ancient to secure him the privilege of riding to the hunt with the King. This last, according to his friend Bouillé, was "a torment to his vanity," a humiliation responsible to a great extent for his repudiation of the royalist cause in favor of the republican at the outbreak of the Revolution in 1789.

With this elegant, cultivated, fastidious, pretentious, narcissistic, egotistical young rake, Marie-Josèphe-Rose went blithely, unquestioningly, gratefully into marriage on December 13, 1779. Her girlish illusions were as short-lived as the honeymoon. By April, Alexandre was off on a house party with his illustrious La Rochefoucauld cousins, leaving his crestfallen bride to console herself as best she could with her resounding new title of viscountess, her jewel case of Beauharnais heirlooms and her position in the family's Paris town house.

"Do not poison the pleasure I take in your letters by reproaches," was his reply to her plaintive messages. "I yearn for nothing so much as a peaceful household and domestic bliss. I am thrilled by your expression of a desire to improve yourself. To join a cultivated mind to your natural modesty will make an accomplished lady of you. If I could kiss you as I wish, your plump little cheeks would glow and show it." He was a hypocrite when he spoke of his yearning for domestic bliss; it was the very last thing to appeal to a man who made a career of amorous dalliance. Still, this first letter of his is a blueprint of his dissatisfactions and disappointments regarding his wife, those which doomed the marriage to failure. Her wide-eyed admiration and her disposition to please and to adore were not enough; shy, virginal qualities were less calculated to titillate the senses of an eighteen-year-old roué than the practiced blandishments of the thirty-year-old matrons upon whom his exploits of gallantry had been concentrated.

Fortunately for him, he could close the boudoir door upon his bride and set off alone for the Château of La Roche-Guyon; certainly he would not parade that gauche, uneducated, still chubby adolescent in those exclusive salons. All the scintillating conversational wit about the social and political scene and contemporary art, literature and drama would be lost upon her; she would look dismayingly blank at discussion of the new liberal philosophy which had inspired Alexandre, the La Rochefoucaulds and a wide segment of the aristocracy to wild enthusiasm.

Her father's letters should have given Alexandre fair warning of Marie-Josèphe-Rose's sexual, social and cultural ineptitude. "Although so well developed as to be taken for eighteen, she has become nubile only within the past five or six months," he had reported from Martinique in the year preceding the marriage. "Her voice is sweet, she plucks prettily at the guitar, and, showing a general aptitude for music, she could with proper instruction perfect her singing, playing and dancing. It is only regrettable that she did not have the advantages of a French education." In France, Creole ignorance was proverbial, according to the Count de Montgaillard, who wrote reminiscing of that time: "We were all acquainted with great ladies of that origin who, while maintaining a place in the highest society, scarcely knew how to read, much less to write.

It was a standing joke, although no one was surprised, so prevalent was the anomaly."

Paris might laugh at other Creoles, but not at Madame de Beauharnais if Alexandre could prevent it. "I promptly proposed to compensate for the sad neglect of the first fifteen years of her life by devising a plan for her education," he explained by letter to his former tutor, Patricol. A student himself (the Collège de Plessis and the University of Heidelberg), his was an ambitious project: "lessons in geography and history, reading aloud of verse by our best poets, memorizing outstanding passages by our best dramatists." There were to be lessons on the harp from Petrini, Paris' fashionable music master, while Alexandre himself would coach his wife in the art of letter-writing—an arrangement which worked out very well, for the reason that he was most frequently off gallivanting, so correspondence proved their sole means of communication. Oddly enough, it was the one subject in which Marie-Josèphe-Rose excelled. She later acquired quite a reputation for the grace and elegance of her epistolary style; even then, in the beginning, Alexandre conceded that she had "made considerable progress and need no longer blush for her compositions, no matter to whom addressed." She was less successful in winning his praise for her accomplishments in other subjects of the curriculum.

In garrison with his regiment for the rest of the first year of their marriage, Alexandre returned to Paris and to Marie-Josèphe-Rose only for a few weeks in the winter of 1780-1781, the period during which their first child was conceived. To a lonely nine months of pregnancy he abandoned her again, rejoining his regiment and, as he himself said, resuming his bachelor life.

He said it to his tutor, Patricol, who reported the conversation to Aunt Renaudin, who had been concerned over the steadily deteriorating relations of the young Beauharnais'. "I thought at first that I could live happily with her," the young husband had confessed, "and pursued my plan [for her education] until I finally recognized an indifference and unwillingness to improve herself which convinced me that I was wasting my time. It was then that I reached the decision to abandon the education of my wife to anyone who cared to take it over. And so, instead of spending my time at home with a creature with whom I can find nothing in common, I have to a great extent resumed my bachelor life."

Alexandre showed no more patience or understanding as a preceptor than as a husband; the honeymoon months and the months of a first pregnancy could scarcely be considered the opportune time to launch a bewildered bride upon a course of higher learning. Yet he was justified in his reproach of her "indolence," which, he wrote her, "has always been the primary cause of your neglect of your duties."

It was a reproach that was consistently to be leveled against her by various intellectuals among her friends and acquaintances throughout her life: a continuing criticism of her intellectual apathy, her general lack of mental curiosity, of reflection and of application. It would be said of her later by a lady in waiting in her retinue, Madame de Vaudey, who meant to be disobliging, that "the only education she possessed had been acquired through conversation." If so, she was to have opportunity to listen to the best conversationalists of her age—scientists, philosophers, artists, savants, literati, diplomats—and she showed cleverness enough to adopt and quote their opinions where lack of study and reflectiveness had kept her from forming any of her own. To have "said little on subjects she did not understand" must surely be interpreted as a sign of native intelligence, no matter how this comment was intended by her friend Laure Permon Junot, Duchess d'Abrantès. And even a bluestocking Madame de Rémusat and a pyrotechnically brilliant Talleyrand were forced to concede that Josephine's prodigious memory and quick learning compensated to a great extent for her deficiencies in those subjects which directly interested her—botany, art and protocol.

She would eventually make herself into just such an "accomplished lady" as Alexandre had set her as a goal: the brightest ornament of Directoire, of Consular and of Empire society, First Lady of Paris, of France, of Europe; and it is conceivable that she found one of her few causes for regret at her husband's untimely death in the fact that it prevented him from living long enough to see her do it. Yet it is not inconsistent to claim that in so doing she modeled herself directly upon those belles of eighteenth-century court and capital who had evoked her husband's admiration and for whom he had rejected, neglected and abandoned her. Alexandre's rejection of her as a woman proved at once the most traumatic experience and the strongest motivating influence of her life.

"My wife has become jealous," he further confided to his tutor, "and has acquired all the qualities of that fatal passion"—a claim of Alexandre's that cannot be denied. Josephine would be subject all her life to a morbid and pathological jealousy, which would be a torment to her second husband even more than to her first. Alexandre, who had aroused it, was primarily disdainful of the emotion. Her jealousy he construed as another of her social blunders, another proof of her ignorance of the manners of that exquisitely refined if decadent *ancien-régime* society in which conjugal love and conjugal fidelity were held to be ludicrous bourgeois concepts.

Beauharnais put in one of his rare appearances at Paris on September 3, 1781, the birth date of their son, Eugène, and, to the gratitude of his wife, "kept her faithful company until the moment of her arising out of childbed," as her lawyers were to phrase it a few years later. By November he was off again, to Italy on a pleasure jaunt, not returning to Paris until July of 1782. Once again he was welcomed with open arms by his wife; "received by her with expressions of the greatest joy, he seemed enchanted at their reunion." He was so enchanted, evidently, as to beget a second child— whose birth it was impossible for him to honor with his presence as he had that of the first; the month of April 1783 was to find him halfway round the world.

In the middle of the night of September 5, 1782, without a word of warning or a farewell embrace, Alexandre had left his wife asleep, preferring to advise her by letter of his decision to join the French forces under the Marquis de Bouillé, as a belated volunteer in action against the British or in concert with the Americans, in the Atlantic or the Caribbean. His farewell was couched in his usual highflown and grandiloquent literary style: "Love of my wife contends with love of glory for supremacy in my heart. If I yield to the latter, it is for your future benefit and for that of our children."

Even as he wrote from Brest, entreating Marie-Josèphe-Rose not to forget him, "not to banish" him from her heart, he had resumed

45

relations with a vivacious, voluptuous and malicious lady of that port, Madame de Longpré, who earlier had borne him a son (christened Alexandre, in a pretty compliment to both her husband and her lover, who conveniently bore the same Christian name). Recently and conveniently widowed, conveniently combining pleasure with business on a trip to Martinique, Madame de Longpré boarded ship in time to sail with Alexandre de Beauharnais for the Antilles.

This series of coincidences taxed his wife's credulity. In the last months of her pregnancy, reading reports from family and friends in Fort-Royal, where her husband was openly flaunting Madame de Longpré as his mistress, Marie-Josèphe-Rose broke off her correspondence with him. He had the effrontery to be nettled at her silence, and at hearing from others of the arrival of their daughter.

News of Hortense's birth on April 10, 1783 reached Martinique by June, and Madame de Longpré was ready with the computation that the pregnancy had fallen twelve days short of the prescribed nine months. When she publicly suggested that the child therefore could not be Alexandre's own, on the highly original theory that the term of gestation may be prolonged but not foreshortened, that otherwise worldly-wise and sophisticated gentleman swallowed the bait and reacted as violently as any despised bourgeois husband might have done.

He set out to avenge the fancied affront to his honor by seeking to establish that Marie-Josèphe-Rose must have been depraved in earliest girlhood, before she had ever come to Paris or to him. To do so, he made research in slander, magnifying gossip, provoking calumny, and resorted to the outright bribery of three Tascher plantation slaves in an attempt to induce them to traduce his wife's reputation. (Maximin, the only slave who did so, was later "put on the chain," Marie-Josèphe-Rose's mother wrote indignantly, but by then the damage had been done.)

Madame de Longpré, who had cast aspersions on Marie-Josèphe-Rose's fidelity, shortly furnished Alexandre with proof against her own: she transferred her affections to a higher-ranking officer, with whom she embarked for the Continent. Alexandre's mistress, on the high seas with her new lover, was invulnerable to her old lover's wrath, but Alexandre's wife could be made to pay twice over for the double blow to his highly developed masculine ego. In an ultimate gesture of perversity and cruelty, his letter of vicious denunciation of his wife was carried back to Paris and delivered to her by courtesy of his ex-mistress.*

3

"If I had written to you in the first hour of my rage," the Viscount de Beauharnais's letter of invective to Marie-Josèphe-Rose began, "my pen would have scorched the paper . . . But now three weeks have passed, and, despite my despair and suffocating fury, I shall be able to control myself, to tell you in cold blood that you are the vilest of creatures and that my sojourn in this island has acquainted me with your abominable conduct here."

He went on to enumerate the intrigues he claimed to have discovered, accusing her of having slipped off at her parents' siesta hour, with the connivance of the slaves, for assignations with army and navy officers, and of having had an affair en route to France. "Any creature who could open her arms to a lover even as she makes ready to join the man to whom her troth is plighted has no soul; she is lower than the lowliest strumpets of this earth. . . . In the light of such excesses, what am I to think of the clouds and conflicts that have marred our marriage, what am I to think of this last child . . . ? . . . I must accept it, but I swear by heaven that it is the progeny of another; another's blood flows in its veins."

In page upon vituperative page, this flagrantly unfaithful husband excoriated his wife for transgressions attributed to her without substantiation, forbade her so much as "a tear or protestation" and demanded that she either return to Martinique or take herself

---

* Incredible as it may seem, the imperial records for the year 1807 show the grant of a pension, at the express instance of the Empress Josephine, to Madame de Longpré, widowed for a second time, in financial straits, and bold enough to apply for assistance to her former rival, the victim of her machinations.

off to a convent. He threatened to show himself "a tyrant" should she dare to defy his orders.

When, with his customary effrontery, Alexandre presented himself for a farewell visit to the Trois-Îlets plantation, Monsieur de Tascher expressed his outrage, categorically denied the charges against his daughter's virtue and pointed out that if his son-in-law had appeared as a belated volunteer for the American War of Independence, his only "action" had been against the reputation of his wife and the honor of her family, and that he had been under fire only once—from an angry gentleman of Fort-Royal whose hospitality Beauharnais had reciprocated by alienating his wife's affections.

Returning to France in late October of that year of 1783, Alexandre had to listen to his own father's stern rebuke and his indignant denial of any misbehavior on the part of his daughter-in-law while under his roof. The young Viscount nevertheless addressed a second vituperative letter to his wife, upbraiding her for not having already retired to a convent, and concluding relentlessly: "No move, no gesture, no attempt at reconciliation on your part can stir or shake me, and I urge you to warn my father and your aunt that their efforts to intervene will prove not only fruitless but even damaging to your cause. For six months now, I have been hardening my heart against you. Resign yourself as I have to a distasteful course of action, to a separation which must be an affliction above all to our children, and believe me, madame, when I say that of the two of us you are not the one most to be pitied."

Marie-Josèphe-Rose had no choice but to place her infant daughter with a foster mother and to retire with her two-year-old son to a convent. But, in retiring, she could choose (with Aunt Renaudin's discriminating counsel) Paris' most fashionable convent, the Pentemont, the resort of ladies of quality in distress— abandoned wives, sisters and daughters, wives in process of separation from their husbands, orphans in search of husbands. Even in distress, these were ladies of the society to which Alexandre, and therefore Josephine, aspired; if she must languish for two years in conventual retreat, she would do so in an exalted company to which she could not otherwise have hoped for entree. As it developed, it was not to Coventry that her husband had banished her, but to the most select of Parisian finishing schools. There she made acquaintance and formed relations with members of France's most illustrious families, and, an attentive observer, she took note of their every word, every expression of opinion, every attitude, every custom, gesture, mannerism. With a good ear and an imitative tongue, she mastered their highly specialized upper-stratum jargon in all its subtlety of cadence and inflection, with all its recondite terms of reference. That magnificent air, that superlative grace and charm of manner which distinguished Old-Regime society and inspired the term *grande dame*, Marie-Josèphe-Rose made her own.

At Pentemont she familiarized herself with the lofty world of the French court, with the intricacies of courtiers' expertise: the endless ramifications of the royal and noble hierarchies (the ranks of the ancient feudal nobility as distinct from the newly ennobled, newly affluent plebeians, who owed their titles to successful careers in law or in finance), the infinite nuances of class distinction (to which peers and peeresses a deep obeisance was due and for which a mere sketch of a bow sufficed, for which aristocrats both panels of a double door were to be swung open and which ones were expected to make their entry into a salon through a single panel). At Pentemont, Marie-Josèphe-Rose furnished her mind with all this paraphernalia of tradition, etiquette and protocol, which—as she could never have dreamed—would prove useful to her in her own court rather than in that of Marie Antoinette.

She must have been, in 1783, at the time she entered the convent, an appealing figure, a picture of injured innocence, this pretty, wistful young woman of twenty with her winsome, ringleted little boy. That "exceedingly sweet disposition" to which her father had referred and which not even her enemies could deny won her many and lifelong friends there. She was genuinely ("divinely," "exquisitely") tactful, as people were to say; agreeable, considerate and invariably good-humored in a society where good humor was a social requisite. And, beyond any shadow of a doubt, she was, after four years in the fashion capital, fashionably as well as becomingly attired; with her impeccably good taste, with her flair for style, her passion for clothes, she could not for long have looked dowdy or provincial.

And she was no longer an ugly duckling, to employ a metaphor as apt as it is irresistible in the case of a woman whose imperial emblem was to be the swan. By the time she came to Pentemont, every trace of awkwardness and adolescence was gone, together with "the plump cheeks" of Alexandre's letter; by then she had become her lovely self, sleek, svelte, shapely, the exquisite and exquisitely graceful creature who delights the eye today on canvas and in marble. Hers was not a classic, not a striking beauty, but the illusion of beauty—mysterious, elusive, and softer, more provocative and more stirring still. Only the biographers, not the artists, could catch the sound of her voice: "low," "silvery," "sweetly modulated," "like a caress"; as caressing and voluptuous as her deep-blue glance, her smile, her walk.

There are few descriptions of her during the years 1783-1785; her biographer-friends had not yet appeared on the scene. But it so happened that the father of one of her legal advisers accompanied his son on a visit to the young Viscountess de Beauharnais and, still fresh from the enchantment of the meeting, described her in a letter to his wife as "a fascinating young person, a lady of distinction and of elegance, perfect of manner, endowed with a multitude of graces, and with the loveliest of speaking voices." He added: "Seeing and talking with her, one cannot understand the outrageous behavior of her husband and his cruelties in her regard"—the latest of these having been the abduction of Eugène, who was restored to his mother only under threat of legal action.

Marie-Josèphe-Rose's first move had been to call in a lawyer, Louis Joron, to prepare a plea for legal separation. The evidence collected was overwhelming: Alexandre's own father gave witness to his daughter-in-law's good conduct, and there came a flood of testimonial letters from Martinique vindicating her girlhood virtue, repudiating the Viscount de Beauharnais's accusations and voicing outrage at his attempts to suborn witnesses to traduce his wife's reputation.

After thirteen months of vain endeavor to collect so much as a shred of evidence against his wife, and confronted by the convincing dossier drawn up by her attorneys, the Viscount de Beauharnais agreed to a settlement out of court. By a document dated March 4, 1785, he accepted in full the terms demanded by the Viscountess: he recognized the justice of her charges of injury and neglect, and he made public retraction of his accusations, apologizing on the ground that he "had been carried away by a youthfully immature impetuosity and temporary irrationality," and further declared that "upon his return to France, the testimony of the public as well as of his father was all in favor of his wife." "Consenting voluntarily to the terms which the lady his wife could therefore exact juridically," he pledged himself "to the payment of five thousand livres annually for her maintenance, plus an additional one thousand livres for the maintenance of his daughter"—legal acknowledgment of Hortense's legitimacy. By the terms of the separation agreement, the Viscountess was awarded permanent custody of Hortense and custody of Eugène until he reached the age of five, when he was to be surrendered to his father's care for education. Her honor vindicated, Marie-Josèphe-Rose lived on quietly and circumspectly in her convent apartment, whereas her husband proceeded to furnish further proof of his libertinage by bringing the list of his known bastards up to three, by a child born in that summer of 1785 to a young woman identified only as "unmarried and of good family"—a daughter, Adèle, for whom the Empress Josephine, long years after Alexandre's death, would generously provide both a husband and a dowry.

In the autumn of 1785, Marie-Josèphe-Rose left Paris, with both of her children, for a several months' visit with her Aunt Renaudin and her father-in-law at their Fontainebleau residence. It is not inconceivable that, with her social ambitions and her natural disposition to gaiety at the age of twenty-two, she timed her arrival to coincide with the court's annual visit to Fontainebleau. And it would have been unnatural had not this attractive grass widow attracted a coterie of noble admirers and—avid as she was for diversion, for masculine attention and admiration—hunted, danced and flirted with them.

A string of noble names, those of the Duke de Lorge, the Chevalier de Coigny, the Count de Crénay and the Chevalier de Brison, have all been tenuously linked with hers, although little or no evidence can be found in substantiation—none beyond the bare facts that she was acquainted with these gentlemen and that their paths crossed in Fontainebleau and Paris during the years 1785-1788. As

for her good offices in their behalf after the Revolution, her efforts
to have their names removed from the proscribed list of émigrés,
royalist spies and conspirators, such intervention need not be an
indication of romantic interest; she did as much for a legion of
friends, friends of friends, and total strangers. Gossip about her
gallant adventures subsequent to her separation from her husband
may have been current at the time, but it was not dignified by
print until after Waterloo. It was after 1815, after Waterloo, when
the Bonapartes first became popular subjects for lampoon, and the
figure of "the voluptuous Creole" a favorite one. After Waterloo,
after the restoration of the Bourbon monarchy, it was as popular
a literary sport to vilify the Bonapartes and glorify the Bourbons as,
after the Revolution, it had been to vilify the Bourbons and glorify
the Bonapartes. The process was reversed again in 1852, when the
last of the Bourbons was swept from the throne of France and the
Bonapartes were restored, in the person of Napoleon III, grandson
of the Empress Josephine.

Marie-Josèphe-Rose departed from France in 1788 and her
subsequent two-year sojourn in Martinique provided another ideal
opportunity for salacious conjecture. The gossip that she had
sought refuge in her remote island home to conceal a pregnancy and the birth of an illegitimate child was founded primarily
in malice, but researchers pounced on an entry in the imperial
records of 1807: the grant of a dowry by Napoleon I to a Martini-
quaise named Marie-Josèphe Benaguette at the time of her marriage to a man named Blanchet. The bride was identified as a
foundling who had been adopted practically if not legally by Josephine's mother and had been listed as "among the household attached to the late Madame de la Pagerie" at the time of the latter's death. In 1870, after the debacle of the Second Empire, after
Napoleon III's abdication and flight, a blackmail letter was found
among his effects in the Tuileries Palace; it was signed by a man
named Blanchet, who claimed to be the son of the foundling
Marie-Josèphe—and the grandson of the Empress Josephine. Discovery of this sheet of paper sent the biographers back over the faint
old trail. Frédéric Masson, France's premier historian of the
Napoleonic epic (but with a stubborn prejudice against Josephine),
gave the incident years of study; writing at the turn of the century,

he first credited the tale, but later he published formal retraction on the basis of insufficient evidence.

As to the Martinique episode, there was actually nothing mysterious or suspicious in the fact that a young wife in matrimonial difficulties should go home to her mother, and to a father and sister who were both gravely ill. Financial difficulties, too, beset the Viscountess de Beauharnais in 1788. The Viscount, living profligately, was remiss in the scheduled payments to his wife and children; and the blockade that the English fleet had clamped down over the Atlantic had caused the decline of Martinique's export trade and with it the Tascher family finances—to the point where remittances to their daughter in France were necessarily interrupted.

Marie-Josèphe-Rose, observing her own contractual obligations, had already surrendered Eugène to the care of his father before she embarked with Hortense in June of 1788 for the Antilles.

"We set out alone, my mother and I, [sailing] from Le Havre, where violent winds almost capsized the ship, and we came close to perishing before we had cleared the harbor," Hortense could still remember vividly twenty-eight years later, when, in exile from France with the rest of the Bonapartes, she set about composing her memoirs. Hortense attributed her mother's departure to the fact that she was "oversensitive," "still brooding over the separation from her husband," and "hopeful of finding a remedy by putting an ocean between them."

"Upon our arrival in Martinique, we were greeted with transports of joy by our family," Hortense continues. "The tranquil life we led, visiting first at one plantation, then at another, doubtlessly suited my mother, for we remained nearly three years far from France."

An exclusively domestic or bucolic way of life was not, however, the one best calculated to suit Hortense's gay and fancy-free young mother—a healthy young woman of twenty-five with a healthy appetite for life and love, who in eight years of marriage had spent a total of eleven months under the same roof and in the same bed as her husband. There were, as might have been expected, livelier interludes at Fort-Royal, a port of call and naval base for the French Fleet of the Antilles. For the carnivals, balls and receptions there, Marie-Josèphe-Rose—already a confirmed Parisienne—sent off to

Aunt Renaudin for fashionable costumes and accessories: "a décolleté and diaphanous ball gown," according to one order, "a dozen fans and five pair of English garters," in another.

Among the officers whom her radiance attracted at the Fort-Royal galas, the name of Captain Scipion du Roure-Brison, a thirty-year-old veteran of the American War of Independence, is frequently mentioned, as a suitor if not a lover. That the captain and the Viscountess were fellow passengers on a French ship of the line which set sail suddenly and unexpectedly on September 7, 1790, is an established fact, but it appears to have come about by accident.

Their hairbreadth escape from Martinique is related by Hortense, upon whom the incident made a lasting impression:

> The Revolution had begun in the colony; the Governor forced us to flee precipitately. We were staying at Government House in Fort-Royal when suddenly one evening my mother was notified that the town was under attack. She rushed out instantly to seek refuge on board a vessel [the *Sensible*] which was commanded by an acquaintance of hers. As we crossed the Savane [a public square] a cannon ball fell close beside us.*
>
> The next day the mutineers, having overwhelmed the town, ordered the French ships to return to port, threatening them with fire from the fort. Our ship's crew shouted out its determination to return to France and hurried to pull out of range of the shore batteries, just as the threat was put into execution. The cannons boomed, but we escaped their shots. Fate had spared us. And there we were unexpectedly on the high seas without so much as an adieu to anyone ashore.

Hortense's "mutineers" were colonial battalions, along with slaves, freedmen, mulattoes and underprivileged whites, all the malcontents of Martinique, in revolt against colonial tyranny and oppression, against caste discrimination and feudal inequalities—an echo of the Revolution that had begun in France on July 14, 1789, with the assault on the Bastille, an echo of the cannon and musket shots at Bunker Hill and Yorktown. Revolution was in the air, even the balmy air of the Caribbean; the winds of discontent

---

* Today a larger-than-lifesize marble statue of the Empress Josephine stands on the spot where, according to island tradition, the cannon ball struck.

had reached even the Islands-under-the-Wind, Martinique and Santo Domingo.

The only report on the stormy fifty-two-day eastbound crossing of the *Sensible* is that of Hortense, who, being fiercely defensive of the reputation of her much maligned mother (as she was of that of her "martyred" father), makes no mention, to be sure, of any shipboard romance between her mother and the gallant captain. Those imaginative historical-fiction writers who do, forget—or forget to mention—that she was a notoriously poor sailor; it is difficult to imagine *mal-de-mer* as conducive to amorousness.

4

By Hortense's account, the *Sensible* pulled into Toulon harbor on October 29, 1790, after a close call in the Straits of Gibraltar, where it ran aground off the North African shore and almost capsized. "Upon our arrival in Toulon my mother learned of the events which had recently agitated France. The Revolution had broken out."

That much her mother had heard even in far-off Martinique; what she could not have known was that she was sailing back into the very eye of the hurricane. She must have been startled, at disembarkation, to hear herself addressed for the first time as "Citizeness" instead of "Viscountess" or "Madame"; to hear the savage chant of the "Ça Ira," the battle hymn of the French Republic, ring out above the din of the dockside disorders; and to see, for the first time, the tricolor flying on the flagpoles of the harbor forts in place of the white Bourbon lilies, the royal fleur-de-lis.

News of the signal events of the preceding year had reached her overseas: representatives of the three Estates (clergy, nobility and commons) summoned to Versailles as a States-General by a desperate, tottering, bankrupt government; the States-General transformed into a National Assembly dominated by the Third Estate (the commons) and proceeding—with the enforced sanction of the King—to frame a constitution for France; the fall of the Bastille. For the shocking developments of recent months, however, an overseas traveler returning along the Paris road in the early winter of 1790 was unprepared: unprepared for the sight of flames and smoke, of châteaux under attack by a peasantry suddenly enraged at absentee landlords and age-old feudal tributes and impositions; unprepared for the ominous sound of the tocsins and of village church bells tolling a summons not to devotion but to insurrection.

Paris, the new seat of the Assembly and the capital and nerve center of a nation in ferment, was the very last place for members of the detested nobility. The Viscountess, quickly discovering this, proceeded direct to Fontainebleau to join the Marquis de Beauharnais and Aunt Renaudin in their modest quarters. There, too, for a joyous reunion with the mother and sister he adored, came nine-year-old Eugène from the Collège d'Harcourt, where he had been enrolled by his father.

"Our father," Hortense noted in her memoirs with some pride, "was already playing a leading role in the party whose cause he had embraced; his brother had chosen the opposite side." Alexandre's elder brother, François, the Count de Beauharnais, a faithful royalist ("the loyal Beauharnais"), crossed the border into exile and into service in the armies of the émigré Bourbon princes; while Alexandre, the Viscount de Beauharnais, joined that band of noblemen who, on the epochal night of August 4, 1789, deserted their Second Estate seats to sit on the benches of the Third and join the commoners, repudiating the feudal system and all its fundamental fealties, and rushing to the rostrum of the Assembly as to an altar of liberty—there, in one of the strangest spectacles of all time, to immolate and to renounce their own splendorous birthright of rank and privilege. (This becomes less phenomenal when one remembers that in many cases, as in that of the Viscount de Beauharnais, these aristocrat-liberal-intellectuals of the eighteenth century were younger sons renouncing the birthright of their elder brothers rather than their own.)

The erstwhile Viscount de Beauharnais, on his sporadic visits to his father and children at Fontainebleau, held forth extensively and pompously on the popular political doctrine of the day, the establishment of a constitutional monarchy. The erstwhile Viscount-

ess listened more or less attentively, less interested in Alexandre's
political theories than in his financial contributions to her support
and to the children's—as sporadic, unfortunately, as his visits.

Elected to the presidency of the Constituent Assembly in 1791,
Alexandre proudly occupied the chair during the final drafting of
the constitution. It was he who on June 21, from that chair, made
the announcement to the delegates and to the nation that the
King and Queen and their children had fled the capital; it was
he who presided over the uninterrupted five-day emergency session of the Assembly, and who served a temporarily leaderless
France as regent. The pursuit of the royal fugitives was organized
by Alexandre; his were the directions for the capture, arrest and return of the abject royal family. He personally instructed their inter-
rogators and composed the remonstrances to be read to the hapless
pair of monarchs upon their arrival at the Tuileries.

With the constitution completed and accepted by the King on
September 14, 1791, the Assembly declared its work accomplished
and its session at an end. But Paris' exultant cry "The Revolution is
ended!" was premature. Before another twelve months had passed,
national rejoicing had turned to national hysteria under the threat
of invasion—by the émigré army of the Bourbon princes, calling
for vengeance on the rebels, and by the coalition forces of European monarchs, preaching the divine right of kings but apparently
less eager to protect the sacred person of the French one than to
snap up several of his tempting border provinces. Whatever the
motives of the invaders, the reaction within France was violent.
By mid-August of 1792, the Tuileries Palace had been mobbed and
the King imprisoned in the Temple, the last wayside station on the
road to the scaffold. By the end of September, the first French Republic had been proclaimed by a defiant National Convention
and christened in blood by rioters of the Paris Commune, who had
dragged hundreds of priests and aristocrats (*ipso facto*, "conspirators in the invasion") from their prison cells to slaughter on the
streets.

Among the victims of these September Massacres were friends of
the Beauharnais'. Terrified by the turn of events and by the
mounting alarms of the winter, Marie-Josèphe-Rose resolved to
send Hortense and Eugène to England in the custody of a friend,

the Princess Amalia of Hohenzollern. But before the children could reach the coast their indignant father ordered them to be returned and, furthermore, to be apprenticed to a trade, like all good little republicans: Eugène to a good patriot of a cabinetmaker, Hortense to a "seamstress"—a Mademoiselle Lannoy, who may or may not have qualified as such but who was undoubtedly her governess.

If General Beauharnais (Alexandre had by then exchanged a lofty legislative role for an equally lofty military one) forbade his family to leave the country, he did not oppose a removal from the capital; the suburbs seemed safer at the moment, less racked by tensions and by alarms. Marie-Josèphe-Rose chose Croissy, apparently tranquil, dozing on the Seine ten miles downstream from Paris.

She was grateful to have been out of earshot of the hideous clamor on Paris' Place de la Révolution on January 21, 1793, when Louis XVI mounted the steps to the guillotine. Her father had served his mother as a page, as she could not forget.

By the summer of that year, General Beauharnais was commander in chief of the French Army of the Rhine, a post in which, for the glory of the Republic, he would issue a gush of patriotic leaflets, pamphlets, proclamations and orations. He came under criticism by the War Ministry not only for his defeats but for malingering behind the lines—"making a fool of himself at Strasbourg by chasing after whores all day and giving balls for them at night," to quote from army commissioners' reports. Under suspicion, furthermore, along with all aristocrats in the Army's upper echelons, General Beauharnais resigned his commission on grounds of illness; the resignation was accepted in August 1793 on grounds of incompetence—and a hint of treason.

Back on the patriarchal acres of former Beauharnais estates in the Loire Valley, not all his show of republican oratorical fervor in the community councils and in the local radical Jacobin club could save Alexandre from the grim surveillance of the Committee of Public Safety, the newly organized executive branch—and instrument of terror—set up by the National Convention. Marie-Josèphe-Rose did her best to dissipate the cloud of suspicion hanging over her husband's head, by writing in his behalf to Vadier, president of the dread committee. She went still further, including a plea in behalf of her imprisoned sister-in-law, the Countess de Beauharnais, with whom she had never even been on terms of intimacy. To sign her name to such a letter to the authorities was to call attention to herself and was thus a violation of the first law of self-preservation in that perilous time when, by the recently enacted Law of Suspects, any former title of nobility was a title to suspicion as "a friend of tyranny and an enemy of liberty"; a title to arrest, to imprisonment and to the guillotine, by then in permanent location and in daily operation on the Place de la Révolution. Those aristocrats who had not fled the borders had gone underground, shrinking back against the walls so as not to cast so much as a shadow on Paris' blood-spattered streets.

Marie-Josèphe-Rose, apostrophizing Vadier as a "former colleague" of Alexandre's in the National Assembly, urged him not to confuse Alexandre with his brother. "You may have reason to doubt the patriotism of the former privileged class," her letter conceded, "but surely among them are fast friends of liberty and equality. Alexandre has never deviated from those principles. At first he doubted my patriotism, but, seeing that I consorted only with republicans, he was convinced. Mine is a republican household, and I can sign myself an out-and-out sans-culotte." (In so doing she was claiming to be one of the most rabid of rabid patriots, who evidenced their extreme left-wing political sentiments sartorially, discarding the knee breeches of court attire in favor of the new long, tight pantaloons.)

If there is a note of panic in her protestations of fervent, fanatic republicanism, the alternative was grim in 1794. Alexandre, in vouching for his wife's patriotism, as her letter to Vadier shows he did, may have flattered himself that his oratory had converted her to his ideology. On the other hand, since she is unanimously described by her associates as suggestible, malleable and pliant, he may have been correct. Certainly she was on good terms, and cultivated the society, as she claimed, of many of his friends in the Revolutionary avant-garde. Her second husband, General Bonaparte, would vouch for her, too, as a good patriot and a staunch republican. Even so, with her "Creole nonchalance" and her "aversion to taking a stand," as she once expressed it in a letter to Aunt Renaudin, there is room for doubt as to whether she was a woman of strong convictions, political or otherwise. Her letter to Vadier proves only that she had achieved fluency in the popular republican patter. Her pattern of thought was subjective rather than objective. "Her attention wandered from any discussion of abstract ideas," as one of her philosophically minded friends, Madame de Rémusat, objected. She fidgeted at dialectics. She could not be enlisted in a cause, but she could be moved to warm, quick response by an individual case, by a personal plea, a human-interest story. So it was with her good offices in behalf of Revolutionary victims, such as her imprisoned sister-in-law and countless others. So it was later with her manifold and tireless efforts in behalf of the émigrés, those pitiful displaced persons of the eighteenth century; she was less apt to have been moved by political convictions or by principle than by her easily stirred emotions, by her ready sympathy and compassion.

Historians are prone to disparage Josephine as an opportunist, to say that she changed her political coloring with every change of regime in France, from Bourbon white to revolutionary red to imperial purple—and consistently to her personal advantage. But that she, a *femme sole* with two minor children, survived such a series of cataclysmic upheavals seems rather a proof of determination, resourcefulness and ingenuity than of political opportunism. During the Revolution in France, as in America, these were times to try men's souls. Josephine's soul must have been of a fiber tougher and more resilient than Napoleon's description of "gossamer and lace," for she endured the long years of Revolutionary torment and managed to emerge with relatively minor neurotic tendencies—tearfulness, fear and a mild hypochondria.

But no currying of favor with the authorities, no scurrying to the countryside into hiding, no "certificate of civism" at Croissy could guarantee security in the epidemic of arrest and death in 1794. The dictatorship of the fanatic Incorruptible, Robespierre, had decreed the principle of "salutary terror," "terror as the order of the day": a bath of blood, red along with blue, as the Revolution, Chronoslike, set about devouring its own children. The Convention, convulsed and paralyzed by its internal struggles, seemingly could find no other measure by which to subdue the counterrevolutionary royalist factions on the rampage in the south and west of France; no other remedy to apply to the national economic collapse. If the people must suffer from famine, inflation and unemployment, at least they were to be diverted by a circus of death, with daily performances in the Place de la Révolution and in every public square of every city of every province.

Word of Alexandre's arrest reached his wife in early March, and she rose again to his defense with oral and written petitions to every old friend of his or hers who had survived the purges. But no one any longer dared, literally speaking, to risk his neck for any other. Marie-Josèphe-Rose, as she was shortly to discover, had too impulsively risked her own.

5

Upon an anonymous denunciation ("Beware of the former Viscountess de Beauharnais, who has secret dealings with government offices"), a search of her Paris apartment was ordered. She must have breathed a shuddering sigh of relief at the first official report, which read: "No evidence of hostility to the Republic, but, rather, a multitude of patriotic letters redounding to the credit of this citizeness."

But that was before the search party had reached the attic. There the discovery of "two chests full of the correspondence and papers of the former General Beauharnais, presently a prisoner of the state" furnished "incriminatory evidence sufficient to justify a warrant of arrest"—as if any justification were necessary. The next night, that of April 22, three red-bonneted functionaries of the dread Committee of General Security returned to claim their victim and to deliver her to the Carmes, the very prison in which her husband was confined.

"Don't wake the children," Hortense quotes her mother as whispering to their governess. "I could not bear their tears. I could not tear myself from their arms." "Our awakening," Hortense concludes, "was cruel—suddenly alone, bereft at one stroke of both mother and father."

The Carmes, the ancient Carmelite convent, was one of the

most hideous of Paris' Revolutionary prisons: dark, dank, its walls dripping with moisture and still blood-smeared from the September Massacres; barred slits for windows, and many of those sealed; open latrines in the narrow corridors; and "crawling with rats, mice, vermin," in the description of one of its seven-hundred-odd anguished human inmates in that spring of 1794, a Mrs. Elliott, an Englishwoman who had been living in France—living too openly with a succession of French and English princes to have escaped republican notice and censure.

It is a tribute to the generally superficial conventions of that *ancien-régime* society that Mrs. Elliott should have found "consolation for the horrors of the Carmes" at finding herself in "the good company of so many delightful, so many great ladies" there. The fact that equanimity and good humor were prime requisites of social intercourse among the French aristocracy accounted to a great extent for the display of high morale and valor in the Revolutionary prisons, a marvel to every contemporary reporter. It is less likely that these effete and pampered noblemen and noble-women were uniformly valorous than that they were uniformly products of their peculiar social code: they demonstrated, in the last extremity, that good manners could reinforce—if not substitute for—character, and that a carefully cultivated insouciance could make an acceptable substitute for heroism.

"Most of the prisoners, like myself," Mrs. Elliott wrote a few years later,

> had little reason to hope they would leave the Carmes but for the scaffold, yet I must own that I passed many pleasant moments there with those very agreeable women, who were all full of talent; none more so than Madame Beauharnais, now Madame Bonaparte. She is one of the most accomplished, good-humored women I ever met with. The only little disputes we had when together were over politics, she being what was called, at the beginning of the Revolution, "Constitutional"; but she was not in the least a Jacobin, for nobody suffered more by the Reign of Terror and by Robespierre than she did. When I first went into the Carmes I slept in a room where we were eighteen in number, and Madame Bonaparte, Madame de Custine and I had our beds close together. We have often made our beds, and

washed the room, for the other prisoners did not take much pains about it.

As for Alexandre de Beauharnais, Mrs. Elliott wrote that she had known him for many years and that he was "a very pleasant man, with much talent, though rather a coxcomb." But when she speaks of his and his wife's "embarrassment" at their death's-door encounter, and of their "perfect reconciliation" ("a small closet with two beds was granted to them, where they slept together"), she ceases to be a credible witness. The estranged couple were on terms of civility and were unlikely to have suffered embarrassment at meeting, having met at his father's house and at that of mutual friends over a period of years, having exchanged reports on the children, and having gone to each other's defense in recent critical times; but there is no corroboration of Mrs. Elliott's story of their resumption of marital relations. Had Marie-Josèphe-Rose, in a weak moment, made any such gesture of reconciliation, she would surely have been discouraged. For, in mentioning the name of Madame de Custine as their cell mate, Mrs. Elliott had already named the "other woman" at the Carmes: Delphine of "the flaxen hair and beryl-blue eyes," who inspired in Alexandre de Beauharnais the most consuming passion (perhaps the only genuine, certainly the last) of his passionate thirty-four-year career; it flared so fiercely bright as to dazzle even that charnel house.

Not that either made any effort to conceal it; Alexandre had never been one to show consideration of his wife, and Delphine, one of Mrs. Elliott's "great ladies" by definition of birth and social distinction, had separated from her husband years previously, to experiment, as Alexandre had, in love. Now he and she divided their time between making love and analyzing it—in curious, interminable, introspective, ecstatic letters to her brother proclaiming that both had had "to come into the shadow of the scaffold to find true happiness."

"That poor Madame Beauharnais," Mrs. Elliott commiserated, "who really seemed to be very much attached to her husband, became very unhappy. Certainly Beauharnais was more in love than it is possible to describe and the little [Custine] woman seemed to have no objection to his attentions."

When Alexandre's attention could be diverted to his children, he joined his wife in letters to them. Hers were tender and spontaneous: "My dear little Hortense, it hurts me to be separated from you and my dear Eugène. I never stop thinking of my two darling little children, whom I love and embrace with all my heart." Alexandre's messages were stilted, in his customary pedantic, self-consciously literary style: "The best way to convince us that you miss and remember us is by assuring us that you are putting your time to good purpose and working hard."

When correspondence with the prison was cut off, the children took to writing out the list of contents affixed to the packages of food and clean linen that were delivered weekly to the Carmes. "Each of us in turn," as Hortense explains the naïve stratagem, "copied out the list so that, at least, our parents would know we were still alive." But a four-footed messenger proved cleverest; Marie-Josèphe-Rose's little dog, Fortuné, with scraps of paper fastened beneath his collar, could dart past the guard in a flash and find his way to his mistress, then back again with her reply.

Once, through some mysterious and friendly agency, Hortense and Eugène were given a glimpse of their prisoner parents.

An unknown woman came one day [as Hortense tells it] and mysteriously led us to the rear of a garden on the Rue de Sèvres and up the stairs of a gardener's house, all the while cautioning us to the strictest silence. Across from us we could see a huge building . . . and then a window opening, in which my mother and father appeared. In surprise and great emotion, I stretched out my arms to them and cried out. They made signs to me to be still, but a sentinel at the foot of the wall had heard us, and began to shout. The unknown woman hurried us out and home. . . . We learned that the window of the prison had been sealed. This was the last time I saw my father. A few days later he was dead.

This incident, a nightmare to haunt all Hortense's childhood, must have occurred in mid-July, for on the twenty-second her father's name was called out by the jailer summoning the Carmes's daily quota of fifty, a sizable number necessary to account for the ghastly total of 1,367 severed heads ("falling like tiles off a roof," in the gleeful, gloating words of the public prosecutor) between the middle of June and the end of July. By that summer's "Great Terror," even the former travesty of trial by jury had been dispensed with at Robespierre's dictate as a luxury the imperiled Republic could not afford; the appearance of the accused before the Revolutionary Tribunal was the sole formality to be observed in the mass executions.

Alexandre de Beauharnais, upon his summons, found time to embrace Delphine and to slip his Arab talisman ring upon her finger as a pledge of his eternal devotion, which, considering the short time remaining to him on earth, could be accepted at face value. To his wife he preferred to write his farewell, from the Conciergerie on the twenty-third, the day before his execution. "My tender affection for our dear children and the fraternal attachment which binds me to you can leave no doubt of the sentiment with which I depart this life," he wrote.

He was said to have been unwilling to subject himself to one of Marie-Josèphe-Rose's emotionally surcharged scenes at a moment when he had need of all his composure. Again he may have flattered himself. Even though, in the very act of widowing her, Alexandre had shown her his customary disrespect, a letter Josephine wrote to her mother reveals a considerable composure, with words to the effect that she "could yet find some reasons for regret" at her husband's death. Perhaps that composure in the face of his final public repudiation of her as wife and woman stemmed from the fact that she had had a prison romance of her own, one as flamboyantly conducted as her rival Delphine's and with a general far more renowned than General Beauharnais.

A dozen generals had paid with their heads upon the scaffold for their defeats on the field of battle, but twenty-six-year-old General Lazare Hoche, hero of the Army of the Moselle, had only victories to his name; it could only have been the lack of recent ones which accounted for his presence at the Carmes. "Handsome, gallant and good-humored," Mrs. Elliott said of him. Tall, muscular but lithe, with a dueling scar like a comma between his brows to emphasize the virility of his regular features, Hoche carried an air of authority. He was precisely the type of male to reassure and comfort a frail and tremulous woman at an hour of crisis, to inspire a responsive passion in an unattached and susceptible woman at any hour.

The exhibition of valor in the Revolutionary prisons was matched only by that of "passionate abandon," to use the words of one reporter, Count Beugnot, who like many another could only marvel at it in the case of "men and women whom I knew to be carrying death sentences in their pockets"; it was, he added, "a species of bravura for which I was not cut out." General Hoche and Madame Beauharnais met in the Carmes courtyard, to which prisoners of both sexes were frequently admitted for the afternoon promenade. But it was the evening which "offered opportunities not to be neglected," according to Count Beugnot's firsthand survey of the romantic side of prison life during the French Revolution. "When shadows lengthened and weary guards relaxed their vigilance, when most of the prisoners were off to bed, and those who remained were discreet, in that moment of peace which came as a prelude to the horror of the night"—it was then that the rendezvous between Marie-Josèphe-Rose and Lazare Hoche took place, in the privacy of the individual cell which was assigned to a general of the Republic as a special dispensation.

Paul Barras, who would later supersede Hoche in Marie-Josèphe-Rose's affections, yet conceded that "of all the men in her life, Hoche was the one she loved the most." The romance was as brief as it was ardent; by calendar count they were together at the Carmes for a total of only twenty days and nights. On May 17 Hoche was transferred to the Conciergerie ("that anteroom to the guillotine," Beugnot called it), presumably to be tried and executed.

Madame Beauharnais gave way to such despair as to "scandalize her companions," according to one report. "She openly wept; she shuffled her pack of tarot cards and told fortunes, and then she wept again. The other prisoners were resigned, but she continued hoping against hope." And, since she had not abandoned hope, it is unlikely that she conformed to the prison custom of cutting off her hair to send as a memento to her family, as well as to avoid its cutting by the public executioner.

By July 23, it seemed inevitable that the name of the Widow Beauharnais would follow that of General Beauharnais on the jailer's roll call. Yet four days passed after Alexandre's execution without a summons for her. The fourth day was July 27—the ninth Thermidor, by the Revolutionary calendar—and to its desperate and gory deeds she owed her life.

Between the twenty-third and the twenty-seventh of July, a desperate effort was under way in the Convention to rally and unite the members in opposition to Robespierre before he should purge them all, individually or collectively. Terrorists now terrified, sinister figures such as Paul Barras and Jean Tallien plotted and connived in the corridors of the Convention and in the political clubs, and galvanized the disconcerted factions into concerted action against Robespierre. On the ninth Thermidor, Tallien seized the rostrum and signaled the attack with a flourish of the dagger and the classic cry of "Death to the tyrant!" The Convention screwed up its courage and condemned Robespierre. (Legend has it that Tallien's beautiful mistress, Thérèse de Fontenay—later his wife —herself a victim of Robespierre and a prisoner awaiting execution, had armed her lover's hand and heart by sending him the dagger with a message that her death would be attributable to his "arrant cowardice." She would later encourage the legend by her claim that "this little hand helped overthrow the guillotine.")

The story of how the news of the ninth Thermidor, the day of Robespierre's overthrow, reached the Carmes and the prisoner Beauharnais can be read in her own words, as recorded by Georgette Ducrest, a lady in waiting who heard her tell it at a tea party eighteen years later:

One morning the jailer came into the room where I slept with the Duchess d'Aiguillon and two other ladies [the Empress Josephine is speaking, according to Mademoiselle Ducrest's memoirs]. He told me that he had come to take away my bed to give it to another prisoner.

"Does that imply that Madame Beauharnais is to have a better one?" Madame d'Aiguillon demanded sharply.

"It means she'll not be needing one of any kind," he replied with a repulsive grin. "It means they're coming to take her to the Conciergerie and from there to the guillotine."

At these words my companions emitted piercing shrieks. Finally, to put an end to their lamentations, I told them that their distress was ridiculous, that not only would I not be put to death, I would live to become a queen of France, as had been predicted to me.

"Then why not begin making out the list of your ladies of the palace?" Madame d'Aiguillon inquired sarcastically.

"Ah, you're right, I hadn't thought of that. Very well, my dear, I'll begin by naming you as my lady of honor. I promise you the appointment." *

At which these ladies' tears began to flow the faster; they were afraid I had gone stark mad. Actually, I was not affecting a show of courage; I was at that moment convinced that the prediction made me by the fortuneteller would be realized.

With Madame d'Aiguillon about to faint, I pulled her toward the window and was opening it to give her a breath of air when suddenly I saw a woman below making vigorous and incomprehensible gestures in our direction. She kept plucking at and pointing to her dress, although we could not imagine what that could signify. But when she persisted I called out, "*Robe?*" to which she nodded a vigorous Yes. Then she picked up a stone, put it in her apron, took it out again, and held it up in her hand. "*Pierre* [stone]!" I cried out, this time to her obvious delight. Next, holding up her dress and the stone together, she began to go through the motion of slitting her throat, and then to dance about and to clap her hands. This singular charade filled us with an inexpressible emotion, for we dared to interpret it to mean that Robespierre had been guillotined, that we had a right to hope and that France was saved! A few moments later, a crowd of our companions in misfortune rushed in and gave us the details of that memorable day. . . .

They brought me back my bed of leather-strip webbing, on which I slept the soundest night's sleep of my life. Before I retired, I said to my friends, "You see, I have not been guillotined, and I shall yet be crowned queen of France."

The memoirs of Mademoiselle Ducrest are not the only ones to quote Josephine and her story of the old mulatto crone who told her fortune when she was a child in Martinique. Both Napoleon and Hortense make mention of hearing her tell it, too. Inclined as

---

* A promise which Josephine tried to keep when she became empress, Mlle. Ducrest reports her as saying; but Napoleon objected because Mme. d'Aiguillon was a divorcee.

she was to superstition, to belief in her star, in signs and premonitions, she may have put faith in that fortune told her in her youth —especially in August of 1794, when the first part of the prediction, that there would be a first, early marriage and an early widowhood, had already come to pass. The part about a second marriage was not unlikely of fulfillment. The final prophecy, however, that she would one day wear the crown of France, must have struck her as patently absurd at a time when revolution had just "abolished monarchy forever."

6

"The regime of Robespierre had ended, but our mother had not yet returned to us," Hortense de Beauharnais wrote, "when a lady of remarkable beauty came one day to call and consoled us with the promise that she would interest herself in our mother's liberation . . . And a few days later she was, indeed, restored to us."

For their mother's release, among the earliest, on the nineteenth Thermidor (August 6), both Hortense and Eugène always credited Tallien, and they expressed their gratitude in the form of a pension to that ignoble "hero of Thermidor" long after he had lost all power, prestige and fortune. Hortense's "lady of remarkable beauty" was Thérèse de Fontenay, the very first prisoner, of course, to be released by her lover, Tallien.

The vise of terror on the nerves and heart had been too long applied to be so suddenly relieved. Paris went from a state of shock into delirium. A typical symptom was the mania for the dance. A dancing plague like that of the Middle Ages seized the capital; Paris commemorated the end of the dance of death by the opening of 644 public ballrooms. "Next to money, the dance is what every Parisian loves, adores, idolizes," wrote Louis-Sébastien Mercier. "Every class, rich and poor, high and low, dances everywhere"—on the Place de la Révolution (hopefully renamed the Place de la Concorde), in the churches, in the former Cemetery of St.-Sulpice (renamed "Bal des Zéphyrs"). In the aristocratic district of St.-Germain, the rage took on a macabre note with its "Victims' Balls"—to which the Widow Beauharnais was eligible on two counts, as a former prisoner and as a surviving relative of a victim of the guillotine; the required accouterments were a coiffure *à la guillotine* (hair cropped short or lifted up off the neck) and a narrow red satin ribbon encircling the throat. The Widow Beauharnais whirled with the rest in the voluptuous undulations of the waltz, recently imported from Germany. She could have waltzed with General Hoche where they had walked together —in the courtyard of the Carmes prison, open again under new management, as another *bal dansant*.

General Hoche's release from the Conciergerie had come on August 4, two days before her own. They must have marveled at finding each other again, still alive and still in love.

Hoche wrote to his little sixteen-year-old provincial bride to discourage her from joining him in the capital. The three weeks remaining to him there, before he set out for his command post with the Army of the West, he could thus devote to the second installment of the romance that had had its origin at the Carmes. He may have led the Widow Beauharnais to believe that he was considering divorce in order to marry her; divorce as well as marriage had been reduced to the sketchiest of civil ceremonies. Certainly the Widow Beauharnais would not have hesitated to marry a man who was highly attractive to her personally and whose prospects were as brilliant as hers were dim. Most gratefully, that autumn, she entrusted to him her thirteen-year-old son, Eugène, to serve on his staff as junior ordnance officer.

In the circumstances in which she found herself in 1794, alone in the world—a world unrecognizably new, dismayingly unstable —she would have difficulty enough in providing for two, herself and Hortense, much less for three. In the famine of that dreadful winter, with people fighting savagely for a place in the ever-lengthening bread lines, Marie-Josèphe-Rose could thank a friend, as she later said in words intended to be taken literally, for "granting me my daily bread"; she was the only guest at Madame Dumoulin's generous board who was excused from bringing a crust of her own. (This frank comment on the vicissitudes of her earlier years, made when she had attained to exalted station, would disarm those who might otherwise have been tempted to speak of her disparagingly as someone they had "known when.") No revenues were to be expected from her husband's estate, his properties having been either confiscated or sequestered by the state; and none from Martinique, presently under English occupation. Little help could be expected from her aunt and father-in-law, themselves suffering in the wild spiral of inflation.

For the three preceding years, the banker Emmery, the Taschers' European agent, had been advancing her small sums against long-awaited remittances. "Without his generosity I don't know what would have become of me," she wrote her mother in January of 1795. "I know your tender heart too well to doubt that you will make all possible haste to provide me with the wherewithal to live and to pay back the sums I owe." And again in October: "I cannot begin to tell you how important it is that you cover this draft, for I have already paid out substantial sums to various friends who have kept me and the children alive."

While she waited, she had been reduced to borrowing—from Hoche, presumably (for he later complained in jealous spite that she had levied heavy contributions on him as a lover), from Hortense's governess and the governess's brother, from casual friends and acquaintances. Signing herself "La Pagerie la veuve [Widow] Beauharnais," she left a paper trail of promissory notes, too many to be considered today as collectors' items. Bills fluttered in her wake like confetti: for carriage hire, for "gray Florentine silk taffeta," for "multicolor, coin-dotted gray silk hose," for (of all things, in that time of want and economic chaos) flowers. She could not live within her means (never could, never would, not even with an imperial treasury at her disposition), so she lived, as was infinitely more agreeable, beyond them.

Her struggle for existence was none the less desperate for being occasionally flighty; her winsome appeal and her sweetest feminine blandishments were dedicated to a pertinacious and effective campaign to recover her own and her husband's properties from national confiscation. Thanks to Tallien and other influential friends in the regime, the government seals were removed from her Paris apartment, and furniture, clothing and jewelry sequestered there since her arrest were restored to her, as were the silverware and books from Alexandre's Loire Valley château; its furnishings having already been sold as national property, the cash equivalent was awarded to her. As for the Beauharnais properties and estates, restitution would not be made until 1796, and then only through her persistent petitioning at government offices.

By the summer of 1795, she could make her daily round of visits to these government offices in a carriage and pair ("two black Hungarian horses") of her own, issued her by the War Ministry as compensation for the horses and military equipment abandoned by General Beauharnais with the Army of the Rhine when he had hastily yielded up his command two years previously. For this favor she was indebted not to Jean Tallien but to Paul Barras, a figure looming suddenly large on the political horizon—and on her own, as was perhaps not entirely a matter of coincidence.

Shortly after his rise to prominence as one of the heroes of Thermidor (as president of the Convention and commanding general of the Army of the Interior) she sent Barras one of the charming little notes she was in the habit of addressing to gentlemen in high public office. This, an appeal primarily in behalf of one of her numerous charity cases, included an invitation to come to call and ended archly: "It is naughty of you to neglect an old acquaintance." Her political flair was excellent. Barras was destined within the year to hold the most powerful position in the nation since the abolition of the monarchy.

The national acclaim and the wild rejoicing at Robespierre's overthrow in July of 1794 had furnished convincing proof that France, anguished, exhausted, drained of blood, resources and energy, required a respite to both terror and anarchy, even at the risk of surrendering some of the gains which had been won by the Revolution against absolutism and tyranny. To give France the breathing spell she demanded, the Convention in November of 1795 delegated the executive powers it had been unable to wield effectively to a five-man "Directoire," with Barras as one of the five Directors—shortly the foremost.

The Widow Beauharnais's liaison with Barras was to be the one most severely reproached her by contemporaries, not to be forgotten even after her consecration in Notre Dame, not even by so loyal a Bonapartist as General Thiébaut, who deplored the fact that "despite her many good qualities and infinite graces, Josephine remained for me, as for so many others, the former mistress of Barras." It was an affair she could never live down for the reason that it linked her name with that of a regime and of a man contemptible to their own generation as well as to succeeding ones: "The most corrupt of men in an era of utter corruption"; "The most dissolute of rakes"; "He would toss the Republic out the window tomorrow if it did not pay for his table and his gambling, his dogs, horses, and mistresses."

Audacity he had, and a sharp intelligence and a great agility at political maneuver; but not an ideal, not a scruple. He did not even seek power for power's sake, but only for the luxuries and privileges it afforded; the principal appeal of the throne he had appropriated was sybaritic—the feel of sitting on velvet. Although he had divested himself of all the trappings of nobility, including the title of viscount, his appearance, tastes, and manners remained those of a *grand seigneur*; handsome, elegant, cultivated, he was the spoiled fruit rather than the flower of that society which he had repudiated in 1789 as a political expedient. In contrast to Louis XV, who relaxed all barriers of caste for beautiful female companions but made no exceptions in the case of males, Barras tolerated the vulgarest and crudest of men, all the parvenu riffraff of place seekers and political intrigants, but showed himself uncompromising as to the ladies of his society; these must be ladies of distinction, elegance and manner—a former Viscountess de Beauharnais, for example.

Even the infamous Marquis de Sade (a cousin, incidentally, of Barras's) took notice of the Director's orgies and debauches, his peculiar collection of male as well as female favorites, his mistresses and minions; Sade's *roman à clef* entitled *Zoloé et ses deux acolytes* depicts the saturnalia of the Luxembourg Palace, with Madame Beauharnais represented as Zoloé, and Thérèse Tallien and Madame Châteaurenaud as the two acolytes. It is by way of a curiosity that no trace of rivalry ever marred this trio's friendship. Thérèse Tallien remained Madame Bonaparte's "*chère petite*" throughout years of correspondence; not even Napoleon's iron will could impose an absolute rupture. Three sultanas in a seraglio could not have more harmoniously shared the favors of a potentate

—if, indeed, there were any favors, in a physical sense, to share. Barras's parade of three mistresses at once would seem to cast doubt on his heterosexuality rather than prove it.

At times, he seemed to protest it overmuch: "Certainly I had enjoyed intimate relations with Madame Beauharnais. In writing my memoirs, I have admitted—to the extent such revelation is possible to a Frenchman brought up in the tradition of chivalry—that she was my mistress." The editor of the Barras memoirs showed Gallic chivalry greater than that of the author by his deletion of a passage in which Barras had expressed his cynical secret scorn at the sight of the sycophantic visitors and petitioners in his salon bowing respectfully low to kiss Madame Beauharnais's hand which was "still moist from the water of my marble tub."

She acted as Barras's official hostess not only in his Paris salon but in her suburban Croissy residence as well. And the neighbors talked. Among them was Étienne-Denis Pasquier, future chancellor and duke, who would write in his memoirs:

> Madame de Beauharnais's house was next door to ours at Croissy. She no longer came there often, but only once a week, and then to receive Barras and the numerous retinue that followed in his wake. Early in the morning we would see the baskets of provisions being delivered, and later the mounted police would appear to clear the road from Nanterre to Croissy for the young Director, who usually arrived on horseback. As is so often the case with Creoles, Madame de Beauharnais's house boasted a certain luxury of appointments, one in which all the superfluities were present and only the essentials lacking. Fowl, wild game and rare fruits were stacked high in the kitchen, and yet there was a shortage of saucepans, plates and glasses, which she came to borrow from our modest household.

A former Croissy neighbor who would also talk later was young Claire de Vergennes, the future Madame de Rémusat—despite the fact that when she wrote her memoirs she had recouped her family fortunes through this same widow whose goings-on she so brilliantly and relentlessly recorded. It was by these superb and disloyal memoirs that she repaid her tremendous debt to the Bonapartes. The very qualities reprehensible in her as a friend and a woman are those most laudable in a biographer; never wholly responsive to Josephine's confidence and generosity, Madame de Rémusat's critical detachment was ideal from the point of view of history.

"Closely associated with the beautiful Madame Tallien, she was introduced into Directoire society, where she became a special protégée of Barras," Madame de Rémusat recounts. "Madame de Beauharnais had little money, and her taste for clothes and luxury rendered her dependent on those who could aid her in satisfying such expensive tastes. From this time on, her reputation for good conduct was seriously compromised, but"—and the "but" is significant in that here, as in most instances of criticism of Josephine's indiscretions, there follows a reference to her kindness, as if to say that both were the product of the same generous, headlong spirit, of the same open heart—"her reputation for kindness, sweetness and grace remained incontestable. Invariably kind and obliging, she more than once, through the agency of her influential friends, rendered valuable services to my father; a fact which accounts for my mother's friendship with her."

If, at this period of her life, the Citizeness Beauharnais "seriously compromised" her reputation by indiscreet relations with men and by exploitation of her charms, the alternative—as she had seen it—was to starve, virtuously and genteelly; at best to eke out a drab, hand-to-mouth existence, beholden to friends for bread and castoff clothing and to her father-in-law for the roof above her head, and with little hope of improving her lot. This, at the age of thirty-one, she was disinclined to do. She had had enough of insecurity, loneliness and neglect in youth and marriage. Now, since her recent brush with death, her longing for life was intensified: a life, in her definition—that of a gay, pleasure-loving woman with expensive tastes—to consist of luxury, revelry and romance. For such a bright new life she was prepared to pay, and she paid, a price. Not that her relations with men were necessarily meretricious or distasteful; Hoche and Barras were two of the most attractive men of their time, and even such an old fogy of an admirer as the Marquis de Caulaincourt was an eminent and charming gentleman of the Old Regime. The moral code of that Old Regime in which she had been bred provided her no bulwark of virtue; it placed no premium on morality, but only upon the amenities to be observed in its violation. Neither had her personal experience fortified her against the decadence of the times; her family circle furnished few edifying examples—certainly not her father, not her aunt, nor her father-in-law, nor her husband.

Her standards of living improved conspicuously at the time of her association with Barras. He taught her to fish in the troubled waters of the post-Revolutionary period, to trade on her influence with her friends in high places. His salon was thronged with profiteers, black-marketeers, munitioneers, financiers, speculators on the Exchange—all eager to pay for information, for an introduction or a recommendation to a minister of war or of finance.

By the autumn of 1795, the Citizeness Beauharnais could afford to enroll Eugène at the Collège Irlandais and Hortense at the Institution Nationale de St.-Germain, that most exclusive of girls' academies, which was under the direction of Madame Campan, former lady in waiting to the "martyred" Marie Antoinette and arbiter of female elegance to the upstart, socially ambitious post-Revolutionary world. By October, Marie-Josèphe-Rose could lease and redecorate a jewel box of a house on the lower slope of the Butte Montmartre, on the Rue Chantereine, complete with garden, stables, porter's lodge and a staff of five.

And undoubtedly she had become, to meet Barras's standards of fashion and elegance, one of the best-dressed women of the capital —or best undressed, in conformity with the latest trend in fashion, the neoclassic, for which the designers had found their inspiration in the scantily draped marble goddesses of ancient Greece and Rome. A filmy knee-length tunic *à la Diane* or a wisp of a shift *à la Cérès* was to be seen any fine day on the Champs-Élysées— and was somehow more startling there than on the Parthenon. Only such reigning beauties as Madame Tallien or Madame Beauharnais would have set such a style, which was, of course, promptly decried as indecent by every contemporary with a figure less flaw-less. Only a Madame Beauharnais would have dared appear in the *costume à la sauvage*, described by its designer as "a tulle skirt over waist-high, flesh-colored satin tights, arms and bosom bare, diamond-studded gold circlets around the leg and thigh."

It was a costume designed for gala evenings, and as such Marie-

Josèphe-Rose might have worn it to a première performance at the Opéra or the Comédie-Française, to a subscription ball in the great circular, gilded and mirrored salon of the Hôtel de Thélusson, to a fete in the Bois de Boulogne at the amusement park of the Bagatelle (formerly the exclusive pleasure ground of the brother of Louis XVI, now open to the public, or that segment of the public which could afford to pay for it)—"a fairyland at night with its hundred violins and its thousand jewel-colored lanterns gleaming through the trees," as Mercier described it.

This was the woman and this the milieu that General Bonaparte would find in the autumn of 1795, when he was first summoned upon the national scene by her lover, Barras, to quell the riot in the Tuileries courtyard, at the doors of the Convention.

III

Buonaparte Before Napoleon

All that I am waiting for is a chance to take part in a battle—to snatch the laurel crown from the hands of Fortune or to die on the field of glory.

LETTER FROM NAPOLEON TO HIS BROTHER
JOSEPH BONAPARTE, JULY 1795

There was a prologue to the career of the Emperor, an unknown Bonaparte preceding the immense Napoleon. Bonaparte's thought was in the world before he appeared on the scene; it set off secret tremors in the earth. It might have been perceptible as soon as Bonaparte arrived—a something formidable, an inexplicable sense of doom. When the globe is threatened by catastrophe, subterranean rumblings give forewarning: men are apprehensive, lie awake listening in the night, staring at the sky, not knowing what affrights them, not knowing what it is that is to come . . .

FRANÇOIS-RENÉ DE CHATEAUBRIAND, *Mémoires d'outre-tombe*

Buonaparte Before Napoleon

1

To SEE NAPOLEON as Josephine first saw him in Vendémiaire, the Harvest Month, of 1795, one must see not Napoleon but General Buonaparte.

One must disassociate the short, slight, shabby young artilleryman from the colossus of the future, efface from one's mind the splendors yet to come: the victories not yet won, battle names not yet carved in stone on the Arc de Triomphe, not yet engraved in bronze or inlaid in marble around the porphyry sarcophagus in the tomb "on the banks of the Seine, among the French people whom I loved so well." * Above all, one must forget the hush and the silence under that vast dome of the Invalides chapel where thousands from all over the world still throng in daily pilgrimage. For the hush and the awe and the glory are in the Napoleonic legend, and the legend was not yet. As yet no crown of laurels, no trace of imperial purple, no golden insignia of bees and eagles, but only a grim, scrawny, down-at-heels young unknown of an officer who began to pay court to the Widow Beauharnais soon after the thirteenth Vendémiaire, and who was not even considered a particularly eligible suitor in that autumn of 1795.

"Who is this General Buona Parte? Where has he served?" Junot's father had inquired in early 1794 of his son, who had just announced his intention of following that general, as aide-de-camp, from Toulon to Paris. "Nobody knows anything about him."

There was very little Junot could tell, very little to be known about "Buona Parte." His chief claim to renown was the role his brilliant artillery strategy had played in dislodging the entrenched British-Spanish fleet from Toulon in December 1793, an achievement which had won him a brigadier-generalship at the age of twenty-four. Except for that, there had not been much in the young officer's past to bring him to the attention of the French public. He himself was French by a narrow margin of time, having

---

* The words are from Napoleon's last will and testament, in which he asked that his ashes be returned from St. Helena. The request was honored by Louis-Philippe, King of the French, in 1840.

been born in Ajaccio on the island of Corsica on August 15, 1769, exactly fifteen months after Corsica had been ceded to France by Genoa. The Buonaparte family had emigrated to Corsica from Italy in the mid-sixteenth century; although fawning Tuscans were later to try to decorate the Bonaparte genealogical tree with royal antecedents, Napoleon more realistically described his family as petty nobility.

He was the second eldest of the surviving eight children born to Letizia and Carlo Buonaparte, a handsome, devoted, spirited and prolific pair. In tribute to the Bonapartes' remote Greek origins, his mother had named him Napoleone—pronounced "Nabulione" in the Corsican dialect—after a Greek saint. His father, who was well-to-do in terms of property and produce but not in cash, engaged in the practice of law. Originally a supporter of the popular Corsican resistance movement against French dominion, Carlo Buonaparte later transferred his allegiance to the French Crown, from which he received substantial benefits: for himself, appointment as assessor (assistant judge) in the law court at Ajaccio, confirmation of his title of nobility, and a financial grant; for his ever-increasing progeny, royal scholarships.

A royal scholarship took nine-year-old Napoleone to France in 1778, to a school in Autun for a few months' study of the French language, of which he spoke not a word, and in 1779 to the royal military academy at Brienne, in north-central France. There for the next five and a half years he devoted himself to preparation for his military career, specializing in history, geography and mathematics. Although he remembered them fondly in retrospect, these were harsh and cheerless years for a lonely, serious-minded, withdrawn youth, an impoverished provincial among affluent French noblemen's sons. Speaking—when he spoke, which was seldom—in a French tinged with a coarse Italian-Corsican accent, he was marked as a foreigner among Frenchmen, which he always would be, even as emperor of the French, even as France's most fabled hero.

He was marked with other signs of his alien origin. The Corsican tradition and way of life differed strikingly from the Continental; they were primitive, crude, in comparison with the polished, sophisticated, exquisite *ancien régime* of eighteenth-century France.

He did not need his supercilious schoolmates to point out that "the Corsican" was different; he was himself all too conscious of it. His isolation facilitated his single-minded application to study, and his examination grades in 1784 warranted the grant of a second king's scholarship, to the Ecole Militaire in Paris, from which he was graduated the following year as a sublieutenant.

Between 1785 and 1787, on garrison duty in various provincial towns, he somehow managed to take on the responsibility for his recently widowed mother and her needy brood, her "pride of lions," as a recent historian euphemistically terms them. But Napoleone, her second son, whose name means "lion of the valley," would prove the only lion of the family; the rest would be no more than a pack of jackals, snarling, clawing, disputing among themselves their brother's kill—the treasure, territories, crowns and titles of his conquests. The title of chieftain of the Buonaparte clan, an appropriate designation in view of the strong Corsican sense of family unity, devolved in theory and by primogeniture to Joseph, but it was Napoleon who assumed the role.

Having attained to the rank of captain by 1792, he was in Paris on June 20 and, with his friend Louis-Antoine Fauvelet de Bourrienne, witnessed the first attack on the Tuileries. "The fool!" was Napoleon's comment on the King to Bourrienne, who had been his classmate and only friend at Brienne and, who was to become his secretary and eventually his biographer. "How could he have permitted that rabble to get to the palace? If a few hundred had been mowed down by cannonfire, the rest would be running still."

After witnessing also the second and fatal attack on the monarchy at the Tuileries in August and the massacres in September, Captain Buonaparte headed back for Corsica to protect his family through those treacherous years. King's scholar, king's cadet, king's officer though he had been, he cast his lot with the new Republic and fought for it in his native island, where the Corsican independence party battled dominion by republican France as it had the royalist. He spent so many months in Corsica as to seem to hesitate between his homeland and France as the scene of his life's career.

In December of 1793 came his first victory on French soil, at Toulon, and a glowing recommendation from his commanding officer, who reported to the Minister of War in Paris on "the virtues of this exceptional officer," his "great intelligence and scientific knowl-edge" and his "perhaps overly great personal courage." But, for all that lavish praise, the Buonaparte star flickered only fitfully; his army career was not yet assured, his rank not secure.

In the confusion of the newly organized War Office of the newly proclaimed Republic, with its ceaselessly shifting balance of power, generals were being demoted as rapidly and as arbitrarily as they had been promoted—if indeed they were not executed, as in the case of Josephine's first husband. It was a fate General Buonaparte narrowly escaped. His promotion had come during the radical, ter-rorist Robespierre regime—reason enough for his arrest and im-prisonment in August of 1794, after Robespierre's overthrow. Buonaparte's coolly shrewd tactics of defense rather than his pro-testations of innocence accounted for his release from prison, but his position in the military hierarchy was still precarious.

The next active assignment offered him, to the Army of the West, which, under the command of General Hoche, was involved in the long and bitter struggle with the royalist guerrillas of the Vendée, was distasteful to General Buonaparte, as civil war is usu-ally distasteful to any career military man; but it was the transfer from his favorite artillery into an infantry brigade which made the assignment unacceptable. His failure to comply with the order came eventually to be construed as insubordination, and only the protection of his newly influential friend and patron, Barras, saved him from the most serious consequences.

But to be without a command and without pay was a serious enough consequence in 1795, and this recalcitrant brigadier flirted seriously with the idea of heading a French military mission to Turkey to assist the Sultan in the reorganization of his armies. Turkey was the jumping-off place for the East, and, like his hero Alexander the Great, General Buonaparte already thought of Egypt as the key to world conquest. But the mission to Istanbul did not materialize, and Napoleon sat waiting or, more probably, pacing the floor in his dingy Paris hotel room in 1795; pacing and waiting for the next assignment, the next opportunity—which was still as far off as Vendémiaire.

Until that month of October in 1795, only an occasional administrative assignment in the Military Operations Department of the Committee of Public Safety kept him from starving—that, and an occasional dinner offered him by Bourrienne or his devoted aide-de-camp Junot, whenever these two were in funds. Fortunately, there were also the Permons, friends from Ajaccio (whose daughter Laure would marry Junot); with typical Corsican loyalty, the Permons had issued Napoleon a standing invitation to their table. He was too proud to presume too often on their hospitality, however. But he was well accustomed to short rations and knew how to forget hunger pangs in concentration on his books and maps.

It was the map of Italy he was studying in 1795—the terrain, the mountain passes, the rivers and the plains—as well as the seasons and the weather, the nature of the political composition of the Italian states, the character of its people. He was convinced that the defeat of the Austrian enemy must come through Italy: by the French Army of Italy joining up, in a pincer movement, with the French Army of the Rhine. The plan he prepared for the strategy of the Italian campaign attracted some interest, then gathered dust in the files of the War Office.

That office was on the verge of cashiering General Buonaparte. And a note of despair sounded in his letters to his brother Joseph in July of 1795. "Life holds very little meaning for me," he wrote. And: "If I continue in this state of mind I may very well end up too indifferent to sidestep the carriages passing me in the street." But that invincible will, that compulsive ambition, that elemental energy could be only temporarily affected by moods of depression: "All that I am waiting for is a chance to take part in a battle—to snatch the laurel crown from the hands of Fortune or to die on the field of glory."

While General Buonaparte waited and brooded in 1795, he contemplated and analyzed the spectacle of France in the final phases of the Revolution, reflecting on the volatility and resilience of the French national character. "The memory of the Terror is no more than a nightmare," he observed to Joseph that same summer. "Everyone seems determined to indemnify himself for what he has suffered; determined, too, in the uncertainty of the future, not to miss a single delight of the present. This great people is giving itself up to pleasure; luxury and the arts have regained their sway in astonishing fashion; dances, theater and the women—who are the most beautiful in the world—have become the great business of life."

One of these women—"a witty young woman" in the words of Stendhal—met General Buonaparte at this period of his life and gave the novelist a vivid description of her impression:

General Buonaparte was certainly the skinniest and most singular creature I had ever seen in my life [Stendhal quotes her as saying]. In accordance with the fashions of the day, his hair hung down in "dogs' ears" so long as to brush his shoulders. That mass of hair looked especially strange in contrast to his extraordinary eyes which often took on a typically Italian somberness. If one's first impression was that here was a fiery man—a man of spirit—one found one's self thinking, next, that here was a man whom one would not care to come across in a lonely wood at night. General Buonaparte's attire was less than reassuring; his redingote was so threadbare, there was such an air of shabbiness about him, that I could hardly believe he was a general. What I could readily believe was that he had a powerful—or, at least, an exceptional—intellect. . . .

The third or fourth time I saw the general with the peculiar name, I could forgive him his over-long "dogs' ears." He might be a provincial, I told myself, with a ridiculously exaggerated hair-dress, but undeniably he had his merit. Young Buonaparte had magnificent eyes that lighted up when he talked. If he had not been so painfully thin—so emaciated as to give the impression of being in ill health—one might have noticed his fine features. The contour of his mouth was especially comely. A student of David's, a painter who frequented the salon of Monsieur N. . . . , where I met the General, described his features as "Grecian," which was enough to make me admire the strange man. . . . The fact is that all he needed to be considered handsome was to have been less miserably attired. . . . I still remember that when he talked about the siege of Toulon, he held our interest; on such occasions, he talked at length, and his face became very animated but, on other days, he maintained a gloomy silence. People said that he was very poor and as proud as a Scot. He had turned down a command in the Vendée because he would not give up the artillery: "That's my weapon," he often said—at which we young women went into gales of laughter, unable to understand how anyone could refer to a cannon in the same terms as to a sword. . . . You would never have guessed him to be a military man; there was nothing dashing about him, no swagger, no bluster, nothing rough. Today it occurs to me that one might have read—in the chiseled, delicate outline of his mouth—the fact that he was a man who scorned danger, that he was a man whom danger would never dismay.

To this "provincial," as Stendhal's unidentified female friend described him, his first close-up view of the Parisiennes was dazzling, as he described them in another letter to his brother:

"Women are to be seen everywhere—in the theaters, in the parks, in the libraries. Even in the savant's study you will find the loveliest creatures. . . . A woman needs to come to Paris for six months to learn what is due her and to understand her own power. Here only, of all places in the world, they deserve to wield such influence. So, of course, the men are mad about them, think of nothing else, live only by and for them."

The writer, as the letter implies, could only observe from a distance, could not afford or aspire to the favors of these "loveliest creatures"; for these, an obscure officer in a powder-burned coat would have to wait, as he was waiting for the laurel crown and his chance.

The chance came suddenly in the middle of the night of October 3-4, in a summons from Barras: the chance to undertake the defense of the Convention against twenty thousand armed insurrectionists converging on its meeting place, the Tuileries. He had "precisely three minutes" in which to decide whether a defense was possible with the four thousand government troops available to his command; whether the Convention was worth defending, in all its ineptitude and corruption, its toleration of a scandalous black market in bread and of a shameless speculation in currency, its total inability to cope with national disorder. But the only alternative carried the threat of civil war—with, on the one side, the radical revolutionary factions demanding a return to terror, and, on the other, the counterrevolutionary factions, including the disgruntled bourgeoisie, demanding a return to monarchy. The October insurrection was royalist-engineered and -financed.

General Buonaparte, a professed republican, rushed in forty cannon and resolved the emergency with the now famous "whiff of grapeshot," his own description (and justification) of his defense tactics against an attacking force with a five-to-one numerical superiority. Two hundred or more of the vanguard fell in the approaches of the Tuileries, but the riot was quelled. And the way was paved for the formation, three weeks later, of the Directory, with Barras at its head.

The Directors' reward to "General Vendémiaire" was to give the holder of that unofficial, popular title an official one: commander of the Army of the Interior, the most powerful post in the military hierarchy. The commander's indirect reward was a meeting with one of those "loveliest creatures" he had until now glimpsed only from afar.

How the Citizeness Beauharnais came to call at his headquarters is part of the "sword story," a charming, pretty and romantic one and in all probability true—although it is still a point of controversy among historians. Barras denies the tale as fanciful, as embroidery on the legend, but his memoirs were written in exile and in anger against the Bonapartes; furthermore, Barras's first version of how they met is contradicted by his second, to the discredit of both versions. On the other hand, the accounts of Napoleon and of Eugène de Beauharnais, the two persons directly involved in the episode, substantially agree; so there seems no reason not to accept their telling of it: that it stemmed from the confiscation of all arms in private hands in troublous sections of the capital, the order for which was issued by General Buonaparte on the eighteenth Vendémiaire (October 10), five days after the coup d'état.

As Napoleon dictated the story, in the third person, to the Count de Las Cases at St. Helena: "Into his headquarters was ushered a boy of ten or twelve,* who said that he had come to entreat the commanding general to return the sword of his father, a former general of the Republic. This young child was Eugène de Beauharnais, the future Viceroy of Italy. Napoleon, responsive to the appeal of youth and sensitive to the nature of the request, granted it. Eugène burst into tears at sight of his father's sword. The general was touched and manifested him such good favor that Madame de Beauharnais felt herself obliged to come, the follow-

* Eugène was fourteen in 1795.

ing day, to express her thanks in person. Napoleon lost no time in returning the visit. . . ."

There is one slight discrepancy between Napoleon's story and the version given by Eugène and Hortense: her children's memoirs claim that it was not Josephine but Napoleon who took the initiative—Napoleon who, expressing a desire to meet "the mother responsible for inspiring such noble sentiments in her son," paid the first call, at the lady's house. But whether the meeting took place at his headquarters or in her salon, Napoleon himself admitted (to Las Cases) that he had been struck by "her extraordinary grace and her irresistibly sweet manner" and that he had lost no time in pursuing an "acquaintance which was shortly to ripen into intimacy."

IV

The Honeymoon

I awaken full of you. . . . Sweet and incomparable Josephine, what is this bizarre effect you have upon my heart?

LETTER FROM NAPOLEON TO JOSEPHINE,
LATE WINTER OR EARLY SPRING OF 1796

Do I love him? . . . Well, no.

LETTER FROM JOSEPHINE TO A FRIEND,
EARLY SPRING OF 1796

1

GENERAL BUONAPARTE "lost no time" in calling at the Rue Chantereine, in availing himself of the invitation extended by the Widow Beauharnais to her Thursdays, her evenings at home. At these receptions he met, among her many friends and admirers, prominent figures of the new regime and the old, celebrities of the world of the theater and the arts: Messieurs the Marquis de Caulaincourt, de Ségur, de Montesquiou, the Abbé Sieyès, the actor Talma, Academician-playwright Arnault, artists Isabey and Prud'hon, Director Barras.

He was immediately enchanted by this lady who dedicated her

life to the cultivation of her enchantments, but he was obviously not immediately enslaved, not yet—in the catch phrase current at the time—"enchained to her chariot wheels." Otherwise she would not have written him one of her charming little letters, dating it merely "This evening of the sixth" (presumably the sixth Brumaire, October 28): "You no longer come to see a friend who loves you. You have forsaken her, which is a great mistake, for she is tenderly devoted to you. Come tomorrow to lunch with me. I must see you and talk with you on matters important to your interests. Good night, my friend. A fond embrace."

Signed "Veuve Beauharnais," it brought a prompt reply from the general, dated "6 Brumaire"—apparently that very night: "I cannot imagine the reason for the tone of your letter. I beg you to believe me when I say that no one so yearns for your friendship as do I, that no one can be more eager than I for the occasion to prove it. Had my duties permitted, I would have come in person to deliver this message. . . . Buonaparte."

Had he been ill at ease, in need of reassurance that he was welcome in the distinguished company that gathered in her salon? ("The most distinguished socially of any house in Paris," he said of it to General Gourgaud.) Unquestionably he would have needed assurance that his attentions to her as a suitor were not to be rebuffed. He required some such assurance even from the prostitutes in the Palais-Royal arcades before he would accost them, his youthful journals reveal. How much more, then, from this first great lady he had encountered, this *élégante*, this sophisticate, this glamorous creature out of a world he had known only from a distance. The *brusquerie* and arrogance that later distinguished his attitude toward his female conquests were camouflage for his basic timidity with women; the contempt he professed for women in all roles save the sexual was another expression of it.

The Widow Beauharnais's motive in beckoning him on is transparent: it required not even her political flair to see him as the new strong man of the capital, and (in the eternally shifting sands of the French political scene) one well worth cultivating as a friend or a friendly protector—or as a suitor, if that was how it should develop. A woman's inventory of admirers could not be too long.

Reassured as to her favor, General Buonaparte became her constant escort at the Opéra, at the theater, at Barras's receptions at the Luxembourg, at the Talliens' soirees in their elaborate thatch-roofed cottage on the Seine. He entertained Madame Beauharnais at dinner in his sumptuous new headquarters on the Rue des Capucines, drove her about the capital and the countryside in his fine new carriage. They exchanged portraits.

And sometime that winter the acquaintance did indeed "ripen into intimacy." Some night in December of 1795 or in January or February of 1796, after a tête-à-tête dinner in the wood-paneled oval dining room, or after a reception, after the last carriage had rolled out of the courtyard and down the long tree-lined driveway to the Rue Chantereine, after chef, maid and butler had retired to their attic, then the hostess and her solitary guest went together up the narrow staircase to the oval bedroom above, and, with the light from the fireplace flickering across the arcs of mirror, that night they became lovers.

No definite date can be established for that first lovers' tryst; General Buonaparte inconsiderately neglected to include the date on the letter he rushed off to the Rue Chantereine early on the morning after—marking it only "Seven in the morning"—in his urgent need to communicate with his beloved even before the appointed hour of their next meeting, at eleven:

I awaken full of you. Between your portrait and the memory of our intoxicating night, my senses have had no respite. Sweet and incomparable Josephine, what is this bizarre effect you have upon my heart? What if you were to be angry? What if I were to see you sad or troubled? Then my soul would be shattered by distress. Then your lover could find no peace, no rest. But I find none, either, when I succumb to the profound emotion that overwhelms me, when I draw up from your lips, from your heart, a flame that consumes me. Ah, it was last night that I realized that your portrait is not you and that . . .

You will be leaving the city at noon. But I shall see you in three hours. Until then, mio dolce amor, I send you a thousand kisses— but send me none in return, for they set my blood on fire.

B.P.

On that same dateless night on which they had become lovers, Marie-Josèphe-Rose had become Josephine.

The portrait to which General Buonaparte referred was one probably painted by her good friend Isabey; one of the well-known fragile profiles, wispy, ethereal. In the line of his letter which ends "and that," those last two words are stricken out. Napoleon's words are sometimes as difficult to interpret as to decipher. The "and that," for example: "and that" she was not so remote a creature as her image? "And that" he had been surprised to find in his arms so sensuous, so passionate, so passionately abandoned a woman, instead of the fragile, ethereal, graciously condescending lady of the portrait?

If he was so surprised, he was naïve; had he not been aware of her "seriously compromised reputation"? Barras says he was: "Bonaparte was as well acquainted with all of the lady's adventures as were we; I know he knew, because he heard the stories in my presence." Her affair with Hoche was known to all Paris, says Barras. "And Madame Beauharnais was generally recognized as one of my early liaisons. With Bonaparte a frequent visitor to my apartments, he could not have remained ignorant of such a state of affairs, nor could he have believed that everything was over between her and me. But where a normal man would have been profoundly disturbed, this one was indifferent; he could rise above such considerations."

Barras's implication is that Buonaparte was so unprincipled, his ambition so overweening, that he encouraged his paramour to use her influence with her former lover to forward the career of her new one. Yet on another page of his memoirs Barras writes that "Buonaparte, artful conniver that he was, looked upon that conniving woman as an angel of truth and candor and flew into such a rage against me as to challenge me to a duel for having attempted an assault on the virtue of his inamorata."

But then, Barras's memoirs, written in exile in the first two decades of the nineteenth century, in consuming anger against the "ingrate protégé" whom he blamed for his own political eclipse and banishment, are a mass of contradictions. All the days of his years were not long enough for a deposed and vindictive Barras to pour out his venom against the Bonaparte pair, male and female.

His defamations of Josephine were those primarily responsible for the cloud that fell over her reputation for all time. It is this virulent hatred which invalidates his testimony, along with his blatant inaccuracies and contradictions. On one page he calls her "a Creole wanton" taking on lovers promiscuously (such as "an aide-de-camp of Hoche's" on a mission to her from the general, or Hoche's "giant Alsatian groom") and "rising superior even to racial prejudice, having intercourse with Negroes." (This last may have had its origin in the report that "a man of color," a mulatto, lived with and eventually married another Madame Beauharnais, the Countess Françoise-Marie, Josephine's sister-in-law.) On the next page he makes her out a cold and venal schemer: "Her heart never played a part in her carnal adventures; her love affairs were the result of sordid calculation; the men who possessed her may have flattered themselves on her apparently passionate abandon with them, but the lubricious Creole had never for a moment lost sight of her mercenary motives. She was one of those women who would have 'drunk gold out of her lover's skull.' "

By Barras's account, she is both "the wanton" and "the venal Creole." And Napoleon is both "dupe" and "pimp."

Barras's word as a biographer is as unacceptable as was his word as a man, but we have Napoleon's own irrefutable testimony to prove that he was in possession of the facts concerning Josephine's indiscretions: "Everything about you pleased me, even to the memory of the errors of your ways . . . Virtue, for me, consisted of what you made it." He could have meant nothing else in this letter of June 8 to Josephine from Milan.

What is truly baffling is the relationship which existed between Barras and the men who loved the women who were ostensibly his mistresses. Tallien never resigned himself to his Thérèse's infidelities, but cringed and fumed at all of her lovers—with the sole exception of Barras, to whom he specifically "entrusted" her when he set out with Bonaparte for Egypt in 1798. As to Generals Hoche and Buonaparte, their hackles rose at sight of each other, out of jealousy over the Widow Beauharnais, yet neither manifested a trace of jealousy toward Barras. Napoleon made Barras the confidant of his courtship of the lady and a witness at the wedding. It is not good enough to say that all three of these men flattered the Director to further their careers; this might have applied to Tallien, but not to an independent and incorruptible Hoche, not to a fiercely proud and fiery Corsican Buonaparte.

The key to Napoleon's attitude toward Barras, to his interpretation of the situation, is to be found in this pronouncement dictated to his chronicler Las Cases: "Barras was a man of the utmost immorality, shameless and debauched. I had no difficulty in believing that he was—as he was generally reported to be—a homosexual." In that frame of mind, Napoleon would have discredited the rumors linking his wife's name with Barras's.

She could not so easily prevent a clash between Buonaparte and Hoche. On the report of his "former lady friend's goings-on in Paris," Hoche became vindictive. "I am desperate at receiving no reply from the woman I love, the widow whose son I have come to regard as my own," he wrote to a friend and confidant in a letter sealed in the design of a bleeding heart. "Vanity has replaced affection in the heart of my former friend. Unfortunately I cannot get leave to go to Paris to see the woman who is the cause of all my distress."

But Hoche had wanted the best of two worlds, marital bliss and extramarital romance; he seemed unable to make up his mind to give up his pregnant wife for the sake of his glamorous widow—or vice versa. It may have been as a sign of her impatience or as some oblique feminine maneuver to bring him to a decision that Madame Beauharnais, in the spring of 1795, recalled Eugène from Hoche's staff. When Hoche finally got leave that December to go to Paris, it was not against Barras but against Buonaparte that his resentment was directed: that upstart, insubordinate officer who had earlier refused transfer to his command, who had so recently flashed to prominence as "General Vendémiaire," and who was now the bulwark of the Directory.

Hoche met Buonaparte, with Madame Beauharnais on his arm, at a party at the Talliens'. As a fellow guest, the banker Gabriel-Julien Ouvrard, tells it in his memoirs: "Bonaparte that evening played the role of fortuneteller, taking Madame Tallien's hand and predicting a thousand improbabilities." (It would have been no improbability had he predicted that Ouvrard would shortly become Madame Tallien's lover and the father of four of her illegitimate children.) "The other guests rushed gaily up for a palm-reading, but when it was the turn of General Hoche there came a sudden change in mood. Bonaparte pretended to study the lines in the hand extended to him, and then in a solemn tone of voice —one with a sharp note of malice in it—he declared, 'Why, General, you will die in your bed.' A quick flush of anger mounted to Hoche's face, but Madame Beauharnais stepped in" (with one of her sweet smiles and tactful phrases?) "and the storm was averted."

"I wrote to demand the return of the letters I had written to Madame Beauharnais," Barras quotes Hoche as saying. "I did not relish the thought of her future husband's familiarizing himself with my amorous style." Apparently, however, no exchange of old love letters was effected between them, for the time would shortly come when not only would Buonaparte's prediction come true, but Josephine would resort to desperate measures to retrieve the packet of her own billets-doux addressed to Hoche.

2

With this glimpse of Buonaparte as jealous lover, it is impossible to credit Barras's horrid story of the general, "hat in hand," waiting in the Director's public outer rooms while the woman he loved was closeted with the Director in his private inner apartments:

> Our interview had been prolonged beyond the time limits of propriety [Barras claims], while Madame Beauharnais effusively assured me that she could not renounce her love for me at even the prospect of marriage with her "little general." While she perpetrated upon my person such advances as are generally made by only the most intrepid males upon their female objectives, I found myself in the same position as Joseph with the wife of Potiphar. But I would be a liar if I pretended to have been as cruel as that young minister of the Pharoah—as must have been clearly discernible when I emerged from my boudoir with Madame Beauharnais. I might have been embarrassed had I not been so revolted by the sight of Bonaparte rushing up to meet her

. . . , fawning rather than reproachful, kissing her hand with an air of passionate reverence. But there you have the picture of a man who will achieve his goal at any cost.

The goal to which Barras referred was the appointment to the command of the Army of Italy. But the appointment was not Barras's to make; it rested on the majority vote of the five Directors. One of these, Larevellière-Lépaux, gave Barras's story a flat denial in his memoirs: "It was said that Bonaparte's marriage to the Widow Beauharnais was the condition upon which he was granted the command of the Army of Italy, which was the object of his fondest dream. But this is simply not the truth! What I can confirm to be the truth is that the Directory, in its selection of Bonaparte, was not influenced by Barras or anyone else."

It was actually Carnot, the military authority of the Directory as he had been for the Committee of Public Safety, who proposed and sponsored General Buonaparte for the post. "Had Bonaparte failed in Italy," Carnot wrote later, "it is I who would have been held responsible for betrayal of the nation; but Bonaparte was victorious, so now it is Barras who claims to have nominated him."

Josephine herself contributed to the impression that she had been influential in the matter. "She liked to think that she had played some small part in his meteoric rise, that she had some small share in his glory," according to General Junot's wife. And Madame de Rémusat observed, "Napoleon came to associate the idea of his wife's influence with every stroke of good fortune which befell him. It was a superstition which she most cleverly fostered and which, for long years, exerted a great power over him."

Furthermore, Madame de Rémusat thought, Josephine "flattered his pride; she represented a step up in the world. He was very young when they met, and she stood out—by the name she bore and by the extreme elegance of her manner—head and shoulders above the circle in which he found her. In the idea of marriage to Madame Beauharnais, Bonaparte envisioned an alliance with a very great lady." Napoleon's words confirm the theory: "Barras did me a service in advising me to marry [Madame Beauharnais], pointing out that she would constitute a link between the old regime and the new and that this would give me substance; that her old French name would offset my Corsican one; that, in sum, my standing would be improved." But these were words spoken to General Gourgaud on St. Helena years later.

Actually, there seem to have been no ulterior motives in General Buonaparte's proposal of marriage in 1796. "He was madly in love, in the full sense of the word, in its ultimate interpretation," his aide-de-camp Auguste Marmont, an eyewitness to the flowering romance, had opportunity to observe. "It was apparently a first love, a primordial passion, that possessed him, and he responded to it with all the vigor of his vigorous nature. Love so pure, so true, so exclusive had never possessed a man."

To have made her his mistress was not enough; Napoleon felt the eternal, ravening desire of the lover to have and to hold, the yearning craving for possession beyond the sexual, one more profound, more enduring—for the lover's ultimate, unattainable closeness, oneness, with the beloved: "to strip from your body the last film of chiffon, your slippers, everything," as he was to write her in June, "and then as in the dream I told you about . . . to swoop you up and enclose you, imprison you within my heart! Why can I not? The laws of nature leave much to be desired."

The laws of nature notwithstanding, she occupied and possessed his heart; was ensconced there, never to be ousted, never to be exiled, even when he would have had it so. He was in thrall to her; she had, as he had written her, enslaved his senses. She was a past mistress of seductions, of the voluptuary arts; he, a raw recruit to the wars of love, his sexual experiences limited to random, sordid encounters with streetwalkers of the Palais-Royal arcades. She "flattered his pride" and must have been, even in her early thirties, a supremely decorative as well as charming creature. Otherwise Barras, with his exacting standards and with all the belles of Paris at his beck and call, would not have installed her as his favorite; and he shows himself not only venomous but ridiculous when he refers to her beauty as "prematurely on the wane." Similarly, when Lucien Bonaparte deprecates her "fading charms" it must be remembered that he, beyond all the rest of the clan, was her openly declared enemy. So one turns to more objective critics. Playwright-journalist Arnault saw Madame Beauharnais as Napoleon must have seen her in 1795 and 1796, and he describes with a profes-

sional's pen the impression she made on him at a Luxembourg
Palace soiree at which she acted as official hostess along with Madame Tallien and Madame Châteaurenaud:

> This trio constituted, in my eyes, the chief attraction of
> Barras's receptions. Of the three, Josephine was doubtlessly not
> the most beautiful, but she was incontradictably the most engag-
> ing: naturally and invariably gracious, ingratiating, the most con-
> genial and sympathetic companion, with an ineffable sweetness
> not only in her expression but in the very sound of her voice.
> And there was a certain intriguing air of languorousness about
> her—a Creole characteristic—apparent in her attitudes of repose
> as well as in her movements . . . All these qualities lent her a
> charm which more than offset the dazzling beauty of her rivals.
> Viewed beside these two, she may have seemed less youthfully
> radiant, but, thanks to the regularity and delicacy of her features,
> to the elegance and grace of her figure, to the sweet expression of
> her face, she too was beautiful.

In proof of that point, the archives yield a frivolous though convincing bit of evidence, a letter from Josephine to her friend "Tallita" Tallien: "Darling, please be sure to wear your peach-blossom
dress to the Thélusson ball tomorrow, and I'll wear mine—with a
Creole turban and three curls on my forehead. In identical costumes, the effect will be devastating to our English rivals." No
woman who was not supremely confident of her attractions would
willfully enter into direct, dress-alike competition with a Tallita "so
beautiful that people gasped aloud at first sight of her." Further
proof, again in terms of feminine logic, is reflected in Josephine's
arcs of mirrors; only a woman supremely confident of the beauty
and grace of her body would hang the bedroom walls with mirrors,
floor to ceiling.

By the first month of the new year, the romance between the
general and his lady had progressed to the point where the Beauharnais children were summoned from their schools in St.-Germain
to Paris. A declaration of honorable intentions, an outright proposal of marriage, from General Buonaparte would account for it.
Eugène had played the role of Cupid to the pair, but Hortense had
not yet met her mother's suitor.

On January 21, 1796, Josephine and the children were invited by Barras to a gala dinner. The idea of a celebration of the third anniversary of the execution of Louis XVI horrified a staunch little royalist like Hortense, who, according to her memoirs, protested:

"How can you associate with such people, Maman? How can you forget the misfortunes which the Republic has brought upon our family?"

"My daughter," my mother replied in that sweet and gentle tone which was never absent from her voice, "what you do not understand is that since the death of your father I have had to try to recover the vestiges of his fortune, which appeared irretrievably lost to us. Would you have me ungrateful to the very persons who have assisted and protected me?"

I recognized my mistake by an apology, and accompanied my mother to the Luxembourg Palace, the seat of government of the Directory. Barras's guests were numerous, but the only ones I knew were Tallien and his wife. . . . At dinner, I found myself seated between my mother and a general, who, in order to talk to her, leaned across my place so constantly and so impetuously that I was exhausted by the effort of leaning back to avoid his shoulder—and finally pulled my chair away from the table. In spite of myself, I began studying his face, which was handsome and highly expressive, although marked with an extraordinary pallor. He spoke fervently, concentrating exclusively on my mother. This man was General Bonaparte. . . .

His marked attentions to my mother gave rise to the saddening thought that she might be considering remarriage. "Maman won't love us as much," I said to my brother, with whom I shared my fears.

When the general came to visit us, he must have noticed our coolness, because he went to some effort to dissipate it—although unsuccessfully as far as I was concerned. I did not understand his humor, took his teasing seriously, and formed a very unfavorable opinion of him. But every time I came to Paris, I found him more and more assiduous in his attentions to my mother, to the point where I could no longer conceal from her my apprehensions. I cried and begged her not to remarry, but her reassurances to me became less and less convincing. The general's influence over her was already stronger than mine, although I do know that my opposition to the marriage added considerably to her indecision.

Hortense's mother could not make up her mind what she thought or felt about her "little general." She was in a state of indecision and indifference—"lukewarmness," as she said sadly in a letter to an unidentified friend:

I am being urged to remarry. You have met General Buonaparte at my house. Well, then, it is he who wishes to serve as father to the orphans of Alexandre de Beauharnais, as husband to his widow. Do I love him? you are going to ask me. Well, no. Do I, then, find him unattractive? Again, no—but, worse still, I find myself in a state of indifference, of lukewarmness, which displeases me, and which is considered by religionists to be the most distressful of all possible states of mind in matters of faith. That which should please me—the force of his passion, of which he speaks with an ardor such as to leave no doubt of his sincerity—is precisely that which makes me hesitate, makes me withhold the consent I am often tempted to give.

Barras assures me that if I marry the general he will see to it that the command of the Army of Italy is awarded to him. Yesterday Buonaparte, in speaking to me of that honor which has already set his brothers-in-arms to whispering, even though the appointment has not yet been confirmed, said to me, "Do they [the Directors] believe that I have any need of their 'protection' to obtain the commission? They will all be only too happy if I accord them mine. My sword is at my side, and with that I shall go far." I don't know why, but sometimes this absurd self-confidence of his impresses me to the point of believing anything possible to this singular man— anything at all that might come into his mind to undertake! And with his imagination, who can guess what he might undertake?

Despite his infectious confidence in his star, his destiny, it was a risky business at best, this military one; the Italian front had frustrated a succession of French generals. A banker such as Thérèse Tallien's Ouvrard was a safer bet, but none had appeared on Josephine's horizon. Buonaparte was no great catch even with the command of the Army of Italy. The fact that General Aubert-Dubayet, the new Minister of War, had advised her against the marriage is evident from a letter she wrote to Madame Tallien six months later: "And whoever do you suppose invited himself yesterday to dinner? An opportunist who fawns presently on those whom he formerly ripped to shreds—you've guessed it, Dubayet! Suddenly calling me his 'darling.' It now develops that I did not make such a fool of myself, after all, in marrying Buonaparte."

Madame de Rémusat writes that her mother "was astonished at hearing that the widow of Monsieur de Beauharnais should have married a man so little known [as Bonaparte]. She [Madame Beauharnais] had hesitated between him, General Hoche and Monsieur de Caulaincourt, who also loved her."

But who were also married. Hoche, newly a father, and Caulaincourt, the father of five and on the eve of a silver wedding anniversary, had made no gesture toward divorce no matter what they may have promised. The Widow Beauharnais's mirror could not promise her how much longer it could reflect so lovely an image; she was a widow of thirty-two with expensive tastes, and with two children to support and educate on the slimmest, most irregular of revenues. She could not waver longer; she would gamble on her general.

3

"My mother's resistance ended when she saw General Bonaparte on the verge of departure," Hortense explains the developments of that winter. "It fell to Madame Campan to break the news to Eugène and me; our mother lacked the courage, knowing what distress it would cause us. I was, it is true, profoundly afflicted, but Madame Campan sought to calm me by pointing out the advantages to my brother; he was eager for a military career and could not begin it under auspices better than those of the general who was to be his stepfather."

In February the general accompanied his fiancée to the office of the notary Raguideau, her *homme d'affaires*, or business manager, for the drawing up of the marriage contract, by which, under a French legal provision still in effect today, each of the contracting parties was to retain control of his or her own estate—nonexistent in the case of both. Even so, Maître Raguideau cautioned his client against her folly, warning her, according to Napoleon's biographer-secretary Méneval, "that her friends were deeply concerned at seeing her enter into a union with a military man devoid of fortune, an adventurer, younger than herself, who might well be killed in action and leave her destitute, with still more children to support," and adding that, while her fiancé was undoubtedly an excellent officer, he nevertheless had "nothing at this point to recommend him save his cape and his sword."

During this interview the general had been waiting in the outer office, but he had overheard, through a partially open door, the notary's remarks to his client, and, reports Méneval, he approved them as the words of an honest man, adding, "I hope that Maître Raguideau will continue as notary for our joint affairs in the future, for he has won my confidence." "Napoleon," says Méneval, "kept the promise made by General Bonaparte, and named Raguideau a notary on the imperial civil list." *

At so late a date as mid-February 1796 there came a lovers' quarrel so "devastating" that Napoleon was still brooding over it four months later, referring to it in his letter to Josephine from Milan on June 8 as "the devastating scene that took place two weeks before our marriage." The morning after the "scene" ("At nine in the morning" is the dateline), he had written her a letter explaining everything save the issue which had necessitated the explanation:

I came away last night in the grip of a painful emotion. I went to bed very angry. It seemed to me that the respect due my charac-

---

* Bourrienne, Napoleon's first secretary, as well as Méneval, his successor, tells the Raguideau story, but there are some slight divergencies in the two accounts. Only Bourrienne includes the amusing sequel in which Josephine is quoted as saying, "Can you imagine my astonishment, Bourrienne, when Bonaparte, on the day of the coronation, dressed in all his imperial regalia, summoned Raguideau into his presence, saying, 'Well, now, Raguideau, have I at last something more to recommend me than my cape and my sword?'"

ter should have prevented such a thought as agitated you last
night from ever entering your mind. *If you continue to harbor such
a suspicion, you will be most unjust, madame, and I most unfortunate! For you even to think that I do not love you for yourself
alone!!! For whom, then? for what? Ah, madame, in that case I
must certainly have changed! How could so base a suspicion have
ever been conceived in a soul so pure? I am still astonished at you,
but still more astonished at myself—back at your feet, this morning, without the will power to resent or to resist. The height of
weakness and abjection! What, then, is your strange power over
me, my incomparable Josephine, that a mere thought of yours has
the power to poison my life and rend my heart, when at the same
time another emotion stronger still and another less somber mood
lead me back to grovel before you? I can clearly see that if disputes
arise between us, my heart and conscience will have to be disquali-
fied for the reason that you have seduced and suborned them—
they are on your side in any quarrel. . . . But what of you, mio
dolce amor, were you able to sleep this night? Or did you give me so
much as a single thought, two at the most? I give you three kisses:
one upon your heart, one upon your lips, one upon your eyes.*

If Josephine had accused him of not loving her for herself alone,
"for whom, then; for what?" For Barras and for Barras's influence?
For her fortune? Napoleon later admitted to a chronicler at St.
Helena that he had paid a visit to the Tascher family agent, the
banker Emmery, apparently to check on the Martinique holdings
and prospects. Emmery may have told Josephine of the inquiry,
but, if so, she gave her future husband very little satisfaction on the
subject, for Napoleon's letter to her on April 24 states that she had
never spoken to him of her business affairs.

Whatever their lovers' differences in mid-February, these must
have been composed by February 28, when the wedding banns
were published, and certainly by March 8, when the wedding contract was signed at Raguideau's office—with the bride subtracting
four years from her age and the groom gallantly adding eighteen
months to his, to further minimize the difference and make them
both a compatible twenty-eight.

On March 2, Buonaparte's appointment to the command of

the Army of Italy was announced publicly. And on March 9 the wedding ceremony was performed—a civil ceremony, as befitted a general of the Republic which had severed all ties with the Church of Rome, a wedding without benefit of clergy, without benefit of guests or celebrations.

Not one of the seven Buonaparte family members had been apprised, much less invited. The groom would wait until after the wedding to seek the pardon of his mother in Marseilles and his eldest brother, Joseph, in Italy, instead of the formal consent he should have sought beforehand in accordance with the strict Corsican tribal custom. Nor had Josephine been willing to risk her children's sulks or tears. The Beauharnais children, however, would become reconciled and devoted to the groom, whereas the Buonapartes never would to the bride.

Josephine, in one of her diaphanous, clinging tunics and with a gold fillet confining her light-chestnut curls, arrived promptly at eight o'clock at the mayoralty of the Second Arrondissement of Paris, on the Rue d'Antin, with Barras, Tallien and Calmelet, her trusted legal adviser. But for two hours it appeared that it might be a wedding party without benefit even of a groom. From eight to ten o'clock Josephine practiced patience, which would stand her in good stead with a man so preoccupied as to be oblivious to time on his wedding night.

As the clock struck ten, the clack of boots and the clank of swords on the stone entry steps roused the mayor from his doze behind his desk. Within a matter of minutes after the arrival of General Buonaparte and his aide-de-camp Le Marois, the gold wedding band had been slipped on the bride's finger—a ring engraved "To Destiny," which would be worn as a talisman on the finger of Josephine's grandson when he entered Paris as emperor in 1851. Before ten-thirty had chimed, the perfunctory civil ceremony had been concluded, congratulations had been offered, the four witnesses had dispersed, and the newlyweds in their carriage were en route back to the Rue Chantereine for their thirty-six-hour honeymoon.

A gifted hostess, Madame Buonaparte would have arranged with the domestic staff to retire early but to leave the salon fire lit and a table drawn up beside it with a cold collation and a bottle of champagne or Chambertin (the general's favorite wine, though he as well as Josephine was abstemious) in which to drink the wedding toasts. The general would be staying on at the Rue Chantereine that night of March 9, his baggage having been deposited earlier by his orderly in the dressing room of the second-floor bedroom suite. Maid, valet, chef, gardener and coachman had all been given to understand that the house had a new master. It was understood by all in the household save Fortuné, the fawn pug dog with the black mask and the corkscrew tail (the messenger of the Carmes), who had obviously in previous weeks been confined in another room until after the general's departure, at which time he was allowed back in the bedroom, on the bed—where he now lay growling at the intruder across the eiderdown.

"My rival!" the general later described the ugly, ill-tempered little beast to Arnault. "He was in possession of Madame's bed when I married her. I tried to put him out—a vain attempt. I was told that I had the choice of sleeping in another bed or sharing that one with Fortuné. The situation rather annoyed me, but it was a question of take it or leave it. So I resigned myself. The canine favorite was less accommodating than I—of which I bear proof on this leg."

The next morning, the tenth, General and Madame Buonaparte drove to St.-Germain-en-Laye to visit the children. Eugène was disposed to bask in the reflected military glory, but one of Hortense's schoolmates said that Hortense had been crying openly in class, sobbing that General Bonaparte frightened her and that she was afraid he would be very strict with her and Eugène. That day he could not have been more charming, visiting the classrooms, walking in the gardens, complimenting Madame Campan on her excellent female academy. Hortense might have been won over then and there—as people generally were whenever Napoleon intended them to be—except for the tweak he fondly gave her ear at parting. His love pats, tweaks and pinches were acutely painful—badges of courage and affection to make even such hero-generals as Junot and Murat wince.

On March 11, with aide-de-camp Junot waiting at the carriage door, General Buonaparte came to "the cruel parting" from his Josephine. Orders from the War Ministry to meet General Berthier, his chief of staff, at headquarters at Nice must have come sooner than had been expected, since his letter of March 14 told of his resenting the haste with which his orders had torn him away from her. Or she had wavered too long in setting the wedding date. Thirty-six hours had not been enough for him of living in her sweet and gentle vicinity, the serene realm her happy nature created all about her. He could not have had enough of her in thirty-six days, thirty-six months. He could think and write of nothing but her embraces; his letters covered her with his "thousand and one kisses," kisses on her eyes, her lips, her hair, her throat, her breasts. "He can talk of nothing but kisses," Prosper Mérimée said in editing these love letters of Napoleon I for Napoleon III in 1859. "He can talk of nothing but kisses, kisses everywhere—and upon portions of the anatomy not to be found in any Académie Française Dictionary."

Until the carriage turned out of the long driveway between the double row of lime trees, General Buonaparte doubtless threw kisses and waved back to Josephine. He resented the haste of his orders, and yet his sword was at his side, ready in its scabbard. He was off for the campaign of Italy, for a campaign that was to stretch beyond Italy across the Mediterranean to Egypt and back again, across the Rhine and the Tagus and the Vistula and the Niemen, across all Europe and into the steppes of Russia, that was not to end until it reached a village near Brussels called Waterloo: the greatest adventure since Alexander had set out across the Hellespont.

4

General Bonaparte was dreaming of love and making war.

"At sight of this young general marching under the triumphal arch of Milan's Porta Romana," wrote Stendhal, "it would have been difficult for the most experienced philosopher to divine the twin passions that ruled his heart."

His strategy for the Italian campaign had struck the former Minister of War, Barthélemy Schérer, as "the work of a madman such as could be executed only by a madman." It was the strategy of a military genius such as could be executed only by a military genius: a lightning-fast strike upon the Austrians, the Sardinians and the Piedmontese, with their two-to-one numerical superiority, climaxed by the capture of twenty-one enemy flags at Montenotte, Millesimo and Mondovi by April 23, and concluded by the Cherasco armistice on April 28—with Junot and Murat off to Paris shortly afterward, to deliver the treaty terms to the Directory.

Junot arrived in Paris by carriage with Joseph Bonaparte on May 6, a few hours after Murat, who had galloped in ahead by the short cut through Turin and the Alpine passes. On May 9 at the Luxembourg Palace, Junot made the official presentation of the battle trophies to the Directors. According to the article in the next day's *Moniteur*, "The Minister of War made the official acceptance speech and a eulogy of the young General Bonaparte, who had won immortality in so few days' time. The sound of martial music further stimulated the enthusiasm of the crowds, who burst into cries of 'Long live the Republic!' "

"It was one of the loveliest days of May," as the poet Arnault saw it. His eyes were focused primarily on his friend Josephine, who was standing on the platform near Barras, between Madame Tallien and Madame Châteaurenaud, "each of the three in the costume best calculated to set off her particular type of beauty, all three with garlands of flowers in their hair—the three months of spring, one might have thought them, gathered together to fete the victory."

Young Laure Permon, the daughter of Napoleon's Corsican friends, had eyes mainly for dashing Colonel Junot, little dreaming that that hero would one day ask her hand in marriage. "Junot, at twenty-five, was a handsome figure in his magnificent hussar's uniform," she was to remember, "and not a little proud to give his arm, at the conclusion of the ceremony, to two such glamorous creatures—Madame Bonaparte on his right, as befitted the wife of his commanding general, and Madame Tallien on his left—as they went down the staircase of the Luxembourg. The immense crowd pushed and jostled for a closer view. 'Look, there's Bonaparte's aide-de-camp! And there's his wife! How pretty she is! Long live

General Bonaparte! Long live Citizeness Bonaparte! She brings us luck!' And 'Yes, yes,' shouted one coarse, fat market woman, 'she's Our Lady of Victories [Notre Dame des Victoires]!' "

The name of the Rue Chantereine was changed to match: Rue de la Victoire. And was immediately clogged with pedestrian and carriage traffic: the people of Paris, personal friends and acquaintances, government and military officials, financiers, speculators—all Paris flocking there to salute the rising star, the meteor in the national firmament. And no one ever knew better than this general's lady how to accept tribute graciously, gracefully to acknowledge the *vivats* and salutes of the throng, the formal speeches, the presentations of ceremonial swords and laurel crowns.

Throughout the weeks of April and May, with every new bulletin from Italy, with every fresh victory from that front, Our Lady of Victories was feted in Paris. Between the fetes and the visits to modistes to select and fit the gowns in which to make her grand entrance at these fetes, she no longer had time to visit the children's schools in St.-Germain. Hortense complained by letter: "I suppose it is the general's victories that keep you from coming. If that is what deprives me of my *chère petite maman*'s visits, I'll start hoping for an end to victories."

Hortense's "dear little mother" could scarcely find time to answer her daughter or her husband. The latter was infinitely more difficult to pacify, becoming daily more importunate, petulant and reproachful of neglect; but there can be no chore more difficult than replying to love letters when one is not oneself in love. His lyric expression of passion embarrassed her, made her uneasy. All very flattering from a lover, but slightly ridiculous from a husband —"funny," from her point of view, which was that of her cynical, ultrasophisticated eighteenth-century social world. She had made a marriage of convenience, but she was discovering that the torrent of his love for her was not to be diverted or dammed up by her indifference or discouragement. That torrent would engulf her and carry her off to Italy if she did not soon find some firm rock to which to cling.

Both Murat and Junot had been bearers of urgent messages to her from the general; both were under orders not to return without her. Until this time Barras, Carnot and the other Directors had agreed—a fact for which she had been grateful—that a theater of war was no place for a woman; only a mad Corsican would have suggested it. But by mid-May Carnot had been obliged to yield to the hero's pressure, writing him on May 21: "The Directory, which has thus far opposed the departure of the Citizeness Bonaparte in the fear that her husband's attentions to her would distract him from his duty to glory and to the nation, agreed with her that she should not set out until after the capture of Milan. That city is now yours, and we of the Directory offer no further objection to her joining you. We hope that the myrtle of Venus with which she will crown you will not detract from the laurels with which Victory has adorned you."

At that point General Murat was enlisted to advise General Bonaparte that his wife was pregnant and "not well enough to undertake so long a journey." Yet Murat's letter was written on May 9, the very day of the Luxembourg victory celebration at which the stellar performance, the one featured by every Paris newspaper, had been hers. And that same week she and Madame Tallien had been seen making the rounds of the gayest Champs-Élysées dance-halls—with none other than Murat acting as proud escort to these two most celebrated of all Parisiennes, a fact that would give rise to gossip and to trouble later.

Was Josephine so flighty, so foolish, as not to realize that her husband would hear of these public Paris activities at a time when she was supposed to be languishing? Was she so reckless as to take no warning from his "dagger of Othello" letter? Or did she not even read those letters of his, not trouble to decipher them, but merely glance through the ink-splotched pages and then tuck them away in a desk drawer with the intention of trying to make them out later, some other day, when she had just a little more time? If so, they flooded in so fast that she could never catch up with her reading; courier after courier from Italy came pounding first up the Rue de la Victoire driveway with letters for Josephine before going on to the Luxembourg to deliver official dispatches to the Directors.

By the end of May, the main Austrian forces had retreated into the Tyrol to await reinforcements, while maintaining a center of resistance at Mantua. General Bonaparte availed himself of the opportunity to make forays against the Venetian Republic at Verona, but he was back in Milan by June 11, in the hope that his wife was on her way.

Josephine [he wrote], where will this letter reach you? If at Paris, then my despair is certain—then you no longer love me, and all that is left for me is to die. . . . No respite, no hope. I respect the immutable law of fate, which has heaped glory upon me only to emphasize my personal misfortune. I shall accustom myself to this new state of affairs, but never to that of no longer esteeming you— no, it is not possible! My Josephine is on her way; she loves me at least a little. Such a pledge of love cannot have been dissolved in two months' time.

I hate Paris, women, love. I am in a dreadful state of mind, and your conduct— But should I reproach you? No. Your conduct is as fate decrees it. So lovable, so beautiful, so sweet, how could you be the . . . instrument of my despair?

The bearer of this letter to you is Prince Serbelloni, the grand seigneur of this land, who goes as deputy to Paris to present his homage to the government. .

Embrace your lovely children for me. They write me charming letters. Since I must no longer love you, I love them the more. Despite fate and honor, I shall love you all my life. Tonight I have reread all your letters, even the one written in your blood. What emotions they have aroused in me!

B——

On June 14 he wrote from headquarters at Tortona to apologize for the letter of the eleventh:

Ever since the eighteenth [of Prairial—June 6], my dearest Josephine, I have been expecting you. I actually believed you had arrived at Milan. I rushed there from the battlefield at Borghetto, hoping to find you. I found you not! A few days later, a courier brought me word that you had not yet set out from Paris, but he brought me no letter from you. Sorrow crushed my soul. . . . My emotions are never moderate. Drowning in sorrow, I wrote you in terms perhaps too violent. If my letters have hurt you, then I shall be inconsolable for life.

Having crossed the Ticino, I came to Tortona to wait for you. Day after day I waited vainly. Finally, four hours ago, there came that scrap of a letter to break the news to me that you are not coming. I will make no attempt to describe my dismay when I learned that you are ill, that there are three doctors in attendance, that you must be in danger since you cannot write to me yourself. Since the moment I read that message, I have been in an indescribable state. . . .

I must know, first of all, that you forgive me the mad, insensate letters I have written you. If you are well enough to reason, you will realize that the ardent love which fills me has perhaps unbalanced my mind.

I must have assurance that you are out of danger. My darling, make your health your first concern. Let nothing interfere with your convalescence. You are delicate, frail, ill, and this is the hot summer season, the journey long. On my knees I beg you, do not risk a life so precious. No matter how short life is, three months will somehow pass.

Three months without seeing each other! I tremble, my dearest. I dare not think of the future. It is a horror, now that my only hope of consolation has been snatched from me. I do not believe in the immortality of the soul. If you die, I shall die immediately, a death of despair and annihilation.

Murat tries to convince me that your malady is not grave—but you do not write to me. It is a month since I have received a letter from you. You are tender, sensitive, and you love me. You are struggling between illness and doctors—unconscious, far from the one who would snatch you from illness, from the arms of death itself. . . . If your illness continues, obtain permission for me to come to see you for one hour. In five days I can be in Paris, and on the twelfth day back with my army. Without you, without you, I can be of no value here. Let him who will seek glory, let him who will serve his country! My soul is suffocating in this exile. And when my beloved suffers, ails, I cannot coolly calculate victory. I don't know how to express myself, what line of conduct to follow.

I want to take the post chaise and come to Paris. But honor, to which you are not insensible, holds me here despite my heart. Out of pity's sake, have someone write to me, so that I may know the nature of your illness and what there is to fear.

Our fate is a cruel one. Scarcely married, scarcely united, and already separated! My tears drench your portrait. That alone remains to me. My brother does not write, doubtless fearing to tell me what he knows must utterly shatter me.

A thousand kisses. Remember that there has never been a love like mine, it will last as long as my life. Think of me, write to me twice daily. Deliver me soon from the grief which consumes me.

Come, come quickly. But take care of your health.

B——

On the next day, June 15, another letter, this time by special courier Lesimple, and with special instructions:

My life is a perpetual nightmare. A fatal premonition stops me from breathing. I am no longer living. I have lost more than life, more than happiness, more than repose. I am almost without hope. I am sending you a courier. He is to stay in Paris only four hours, and then to bring me your reply. Write me ten pages. That alone can bring me a measure of consolation.

You are ill, you love me, I have hurt you, you are pregnant, and I shall not see you! The thought overwhelms me. I have been unjust to you, done you injustices so many I don't know how to expiate them. I have accused you of lingering on in Paris, and all the while you were ill. Forgive me, my darling. The love you have inspired in me robs me of my reason; I shall never regain it. One never recovers from that condition.

My premonitions are so dire that I limit my hope to seeing you just once more, to holding you in my arms, against my heart, for just two hours—and then dying together. Who is taking care of you? I imagine that you have sent for Hortense. I love that sweet child a thousand times more for the thought that she may bring you comfort.

As for me, no comfort, no rest, no hope until the courier I have sent to you has returned—until, in a long letter, you explain to

"My life is a perpetual nightmare . . ." Napoleon's letter to Josephine chiding her for not answering his letters. Translated on page 112.

me the nature of your illness, and to what extent it may be [illegible word]. Should you be in danger, I warn you, I am leaving at once for Paris. My presence will conquer the disease. . . . I have always been able to impose my will on destiny. But today I am struck down through another, the only one in all the world about whom I care.

Josephine, how can you go so long without writing to me? Your last letter, dearly beloved, was that of the third [May 22], and one, furthermore, that hurt me deeply. I keep it nonetheless in my pocket. Your portrait and your letters are constantly before my eyes.

I am nothing without you. I do not know how I managed to exist before I knew you. Ah, Josephine, had you had my heart, would you have put off leaving from the twenty-ninth to the sixteenth [29 Floréal to 16 Prairial—May 18 to June 4]? Would you have listened to perfidious friends who wished perhaps to hold you back from joining me? I suspect everyone. I resent all those who surround you. I counted on your departure on the fifth [May 26], on your arrival at Milan on the fifteenth [June 4]. . . . I cannot bring myself to tell you not to undertake so long a voyage in this heat—not, at least, if you have come to the decision to make the trip. Travel by short days' journeys, write to me at every stop along the way and send your letters on ahead.

All my thoughts are concentrated within your alcove, upon your bed, upon your heart. Your illness, that is all I can think of, day and night. Without appetite, without sleep, without interest in friendship or in glory or in country—thou, thou alone; and the rest of the world has no more reality for me than if it had been annihilated. I value honor only because you do; victory, only because it gives you pleasure. Otherwise I would have abandoned it all to come and throw myself at your feet.

Sometimes I tell myself: I am alarmed without reason; she has already recovered, she is leaving, she has already left, she may already be in Lyons. Vain imagination! You are in your bed, suffering, more beautiful, more fascinating, more adorable than ever; you are pale, your eyes even more languishing. But when will you be well again? If one of us had to be ill, could it not have been I? More robust and more stalwart, I could better have withstood illness. Destiny is cruel, she strikes me through you. There is some small consolation in the thought that, though fate may have the power to make you ill, no power can force me to live on without you. . . .

When you write, dearest, assure me you realize that I love you with a love beyond the limits of imagination, that every minute of my life is consecrated to you, that never an hour passes without my thinking of you, that I have never thought of another woman, that they are all, in my eyes, lacking grace, wit and beauty. That you, you alone, and all of you, as I see you, as you are—only you can please me, absorb the faculties of my soul; that you pervade my soul to its farthest reaches; that there is no corner of my heart into which you do not see, no thought of mine which is not subordinate to you. That my arms, my strength, my mind are all yours. That my soul lives in your body, and that the day upon which you should change or cease to live would be the day of my death. That the world is beautiful only because you inhabit it. If you do not realize and believe all this, you do not love me. A magnetic fluid flows between persons who love each other.

You know very well that I could never bear your taking a lover— much less, seriously suggest one to you. To see him and to tear out his heart would be one and the same thing. And after that, if I could ever bring myself to raise my hand against your sacred person— No, I never could, but I would depart a life wherein all that I know as virtue had deceived me. But I am sure and proud of your love. These misfortunes are the trials whereby the force of our passions is mutually revealed. A child, adorable like its mother, will see the day and be so fortunate as to spend long years in your arms. Unfortunate that I am, I would be satisfied with one day there!

A thousand kisses upon your eyes, upon your lips, upon your tongue, upon your c——. My adorable wife, what is your power over me? I am ill of your illness, burning with your fever. Do not hold Lesimple in Paris more than six hours, then let him return immediately to bring me the cherished letter from my sovereign.

And in the event the commander's sovereign could not or would not reply, Lesimple carried in his pouch a letter for the commander's brother Joseph, a "plea in the name of our blood bonds and tender friendship to write to me, tell me the truth, reassure me about my wife's condition, . . . lavish your cares upon my Josephine, the first woman whom I have ever loved—and whom I love to distraction."

And another letter to be delivered at the Luxembourg, to Barras, beginning formally as a notification of the petition of the kingdom of Naples and the Papal States for armistice terms, but ending informally, on a personal, confidential note: "I hate women. I am in despair. My wife does not come—she must have a lover who is holding her in Paris."

The words are echoed in the memoirs of Bonaparte's friend General Marmont, a former École Militaire classmate, who was with him that week in June at Tortona. "His wife's continual postponement of her departure tormented him grievously," says Marmont, "and he began to show symptoms of jealousy and of a superstition which was a marked trait of his character. One morning, during an inspection tour of the Piedmontese strongholds on which I accompanied him, the glass of the portrait of his wife shattered in his hands. His face turned so white as to alarm me, and his reaction was distressing to behold.

" 'Marmont,' he said to me, 'my wife is either ill or unfaithful.' "

V

Charles

Charles Something or Somebody Charles! . . . A shadowy figure, an unknown, a phantom, a Monsieur X.

BARON DE MÉNEVAL, *Mémoires*

1

APPARENTLY it was the latter. Apparently with a man named Charles—whether this was a first name or a last, whether Charles or Charles Quentin or Hippolyte Charles. Apparently a man in the military service, in either the guides—elite guards—or the hussars; a lieutenant or a captain, apparently attached to the Army of Italy. For more than a hundred years it was difficult to identify or to place the man precisely. There was certainly talk enough at the time, contemporary gossip which would be preserved in black and white through nineteenth- and twentieth-century printing presses; but historians were to find later that the dossier of the officer named Charles was missing from the archives of the War Ministry, and so little actual fact could be established about him that some biographers relegated the whole story to the realm of myth and malice. "Charles Something or Somebody Charles!" exclaimed Méneval, who became Napoleon's private secretary in 1802. "With that insignificant, enigmatic name of his, he seems to belong to legend rather than to reality. A shadowy figure, an unknown, a phantom, a Monsieur X."

If Napoleon's secretary did not believe in a Monsieur Charles, General Junot's wife surely did, mentioning him pointedly and repeatedly, in her memoirs, as a dear friend of Josephine's and a good friend of General Junot's. "A quasi-historical character whose obscure name was linked with a great one," she says of him, adding: "It is curious how the life trajectory of a virtual unknown, in crossing that of a luminary, can be at that point caught up in the glare of history and, shining originally only in a reflected glory, eventually give off a light of its own by which the central figure is clarified."

Only in recent years, however, has enough light been shed on the figure of the romantic cavalier himself to confirm his identity officially and positively. In the 1950s the researches of the French historian Louis Hastier in the day-by-day records of the Army of Italy established beyond a doubt that in the spring of 1796, at Paris, the life trajectory of Lieutenant Hippolyte Charles of the First Regiment of Hussars, born twenty-four years earlier near Romans-sur-Isère in southeast France, did indeed meet that of the wife of his new commander in chief.

Lieutenant Charles was "utterly charming," Laure Junot thought; "elegant in his person; dashing in a hussar's uniform resplendent with gold braid." If he was the wolf in the fold, he was a gallant little wolf, and the shepherd himself had opened the gate. Lieutenant Charles owed his entree to the house on the Rue de la Victoire to his good friend Adjutant General Leclerc, whom he himself served as adjutant; and Leclerc was, in turn, the good friend of General Bonaparte, with whom he had served at Toulon two years previously and whom he now planned to join in Italy. Charles and Leclerc had come up together from Marseilles on April 19 and gone together immediately to pay their respects to Josephine and to bring her news and messages from the Bonaparte family, then living in that southern seaport city.

Napoleon's superstition (or intuition), his faith in his "presentiments," his "dire premonitions," seems to have been justified: Charles had been introduced to Josephine on April 20 or 21, and within the next weeks Napoleon was writing: "There is no one else, no one but me, is there?"; "I am not jealous, but sometimes anxious"; "I have the feeling that you have made a choice and that you know to whom you will turn to replace me." He had cause for anxiety. In May, Josephine wrote a breathless little note to Talleyrand, inviting him to meet her new protégé, the latest addition to her social gatherings: "You will be wild about him. Mesdames Récamier, Tallien and Hamelin have all lost their heads over him, he is so handsome. And such taste! He is so superbly accoutered, I am convinced that no man has ever before known how to arrange a cravat. I shall present him to you; you will hear him talk and he will give you ideas. He astonished even Madame Despaulx"—a reference to the modiste Madame Despeaux, the fashion authority of the fashion capital.

It was not Madame Hamelin—another Creole member of the Directoire smart set—who had lost her head over the hussar Charles, but Madame Bonaparte. At least that was how Monsieur Hamelin saw it; he saw Charles as the new favorite in her salon, "enjoying a decided preference on the part of the hostess, a signal favor which she did not adequately dissimulate. This Hippolyte Charles was a captain [sic] attached to the general staff [of the Army of Italy], a small man with a charming face and a knack for puns and jingles, at which she laughed until she cried—never forgetting, however, to put her handkerchief to her lips to conceal her dreadful teeth." Hamelin was always resentful of the fact that, although Madame Bonaparte most kindly arranged for him to traffic in army contracts in Italy, he could never manage to make the success of it that others would. Hamelin is spiteful and malicious, but not a liar as concerns either Charles's favor with the hostess or the hostess's bad teeth. The latter fact is corroborated by Madame de Rémusat, among others: "Her very small mouth artfully concealed her bad teeth." Josephine had long and carefully consulted her mirror to make certain that her sweetest smile revealed no trace of this less attractive feature.

Charles's height—or lack of it—was his only point of similarity with Napoleon. "Impossible to find a droller, more amusing fellow" than Charles, Laure Junot said. Playwright Arnault heartily agreed: "The gayest, most even disposition—a delightful companion." All the things Napoleon was not, all the things Josephine missed in a husband. She, whose element was society—the principal distraction to her idleness—had as husband the most unsociable of creatures, never then or later at his ease in a crowd or among strangers, brusque, boorish, preoccupied. For small talk, which was her forte and Charles's, Napoleon had neither talent nor inclination. When he talked, it was with savants or with generals, diplomats, jurists, scientists; "he never conversed, he held forth in brilliant monologue" (as an erudite Madame de Rémusat could appreciate) on the topics of war, mathematics, politics, philosophy. Where Charles hummed airs or cracked jokes from the latest stage successes, Josephine's husband recited verse from the melancholy Ossian or the more lugubrious passages from Racine. Charles was the life of the party, Madame Junot said; Napoleon, "the Unamusable," as Talleyrand called him to his face as well as behind his back. When Napoleon was roused to open mirth, "which was seldom," said Laure Junot, his laughter "had the disconcerting sound of a ventriloquist's dummy."

Charles was, by instinct and predilection, a lady's man, fastidious in his dress, a dandy in his tasseled red leather boots, with his silver-embroidered, red-fox-trimmed cape slung jauntily over the left shoulder—in contrast to a General Bonaparte who was negligent in his dress, almost oblivious to what he wore, affecting the simplest *guides* uniform in the midst of his flamboyantly arrayed staff.

Above all, Charles must have been a deft suitor, an experienced, skillful, considerate, rewarding lover—which Napoleon never was, despite a record of amorous exploits more extensive than that of his military ones. Napoleon's sexual proclivities were prodigious; but women were consistently dismayed at his approach, or, rather, his lack of it—at his tactics in love or in passion, which were anything but endearing. An awestruck Stendhal hailed him as "the successor, after all these centuries, to Caesar and to Alexander"—but not to Casanova, not to Don Juan. Stendhal, when he was still Henri Beyle and in the diplomatic service, met General Bonaparte in Italy in 1796 and came to admire him lavishly as a "born warrior"—but not as a born lover.

The Emperor [Stendhal wrote, referring to a later period, the Empire], usually seated at a small table, his sword at his side, would be signing his endless decrees. When a lady was announced, he would request her—without looking up from his worktable—to go and wait for him in bed. Later, with a candlestick in his hand, he would show her out of the bedroom, and then promptly go back to his table to continue reading, correcting and signing those endless decrees.

The essential part of the rendezvous had not lasted three minutes.

To dismiss these gallant visitors after a mere three minutes of his time, to go on signing decrees, and often without so much as unbuckling his sword, struck these ladies as an outrageous procedure.

Allowing for some slight exaggeration on Stendhal's part, the delineation is basically accurate, as others of Napoleon's male intimates and several of his mistresses confirm. Frédéric Masson, Napoleon's distinguished and reverent biographer, concedes the Emperor's relations with women to have been "brutally abrupt," with no waste of time on preliminaries. Masson interprets this as another reflection of the Emperor's inherent timidity with women; this was the man who described his youthful approach to prostitutes as invariably heralded by the question "Would you be so kind as to tell me the story of how you lost your virginity?" The answer to this ritual query served to reassure the eighteen-year-old officer of the woman's accessibility to his fumbling advances. At St. Helena, in years of endless reminiscence and introspection, Napoleon analyzed himself to General Gourgaud, to the effect that sexually he was instantly stimulated in the proximity of a "pretty and agreeable woman" ("agreeable," in his use of the word, meaning compliant), and that "the lady's role in the proceedings was concluded in the very minimum of time."

Certain findings in the autopsy report issued at St. Helena are cited in proof of Napoleon's deficiencies as a lover, and as substantiation of a "physiological weakness." But modern medical opinion would construe his haste in love-making as having been due to psychological rather than physiological causes—to timidity and indifference to a partner's pleasure.

It is, to be sure, unlikely that Napoleon showed himself such a peremptory and indifferent lover with a woman he so loved as he did Josephine. His letters to her in reminiscence and in evocation of their embraces are evidence to the contrary. She had surely taught him a tenderer communion, although even under her gentle and deft auspices he could not have entirely altered his basic pattern. A courtesan's role is to simulate a pleasure she may not genuinely share, but Josephine was more than that: she was so genuinely tender, so sensitive to the sensibilities of others, that it is unlikely she would ever have wounded his pride by allowing him to guess that she did not enjoy his embrace.

Yet neither did she choose to go to Italy to receive it. Here again she was reluctant to show herself unkind by disappointing him, but apparently she could not at this point control her own heart and keep it from turning to Charles. Apparently she was moved by love as she had never been before—not even by Hoche, Barras's opinion notwithstanding—to the point now of a rashness quite unlike her, a total disregard of her own best interests.

To avoid hurting her husband, she may have resorted to the plea of illness, pregnancy, even a miscarriage. A month after the capture of Milan, she was under pressure not only from her husband but also from the Directors, now fearful that their temperamental military genius might carry out his threat to desert the battlefield for the bedside of his ailing wife. General Murat had been obliged to return to his post in Italy without Madame Bonaparte, despite his commanding general's orders to the contrary. And Colonel Junot was still waiting in Paris to escort her across the Alps, but growing restive at her postponements. General Leclerc and Charles had received their official assignment to the Army of Italy on May 5 and had entered a request with the War Ministry for four horses for the journey. But Leclerc set out alone in May.

It could only have been as an especial favor to his commander's wife that Leclerc permitted his adjutant to linger on in Paris and to join Madame Bonaparte's cavalcade, as her special cavalier in addition to the cavalry detachment assigned her as a protection against the *barbets,* bandits who harassed the Alpine roads.

Barras sent word to his fiery, touchy Bonaparte that the month of June would not pass without his wife's departure. Arnault comments: "Her distress was acute when she saw that she had exhausted her last excuse. Thinking of what she was leaving behind rather than of what she had before her, she would gladly have forgone the palace prepared for her reception in Milan—would have forgone all the palaces in the world!—for the sake of her little house on the Rue Chantereine."

By June she was at last making preparations for the journey, assembling an elaborate trousseau, to judge by Hamelin's report that she borrowed two hundred gold louis from him for her purchases, plus an additional thirty louis for a cobwebby English lace scarf—and considered herself acquitted of the debt in having arranged for his transportation in her suite across the Alps. During those weeks of June, she also commissioned the most fashionable of Paris decorators to refurbish her house. In June, too, she prepared her children for the parting, treating them to a trip to Fontainebleau on the occasion of a family wedding, perhaps in consolation for their having missed her own. The bride this time was none other than Aunt Edmée Renaudin, and the groom the octogenarian Marquis de Beauharnais; these two were exchanging the enduring bonds of a forty-year-old illicit liaison for the tenuous ones of holy matrimony.

On June 25 Director Barras honored Madame Bonaparte at a farewell dinner party at the Luxembourg, and it was from there that she made her departure, Arnault recalls. "In leaving, she gave me fresh proof of her kindness, promising to intercede with her husband to procure a post with the Army of Italy for my brother; in this instance she kept her word, and this deserves special mention, since, not always able to shake off that Creole indolence of hers even when most eager to do you a favor, she was apt to forget her promises as easily as she made them. Poor woman, she burst into tears that night when the other guests accompanied her to her waiting carriage in the courtyard, and when Barras helped her in. She sobbed as if she were going to the torture chamber, whereas she was going to Italy to reign as a sovereign."

On June 24 the Directory had issued orders for the passports to be delivered for "the Citizeness Josephine Lapagerie, wife of General Bonaparte"; for her maid, Louise Compoint, and two menservants; for Colonel Junot and Joseph Bonaparte; for financier Hamelin (in fulfillment of Josephine's promise); and, of course, for "Citizen Hippolyte Charles, assistant to Adjutant General Leclerc of the Army of Italy"—who would ride in Madame Bonaparte's carriage with her, with Junot and with Joseph. The fifth occupant had no passport, but was identifiable by a silver plate affixed between the silver bells on his pretty leather collar, reading: "I belong to Madame Bonaparte." This was Fortuné, the pug, the only rival as yet acknowledged by Napoleon or known by him to be riding in his wife's carriage.

Although Napoleon may have been warned by another of his "dire premonitions." Director Carnot had sent him a message on June 22 that "Madame Bonaparte, though still not completely recovered from her illness, will set out on June 26." On that very date, before Carnot's message could have reached him, Napoleon wrote Josephine from Tuscany—still addressing her at the Rue Chantereine—a letter in which, for the first time, a note of serious mistrust and suspicion, of sarcasm and of irony, crept in between the lines of his customary rhapsodizing:

In a month I have received only two notes of three lines each from my sweetheart. Are there other matters claiming her attention? Is not that of writing to her husband a claim upon her? That of thinking of him, at least? Not to think of Josephine—for her husband, that would mean death, denial of his very existence. Your image embellishes my thought, brightens the dark and sinister face of melancholy and of sorrow.

A day perhaps will come when I shall see you. . . . Well, then, on that day I will show you my pockets stuffed full of letters which were too foolish to send; yes, that's the word for it—foolish. Good God! Tell me, you who know so well how to inspire love in others' hearts without feeling it in your own, would you know how one cures oneself of love??? I would pay a handsome price for such a remedy.

You were supposed to have left on the fifth Prairial [May 30]; fool that I was, I was expecting you on the thirteenth [June 7]. As if a pretty woman could be expected to abandon her pleasant way of life, to run off and leave her friends—her Madame Tallien, her dinners at Barras's, her first-night theatrical performances, her Fortuné; no, not even her Fortuné could she give up! *You love them all better than you do your husband*. For him you have only a mild esteem; he can claim only a share of that sweet good will of which your heart is a wellspring.

Recapitulating your faults, your frailties, I flagellate myself in an effort to stop loving you. Bah! I wind up loving you all the more! In brief, my incomparable little darling, I shall let you in on my secret: Make mock of me, stay on in Paris, take lovers, let all the world know it, never write to me—and then? And then I shall love you ten times more than I did before! If that is not folly, fever, delirium! What is more, I shall never recover from it—but oh! if by chance I should!

But don't go on telling me that you are ill; don't go on trying to justify yourself. Good God, you are forgiven; I love you to distraction; never will my poor heart cease to give you all its love. If you should not love me, my fate would be indeed bizarre. So you have not written to me; so you were ill; so you have not come. So the Directory has opposed your coming, and then there was your malady, and then the baby that stirred so strong within you as to make you ill? But now you have passed beyond Lyons; you will be in Turin by the tenth [June 4]; on the twelfth at Milan, where you will await my coming. You will be in Italy, but I will still be far away from you! Adieu, my beloved, a kiss upon your mouth, another upon your heart, another upon your little ——.

We have made peace with Rome, which brings us money. I will be tomorrow at Leghorn, and as soon as I can in your arms, at your feet, upon your breast.

2

The disillusionment slowly dawning upon Napoleon even in his delirium may have been the result of an inadvertent or careless word from General Murat or General Leclerc upon their return from Josephine's "shrine"—some word about her Paris social whirl, her radiance and exuberance at a time when he had thought her ailing and suffering.

Much has been made in history books of that "false pregnancy" —whether it was a fact or an honest mistake on her part or an outright invention. When biographers deride the idea that she had felt life—as, to judge by Napoleon's letters, she had told him—only two months after the wedding, they evidently choose to forget that the March wedding date was no indication of the beginning of their intimacy. If Josephine was truthful in mentioning the symptom, the pregnancy would have been in an advanced stage, and a miscarriage—if there was one—sufficiently serious to have warranted the "three doctors in attendance." But the episode remains forever in the realm of conjecture and controversy.

Napoleon's letter of June 26 did not reach Paris until after Josephine's departure. By General Bonaparte's orders, she was conveyed under armed and mounted guard, with his special courier, Moustache, detailed to ride ahead to arrange for horses at every relay station, as the three-carriage caravan rolled south to a first halt at flag-and-flower-bedecked Lyons, and then veered east toward the Mont Cenis Pass.

"The journey would have been very gay," says fellow traveler Hamelin, "for Junot would have kept us laughing with his sallies of robust military wit—had not that little Charles taken to jealous sulking whenever another enjoyed the favor he sought to monopolize."

Laure Junot hints that Josephine's favor was unwelcome and embarrassing to a loyal Junot, and that as a tactical diversion he affected an interest in Louise Compoint, her soubrette of a maid. Or such is the version of the story that Laure heard later from her husband. Junot, great, hulking, swaggering officer that he was, may have been the type of man who flatters himself that every woman is flirting with him. Or Josephine may have been the type of woman who created that impression on every man upon whom she turned her gaze, that "languorous look" of hers—the arched lids and the slightly curling, long, dark lashes seductively veiling the dark-blue eyes—which may have been the result less of intention than of ocular conformation. What is certain is that, on Junot's part, an ill will developed which would melodramatically erupt two years later in Egypt.

Hamelin's tongue and pen wagged about the pairing off at the overnight stopping places along the road: "Charles with Josephine, Junot with Mademoiselle Louise. . . . Joseph [Bonaparte] off to a room by himself, still smarting from the painful souvenir of his indiscriminate Paris love affairs." It is difficult to credit Hamelin's scandalmongering. Even if Josephine was so reckless as to flaunt her relations with Charles in the face of her husband's brother, even if she so dared to brave her husband's wrath, surely Charles must have had misgivings about such an affront to his notoriously jealous and all-powerful commander in chief.

Once that commander in chief knew as a certainty that his wife was on her way, he knew fresh torture in the thought that he might not be on hand to greet her when she reached Milan. Called to Florence and to Bologna to treat with emissaries of the Pope, he arranged with General Lespinoy to "rush off a courier to me the moment my wife arrives." And he dispatched General Marmont with an honor guard to Turin, where the court of Sardinia gave her a sovereign's welcome, Marmont reports.

On July 13, General Bonaparte rushed back from Roverbella in time to give her a lover's welcome to Milan, to the colonnaded Palazzo Serbelloni which he had chosen as their residence, a palace described by Arnault as one of the most magnificent in Milan, "a palace in Cockaigne—a pile of rosy, crystal-specked granite that sparkled in the sun like sugar candy." In its great loggia Colonel Junot and Joseph Bonaparte, who descended from the carriage after Josephine, stood patiently waiting until Napoleon should release her from his embrace long enough to turn and greet them.

There in Milan, with her husband at last, Josephine gave herself to him—if not out of love, then out of her warm unfailing sympathy, her eagerness to please—to try to meet his burning need of her. "Once reunited with his wife at Milan," General Marmont observes, "General Bonaparte was supremely happy, for he lived then solely for her. And so it was for a long time; a love so true, so pure, so exclusive had never possessed the heart of a man, and that man of so superior an order."

So little time he had to enjoy the happiness of that reunion—

forty hours only before he must return to direct the assault on Mantua, and even those forty hours not uninterrupted. On July 14, Bastille Day, the city honored Madame Bonaparte with a gala performance at La Scala, followed by a ball at which all the notables of Lombardy were presented to her. It served, as well, as an occasion for her to present her protégé Hamelin to Bonaparte, and perhaps Lieutenant Charles, unless he had already departed for headquarters at Verona.

By July 15, Napoleon was back at the battle front, writing to Josephine from Marmirolo that night at nine:

Thank you, my darling, for your letter. It filled my heart with joy, and I am grateful to you for going to the trouble of sending me news. You should be feeling better today?

I have been sad every moment since our parting. I know no happiness save when I am with you. I think incessantly of your kisses, your tears, your teasing jealousy. The charms of my incomparable Josephine kindle a flame that burns unceasingly in my heart, through my senses. When shall I ever be free of anxiety and responsibility, free to spend all my time with you, with nothing to do but to love you, nothing to think of but how to tell you of my love, how to prove it to you?

A few days ago I thought I loved you, but now since I have seen you again I love you a thousand times more. Every day since I met you I have loved you more—just to disprove La Bruyère's maxim that love comes in a lightning flash. . . .

Ah, I implore you, let me see that you have faults. Be less beautiful, less gracious, less kind, less tender. Above all, never be jealous, never weep. Your tears rob me of my reason, set my blood aflame.

Take your rest. Gain back your strength and your health. Come quickly to join me—so that at least before we die we can say, "We have had this many joyous hours together." Thousands of kisses—one even for Fortuné, wicked beast that he is!

All the night of July 17 he had "spent under arms" before the walls of flaming Mantua ("a horrible if impressive spectacle"), but he found time to write her the next morning to describe a pilgrimage he had made (fancying it would hold literary and romantic significance to her as to him) "to Virgil's village on the lake shore, in the light of the silvery moon, and thinking of my Josephine at every moment"; also to forward to her a letter from Eugène and to ask her to assure her "darling children" that he loved them as if they were his own. "My heart is incapable of distinguishing between what is mine and what is thine." For having opened other letters addressed to her from Paris, the intrepid warrior confessed to such trepidation that he had been tempted to reseal them—

but fie! that would be shameful. I wish you would give me explicit permission for the future, though. If you are angry, I apologize. I swear that it was not out of jealousy. I have too lofty an opinion of my darling for that.

A thousand kisses as fiery as my heart, as pure—and cold—as thine. A courier returning from Milan reports that you told him you had no order, no letter, no message to send to me. Shame on you, you wicked, ugly, cruel tyrant, you pretty little monster! You laugh at my threats and at my follies. Ah, if I could only imprison you, shut you up in my heart! When can you come to join me?

On July 21 he was "still waiting for that letter" from her, but heading for the northern border to check on a concentration of Austrian forces that posed a threat from the Alps. He supposed she was still sleeping at the early hour at which he wrote,

. . . and I not there beside you to breathe in your breath, to contemplate your beauty, to overwhelm you with caresses! Separated from you, the nights are wearisome, mournful, long. When I am with you, my only regret is that the nights are not eternal!

By this time you are well acquainted with Milan. Perhaps you have even found that lover you were seeking? The thought of such a thing never ceases to [illegible word]. But no, let me think too well of myself for such a possibility.

I hope that you are feeling completely well by now and that you can come to stay with me at headquarters, never to part from me again. Are you not the life of my life, the heart of my heart? . . .

Adieu, my beautiful and good, my utterly incomparable, utterly divine Josephine! A thousand impassioned kisses, everywhere, everywhere!

On the twenty-second of July two letters went off by courier to bring her word that she should come on the twenty-fifth to the southern shore of Lake Garda, to Brescia, where "the tenderest of lovers would await" her.

I count the days until then—and well know which of us will be the promptest at the rendezvous! Your letters are cold. The warmth of your heart is not for me. Pardi! I am only your husband. Another must be your lover! After all, that's the fashionable way of the world—though let the man beware who would claim your love. But here I am, being jealous again! Good God, I don't know what I am! The only thing I know is that without you there is no happiness, no life for me. The seventh at Brescia, then—is it agreed?

Agreed, but not agreeable to Josephine, as is clear from her letter to her "darling little Thérèse" (Tallien) dated July 23, just before her departure from Milan:

The trip here was the most arduous and uncomfortable imaginable. I was eighteen days on the road, and entered the carriage with fever and a pain in my side. The fever has subsided, but the pain persists. I am bored to death here. In the midst of all the superb fetes given in my honor, I long constantly for my friends at Chaillot [the Talliens] and my friend at the Luxembourg [Barras]. My husband doesn't love me—he worships me! I am afraid he will go mad with love. I have seen him only for a moment; he is involved in the siege of Mantua. I leave tomorrow night to go to Brescia. That will bring me closer to headquarters.

That is to say, closer to Verona, where, presumably, Charles was stationed—if that is what she meant to say.

She took Louise Compoint and Hamelin with her on the twenty-fourth; a maid was indispensable to Madame Bonaparte even at the front lines, and Hamelin's presence would serve as a reminder to

Bonaparte that she had promised that protégé an army post. Her "tenderest of lovers" was awaiting her at Brescia, and on July 29 they went on east together to Verona. There, that very afternoon, General and Madame Bonaparte and Hamelin, taking their after-luncheon coffee on the balcony of a palace overlooking the Adige River and the foothills of the Alps to the north, espied curious specks of white moving toward the city—white-uniformed Austrian troops in a sudden descent through the passes after outflanking the northernmost French outposts.

General Bonaparte's first move was to rush Josephine to safety. Milan and Brescia were out of the question, for, as he correctly reasoned, Field Marshal von Wurmser would have sent another column down the western shore of Lake Garda. Bonaparte therefore chose walled and fortified Peschiera, halfway between Verona and Brescia, at the southernmost tip of the lake, as the safest place in the emergency.

But when Josephine's carriage jolted into Peschiera the panicky commanding officer, Guillaume, urged her to seek refuge elsewhere; he did not choose to answer for her safety with the invaders at the gates and their gunboats patrolling the lake shore. Madame Bonaparte displayed admirable presence of mind in rejecting General Guillaume's suggestion. She had confidence in her own general and, despite the chatter of muskets and the flicker of enemy bivouac fires in the night, insisted on staying where he had sent her until further word should come from him. She slept in her clothes but also in the certainty that—though it might require the entire French army in Italy—General Bonaparte would fight his way through the Austrian encirclement to Peschiera and to her.

When morning came, Junot—most redoubtable of all Napoleon's redoubtables—galloped in through the last open gate of the town with a company of dragoons to escort her to her husband at Castelnuovo, where his new command post had been established during the night. Within the first few miles, however, as her carriage hurtled west along the Garda shore, it came under fire from an Austrian patrol boat. Two of the carriage horses fell between the traces, and one of the escorting dragoons tumbled dead from his mount. Junot unceremoniously shoved Josephine, Louise Compoint and Hamelin out the land-side door of the coach, onto their knees in a ditch beyond the road, and whipped the four remaining horses to make them dash on with the empty carriage and so divert the patrol boat's fire. Herding his trio of civilians along the ditch and out of range, Junot finally commandeered a peasant cart to convoy them the rest of the way.

This was Josephine's second baptism by fire—as unwelcome as the first, six years previously, in the Savane at Fort-Royal, in Martinique. She clung to her courage and her composure even while they lurched through Desenzano, scene of the previous night's hottest fighting, littered with the corpses of men and of horses, redolent with the stench of death and powder—only to dissolve into tears in her husband's arms when he snatched her from the cart at Castelnuovo.

"Wurmser shall pay dearly for your tears," General Bonaparte promised, and he kept the promise before the autumn was out. At the moment, however, the French were on the defensive and fighting against odds that would have been considered insuperable by any commander save a Napoleon. At the moment, Brescia had been lost, and with it access to Milan. Bonaparte had no choice but to send his wife and her party along the road to the south— detouring past beleaguered Mantua—through Parma, to Florence, where the Grand Duke of Tuscany, who had already signed a peace treaty with General Bonaparte, showed proper courtesy to his wife (just in case the tide of battle should turn back again in favor of her husband). She continued on as far as the west coast at Leghorn before turning back north once more to Brescia on receipt of a message delivered by Moustache, announcing sensational French victories southeast of that city, at Castiglione and Lonato.

> When we reached Brescia, [her traveling companion Hamelin wrote] we did not find the general as we had expected, but instead a letter to advise that he was awaiting us at Cremona. Despite my urgings to follow him there, Madame Bonaparte insisted on spending the night in Brescia, pleading that it was getting late and that she was too exhausted to travel farther. She took the apartment General Bonaparte maintained in the town, and I that of his aide-de-camp.

"Go on up to your room," she said to me. "I am going to bed, but I shall order a table placed beside it, and we can dine together."

When I came downstairs again, I saw that three covers had been laid at table, and inquired as to the third.

"It's that poor Charles," she replied. "He is just returning from a mission and happened to stop at Brescia, where he heard of my arrival."

At that moment Charles came in, and we three had dinner together. The meal soon over, we were both on our way out of her apartment when, just as we reached the door, a languishing voice was to be heard recalling Charles. I continued on my way, and it was not until I made ready to undress that I realized I had left my hat and side arms in the sitting room that preceded her bedchamber. I wanted to retrieve them, but the grenadier sentry at her door told me that no one was permitted to enter.

"Who gave you that order?"

"Madame Bonaparte's maid."

Then it was I understood that the heroine of Peschiera had reverted to type—had become once again the frivolous and giddy Parisienne.

A report in which Hamelin showed himself grossly ungrateful, for within the next few days, at Cremona, he was handsomely rewarded for his escort duty to the general's wife by an appointment as national agent for collection of reparations in conquered territories around Ferrara—a literally golden opportunity, though he muffed it (and never forgave the Bonapartes for his own ineptitude).

As for Josephine, at the end of that frantic three-week carriage flight, after careening some three hundred and fifty miles across miserable roads in and out of battle zones, up and down north and central Italy, she would have shown superhuman control had she resisted the temptation to gasp out a breathless "I told you so—I told you a theater of war was no place for a woman!" To which Napoleon must have agreed, for he would never again allow her to enter one, not even when the time came when she would plead to do so.

He escorted her back to safety, to Milan, on August 24 and then turned around on the twenty-seventh to drive the northern Austrian line back into the Alps, in order to concentrate his forces on the assault of Mantua. He was haunted by the sight of Josephine at their parting: "sad, upset, half sick." She herself dated the onset of her migraine headaches from that period, and she was in no happy mood when she wrote from Milan to Aunt Edmée Renaudin Beauharnais on September 4:

Monsieur [Prince] Serbelloni will bring you this letter and tell you something of the way in which I have been welcomed to Italy. I am feted wherever I go; all the princes of Italy have entertained in my honor, even the Grand Duke of Tuscany, brother of the Emperor [Francis of Austria]. Very well, then, I would rather be a simple private citizen in France! I care nothing about the honors paid me in this country and am terribly bored. It is true, of course, that my poor health contributes to my melancholy. I am often indisposed. If good fortune could ensure good health, I would be feeling fine. I have the most amiable husband it would be possible to find. My wishes are granted before I have time to voice them; my desires are his desires, my will his law. He spends his days in adoration before me as if I were a divinity. No one could be a better husband. Monsieur Serbelloni will tell you how I am loved. He is bringing the children gifts from Bonaparte: a handsome enameled repeater watch set in fine pearls for Hortense, a gold one for Eugène. He loves my children, writes them often. I embrace my dear Papa and you, my dear Aunt. I will try to send you the money you have requested at my very first opportunity.

The Prince carried a letter for Hortense, too, urging her to write often to her mother ("Your letters and those of your brother console me in my separation from my precious children"), and a letter for Barras, and one for *chère petite* Thérèse Tallien.

Only General Bonaparte was left to complain of Josephine's remissness as a correspondent: "No letters from you, which seriously disturbs me, although I hear that you have been well enough to take a drive to Lake Como recently." On the seventeenth of September, he still had received no word:

Charles

I write so often; you, so seldom. It's perfidious to deceive a poor husband, a tender lover. Should he lose his rights just because he is far away, burdened down with responsibility, with fatigue and anxiety? Without his Josephine, without the assurance of her love, what remains to him on this earth? . . . Yesterday's was a bloody business, but the enemy was beaten and we occupy the suburbs of Mantua. Adieu, Josephine, and take care: one of these fine nights your doors will come crashing open and there I'll be, your jealous lover—there I'll be in your arms!

(It could not have been Charles he would have found with her in Milan, not Charles who had escorted her on that tour of Lake Como, because Charles had himself been involved in that "bloody business" at Mantua on the sixteenth, as is established by a citation, a "special mention" to the Directory, signed by none other than General Bonaparte on the seventeenth: "Charles and Sulkowski, assistants to the adjutant general's staff, acquitted themselves superbly in this action.")

Mantua had not yet been reduced, but, with the situation under control, General Bonaparte could come into Milan on September 19 for a three weeks' stay with Josephine. His forces already outnumbered, he urged the Directory to send him reinforcements to meet those that would shortly be coming south from Austria, but letter upon letter proved unavailing.

Restless, pacing like a lion, he would leave his letter-writing, his desk, maps and conferences to dash into Josephine's room, to refresh himself with the sight and sound and touch of her. "He would burst into the room," says Hamelin, who was often a guest in the Bonapartes' private apartments, "and, without a word to me, he would stride over to Madame Bonaparte and begin to play with her like a child, teasing her until he made her cry, caressing her so boldly, so heartily that I considered it best to walk away to the window and pretend to be checking on the weather. He was passionately in love with his wife. As for her, she was never in love with him, for the reason that she was already in love with someone else. I knew what to expect from Sir Charles, and felt positively uncomfortable at the thought of this young general—already covered with a glory which reflected on his wife—in a losing com-

petition with a little fellow who had nothing to recommend him
except a pretty face and a hairdresser's elegance."

3

From that unworthy—if unsuspected—competition, General Bonaparte was forced to withdraw on October 12 to return to the
front in order to cope with reinforced Austrian columns pouring
down through the Alpine passes, where the barefoot, battered
French outposts had been unable to hold them. At Vicenza, Bonaparte himself fell back under the enemy advance, his first defeat on
Italian soil. On October 17, from Modena, he wrote of a dream
that had comforted him amid his military tribulations, amid the
disturbing memories of Josephine's strange moodiness in the days
prior to his departure from Milan:

*I dreamed that you were close to me—not moody and capricious,
but sweet and tender, with that ineffable sweetness and tenderness which is a balm you alone can dispense. Your letters are as
cold as those of a woman of fifty, such letters as might be expected
after fifteen years of marriage. All that is to be read into them is
friendship, the sentiments of the winter of life. For shame, Josephine! It is wicked and traitorous of you. What is left for you to do
to make me utterly wretched? Stop loving me? Ah, that's already
done! To hate me?? Perhaps it's that for which I should hope.
Hatred, at least, is not humiliating. But, oh, indifference—the
pulse of marble, the vacant glance, the distracted air!*

With the military crisis in November, he veered from recriminations against Josephine to recriminations against the Directory for
its failure to provide him reinforcements. "It may be that we face
the loss of all Italy," he wrote Paris on the fourteenth. "The army
is exhausted, reduced to a handful, and nothing is left to these few
surviving heroes but their reputation and their pride."

Their pride was stung by what appeared to be a general retreat
west from abandoned Verona—until the genius of their great com-

mander produced the necessary miracle: a brilliant maneuver to cut back of the enemy lines, across marshy land deemed impassable and thus unguarded, the only terrain upon which twelve thousand could oppose forty-five thousand. The fantastic victory at Arcole was inspired, of course, by Bonaparte's personal heroism, his charge across that famous, bloody bridge with the tricolor in his hand, at the head of the French troops, into withering enemy fire.

On the nineteenth of November, when he was back in possession of Verona, his letter to Josephine rang with the sound of trumpets, with life and joy: "At last, my adorable Josephine, I am reborn! Death is no longer in my eyes; glory and victory are in my heart. The enemy has been defeated at Arcole . . . some six thousand killed, five hundred taken prisoner. Mantua will fall to us within the week—and then I can be back in your arms!" A postscript reads: "Be sure to give me news of your little belly," an indication that Josephine may again have suspected pregnancy or offered it as cause of indisposition and as explanation of her aloofness in Milan in October.

By the twenty-first of November, with the crisis of the war resolved, General Bonaparte could abandon himself to his other love:

I go to bed, my heart full of your lovely image, but frantic at this long separation. . . . Good God, how I wish I could drop in on you tonight and watch you at your dressing table, with one little shoulder bare and one little white breast showing, firm, elastic, and above all that your adorable little face, under a bright kerchief knotted à la créole—sweet enough to eat! You well know that I never forget the little visits to the little black forest. I give it a thousand kisses and impatiently await the moment of my return, to be yours, utterly yours. . . . To live in Josephine, that is to live in Elysium. A kiss upon your lips, your eyes, your shoulder, your breast, everywhere, everywhere, everywhere!

Two days later, the twenty-third, he was raging at her neglect:

I no longer love you. . . . You are wicked, horrid. . . . You never write—not so much as six little lines scribbled at random, though you know what your letters mean to me. What, then, are you doing all the day, madame? What business is so important as to deprive you of the time to write to your devoted husband? What other affection interferes with the tender and constant love you promised him? Who can he be, this marvelous new lover who monopolizes your every moment, tyrannizes over your days and prevents you from thinking of your husband?

The cliché was already a cliché in 1796: the husband is the last to know.

"The situation was known to all the army, as to everyone in Milan; Lieutenant Charles appeared as a luncheon guest at the Serbelloni Palace as soon as the general left the city," according to Laure Junot. "Josephine's interest in the young officer was no secret; if only a tender friendship, it occupied much of their time." So Madame Junot was to hear it from her husband. So Madame de Rémusat was to hear it, from others: "Despite the prestige of love and glory with which her husband had enveloped her, in the midst of that life of triumph and victory and general license, Madame Bonaparte sometimes gave cause for anxiety to her conqueror husband."

And: "Take care, Josephine!" came another message from the general's Verona headquarters. "Take care, for one of these fine nights your doors will burst open, and there I'll be. Seriously speaking, however, I am deeply concerned at your silence, and hope before long to clasp you in my arms, to cover you with a million kisses as torrid as the lands below the equator."

That was on the twenty-fourth of November; on the twenty-fifth General Bonaparte set out for Milan, where he wrote on the twenty-seventh:

I arrive in Milan. I rush into your apartment. I have abandoned everything to see you, to hold you in my arms . . . You are not here! You are off gadding about from city to city, fete to fete. You leave Milan just as I arrive. You no longer concern yourself with your dear Napoleon. You loved him out of a caprice; inconstancy renders you indifferent. . . . The distress I experience is incalculable. I had a right to expect other than this.

Charles

*I will be here until the ninth [of Frimaire—November 29]. But
don't upset your itinerary. Continue on your pleasure-seeking
rounds. Happiness is your especial province. The whole world is
only too eager to please you. Only your husband is in distress.*

If he rushed into her apartments, into her boudoir, into her armoires, and buried his face in the delicately flower-scented folds of
her gowns, he was catching at a froth of chiffon, a wisp of "gossamer and lace." The woman herself he had never held; herself
she had never given him, but only her "beautiful body"—and that
not always too willingly.

As to whether Lieutenant Charles had accompanied her on this
pleasure jaunt to Genoa, contemporary witnesses, usually so volu-
ble, are silent; and Sir Walter Scott makes no mention of an escort
at the great ball "tendered her with studied magnificence by that
ancient state," but only of the orchestra playing so late into the
night and morning as to shock the Genoese Senate, which had decreed that particular Friday to be a holyday.

Too late for Madame Bonaparte to undertake the journey back to
Milan, to her husband, on that Friday; too late even to write. On
November 28, Napoleon wrote that his courier had returned from
Genoa empty-handed and added:

*I understand, of course, that you cannot find time to write in
the midst of galas and celebrations. I do not expect you to derange
your social calendar . . . I am not worth the trouble. The happiness of a man you do not love cannot interest you. . . . I am wrong
to demand of you a love such as mine for you. How expect lace to be
as strong as gold? . . . I am yielding to the empire which your
charms, your personality, your whole person have achieved over
my poor heart. I am wrong to expect the same of you, since nature
has not endowed me with the attractions to captivate you. What I
do have a right to expect from Josephine is consideration and esteem, for I love her alone and love her to distraction. . . .*

I reopen my letter to send you a kiss. Ah, Josephine! Josephine!

When she came back to him in Milan on December 2, Napoleon
was flattered that she came with an artist in tow and with pretty

pleadings that he sit for a portrait for her—as the hero of the Arcole bridge, flag in hand. When he yielded to this along with all
her other blandishments, she arranged a studio in the Serbelloni for
Antoine Gros, the French master David's star pupil, who wrote his
mother that this patroness of the arts was "a very angel of kindness." The problem of inducing their model to desist from his
eternal pacing and his nervous fidgeting and hold his pose for the
necessary series of sittings was solved in Josephine's typical beguiling, feminine fashion: by pulling the hero, flag and all, into a
chair beside her or onto her lap, and pinioning him with embraces
he would not care to break, while Gros proceeded to his sketching.
If only young Gros had had the sense of humor to sketch his subject in that pose instead of in the standard, stilted military one!

"I was present at three of those after-breakfast sittings," said
aide-de-camp Lavallette. "The youth of the happy couple and the
artist's modesty and enthusiasm for the hero excused such familiarities. Gros achieved an amazing likeness of Bonaparte as he was at
the time"—the intensity of the set of the jaw, the exaltation in
the eyes, the brown hair lank to the shoulder, the classic features
of "an antique Greek or Roman coin" (a simile to which Madame
de Rémusat resorts three separate and distinct times). The "essence of the extraordinary man," however, in the opinion of his
secretary-friend Bourrienne, was no more captured by Gros than by
any other of the countless artists who would attempt it; "impossible to reproduce the mobility of his face, that quick and piercing
eye, that lightning glance, that expression now tender, now stern,
now terrible, at times even caressing."

Yet Gros's canvas won Napoleon's approval, for he appointed
the young painter to head the French art commission charged with
the selection and collection of Italian masterpieces "offered in tribute," to put it euphemistically, to the conquerors—and destined to
form the nucleus of the Musée Napoléon in the Louvre.

"It was during this short sojourn in Milan"—from November 27,
1796, to January 7, 1797—"that Gros made the first formal portrait
that exists of the general," Lavallette continues. "The commander
in chief was, at that period, supremely happy in his wife's company. Madame Bonaparte was charming, and not all the cares of

the high command, not all the duties of government, could prevent her husband from enjoyment of that domestic bliss."

Another glimpse of that "domestic bliss" was caught by French Ambassador Miot de Mélito, who accompanied "the happy couple" on an "enchanted two-day holiday at Lake Maggiore, at the magnificent Palace of Isola Bella, where the snowy summits of St. Gotthard and of Simplon were mirrored in the limpid blue waters around the island. I drove there in the carriage with Bonaparte, his wife and his chief of staff, General Berthier. All along the road, the general [Bonaparte] proved a gay and animated companion, entertaining us with anecdotes of his early life. He showered his wife with attentions and indulged himself in conjugal liberties so marked as to constantly embarrass us." Miot could appreciate the general's infatuation with his wife, if not his deportment, for the diplomat was himself enchanted with Josephine: "Never has a woman combined greater kindness with so many natural graces; never has a woman done so many good deeds as she—with greater pleasure in the doing."

4

The Bonapartes' idyl of island love was necessarily brief, and, as Miot de Mélito puts it, "the calm of the Italian lakes stood out in striking contrast to the terrible scenes of battle" to which the youthful general was recalled in January. Never had he "been so annoyed with this confounded war," Napoleon wrote to Josephine. But after the resounding victory over the Austrians at Rivoli on January 14 he could focus his attention on a whirlwind invasion of the Papal States, with the result that by mid-February the plenipotentiaries of Pius VI arrived, biretta in hand, to sue for peace at Tolentino.

They discovered that this young general, in his tent, read not only Caesar, but also Plutarch and Machiavelli. The extraordinary versatility of Napoleon's genius—that of a diplomat as well as a warrior, alternately terrifying, insinuating, fascinating and consummately cunning—was demonstrated to the Roman Curia, itself the most diplomatically adroit of all the powers of Europe.

General Bonaparte's proclamation to his Army of Italy rang with triumph:

> You have been victorious in fourteen pitched battles, seventy combats; have taken more than a hundred thousand prisoners.
> . . . The contributions levied on the lands which you have conquered have financed and maintained the army during the entire campaign. You have furthermore contributed thirty millions to the national exchequer. You have enriched the museum at Paris with more than three hundred art objects of ancient as well as modern Italy—masterpieces thirty centuries in the making. You have conquered, in the name of the Republic, the fairest lands of Europe. The Lombard and Cisalpine republics owe you their liberty; the French colors fly for the first time on the shores of the Adriatic, across from ancient Macedonia [significant as the birthplace of his hero, Alexander]. The Kings of Sardinia and of Naples, the Pope, the Duke of Parma have been detached from the coalition of our enemies and have solicited our friendship. You have driven the English out of Leghorn, Genoa and Corsica. But a greater destiny still awaits you. . . .

General Bonaparte had found it easier to impose his terms upon the Pope and assorted Italian potentates than upon his Josephine. "Not a word in your own handwriting. Good God, what have I done? Nothing but think of you, love you, live for you. So you are sad, you are ill. So you want to go back to Paris!"

Josephine was languishing with fever and migraine in Bologna. So, "I am rushing [Dr.] Moscati there to attend you," her husband wrote in that same letter of February 19.

Josephine was sulking. If at the fact that Charles was to be away for two long months, she was extremely silly, because the mission for which he had been chosen was an honor: accompanying General Marmont to Rome, to deliver the Treaty of Tolentino to the Pope for ratification. And since it was General Bonaparte who had appointed him to accompany Marmont, it was possible proof that her husband as yet harbored no suspicion of Charles's relations with her.

Above all, Josephine was homesick, homesick for her children, writing Hortense: "I am bored in Italy. Despite the flattering reception given me by all the peoples of this beautiful country, I cannot adjust to such long separation from my darling children." She was also homesick for Paris, this Creole from the Islands-below-the-Winds, as she would always be, all her life, whenever she was called upon to leave her City of Light. The history-rich soil of Etruria and of Rome, the classic tradition could not entrance the woman who, as a girl, had been unable to plow through the four-volume history of Rome which her first husband had assigned her as required reading; whereas such ultimate refinements as modern Italy had to offer were available in Paris: Maestro Ruggieri, "genius of pyrotechnics," nightly starred the Paris skies above the public pleasure gardens of the Tivoli; Maestro Tortoni concocted and dispensed his ices, sherbets and *biscuits* to Parisian gourmets.

The company at Bologna offered Josephine little consolation except for the beautiful Italian Signora Visconti, General Berthier's lifelong love.* Certainly the presence in Bologna of that seventeen-year-old minx Pauline Bonaparte could not be counted among her sister-in-law's blessings. Throughout her life Josephine liked and enjoyed young people, included them in her honor household and social circle; and young people liked and enjoyed Josephine, with her blithe and romantic spirit, her indulgence and understanding. But she was baffled by Pauline, who rebuffed her every overture of friendship. She could not dream that little Pauline had joined the other members of the Corsican Bonaparte clan in a vow of vendetta against "the interloper," "the foreigner," "the Creole" whom brother Nabulione had dared to marry without so much as a consultation with the tribe.

Gauche and provincial, in her frumpish homemade wardrobe, Pauline was envious, overawed and discomfited by her brother's wife, so poised, so elegant of manner and of dress, the center of

---

* Berthier never abandoned Signora Visconti, not even after his marriage to a German princess on the Emperor's orders; the three of them kept house together in utmost congeniality.

attraction. Not that Pauline lacked attractions of her own; she was the beauty of the family, the greatest beauty of her age in the opinion of her own generation—and in that of succeeding ones, which are enabled to evaluate the flawless perfection of her face and body in the famous undraped marble statue by Canova, the *Imperial Venus*, first among the treasures of Rome's Villa Borghese. "Nymph" was her contemporaries' word for her, reaching for the twentieth century's clinical term *nymphomaniac*. The sexual appetites of the female Bonapartes were as notorious as those of the males, but Pauline's was perhaps the most insatiable of them all. Even a broad-minded Josephine recognized the need of exercising a strict surveillance over this amorous and amoral hoyden. Pauline retaliated "by sticking out her tongue at her sister-in-law whenever the latter looked the other way," says Arnault; by eavesdropping and spying on her, by tattling on her to Nabulione.

The Bonaparte vendetta against Josephine was no less lethal for being waged by tongue instead of stiletto. It was apparently Pauline's venomous tongue that relayed to Napoleon the gossip linking Josephine's name with General Murat's—although it was Murat's own braggadocio which set off the rumor in the first place.

Swashbuckling, swaggering Murat was the type to kiss and tell, priding himself no less on his conquests in the boudoir than on his victories on the field of battle. The word *panache* might have been coined expressly for (or by) him; his bills for helmet plumes and feathers stagger the imagination. From under the plumed helmet, his black ringlets fell to his broad gold-braided, gold-tasseled shoulders; his famous saddlecloth was a tiger skin; no wonder the army dubbed him "General Franconi" (for Franconi, Paris' gaudy circus master). It was this brawny, fearless Murat who, upon his return from Paris to Italy in the spring of 1796, played host to a group of fellow officers at a rowdy champagne breakfast and, to top off the champagne, proposed concocting for his guests a Caribbean rum punch, the recipe for which, he boasted, he had learned in Paris from "a charming Creole"—with the innuendo that if he could but divulge the full particulars of his "education at that lovely lady's hands, the story would be sensational." Or so the story was told later by General Junot to his wife, although Junot himself, she says, did not believe that Bonaparte had any real cause for jealousy of Murat.

"The young fools," Laure Junot writes, "seized hold of the vermeil lemon squeezer" (which Murat claimed had been a gift from his indulgent Creole friend, along with the punch recipe), "and they thought they read the monogram etched into the silver gilt as 'J.B.' Murat, suddenly sobering and repenting of his rashness, snatched it away, insisting that the initials were his own: 'J.M.,'" which was how two of his guests, aides-de-camp Lavallette and Duroc, later claimed they had read the marking.

But the damage was done, and there is no doubt that Napoleon was disconcerted and offended by the gossip; his attitude to his foremost cavalry officer became anything but cordial. Bourrienne, who had by then joined Napoleon in Italy as his secretary, remarked that Napoleon manifested distinct relief, three years later, when Josephine pleaded Murat's cause as suitor for Caroline Bonaparte's hand. "I am well content," Bourrienne quotes Napoleon as saying in 1800, "to find my wife the sponsor of this marriage. You should be able to understand why." "I concluded," Bourrienne adds, "that Napoleon interpreted his wife's eagerness to promote the match as a proof that the rumors of her intimacy with Murat had been slanderous and unfounded."

Curiously enough, it was Josephine, in the late winter and early spring of 1797, who was making a show of jealousy. Or so it appears from a letter that General Berthier wrote to reassure her about his commander in chief: "No, your husband is guilty of not a single offense against you. He loves you, adores you, and is afflicted by these chimeras and fantasies which lead you to believe in a situation which simply does not exist. How many times he has said to me, 'I am mad about my wife, think only of her. You well know what injustice she does me by such suspicions.'"

It is difficult to know what to make of her sudden display of mistrust—whether Josephine was making a show of these "fantasies" or whether she was really jealous. She had returned to Milan from Bologna in March, and certainly she was depressed, homesick and lonely there. General Bonaparte had gone north in a final offensive against the Austrians, driving them out of Italy and pushing deep into Austria as far as Leoben, where, on April 13, the enemy agreed to call a truce and begin peace negotiations. Perhaps Josephine in her loneliness remembered that a year earlier the youthful conqueror had been hailed at every city gate by Italian beauties who vied for his favor; that La Grassini, the *prima donna assoluta* of La Scala, with face and body as glorious as her voice, had parleyed with General Bonaparte on his entry into Milan to persuade him to accept her on terms of unconditional surrender; perhaps Josephine remembered that she herself had given him little reason to be faithful now.

Still, she must have known that there was no real justification for her suspicion, as Berthier had assured her. It may be that Josephine, with an uneasy conscience, sought to establish guilt on the part of her husband to offset her own, in the classic maneuver of feigning jealousy to cover up her own infidelity; she may have learned enough of military strategy from her association with a succession of generals to know that the best defense is a good offense. Or it may be that she was one of those women to whom jealousy serves as a spur to competition, and that she sought subconsciously to rake herself out of her indifference.

Or could it have been that Josephine was coming slowly to a realization of the "singularity," the "extraordinary" quality, the greatness of the man—the odd little man—she had married so off-handedly a year ago? Was she coming to see him as he was seen by General Junot, who was to say about Napoleon that "there was something of a god about him," that he was "one of those men of whom nature is sparing—such a man as is vouchsafed to the world only once in the course of centuries"? Josephine may have come at last to be stirred, as Madame de Rémusat says she admitted to having been, "by the impressions of that year [in Italy] when love came to lay a daily tribute of victory at her feet, a fresh conquest daily over a people entranced by its conqueror."

Another who was stirred by impressions of General Bonaparte in Italy was Josephine's intellectual admirer Arnault, who deserted the greenrooms of Paris for Milan in the early summer of 1797. Arnault came straight to the Serbelloni Palace to kiss the hand of his dear friend Madame Bonaparte, finding her radiant among her ladies, ensconced on a settee at the far end of the lofty colonnaded gallery. Beyond the archway, in the great central hall, he was presented to the commander in chief, "surrounded by his highest-ranking officers, by army administrators, city magistrates, Italian government ministers, all standing about him, though at a respectful distance, all waiting until he should address them. Nothing could be so remarkable as the sight of that small man in the midst of giants all so dominated by his personality that none with whom he spoke appeared taller than he. Never did military headquarters so closely resemble a royal court; the *ambiance* was exactly that of the Tuileries Palace a few years later. There was nothing prideful in his attitude, but one recognized in it the confidence of a man who knows his own worth, knows that his place is rightfully his. He held us, standing there entranced, for at least two hours"—Arnault aware, like all the rest, that he stood "in a presence."

"That man is a man apart," Arnault said to a friend as they left the palace. "Everyone, everything succumbs to the supremacy of his genius, to the impact of his personality. Everything about him bears the imprint of authority. . . . He is a man born to dominate, as so many men are born to be dominated. Within four years' time he will be in exile or on a throne, if he is not lucky enough to be carried off by a bullet." Always men reached for the same words in reaction to Napoleon. "You dominate our age," Victor Hugo's verses run in the poem "Lui." "Always Napoleon, Napoleon everywhere, dazzling and somber,/Astride the threshold of the century." Surely a littérateur such as Arnault, after his first encounter with the general, must have told Josephine that her adjective "funny" in description of her husband was scarcely the *mot juste*.

The immediate occasion for Arnault's journey to Italy was the marriage of his friend General Charles-Victor Leclerc to Pauline Bonaparte. Malicious gossips (Madame Junot, for one) had it that this was a "musket wedding"; that Napoleon, discovering his sister and his adjutant general "behind a screen in a highly compromising situation," had decided that the month of June was none too soon to marry off his sexually precocious sister.

5

For the occasion of that wedding and in anticipation of the arrival of his family, General Bonaparte had leased the pleasant summer castle of Mombello in its extensive, elaborately landscaped park some eight miles outside Milan.

Again Josephine was disposed to be friendly, her sweet and gracious self, to her husband's mother, sisters and brothers. "Josephine's attitude toward her husband's mother left nothing to be desired," her husband is quoted as saying by one of his chroniclers at St. Helena. "She showered her mother-in-law with courtesies and attentions, and was no less considerate of her sisters-in-law." She simply could not believe that, in time, her genuine good will and warmth would not dispel the baleful glare from those unblinking, obsidian Bonaparte eyes.

With them it had been hate at first sight of this exotic hothouse flower—parasitic and past full bloom, from their point of view. Lucien Bonaparte had reported maliciously from Paris in the preceding year on the dubious reputation of the Widow Beauharnais; Joseph, on her indiscretions during the carriage ride from Paris to Milan; Pauline, on the results of her own eavesdropping and spying in the Serbelloni Palace.

The entire clan had hooted at Josephine's pregnancy reports in the spring of 1796. Surely there was not presently discernible to her mother-in-law's eye so much as a bulge or a wrinkle in Josephine's clinging neo-Grecian gowns, no suspicious swell of bosom at the deep and revealing neckline. And to a Corsican matriarch the success of a marriage was gauged by its prolificity.

This Corsican matriarch, Madame Letizia Bonaparte, still handsome at forty-seven, ramrod stiff with dignity, stern, dour, parsimonious, could find no inch of common ground upon which to meet her frivolous, prodigal fashion plate of a daughter-in-law. Scarcely could they be said to have spoken the same language; Napoleon's mother's French was so execrable in both grammar and pronunciation that her son later complained of it to his brothers as an embarrassment to the Emperor of France. If Madame Letizia recognized her own lack of the social graces, she considered that her daughter-in-law substituted them for the moral virtues.

Joseph Bonaparte's wife, the plain and mild, the unassuming and long-suffering Julie, was the only one among Josephine's guests who responded to her gestures of friendship. Of nineteen-year-old Louis Bonaparte, to whom Napoleon had served as second father, it could only be said that he was not yet overtly hostile to his brother's wife. As for sister Elisa, she dared not show her rancor, for the reason that she needed Josephine as an ally to win Napoleon's pardon for her recent marriage to one Felice Bacciocchi, a nonentity with nothing to recommend him beyond his Corsican blood and his willingness to marry the eldest—twenty years old—and least attractive of the three Bonaparte girls. Captain Bacciocchi had displayed more talent in the music room than on the parade ground, but, thanks to his brother-in-law, was shortly promoted to the rank of major and to command of the fortress at Ajaccio. Pretty, blond Caroline, at fifteen, and Jérôme, at thirteen, as yet too young properly to hate the Beauharnais', romped in the gardens with sixteen-year-old Eugène, whose recent arrival in Italy compensated his mother for the horde of Bonapartes descending upon her.

To Josephine's delight, her son had been summoned from school in the spring to begin his military training under the direct supervision of his distinguished stepfather. Happily, Josephine's protégé Gros was still on hand to paint her boy in uniform, with his high plumed hat and his aide-de-camp's insignia, the white, fringed scarf, puffed and knotted just above the elbow. From that Gros portrait Eugène looks out straightforward and serene, his youthful countenance, if not strictly handsome, fine and sweet and appealing—as he was and always would be. Genuinely genial, kindly, blithe of spirit, courageous, loyal, honorable, he was the only "normal," only non-neurotic member of the whole Bonaparte-Beauharnais congregation, the only one for whom the chorus of malice and venom after Waterloo could find no word of disparagement.

Josephine's arrangements for the nuptial festivities and ceremonies were both tasteful and lavish; the nuptial Mass for Pauline and Leclerc was followed by a benediction for the Bacciocchis. There is cause for wonder in the fact that the Napoleon Bonapartes did not kneel beside the Bacciocchis in the Mombello oratory for that benediction. One must conclude that Josephine, never devout in her Catholicism, felt no religious urge toward sanctification of her civil marriage vows; for certainly Napoleon, in his state of abject devotion, would not then have denied her such a request. When the time came that she would feel the need to fortify the bonds of her marital status by the blessing of the Church, Napoleon would no longer be in the frame of mind or heart to accede to her wishes.

In June of 1797, the relative security or insecurity of her union with General Bonaparte was apparently not foremost among Josephine's concerns. It so happened that, all that halcyon summer, Lieutenant Hippolyte Charles was quartered at Mombello, as a member of General Berthier's staff. Charles would surely have been included in the party of thirty-odd friends and relatives who helped the Leclercs celebrate their honeymoon at Lake Como.

Napoleon's eagle eye (upon which he prided himself and which "encompassed everything in a flash," according to Laure Junot) evidently surprised no sidelong smile or glance, no clinging touch, no clasp of hands between his wife and Berthier's aide-de-camp, for on June 24 the commander in chief personally signed Charles's commission as a captain in the First Hussars, that "premier regiment of the world." With that host of Bonapartes on patrol, Josephine and Charles, if they managed to meet or communicate at all, could have found occasion only on the long, warm June evenings, in the pools of darkness beyond the torchlit Mombello terraces, in the dusky groves and grottoes of the park, where the guests all wandered after dinner to marvel, as did Arnault, at "the phenomenon of the fireflies—those wingèd sequins that made a fairyland of the Italian summer night."

Arnault undoubtedly knew, as others did, that it was Charles who had presented to Josephine a new pug-dog puppy to console her for the loss of Fortuné, whose death had constituted "the major tragedy" of the Mombello sojourn. As Arnault tells the tale, "A mastiff belonging to the chef at the summer castle fell upon the arrogant little beast and destroyed him—dogs being not so clever as humans in distinguishing their betters. The conqueror of Italy could not fail to sympathize, expressing his distress at the accident which restored him to full possession of his conjugal bed." The new pug, "heir to all the privileges and defects of his predecessor," had become the reigning favorite when the general, on a stroll one day along a remote garden path, came upon the unlucky chef, who stammered out his excuses and a pledge "never again to allow his wicked mastiff to set foot in the castle gardens—above all, not now, when Madame had acquired another puppy." To which Napoleon replied, "Let your dog run loose, and perhaps he will rid me of this new one as well!"

This story Arnault found "an amusing and characteristic story, providing an excellent example of the empire exercised by the gentlest and most indolent of Creoles over the most willful and despotic of men. His determination, before which all men quailed, could not resist the tears of a woman. And he, who dictated the law to all Europe, dared not evict a dog from his bedroom."

The pastoral interlude at Mombello was rapidly drawing to a close. By July 1 the visiting Bonapartes had scattered, and on the fourteenth the general and his lady appeared as guests of honor at Milan's Bastille Day fete, the newly inaugurated Cisalpine Republic joining with its French "liberators" in the celebration. The commander in chief seized the opportunity to thunder a warning to the reactionary, counterrevolutionary factions which were once again menacing the central government in Paris.

On August 22, General Bonaparte was called from Milan to Passeriano to meet with representatives of Austria in the final drafting of the Treaty of Campoformio. Josephine—for some reason or another, some reason of her husband's or her own—did not accompany him on that date, but joined him ten days later, having postponed her departure from Milan until September 1. It may or may not be significant that Captain Charles was in Milan until August 31, upon which date, according to cavalry furlough records, he set out for France on a forty-day leave. For once, there is no contemporary comment.

There *was* comment on September 19 when word of General Hoche's sudden death shocked the nation; gossip recalled that Hoche had been a former lover of Madame Bonaparte; people who had been at the Tallien party in 1795 recalled General Bonaparte's curious prediction that Hoche would die not on the field of battle but in his bed—as he did, at the age of twenty-nine. "The circumstances gave rise to conjecture," Napoleon himself would tell Dr. O'Meara at St. Helena. "The rumor spread that I had had him poisoned. But since I scorned to dignify the talk by my attention, it soon died down."

An observer at the Castle of Passeriano remarked that there were tears in Josephine's eyes when the news reached her toward the end of the month; but she was conspicuous by her absence from the Italian memorial services arranged by General Bonaparte for his onetime rival in love and war.

Hoche's untimely death left Josephine in a predicament: he had died without returning the love letters she had written him in 1794 and 1795. And if at first she feared lest these fall into the unfriendly hands of Hoche's widow or of her own malevolent brothers-in-law, she was still more alarmed at the news that a man named Alexandre Rousselin had been appointed by the Directory to take charge of Hoche's private papers in preparation for the writing of a biography of the hero.

Josephine turned in this emergency not to her husband, nor yet to her friend Director Barras, but to a valiant Polish officer, Brigadier Sulkowski, an aide-de-camp of Bonaparte's and a close friend of her close friend Captain Charles. Sulkowski, successful in the delicate mission assigned him, never betrayed Josephine's trust. (Rousselin, however, wrote Napoleon in 1810 to suggest that his services to the wife of General Bonaparte deserved a more signal reward than any thus far extended him by the Emperor.)

The treaty terms with Austria concluded, and ratified by Paris, General and Madame Bonaparte returned to Milan on the first of November. By the sixteenth, the general was off for Rastatt to represent the French Republic at further European peace parleys.

Josephine, who had been longing for months to get back to her beloved Paris, evinced a sudden desire, in November of 1797, to see more of Italy—Rome, for example; although no sooner had General Bonaparte made arrangements for her reception at the Lateran than she changed her mind and plans in favor of Venice.

While there is no evidence to support or to contradict the supposition that Captain Charles met her there, certainly he was close by, in Milan, having returned to Italy in mid-October from his furlough in France.

A city in a perennial state of fete, the Bride of the Adriatic outdid herself in feting the bride of Bonaparte, devising for her, says Marmont, "the most brilliant, the gayest, the most splendorous entertainments" in all Italy: "every theater ordered to open," a glittering ball in the Doges' Palace, the torches flaring until sunrise on the Piazza San Marco, the canals alive with song and fireworks throughout the night, "every palazzo, every building illuminated, reflecting in the waters—a sea of flame." (Only the famous bronze horses pawing at the air over St. Mark's Cathedral were missing from the fabled décor; by command of the conqueror they were en route to Paris, where they would later—if briefly—decorate the Arc de Triomphe du Carrousel.) Decorative, willowy Madame Bonaparte must in turn have delighted the eyes of "the 150,000 Venetians lining the canals" to catch a glimpse of her as she floated past—surely one of the few female tourists in all the history of that ancient city to master the art of stepping gracefully in and out of a gondola.

Some report came somehow from the Adriatic, in November, to disquiet General Bonaparte on the Rhine. Napoleon's secretary Bourrienne claims that Joseph and Lucien Bonaparte were the troublemakers at Rastatt: "Seeking to diminish Josephine's influence over the general for the purpose of heightening their own, the Bonaparte brothers took advantage of her remaining on in Italy after our departure to inflame his jealousy, even though he himself had authorized her sojourn there."

On November 30 Napoleon rapped out an order to be signed by General Berthier: "The Citizen Charles, aide-de-camp, to depart Milan at once upon receipt of these papers; to report forthwith to Paris; there to await further instructions . . ."

"At headquarters in Milan a rumor suddenly went the rounds," according to Madame Junot, "to the effect that the commander in chief had ordered the arrest of Captain Charles and that an order for his execution by a firing squad was shortly to follow. As it developed, Charles was instead ordered back to France. His narrow escape can be attributed to the good offices of his close friends Duroc and Junot, who were instrumental in extricating him from this scrape." And so Junot must have told it to his wife, although there is no scrap of evidence to substantiate the story.

VI

Crisis

. . . the most unfortunate of women and the unhappiest!

LETTER FROM JOSEPHINE TO CHARLES, MARCH 1798

1

GENERAL BONAPARTE, arriving in Paris from Rastatt on December 5, assumed that his order concerning Captain Charles had by then been executed in Milan.

He had further assumed that Josephine would be awaiting him in the capital, but she was not. He was disappointed that she had not yet arrived on December 12 to share his triumph at the giant victory celebration at the Luxembourg Palace at which he made formal delivery of the Treaty of Campoformio to the assembled Directors, ministers, and national legislative bodies. ("A peace," he termed it in his speech from the Altar of the Nation, "to assure the liberty, prosperity and glory of the Republic, a peace from which to date the era of representative government in Europe"; and he concluded with the promise, "When the good fortune of the people of France shall be ensured in a formal system of law, all Europe shall be free.")

Josephine had still not reached Paris on December 26 to

see him installed a member of the Institute of France.* Of all the honors accorded him, this was the one of which he was most proud; it was listed foremost on his letterheads, superseding even his military titles.

"All Paris rang with his name," wrote Hortense, "and thronged in such vast numbers to acclaim the 'Conqueror of Italy' that the sentries posted at the gateway to the house on the Rue de la Victoire could scarcely deal with the crowds which fought for a chance to see him"—although the new national idol shunned the spotlight and avoided the ovations of the fickle Parisian populace, of whom he said contemptuously to Bourrienne, "Bah! They would flock just as eagerly to see me if I were on my way to the scaffold." He furthermore avoided any appearance of close association with the corrupt and unpopular Directory; there were undercurrents of distrust and discord between him and Barras, although neither could, as yet, see a way to eliminate the other.

One of the few visitors permitted by the sentries past the gates was fourteen-year-old Hortense, escorted by her grandfather Beauharnais to greet her stepfather Bonaparte. "What a change in our little house," she was to write. "Formerly so tranquil, it was filled now with generals and officers. At last, despite the crowds, we reached the general, who was surrounded by his staff. He gave me the fond and tender welcome of a father, telling me that my brother had been sent to Corfu and to Rome to bear the news of the peace."

But when she asked him the whereabouts of her mother, he could not satisfactorily explain—to himself or to her—Josephine's strange tarrying along the way.

It is as difficult for the historian as it was for Napoleon to establish precise dates for Joephine's itinerary subsequent to her four-day Venice visit in late November. Heading west, though slowly, she came through Turin on December 15, a date supplied by

---

* Napoleon's election to membership was under the category of mathematician. The National Institute of French Arts and Sciences had been established by the expiring National Assembly to replace the ancient, aristocratic, exclusively artistic Académie Française, which had been abolished during the Revolution. The arts and the sciences would shortly be separated again, and the literary Academy revived under its original title.

French Ambassador Miot de Mélito, who entertained with a dinner that night in her honor, remarking that she was "carrying her jewel case clutched in her hands"—as well she might, considering that it contained the treasure of Italy: the superb pearl necklace presented her by the Cisalpine Republic; magnificent gems and ornaments sent by Pius VI to the wife of the conqueror who had spared the Eternal City; a collection of the rarest cameos ever assembled in the peninsula. Her husband had tried to impress on Josephine the importance, in his position, of "observing the utmost scrupulosity" in accepting gifts of value; he had urged specifically, by letter, that she return the box of ancient medallions sent her by General Miollis, for the reason that "men have wicked tongues." But it is unlikely that Josephine would have ever relinquished anything that adorned, glittered or shimmered, and upon her return from Italy her jewel case was bulging and her carriages were heavy laden with her collection of paintings, bronzes, marbles and "Etruscan" vases—*oggetti d'arte* bestowed by various and sundry "grateful" Italian states and principalities.

By happy accident, in the midst of a perilous midwinter crossing at Mont Cenis, Josephine on her way up the Alpine pass met General Berthier on his way down, on his way back from France to assume command of the Army of Italy, and she seized the opportunity to urge him to soften the terms of the orders sent to Captain Charles from Rastatt three weeks previously. Berthier was susceptible to her persuasions, and, back in Milan on December 22, he issued new orders to read: "Upon the request of the Citizen Hippolyte Charles, adjutant to the general staff, for permission to return to France to attend to urgent family business, Alexandre Berthier, Commander in Chief, authorizes the Citizen Charles to present to the Minister of War in Paris this recommendation for a three months' leave of absence."

If Captain Charles set out from Milan on that same date, December 22, he could have—riding alone and riding light—caught up with Madame Bonaparte's carriage train some two or three days after Christmas, somewhere on the road between Lyons and the capital.

The lights of Lyons ("a candle in every window of every story of every house") shone out through the winter dusk on the evening of December 19 in official welcome to Madame Bonaparte, and "a crown of flowers was placed upon her brow in homage to her virtue by an admiring citizenry." That "wreath of immortelles and roses" she would have doffed by the morning of the twentieth, when she sat down to a business conference with the astute Louis Bodin, at a meeting arranged by a mutual friend, Captain Charles. Through her influence with Director Barras, Josephine could assure Bodin a lucrative contract as official purveyor of supplies to the Army of Italy. Bodin, in turn, could assure his patroness of his gratitude—to take the form of a cash payment to her and a partnership in the newly organized Bodin Company for that same mutual friend of theirs, Captain Charles. (Madame Bonaparte had learned by then to exact full value for such services.)

For several days the municipality of Moulins, only 110 miles north of Lyons, expected the wife of the hero, and a pyramid and a tree of liberty, festooned with colored lanterns, gleamed in the main square. But the two cannons installed there to signal her approach did not boom out until Christmas Day.

Paris had expected her the day before; "The Free Men's Journal" published a premature report of her arrival on Christmas Eve and announced the date of the ball to be given in her honor at the Ministry of Foreign Affairs as December 25. Talleyrand, the high-born Minister of Foreign Affairs, as polished a host as he was a diplomat, was obliged to notify his guests of three postponements. The leaves and petals of the 930 trees, aromatic shrubs and floral decorations installed at the Hôtel Gallifet had drooped, faded and been replaced three times before Madame Bonaparte finally drove into Paris, on January 2.

If the florist-decorator Müller began to fret at the fourth replacement, so did General Bonaparte, unable to understand how it could take Josephine eight long days to cover the 174 miles between Moulins and Paris, granting even a series of mishaps to the carriages. The report would shortly circulate—though it was not to reach the general's ears until six months later—that Captain Charles had caught up with Madame Bonaparte just beyond Moulins, at Nevers, on December 27 or 28, and that they had celebrated the *réveillon*, the observance of New Year's Eve, together, parting only at Essones, "within three posting stations of Paris," as Josephine's son was to hear it.

Although still unaware on January 3 of the recent cause his wife had given him for jealousy, General Bonaparte was observed scarcely to leave her side at the Talleyrand gala, "making no secret of the fact that he was insanely jealous, head over heels in love," according to Stanislas de Girardin, one of the guests who carefully observed "the idol of the nation." The general relinquished Madame Bonaparte's arm only to escape the line of guests waiting to be presented to him, and to link his arm instead with that of fellow Institute member Arnault, suggesting, says the latter, that they two "walk, and talk together so intently as to ward off the importunities of those seeking to assail him."

There was only one woman in Paris—in all France, all Europe— so importunate, so brash, as to have "assailed" General Bonaparte when he made himself unassailable: a celebrity in her own right, a bold innovator in the fields of literature, politics and love—the dynamic, overpowering Germaine de Staël, who cornered Arnault, demanding to be presented to the general.

She had failed, in a barrage of her justly celebrated letters, to convince the general that they two "had been created for each other," says Bourrienne; that "nature had destined a soul of fire" (such as hers) "to the adoration of a hero" (such as he); that, to this divinely destined union, he should now "set aside a bland beauty such as Josephine, to whom he could have united his life only through some human error." "What effrontery!" Napoleon had exclaimed, ripping one of Madame de Staël's letters to shreds. "To dare to compare herself to Josephine!" What Madame de Staël could never get through that formidable head of hers was that a formidable head on female shoulders was one of the very last things to appeal to Bonaparte, that blandness and beauty, such as Josephine's, were the very first.

As Arnault remembered the scene in the glittering Hôtel Gallifet ballroom:

A crowd instantly collected to catch the exchange of words between these two illustrious protagonists, as if it had been the meeting between the Queen of Sheba and King Solomon. Making it clear that she considered him the foremost man among men, and undismayed by the hostile reserve manifest in the foremost man's eye and voice, Madame de Staël persisted in plying him with questions:

"Who is the woman, General, whom you could love the most?"

"My wife, madame."

"Yes, yes, of course, but which is the one whom you could most admire?"

"The one who best manages her household."

"Very well, then, granted. But who is the woman whom you would consider pre-eminent among her sex?"

"The one who gives birth to the greatest number of children."

It was an encounter to set all Paris talking.

Undauntedly optimistic, Madame de Staël professed admiration, publicly at least, for the general's repartee. "Which only proves the difference of opinion," he told his brother Lucien. "Josephine, on the other hand, reproached me. She said Parisians would accuse me of behaving like a celibate friar." But then, Josephine always deplored her husband's antisocial tendencies, his social ineptitude, his boorishness. In this instance, she apparently found it easier to forgive her friend Madame de Staël for her designs upon her husband than to forgive her husband for his tactless public tribute to fecundity. After almost two years of childless marriage, Josephine was growing touchy on the subject.

Which may have accounted for the fact that, as one reporter had it, Talleyrand's guest of honor did not that night, for all the elegance of her attire—a white, jeweled Grecian tunic—appear at her serene and gracious best. Though the dancing went on until sunrise of the fourth, the Bonapartes withdrew immediately after the midnight supper.

There had been several subjects for domestic discord since Josephine's arrival at the Rue de la Victoire on the second. An inquisition on the snail's pace of her caravan from Italy was followed by one equally unpleasant on the outrageous total of the decorators' bills for the refurbishing of their small leased residence. Not even the subtle flattery of the military motif of the décor—the drums transformed into stools, the cannon into bedposts, the canopy in the form of a tent to drape the twin beds, which sprang apart and together again by means of an ingenious spring device—could appease the general. Josephine's bills would provide the eternal theme for bickering between them.

But there was one still more grave in January of 1798, as Napoleon had not forgotten twenty years later, when he told General Bertrand at St. Helena, "A former maid of Josephine's [Louise Compoint] who had had to be dismissed when it was discovered that she was sleeping with Junot, decided to revenge herself on my wife for the dismissal. She came to me, upon my return from Italy, and told me that a young adjutant on the general staff, a fellow named Charles whom you must have come across in Italy—the type of little dandy who appeals to hussies—this fellow Charles, according to the maid, had followed Josephine to Italy, had ridden with her in her carriage and had slept in the same inns at night. These were confidences I could well have done without."

Napoleon, as he told it, had quizzed Josephine on the subject without revealing the source of his information, urging her, "Tell the truth. There's no great harm in all this. A man and woman can travel together and sleep in the same inns without—" But she had insisted, "No, no, it's not true!" and begun to cry.

"But then, Josephine invariably resorted to the negative," Napoleon added. "It was invariably her first impulse, her first reaction. Her first word was always 'No'—a 'No' that was not precisely a lie, but, rather, a precaution, a defensive measure." On what other line of defense could she have been expected to fall back, this mildest, blandest, most indolent of women, under attack by this Earthshaker? Even a woman of stronger character, more self-assertive, might well have "bent before him as before a phenomenon of nature"—as Emerson says all men did.

2

If Josephine's categorical denial of the Louise Compoint charges —plus her facile and highly becoming tears, traditionally her most effective weapon in any contest with the general—succeeded momentarily in stilling his jealousy in January, she could not trust to having totally dissipated his suspicion. She had reason to fear that he would carry out his threats to break Charles, and she could congratulate herself on having paved the way for a civilian career for him with the Bodin Company of Lyons.

Charles had reported on January 8 to the Ministry of War in Paris and had been granted his three-month leave of absence—none too long a period of time for Josephine to fulfill her part in the agreement by producing the contract for army provisioning on which the Bodin deal was predicated. On January 25, in what must have been a highly irregular procedure even for a regime noted for irregularities, Barras's secretary Bottot signed an authorization for the grant of a personal loan of four hundred thousand francs* to Madame Bonaparte from the executive funds of the national treasury. A portion of that sum was presumably to be applied to liquidation of Madame Bonaparte's tremendous personal debts; another portion was presumably allocated to financing the Bodin venture, the purchase of an interest in that company for Captain Hippolyte Charles.

---

* Any attempt to equate the value of a French monetary unit in the late eighteenth and early nineteenth centuries with that of an American monetary unit in the mid-twentieth century represents, at best, an approximation. The French franc was subject to wild fluctuation during and after the Revolution, though it was stabilized to some extent during the Consulate and the Empire; the fluctuation of the American dollar in recent years is too well known to require comment. For a basis of comparison between the value of the franc in the Napoleonic era and that of our dollar in the 1960's, economists can rely only upon the relative purchasing power of the two units of currency in the two periods of time, and even on that basis estimates differ widely. For lack of any precise way of evaluating the sums quoted in French francs in this book, a very rough estimate is suggested: that the franc be considered the equivalent of the dollar.

Such haste did Madame Bonaparte make in January in her appeals to Barras, to Bottot and to General Schérer, the Minister of War, that she could report by February 5 to Charles, in one of the few of her letters to him which have come down to us:*

Barras sent Bottot to see me this evening to assure me that the Bodin contract is under consideration, that the Minister of War had told Barras of my personal interest in the matter, and that Barras had taken advantage of the opportunity to urge Schérer to consummate the negotiation. Barras has sent word for me to meet with him tomorrow.

In the course of that meeting on the morrow, Barras invited Josephine to dine with him on February 17 for a final discussion of arrangements.

During the night of February 16–17, as it happened, General Bonaparte returned suddenly to Paris from the Channel coast, where he had spent twelve days inspecting the naval and military installations that were being readied for a possible invasion expedition against England, the command of which had been recently offered him by the Directory. His return obviously took Josephine by surprise, to judge by the note she dashed off to Barras's secretary next morning: "Bonaparte arrived last night. I beg of you to express my regrets to Barras at being unable to dine with him tonight. Tell him not to forget me! You understand better than anyone else, dear Bottot, the delicacy of my position."

Before the end of the month the prize was hers: a contract issued to Bodin and Company for the supply of foodstuffs to the Army of Italy. If Josephine, for her exertions, could expect to share with Charles in the profits, General Schérer, for his signature, and Barras, for his co-operation, could each expect a handsome commission—or, to use the French term for "payoff," *pot-de-vin* (wine keg).

The question that inevitably comes to mind is how Josephine and her protégé could have been so naïve as not to realize—or so

---

* These letters to Charles were discovered in the 1950s by historian Louis Hastier among old business documents in the archives of Charles's ancestral home, the Château of Génissieux.

reckless, so brazen, as not to care—that her role in the affair and his connection with the Bodins could not be long kept secret. General Junot's wife heard it—that "Monsieur Charles was associated with the Bodin Company in the purveying of foodstuffs," that "it was Madame Bonaparte who had arranged for him to secure an interest in that enterprise, which was the origin of his fortune." Antoine Hamelin heard, too, that "Sir Charles had quit the military service when peace was concluded, at which time, through his influence with Madame Bonaparte, he arranged for purveyors' contracts to be issued to Bodin of Lyons on the condition that he receive a half interest in the company profits." It was inevitable that the news would come to General Bonaparte's ear.

It came in the third week of March. The story of what happened on "the day of the catastrophe" is told by Josephine herself in this distraught undated letter to Charles written the following day:

Joseph [Bonaparte] had a long talk yesterday with his brother, and afterward he [Napoleon] asked me whether I knew the Citizen Bodin, whether it was I who had procured him the purveyor's contract with the Army of Italy which he had just heard about, and whether it was true that Charles was living at the Citizen Bodin's house at No. 100 Rue du Faubourg St.-Honoré and that I went there every day. I replied that I had no knowledge of any of the things he was talking about; that if he wanted a divorce, he need only say so, that he had no need to resort to tactics such as these, that I was the most unfortunate of women and the unhappiest.

Yes, my Hippolyte, they have all my hatred. You alone have my tenderness, my love. They should be able to see how I abhor them from the frightful state I have been in for several days. They must see the regret and the despair I experience at being deprived of seeing you as often as I wish. Hippolyte, I shall kill myself! Yes, I prefer to end [a life] which would henceforward be a burden if it cannot be consecrated to you. Alas! What have I done to these monsters? But still, no matter what they try, I shall not fall victim to their atrocities.

Please tell Bodin to say that he does not know me, that it was not through me that he obtained the Army of Italy contract. And tell him to tell the porter at No. 100 that if anyone should ask whether Bodin lives there he is to say that he does not know anyone by that name. And tell Bodin, too, that he should not make use of the letters I gave him for Italy until after he has been in that country for some time, and then only if he has need of them. —Ah, no matter how they torment me, they shall never separate me from my Hippolyte! My last sigh shall be for him.

I will do everything in the world possible to see you during the day. But should I be unable to do so, I will come by Bodin's this evening, and then tomorrow I will send Blondin to tell you what time I can get away to meet you in the Mousseau [Monceau] Gardens.

Goodbye, my Hippolyte, a thousand kisses as fiery as my heart, and as loving. If you have anything to send me, give it to Blondin.

They also said, the day of the catastrophe, that you had been at the War Ministry to hand in your resignation.*

This letter holds extraordinary significance in that it throws light upon the nebulous and delicate area of the degree of intimacy of Josephine's relations with Captain Charles, as well as the state of her affections during the early years of her marriage with General Bonaparte. For the first time the heart of Josephine is revealed to us. The heart that at the time of their marriage in 1796 was in what she herself honestly defined as "a state of indifference, of luke-warmness," was never truly accessible to her husband's ardent wooing. The element of tragedy in their relationship stems from the fact that the siege he laid to it was doomed to failure; her heart was never his to win, having been surrendered, within two months of their wedding date, to another.

Ironically, Josephine's letters to Charles ring with that very note of delirium which she found so naïve, so "funny," in her husband's letters to her. Here is evidence that this ultrasophisticate of thirty-four, a widow with two adolescent children and with at least two extramarital liaisons to her account, may have been as lovestruck as

* General Schérer's official memorandum on Charles's resignation in the files of the Ministry of War shows that it was tendered on March 17, 1798. The "day of the catastrophe" was probably March 18 or 19, which would make the date of Josephine's letter March 19 or 20.

any girl at her encounter with Charles; evidence that, with him, she may have been experiencing the exquisite torment and rapture of first love.

Then why, despite her protestation to Charles that she stood ready to renounce position and security for herself and for her children, ready to grant her husband a divorce should he "only say so" —why, then, did she call it a "day of catastrophe," resort to tears, and deny Joseph's charges as she had denied those of Louise Compoint? It is not enough to recall her tendency to tears and to "the negative," to say that she always bent like a weeping willow before Napoleon's wrath. It may have been Charles, less reckless than she, who urged her at that point to caution. Charles may have been justifiably fearful, if not of the physical violence implicit in the "dagger of Othello" letter, then of other forms of reprisal available to a vengeful Corsican with tremendous influence in the regime.

The Bonapartes' domestic crisis was, at any rate, resolved—or averted or postponed—in the spring of 1798, apparently upon a pledge extracted by Napoleon from Josephine that she would break off with Charles, as Josephine's own letter implies, and as Laure Junot states on the authority of her friend Pauline Bonaparte Leclerc. "My sister-in-law nearly died of vexation," Madame Junot quotes Napoleon's sister as saying. "Now, you know that we do not die of vexation merely at being parted from our friends, so there must have been more than mere friendship in that relation. As for me, I tried to comfort my brother, who was exceedingly unhappy. He was aware of the situation when he returned to Paris [from Italy], before he went to Egypt. Poor brother!" ("Whereupon this devoted sister sympathized tenderly with the brother to whose distress she herself had in all probability contributed," comments Madame Junot, who was of the opinion that Pauline had joined with Joseph Bonaparte in a determined effort to shatter their brother's illusions about his wife.)

Bourrienne, at this time Napoleon's confidant as well as his secretary, saw a number of reasons for the reconciliation with Josephine and the postponement of their domestic crisis: "His love for his wife, his inspection tour of the coasts, his preoccupation with plans and preparations for the Egyptian campaign, the brevity of his sojourn in Paris—these were the factors which prevented him from giving vent to his suspicions at the time." Above all, first and foremost, came his love for his wife. "In our intimate conversations," says Bourrienne, recalling the long six weeks on shipboard across the Mediterranean to Egypt, "Josephine almost always formed the subject. As passionately as he loved glory—France's and his own—still Josephine engrossed much of the thought in a soul dedicated to vast designs. His attachment to her bordered on idolatry."

Napoleon was still desperately in love; Josephine's hold on his heart, his emotions and his senses was undiminished after two years of marriage, out of which he could count fewer than nine months in her arms. He had not even begun to have enough of her. She haunted his flesh. As keen and penetrating as were his powers of analysis, Napoleon accepted Josephine's stammering refutation of the charges made by Louise Compoint and by Joseph and Pauline, accepted her lame and faltering explanations of her dealings with Charles—because he wanted to.

Because he wanted to, Napoleon took her word that she would discontinue communication with Charles, while every sympathetically inclined biographer and reader must wince at the evidence contained in Josephine's own letters that, in violation of her word, she continued to pay clandestine visits to the Bodin house on the Rue du Faubourg St.-Honoré, continued to arrange (through the connivance of a servant, Blondin) to meet her lover, like any little Paris midinette, in the shadowy bypaths of the Monceau Gardens —then a popular suburban pleasureground of none too savory repute, patronized by a segment of the Parisian populace least likely to recognize the veiled face and form of the wife of France's premier general.

Romance and finance, the love affair and the business affair, are in such a jumble in a second undated letter of Josephine's that there can be small wonder that Charles filed it where it was found some one hundred and fifty years later, among his business papers:

I have just written to the Minister of War to tell him that I cannot see him today because I am going to the country, but that I will visit him tomorrow to deliver a packet which has been given to me to pass on to him. I have also written to Barras, urging him to send me the promised letters. I am awaiting his reply.

I am going, my dear Hippolyte, to the country. I will be back at five o'clock and will come at five-thirty or six to Bodin's to see you. Yes, my Hippolyte, my life is a constant torment! Only you can restore me to happiness. Tell me that you love me, that you love me alone! That will make me the happiest of women.

Send me fifty thousand livres by Blondin, out of the funds on hand. Collot* is asking me for the money.

Adieu, I send you a thousand tender kisses—and I am yours, all yours.

In keeping her assignations with her lover and her appointments with her business agents, it required no extraordinary talent on Josephine's part to escape Napoleon's surveillance. Throughout the months of February and March, he was closeted in his study all day and late into the night with his chiefs of staff and with naval as well as military experts, amid tables and desks littered with maps of Egypt—or, rather, such fragmentary, inaccurate, inadequate ancient and medieval specimens as existed prior to his own expedition up the Nile.

For General Bonaparte had rejected the command of France's Army of England after concluding that the chances of success were insufficient to warrant the risk of an invasion. As an alternative, he had proposed to the Directory that England be attacked along her commercial lifeline to the East, to India: by an expedition across the Mediterranean, against Malta and Egypt. Here the calculated risks were staggering, too, but the odds of success, as Napoleon had meticulously calculated them, were infinitely higher. The English Mediterranean fleet had been weakened by the withdrawal of much sail to protect the British Isles against the threatened invasion; the Ottoman Empire sprawled like a flabby giant, its province of Egypt in the hands of the openly mutinous Mamelukes—a legendary and ferocious fighting force, but as outmoded in arsenal and tactics as the Crusaders, its most recent challengers of any note. As for Europe, in early 1798, French victories in Italy and Austria had ex-

* One of the Army of Italy's civilian contractors, from whom Josephine apparently borrowed heavily during her Italian sojourn.

tended and ensured the borders of the new Republic; Austria was licking its Italian wounds, Russia was not yet stirring, and England was preoccupied with self-defense.

Still, over and above the validity of the military and economic objectives of the Egyptian campaign as General Bonaparte had outlined them to the Directory, it was the East which was exercising its inevitable magnetism, its lure of adventure and glory, over his mind, as it had over the minds of Caesar and Alexander, the two other great adventurers of history who preceded him there. "Europe is a molehill!" he had scoffed a year earlier at Passeriano in Bourrienne's hearing.

Now in 1798, chafing within the narrow Continental confines, he confided to Bourrienne, "This little Europe cannot provide enough of glory. Everything wears out here. My fame is already fading; I shall seek it in the East. If I stay on here without further achievements, I am lost."

If he could not become a Director (the minimum age was constitutionally specified as forty, and he was not yet twenty-nine), neither would he linger on the fringes of power to tarnish his lustrous name and reputation through association with the disreputable and doomed Directory. "The pear is not yet ripe," Napoleon is quoted as saying by Barras, himself so fearful of the new strong man, the man so obviously the people's choice, that he persuaded his fellow Directors to rid themselves of Bonaparte at any price— even to giving him an expeditionary force thirty-five to forty thousand strong, with the entire French fleet as convoy.

"A matter of months or six years," was Napoleon's estimate to Bourrienne of the possible duration of the expedition. "Everything depends upon developments. We"—he was already speaking in the imperial first person plural—"are only twenty-nine; we would then be thirty-five—not too advanced an age. These six years will suffice, if successful, for me to go to India." And, referring again to Egypt: "I shall colonize that land, send for craftsmen of all sorts, women, artists, actors."

In the interest of the ultimate goals of colonization and scientific investigation and recording, a 167-member Commission of Arts and Sciences was signed on: engineers, mathematicians, chemists, botanists, zoologists, physicians, pharmacists, cartographers, Orientalists, antiquarians, Arabists, artists, lawyers, historians—fellow members of Napoleon's from the Institute of France recruited for the "Institute of Egypt," a corps of *penseurs* ("thinkers," the eighteenth century's catchword for "intellectuals") rallying to the banner of this *penseur* in uniform who translated thought into action. The publication by this "Living Encyclopedia" of the monumental, comprehensive, illustrated twenty-four-volume *Déscription de l'Égypte* marked the emergence of Egyptology as a science; the discovery by Napoleon's archaeologists of the Rosetta Stone furnished the key for the deciphering of hieroglyphics.

For the enlistment of Dominique Vivant Denon, art expert, artist and author (among his host of talents), one of the most productive of all Napoleon's savants, the commander in chief had Josephine to thank, though she most carefully kept him from suspecting it. Denon's mistress, Madame de Krény, was Josephine's dearest friend, but, as Arnault noted in this instance, "to be in the good graces of Madame Bonaparte was no passport to those of her husband; his ill will toward the lady [Madame de Krény] extended to her cavalier"; and Josephine was obliged to enlist Arnault—himself one of the savants accompanying the expedition—to plead Denon's cause with her husband.

The question of whether or not Josephine too was to accompany the commander in chief to the Levant was still under consideration when their carriage rolled south from Paris in the predawn hours of May 4, departing so suddenly and secretly as not to permit even a farewell kiss for Hortense—in accordance with the strict security measures established to prevent any leak of news to Admiral Nelson and the British fleet concerning the expedition's destination or its embarkation date.

3

The mighty armada lay fully assembled and tugging at anchor in Toulon harbor when General and Madame Bonaparte, accompanied by the indispensable Bourrienne and by young Eugène, proud in his aide-de-camp's uniform, drove into that port on May 9, 1798.

During the six days' wait for the abatement of a storm, Josephine went out one afternoon, escorted by Vice-Admiral Brueys and high-ranking army officers, for a tour of the flagship, the *Orient*, and an inspection of her husband's quarters—including the library, with its 287 volumes of history, philosophy and poetry, which had been assembled by Arnault in conformity with the commander's tastes and orders. Articulate and witty Arnault includes in his memoirs an amusing account of the preliminary skirmish between Napoleon's military and literary cliques which enlivened Josephine's visit. It was set off by General Lannes, who, upon being introduced to Arnault, roared, "Were I in command here, I would order the whole lot of savants tossed overboard!" At which point General Junot spoke up in defense of the librarian:

"What do you mean by calling Arnault a savant? He's no more of a savant than you or I. Why, Arnault was with the Army of Italy."

"Yes," Josephine joined in, evincing her displeasure at the turn the conversation had taken, "Arnault belongs to the Army of Italy."

The statement having been confirmed by Berthier, Murat, Eugène and even the worthy vice-admiral, Lannes exclaimed, "That's different! If he's not a savant, he's one of us, and I hope he will be my friend."

Arnault was one of the select few in the commander's personal entourage, boarding ship with him at daybreak on May 19. "An hour later the *Orient* raised her sails," he wrote,

but, with her overload of 120 cannon and her exceedingly deep draft, she dragged bottom and listed so sharply as to cause alarm to the throngs of spectators lining the shore—above all, to Madame Bonaparte, who, from the balcony of the Marine Intendancy, stood watching the movements of the fleet. She was speedily reassured when our ship righted itself and pulled out majestically into the open sea, to the accompaniment of wild shouts of acclamation from the shore, the fanfare of the regimental bands blaring away on deck and the boom of cannon from the city forts and from the battleships.

Emotion ran high at sight of that great fleet with its thousands of men, setting out on an expedition of which the destination was unknown to most—and all of those thousands staking their fortunes on the fortune of one!

It was that one man's good fortune that the recent storm had dispersed the squadron of thirty English ships patrolling the Mediterranean off Majorca, and his lucky star would shine through the six weeks of the perilous crossing while Nelson and another squadron of fourteen ships vainly chased him.

Napoleon surely watched, as did Arnault, for the last flutter of Josephine's scarf from the balcony over the port at Toulon. "Their parting had been affecting in the extreme," as Bourrienne recalled the scene. "Those who knew Madame Bonaparte are aware that few women were ever more delightful or more fascinating; and Napoleon, passionately in love with her, had brought her with him to Toulon to enjoy her company, to put off the cruel parting until the last possible moment."

Enjoying her company until the last possible moment in bed was how General Alexandre Dumas found his commander early one morning in Toulon. The handsome, swarthy Dumas—a mulatto giant from Santo Domingo, father of the Dumas *père* of *The Count of Monte Cristo* and *The Three Musketeers*—having been summoned by General Bonaparte to take over command of the expedition's cavalry, was ushered unceremoniously into the Bonapartes' bedroom, where he found Josephine in tears—and little else, "to judge by the luscious curves discernible beneath the sheets."

The tears Napoleon explained by saying that his wife was weeping because "she wants to accompany me to Egypt." When Dumas observed that his wife was not accompanying him either, Bonaparte consoled Josephine with the comment that it was traditional for soldiers' wives to follow later, adding, "If we are there for several years, we will send for our wives. Dumas, who has thus far made only daughters, and I, who have not even done that well, will each do our best to make a son. He will stand godfather to mine and

I to his," Bonaparte concluded, punctuating his remarks with a resounding smack on his wife's bare and shapely buttocks.

The decision as to whether they would part at Toulon or sail together seems, then, to have been put off until the last, and to have been made finally by Napoleon. The historians' theory that Josephine made the decision, never intending to go, refusing point-blank to leave Paris (or her lover), is untenable in the light of the evidence to the contrary—for example, her letter to Barras dated May 26 from Toulon, which indicates that when the Bonapartes had dined with him on the eve of their departure from Paris they had left him under the impression that Josephine was to accompany the expedition: "I have stayed on at Toulon, my dear Barras. Bonaparte was fearful of an encounter with the English, and did not wish to expose me to that risk. If I do not sail from here within two weeks to join him, I shall go to Plombières for the waters, and then leave within the next two months to meet Bonaparte in Egypt." And in postscript the notation: "I have only this moment received a letter from Bonaparte. He was feeling very well" —not seasick, as he had fully expected to be—"and the fleet was safely off Cap Corse."

Off the coast of his native isle on May 23, Napoleon notified brother Joseph as well as Josephine: "My wife will wait several days longer at Toulon, until she has received word that we have passed Sicily, after which she will go to take the waters."

Hope in "the waters" as well as fear of the English had influenced General Bonaparte's decision. Europeans' faith in the therapeutic virtues of their watering resorts continues undiminished into the twentieth century, certain mineral springs being renowned for their benefit to the liver (perennially the crankiest of Gallic organs), others specified for the kidneys, the spleen or the stomach, or for rheumatic or arthritic aches and pains. Plombières, in the Vosges Mountains, is noted for its "waters of fertility." Josephine no less than her husband, after two years of childless marriage, wished for a child. Napoleon's wish was inspired not only by his natural love of children, but also by his Corsican tribal spirit; begetting a numerous progeny was a duty to the clan. As for Josephine, the more the Bonapartes whispered about the possible sterility of Nabulione's wife, the more sensitive she became to the difference in their ages: Napoleon, at twenty-nine, could expect to father a sizable family; at thirty-five, Josephine's time for child-bearing was running out.

And so, early in June, on receipt of the news that the French armada had successfully eluded Admiral Nelson even beyond Sicily, Madame Bonaparte turned north, up the Rhone Valley, for the highly recommended waters of Plombières.

From Lyons, on June 10, she sent off an urgent message to Barras in behalf of the Bodins and Charles: "I have just learned, my dear Barras, that General Brune [in Italy] is making a determined effort to break the Bodin contract. Write to him in their behalf, I beg you, and lose no time! We are, both you and I, obligated to them, and I hope that you will oppose any action detrimental to their interests. You know what a great interest I take in these persons."

Whether it was Charles who met her at Lyons and gave her this news or whether she learned it there through the Bodins, she does not say; but there is no indication, from her or from contemporary gossip, to indicate that Charles was with her at Plombières when she arrived in mid-June. Indeed, her letter to Barras dated June 19 makes a point of the fact that she was alone:

I have come here solely for reasons of health and devote all my time to the cure. There is no social life.

I beg of you, my dear Barras, to keep me informed about yourself and to pass along news of Bonaparte as soon as it reaches you. I need to hear regularly. I am so upset at being separated from him that I am overwhelmed by a sadness I cannot shake off. Besides, his brother [Joseph], with whom he maintains an assiduous correspondence, is so vicious about me that I am always anxious when I am away from Bonaparte. Joseph told one of his friends—who repeated it to me—that he would not rest until he had succeeded in bringing about a rift between my husband and me. Joseph is a vile, abominable creature, as you will one day discover.

I am sending you a letter for Bonaparte which I ask you to send on to him at once. I shall send all my letters to him* through you,

* None of Napoleon's and Josephine's letters to each other during the Egyptian campaign has ever been discovered.

*and I urge you to be sure to see that they are dispatched to Egypt
as speedily as possible. You know him, and you know how angry he
would be if he did not hear from me regularly. The last letter I received from him is very tender, very touching, shows great feeling.
He tells me to come as quickly as possible to join him, that he cannot bear to be separated from me. So I am hurrying to complete the
cure prescribed for me so that I can go as soon as possible to join
Bonaparte—of whom I am very fond, despite his little faults.*

"Little faults"! In all the billions of words written about Napoleon during his lifetime and in the ensuing centuries (there are
more than two hundred thousand printed items to date on the
man and the legend), no one, neither friend nor foe, save his wife
has ever accused him of "little faults." His vices and his virtues have
been theme for vituperation or eulogy on the grand scale only. (As
in Hugo's "Lui": "Angel or demon!—it little matters which.")

Even so, in Josephine's letter to Barras of June 19 there is evident
a hint of change in her perspective on the marriage, in her attitude
toward her husband: she speaks for the first time of "sadness" and
"anxiety" at separation from him. She was coming slowly to take
the measure of the man she had so nonchalantly married; something had somehow, finally, shaken her out of her "Creole nonchalance," stirred her indolent imagination—touched perhaps
even, at last, her indifferent heart. It may have been the crescendo
of national acclamation in recent weeks and the rousing cheers of
Napoleon's fanatically devoted troops which had finally pierced her
ear, the sight of that formidable amphibian operation—his in conception and execution—which had opened her eyes to the colossal
stature of the man, so that the figure of Charles, seductive, attractive and amusing as he was, began to diminish in comparison to
the figure of the man she had strained her eyes to discern on the
prow of the *Orient* as it disappeared over the eastern horizon.

Heading east, the *Orient* reached Malta on June 9. By the nineteenth, General Bonaparte had taken possession of that island, in
the name of France, from the Knights of Saint John of Jerusalem
—the Knights Hospitalers—and had ordered the four hundred sail
of the armada set for Alexandria. Elated at these auspicious begin-
nings, the general dispatched the *Pomona*—which, as it happened,

had served as convoy on Marie-Josèphe-Rose's first sailing from Martinique in 1779—back to the mainland to fetch his wife.

But by the time the *Pomona* had reached Naples, Josephine had suffered a serious accident. At Plombières on June 20, while she sat decorously hemming Madras handkerchiefs on her second-story balcony overlooking the street, that wooden structure collapsed and fell, a drop of twenty feet that might have proved fatal. As it was, she escaped with severe shock, sprains and contusions. The local physician wrapped the wife of the nation's hero in the skin of a freshly slaughtered sheep. Then, suspecting spinal injury or concussion, and nervous about making a mistake in the case of so celebrated a patient, he called into consultation several renowned regional colleagues, whose prescriptions included "bleeding, leeches, compresses of hot boiled potatoes and of camphor, liniment rubs, arnica infusions and warm mineral-water baths."

Under the wing of Euphémie, her old mulatto nurse from Martinique, Hortense de Beauharnais came flying from St.-Germain to her mother's sickroom, which provided, if only incidentally, the opportunity for a reunion rarely enjoyed by the girl since her Maman's remarriage. Hortense's solicitude for Josephine seemed, not only then but all her life, maternal rather than filial. Josephine's perennial air of feminine fragility and helplessness evoked the protective instinct in both her children; even with them she coquetted.

Hortense, at fifteen, was still gay and animated, as she would be until the blight of her brilliant marriage fell upon her; still all eyes (violet blue), which dominated her little face and betrayed her schoolgirl secrets, her romantic notions and noble aspirations, as well as the painful hypersensitivity and the tender sensibility which distinguished her even in an age when *sensibilité* was cultivated. Hortense's nimbus of fair hair was another distinguishing feature, redeeming her from plainness, as did her lissome figure, graceful and lovely like her mother's. Like her mother, too, Hortense was kind and gentle, gracious and considerate; the best-loved girl in Madame Campan's female academy as well as its star pupil, amenable to reason and suggestion, earnest in application to study and to duty.

To Plombières, to cheer Josephine's convalescence, came her dear friend Madame de Krény, another grass widow of the Egyptian campaign, whose lover Denon was off on the Nile sketching tombs and temples and dodging Bedouin bullets.

Still another widow—this a morganatic one—summering at that spa in 1798 was Madame de Montesson, venerable relict of Duke Louis-Philippe d'Orléans, prince of the blood and cousin to the Bourbon kings as well as father to the late Revolutionary leader and regicide Philippe-Égalité. If Madame de Montesson had never been officially received by Louis XVI and Marie Antoinette at the court of Versailles, she and the Duke had held court of their own in his numerous châteaux, and her visits infinitely flattered the invalid Citizeness Bonaparte, who, as the Viscountess de Beauharnais, had so wistfully eyed the court circular, the titles and the doings of all that exalted, exclusive, glittering pre-Revolution world to which she had never had entree.

Madame de Montesson's high injunction on the subject of General Bonaparte, "Never forget that you are married to an extraordinary man!," greatly impressed Josephine. She had heard the pronouncement from military scientists, intellectuals, statesmen and diplomats, foreign and domestic, but it had perhaps never struck her so forcibly as now, coming from a pseudo princess of the blood.

Josephine was now willing, once she recovered her health, to undertake the long and perilous journey to Egypt for reunion with that "extraordinary man," as she notified Barras by letter early in July:

I have just received a charming letter from Bonaparte in which he tells me that he cannot live without me and that I should go to Naples to embark [for Egypt]. I so wish that my health permitted me to leave at once, but I can as yet see no end to my confinement. I cannot stand up or sit down for ten minutes at a time without suffering terrible pains in my kidneys and lower spine. All I do is cry. The doctors assure me that within a month I shall have recovered, but meanwhile, my dear Barras, you have no idea of how I suffer. . . . Enclosed you will find a letter for Bonaparte. Send me all news of him. . . .

Within the month, she was making definite plans with the young bride of General Marmont to travel together to join their husbands, writing on July 23: "I hope to be in Paris by the end of the month.

Bonaparte advises me to go to Naples to take ship, so, you see, we shall cross Italy and sail from there to Malta, and from Malta to Egypt." A plan that was never to be carried out, that was to founder in the wake of twin disasters.

To whatever re-evaluation of her marriage Josephine may have come in 1798—to whatever new resolutions regarding her husband —the moment for going to him had been lost irretrievably.

4

Before the generals' ladies could even meet in Paris to proceed to their port of embarkation, the Mediterranean had become what it would remain until modern times, an English lake, and the French fleet lay fathoms deep beneath the waters of Abukir Bay, off Alexandria, where the English had surprised it at anchor, in a helpless huddle, on August 1. Sunken there, along with most of those proud ships of the line, were all General Bonaparte's hopes of reinforcing or supplying his expeditionary forces.

But even had the French frigate *Pomona* dared venture out of Naples harbor, Josephine would no longer have been assured of a welcome from her husband. Even before Admiral Nelson had blasted Napoleon's dreams of Eastern dominion, General Junot had blasted his last illusions about his wife, his love, his marriage. The debacle on the sea had been preceded by a debacle in the desert and in the personal lives of the Bonapartes, though Josephine would long remain ignorant of both.

Weeks were required for news to travel to France from Egypt; in late July, she could not yet even have heard of the army's successful disembarkation at Alexandria on the first and second. That port city speedily invested, General Bonaparte had marched immediately south to engage the main body of the Mameluke forces drawn up at the approaches to Cairo. It was a march of only one hundred miles in actual distance, but under murderous conditions —under a searing sun and over scorching sands—that were so devastating to morale that officers as well as men had grown sullen and mutinous. It was here, on July 19 at El Ouardan, that General Junot, strangely moved (out of desperation, anger, pity, spite, a sense of honor or of justice?), played out his strange role of informer against his beloved commander's beloved wife.

Secretary Bourrienne, plodding along on foot, spitting out sand like all the rest, glimpsed Bonaparte and Junot out of the corner of his eye. What he saw snapped him to attention:

I noticed Bonaparte walking alone with Junot. I was only a short distance away, but I do not know why my eyes fastened on him during that conversation. The general's pale face had turned paler than ever. His features were suddenly convulsed, a wild look came into his eyes, and several times he struck his head with his fists!

Some fifteen minutes later, he left Junot and came toward me. I had never seen him so distraught, preoccupied. As I went to join him, he burst out with: "You are not genuinely devoted to me, or you would have told me what I have just learned from Junot. There's a true friend for you. Josephine! And I six hundred leagues away! You should have told me! Josephine—thus to have deceived me! Damn them, I shall exterminate that whole breed of fops and coxcombs! As for her, divorce! Yes, divorce—a public divorce, open scandal! I must write immediately. I know everything. It's your fault, you should have told me!"

These violent and disjointed exclamations, his anguished look and his unnatural tone of voice informed me all too well of the subject of his conversation with Junot. I saw that the aide-de-camp had been drawn into an unpardonable indiscretion, and that if Josephine had committed mistakes they had been cruelly exaggerated.

The situation was one of extreme delicacy, but fortunately I retained my self-possession, and, as soon as some degree of calm had been restored, I replied that I knew nothing of the reports which Junot might have made to him; that even if such reports, often the product of calumny, had come to my ear, and even if I had considered it my duty to inform him of them, I would certainly not have chosen a moment when he was six hundred leagues from France. Nor did I make any effort to conceal how reprehensible I considered Junot's conduct, how unfair thus recklessly to accuse a woman who was not present to justify or defend herself; that it seemed to me no great proof of friendship or devotion to add domestic anxieties to those already confronting a commander at the outset of a hazardous military enterprise.

Despite these observations, to which he listened with some attention, the word "divorce" continued on his lips. Unless one is familiar with the violence of the wrath of which Bonaparte was capable when aroused, it is impossible to conceive of what he was like during this terrible scene. Nevertheless, I stood my ground, repeating what I had said. I implored him to remember with what facility rumors are fabricated and circulated, and that gossip such as had been repeated to him was the diversion of idle minds, contemptible to strong ones. I spoke of his glory.

"My glory!" he cried. "Oh, what would I not give to have that which Junot has told me untrue! So deeply do I love that woman! But if she is guilty, then divorce must separate us forever. I will not be the laughingstock of Paris! I will write to Joseph and tell him to have the divorce pronounced."

Although his agitation continued, moments of comparative calm succeeded, and I took advantage of these to combat the idea of divorce which seemingly obsessed him. I pointed out that it would be especially imprudent to write to his brother in reference to a report which was in all probability false, for the reason that the letter might be intercepted and would betray the wrath which dictated it. "As to a divorce," I said, "there is plenty of time to think of that later, after due consideration."

These last words of mine produced an effect on him for which I had not dared to hope so soon. He quieted down, listened to me as if he had suddenly felt the justice of my observations, dropped the subject, and never returned to it again—except about a fortnight later, when he expressed a great dissatisfaction with Junot, complaining of the injury done him by such indiscreet disclosures, which he had come to regard as malicious inventions. It is my opinion that he never forgave Junot for this indiscretion, and I can state almost with certainty that this was one of the reasons why Junot was never created a marshal of France, like so many of his comrades whom Bonaparte loved far less. And there is ground for the supposition that Josephine, who was later informed by Bonaparte of Junot's revelations, would have been little disposed to favor him.

On the march up the Nile, Napoleon's personal problems could not be permitted to distract him from his military ones. The sight of the Sphinx and the Pyramids of Giza through his field glasses on the morning of July 21 reminded him—as he reminded his soldiers, in his famous order of the day—that "forty centuries look down upon us from the height of these monuments."

In the Battle of the Pyramids, the Middle Ages collided with modern times; before the sun had set, the Mamelukes had discovered that their hitherto formidable spears and lances were pitiful relics of the past. One thunderous, awesome, savage, shrieking cavalry charge by the turbaned desert warriors into the withering fire of the French army's modern artillery and infantry units, deployed alternately in General Bonaparte's lethal "squares," and then: "It was no longer a battle," as Denon shudderingly described it, "but only a massacre." And by July 23 the French commander of the Army of Egypt made his triumphal entry, unopposed, through Cairo's Gate of Victories, Bab el Nasr.

But the disillusionment in the desert had left a bitterness that not even the victory at Cairo could sweeten, as the victor wrote on July 26 from his palace on the Nile to his brother Joseph in Paris.

You will read in the newspapers the outcome of the battles and the conquest of Egypt, which was sufficiently contested to have added a page to the military glory of this army. . . . I am undergoing acute domestic distress, for the veil is now entirely rent. It is a sad state when one and the same heart is torn by such conflicting sentiments regarding one and the same person. You know what I mean. . . . It is possible that I may be back in France within two months, and I entrust my interests to you. Make arrangements for a country place to be ready for my arrival, either near Paris or in Burgundy. I expect to shut myself away there for the winter. I am disgusted with human nature. I have need of solitude and isolation. Grandeur palls on me. My emotions are spent, withered. Glory stales. At the age of twenty-nine, I have exhausted everything; life has nothing more to offer. Nothing remains for me but to become a complete egoist. I intend to keep my house [the house on the Rue de la Victoire]. No one else shall have it, no matter who. . . .

In the same dispatch pouch, for transmittal by courier to Alexandria and thence by ship to France, went a letter addressed to Josephine from her son Eugène, under a July 25 dateline.

My dearest mother, I have so many things to tell you, I don't know where to begin. For the last five days Bonaparte has appeared exceedingly sad, and this came about as the result of a talk he had with Junot and Jullien—even Berthier joining in.* He was more seriously affected by this conversation than I had realized. From the few words I could catch, it all goes back to Charles, to the fact that he returned with you [from Italy] in your carriage to within three posting stations from Paris; that you have seen him since in Paris; that you have been going with him to the Italiens [the Théâtre Italien], to the fourth-balcony loges [the upper, discreetly grilled private boxes]; that it was he who gave you your little dog; that he is with you even at this moment. . . .

There, from the snatches of conversation I have overheard, is all I can make out of it. As you can well imagine, Maman, I do not believe a word of this, but what is certain is that the general is deeply affected by it. Still, he redoubles his kindnesses to me; he seems to be saying, by his actions, that children cannot be held responsible for their mothers' frailties. But your son tells himself that all this gossip has been fabricated by your enemies, and he loves you no less, no less yearns to embrace you. I only hope that by the time you arrive here all this will be forgotten. . . .

A letter of amazing delicacy, tenderness, chivalry and tact from a boy of seventeen. Yet neither this poignant message from Eugène to his mother nor the letter from Napoleon to his brother Joseph was ever to reach its destination. Dispatched from Cairo in the last week of July, they were intercepted by a quirk of fate—and Admiral Nelson—after the naval "Battle of the Nile" on August 1.

Word of that naval disaster came to France by the middle of the month, and Josephine had no sooner driven into Paris from Plombières than she sought to contact Barras. "I arrived during the night,

---

* Eugène adds two more actors to the scene at El Ouardan described by Bourrienne. It may be that Napoleon queried the others on the subject Junot had opened.

my dear Barras," she wrote in a letter dated August 16, "and my first thought was to send a messenger to inquire about you—only to learn that you were in the country and would not return until very late. I am so disturbed about the news which has just come in via Malta that I must ask to see you alone tonight at nine. Give orders, please, that no one else is to be admitted."

Director Barras could only confirm the fact that Bonaparte was cut off from Europe and that the military situation was ominous; he could offer Josephine only cold comfort on the score of her husband's and her son's return to France within the foreseeable future.

The first hint of the embarrassment in store through the interception of the highly personal, confidential letters written by Napoleon and Eugène came to her from the pages of a Paris newspaper in October. *La Clef du Cabinet* reported a rumor then current in England to the effect that a small French mail ship captured at Abukir had carried a racy cargo—as to which, however, "Admiral Nelson had given faithful assurance that all nonmilitary communications—all letters of confidential, personal or romantic nature—would be released and forwarded to their addressees."

By November, Josephine had learned the worst: the British government was publishing an official collection of all the letters in the confiscated Egyptian mail pouch—the complete text, both in the original French and in English translation. This she learned from the November 24 issue of the *London Morning Chronicle*, which declared, in a high editorial dudgeon:

> The publication of the confidential letters written by Bonaparte and his men to friends and family in France (letters intercepted by our navy) does little credit to the ethics of our Cabinet.* Such scandal-mongering cannot serve to enhance our national dignity. One of these confiscated letters is from Bonaparte to his brother, a lament on his wife's *coquetterie*; another, from young Beauharnais, expresses the hope that his *chère maman* is less of a coquette than she had been depicted. . . .

---

* Nor, presumably, would the indignant editor of the *Morning Chronicle* have approved the display of the two letters in question under glass today in the British Museum; the one from Bonaparte to Joseph is labeled "Found upon the person of the General's courier."

In view of the fate of this correspondence, Josephine would assuredly not have dared entrust another letter to the British-dominated Mediterranean, even had it been her impulse to write to her husband in an attempt to propitiate him or to justify herself. Prompt action by some influential party—in all probability, Barras—forestalled the publication of those two telltale letters in the French edition of the English volume, a best seller in Paris by December. But it was bad enough as it was: the French edition, published by Garnéry, carried a reprint of the London Morning Chronicle article, and the news was out; the Bonapartes' domestic crisis became a public scandal.

Madame Bonaparte had every reason to believe that if her husband ever succeeded in returning to France he would repudiate her legally. Otherwise she might not have lapsed back into her former intimacy with Hippolyte Charles.

Charles had recently returned from a trip to Italy on company business, and those Bodin interests were now of prime importance to Josephine. The annual allowance of forty thousand francs allotted to her by the general had struck her as "stingy" from the beginning—at least, so Barras quotes her; it was adding insult to injury that this allowance was now being doled out to her by the hand of that "vile and abominable" Joseph, in charge of his brother's affairs during his absence, and outrightly antagonistic now, contemptuous of his brother's publicly dishonored wife.

Cringing at the notoriety, Josephine could not guess that the general, once he had recovered from the first shock of Junot's ugly disclosure, was beginning to show signs of "an inclination to pardon," in Bourrienne's opinion and upon Bourrienne's urging. That inclination may have been induced by the mute plea in Eugène's unhappy eyes as well as by Bourrienne's glib tongue; the son, blushing for the mother, was as appealing and disarming as she. A glimpse of the intricacy and the poignancy of the relationship between Josephine's son and her husband at that uncomfortable hour comes down to us in Eugène's memoirs:

> The general, at that period, found cause for keen anxiety, whether the result of widespread discontent among certain divisions of the army—especially among the generals—or the result

of reports sent to him from France to the purpose of troubling his domestic happiness. Although I was very young, he trusted me sufficiently to share his problems with me. It was usually at night, pacing back and forth across his tent, that he gave voice to his complaints and made me his confidences. I was the only one to whom he could unburden himself. I sought to alleviate his resentments. I consoled him to the best of my ability—to the full extent possible in view of my youth and of the profound respect which he inspired in me.

By October Napoleon's heart had softened to the point where, writing to Joseph, he urged: "Show some courtesy to my wife, go to see her occasionally. I am likewise asking Louis to give her some good counsel." Louis Bonaparte was the bearer of this message; in ill health, he was running the gauntlet of the English fleet for the sake of home and a more moderate climate.

Napoleon might have come around to reinstating his wife in his affections had not the crisis in their private lives become public property and an international incident. Not even the Egyptian voices hailing him as "Sultan Kebir" (Grand Sultan) could drown out the whisper of "cuckold." If he was not to be, as he had said he feared, "the laughingstock of Paris," and of London and the Continent as well, then the infidelity of his wife must be offset by one of his own, more flagrant still—the first, beyond the shadow of a doubt, since his marriage, and perpetrated grimly, even ruefully, in deliberate reprisal.

With Bourrienne playing the role of procurer as well as that of confidant, "a half-dozen Asiatic women most highly recommended for their beauty were summoned up for the general's inspection. They were all dismissed, however; their lack of grace and their obesity were displeasing to him. He had an unconquerable aversion to fat women." Napoleon's dream of fair women, as he told it to Bourrienne: "tall" (tall by a short man's standards, and so probably of medium height), "slender and graceful, in the palest gowns, walking on shadowy garden paths." Like Josephine. Like Josephine, always in white in the early days, strolling the tree-lined *allées* of Malmaison. No wonder he was disappointed in the opulent charms of the tattooed houris, disappointed in the delights of the Mohammedan Paradise as promised in the verses of the Koran, which had formed part of his precampaign curriculum of reading, the religion of a country destined for invasion being as significant to him as its history and geography.

European women were few at Cairo; few had been authorized to accompany the expedition. Lieutenant Fourès' recent bride, Pauline, had come aboard at Toulon as a stowaway, disguised in the uniform of her husband's regiment of *chasseurs*. A twenty-year-old blue-eyed blonde was the very one to catch the roving eye of General Bonaparte.

The seduction scene was pure *opéra-bouffe*. With the Lieutenant conveniently on patrol upriver, Madame Fourès was honored with an invitation to a dinner party at the palace of the commanding officer, and when her host, with skillful clumsiness, spilled a carafe of wine on her skirt, he ushered her gallantly into his private quarters to repair the damage. Upon their return to the salon, late in the evening, the happy and unblushing pair were greeted by broad smiles and applause from the assembled company.

"Gossip about the affair set headquarters buzzing," according to Bourrienne. "Pauline Fourès was certainly very pretty, but her charms were just as certainly enhanced by the fact that the sight of a woman pleasing to the European eye was a rarity in Egypt. Bonaparte would shortly install the lady in a palace adjoining his own. . . . But first, prompted by a sense of delicacy as concerned her husband, he would ship that officer off to Paris on a mission to the Directory."

It was a foregone conclusion that Fourès would spend the rest of the campaign in an English or Turkish prison. But although the vessel on which he sailed was captured, as expected, the English captain proved unaccommodating, and well aware of the romantic complication (as Bonaparte intended the world should be), he maliciously set the captive free—back on Egyptian soil. The general, at Cairo, had no choice but to order a military tribunal to hand down a divorce decree, and Lieutenant Fourès had no choice but to abide by it.

If Napoleon, in December of 1798, flaunted the liaison, certainly his mistress made no objection. As brash as he, she rode beside him in his coach-and-six or astride a white Arabian horse matching his, in a "general's" uniform gaudier than any he affected: form-fitting white pants, gold-braided sky-blue coat, sash of red and gold and a red, white and blue plumed bonnet—all to the vast amusement of the army, which nicknamed her, variously, "Madame Générale," "Cleopatra" and "Our Lady of the Orient." Less amused was Eugène:

The perfect harmony and understanding that reigned between my father and me came close to being disrupted. General Bonaparte had singled out for his attentions the wife of a certain officer, and went out driving with her in his carriage. This woman was endowed with wit and certain physical attractions. From that time on, there was talk that she was his mistress, so that my position, both as his aide-de-camp and as the son of his wife, became embarrassing. Since one of my duties was to accompany the general, who never went out without an aide, I found myself several times riding escort behind their carriage. No longer able to endure the humiliation of the situation, I went to General Berthier to apply for a transfer to another regiment. As a consequence of that application, a rather heated scene ensued between me and my stepfather; but from that moment on he discontinued his public promenades with the lady in question.

5

Meanwhile, in Paris, Eugène's mother was beset by humiliations and vexations of her own, even before the news of this eighteenth-century version of the Caesar and Cleopatra story could travel from the banks of the Nile to those of the Seine.

Josephine's only solace, on hearing it, was that no Caesarion was forthcoming. Bourrienne reported that Bonaparte had promised Pauline Fourès marriage if she produced one, and he quotes the lovers in an unloverlike dialogue: Napoleon with "The little idiot doesn't know how to have a child!"; Pauline with "Good Lord! the fault isn't mine!" The latter comment was one to undermine Napoleon's confidence in his virility and to discourage the Bonaparte family's whispers that it was Josephine's age which accounted for the three years of childless marriage.

The last year of the eighteenth century dawned most unhappily for Madame Bonaparte, for her name was linked in January to another open scandal. Now it was the Bodin Company that was in the news. The firm was in serious difficulties and Bodin himself in jail, as the result of a War Ministry inquiry into the company's shameful practices in the execution of its army contract: delivery of horses unfit for service and of meat unfit for human consumption—requisitioned, in both instances, from breeders as yet unpaid and now threatening legal action.

In behalf of Bodin's (her company and Charles's), Josephine solicited in person and by letter every friend of hers or her husband's in the Ministries of War and Marine—General Sarrazin and Admiral Bruix, among others—and, of course, Director Barras:

My Dear Barras,

A report on the Bodin Company is to be made today to the Directory, and I implore you to intervene in their favor. I hesitate to distract you from your weightier duties, but the firm is in such dire straits that it cannot survive without powerful sponsorship. I am so dependent on your friendship, dear Barras, that I frequently impose upon it, but the disposition you have always shown to oblige me seems a guarantee of your indulgence. I count on your good offices. The Bodin Company never stood in greater need.

Lapagerie-Bonaparte

To have his wife involved in a profiteers' scandal could not but further outrage General Bonaparte, who consistently deplored the abuses of the system whereby civilian companies were chartered to supply the Army and Navy with foodstuffs, apparel, field equipment and ammunition. "The scourge and leprosy of the services," he called these unprincipled army contractors in a letter from Italy in 1797 to the Directory. "Their thievery is so impudent that not a single offender would escape from justice if I had as much as a month's time to deal with the situation."

By early 1799, Josephine's security seemed threatened from every side: financially, maritally, and now extramaritally—in February a lovers' quarrel. Her relations with Charles showed signs of strain in the wake of the Bodin disgrace and bankruptcy, from which Barras had failed to save the company despite Josephine's appeals. Did Charles reproach his mistress for this? Or was it that he feared Bonaparte's return, Bonaparte's reprisals against the man now conclusively identified as his wife's lover? Paris seethed with rumor that the general was to be recalled, either officially, by the Directors, to bolster their tottering regime, or unofficially, by various subversive factions, to join in a coup d'état to seize power from the Directors' inept and rapacious hands.

Whether because of fear or of waning passion in this third year of their liaison, Charles's attitude toward Josephine in the winter of 1799 caused her a sharp pang of anguish, as is evident in this letter of hers written to him in February:*

I have arranged for Bodin's appointment with Bodard, and I now request you to advise me whether I may come to see you tomorrow at noon. I want to bring you a letter of introduction to Citizen Laumont, who is also an acquaintance of mine and who has just been appointed by the Directory as commissary of Schérer's army. Laumont has just this moment left my house, after promising me to give Bodin a courteous reception. So now I am asking you to grant me a moment of your time to speak to you on a matter of importance to me. You may rest assured that after this interview, which will be the last, you will be no further annoyed by either my letters or my presence. A self-respecting woman finding herself the victim of deceitful practices quietly withdraws, without a word. Please be so kind as to hand your reply to the bearer of this letter.

The reply (unfortunately undiscovered) so disturbed Josephine that she forwarded it in tearful indignation to her confidante, Madame de Krény, writing:

Please do me the favor, darling, of reading the enclosed letter, which has been handed to me this very moment—and then ask this person to come to you, and try to discover what motives could have prompted such a message. I find it so unreasonable, so unmerited, that I am not even taking the trouble to reply. Of course, since I

* Another of the letters discovered in the 1950s among Charles's business papers.

have done nothing with which to reproach myself, it is obvious to me that the intention is to bring about an open breach. I have the feeling that such has been the intention for quite a while, but methods more straightforward, less hypocritical, than these should have been employed. Forgive me, darling, for upsetting you with this, but you can imagine how horribly distressed I am to impose my distress on you. It is proof, as well, of how greatly I rely upon your friendship. I am so unhappy!

"So unhappy," "miserable," "unfortunate"—words to be found over and over again in her letters throughout that critical year. She could have had no feeling of security about even the roof over her head; the little house on the Rue de la Victoire, originally rented by her, had been purchased by Napoleon—in his own name, not hers—and brother Joseph undoubtedly reminded her that in the event of a divorce Napoleon intended to evict her and claim it for himself.

Josephine's purchase of the Château of Malmaison, near the village of Rueil, ten miles down the Seine from Paris, may have come as the direct result of Joseph's threats, although it is probable that those three hundred rolling acres of lawns, woodlands, vineyards and farmland bordered by the silver ribbon of the Seine had been coveted by Josephine for years, that she had admired them from the windows of the house across the river in Croissy which she had rented during the Reign of Terror. Later on, Malmaison was to be enlarged and embellished almost beyond recognition, but originally the term *château* applied to it was euphemistic; *manor house* would have been more appropriate to its rustic charm and simplicity. In no way was it so pretentious as the princely residences the other Bonapartes were presently acquiring throughout the Île de France, the beautiful French heartland environing Paris. But then, Josephine's tastes were always more appropriate and less ostentatious than theirs.

Even so, the comparatively modest investment of Malmaison represented three hundred thousand francs; and lenient as were the terms of credit extended to the wife of Bonaparte, even so, the down payment of fifty thousand francs was far beyond her means, which were currently nonexistent—her allowance having been cut off by Joseph and her revenue from Bodin's discontinued. But she was never one to allow such practical considerations to stand in her way when her eyes and heart had fastened on an object—as on Malmaison, the only one among the countless costly fancies of her life that was not a passing one.

Since she could not look for assistance to Joseph or to Bodin, there remained only Barras to be laid under contribution, but—still another of her misfortunes of the moment—their warm friendship had recently cooled. It was not only, apparently, that the Director had resented being dragged into the Bodin affair—"I would die of sorrow, my dear Barras, if I thought you had been compromised by my actions!"; it was also that some malicious friend had deliberately made trouble—"Just allow me to come face to face with that woman and you will see, my dear Barras, that my fondness and esteem for you have never wavered!" In a letter dated April 10, with the Malmaison contract drawn up and awaiting signature, she energetically followed up these conciliatory approaches: "It is so long since I have had the pleasure of seeing you, my dear Barras. I have come several times lately to the Luxembourg without finding you in. You would be most kind if you would invite me to dinner. Any day except tomorrow—just let me know which you have chosen. You well know the sincerity of my attachment."

Barras again proved the sincerity of his. When the Malmaison contract was signed on April 21, and the deed to the property delivered to its new mistress, the deposit of fifty thousand francs had ostensibly been paid, having been supplied by him—or so he claims in his memoirs, and there is no evidence to contradict him.

Josephine took possession of Malmaison at the time of year when it looked its loveliest. The gardens were nothing to compare to the splendor to which she would bring them later, but venerable chestnuts were blossoming pink and white and willows reached out tentative, delicate chartreuse streamers to the brook that meandered the greening lawn. Malmaison, her first home all her own, was in full panoply of April—and her first guest was Charles, spring having reconciled their differences.

"Monsieur Charles sojourned at Malmaison in the capacity of master—friends, as we know, being privileged characters," is the tart comment of that talented gossip Laure Permon Junot, Duchess d'Abrantès, here retailing a scandalous titbit she had heard when still a girl, "from a friend of my mother's who lived at the time in nearby Rueil":

> She told us that she used to see "Madame la Générale"—the name by which Madame Bonaparte was known to the villagers—walking late at night in the garden.
>
> "One can see into the garden from the road," said our friend Rosalie, "and in the moonlight the sight of those two figures—she in her white gown and veil, upon the arm of her son, he in somber attire, black or blue—create an effect that is nothing short of fantastic. Two phantoms, one might think! Poor woman, perhaps she wanders the shadows thinking of her first husband, lost to the Revolutionary executioners—or perhaps of her second husband (with whom a merciful Providence replaced the first), whom she may lose as well, carried off at any moment by a cannon ball. Which reminds me, Mademoiselle Laure," the pious girl exclaimed, "whatever do you suppose the general does about attending Mass over there among all those heathen Turks?"

The joke, of course, was on Rosalie, naïve as well as pious, who obviously had not heard that Madame Bonaparte's only son was off with her husband among the heathen. It was just the joke to appeal to the Permons' fellow Corsicans, the Bonapartes.

6

If General Bonaparte was not "attending Mass over there among all those heathen," neither was he worshiping in their mosques—contemporary reports notwithstanding. What was true was that his proclamation to Egypt, as to all conquered nations, carried his promise of "respect for religion, humanity and property." He had entered Cairo, literally as well as figuratively, with the Koran in one hand and Paine's *Rights of Man* in the other, announcing himself, as in Italy, the Liberator (Egypt was to be liberated from the Mameluke yoke as Italy had been from the Austrian) and reiterating "the Republican Army's pledge of friendship to the peoples it has set free. . . . We have given you liberty and you will know how to preserve it."

That neither the Italians nor the Egyptians did know how, came as a disappointment to this eighteenth-century "liberator," just as it would come as a disappointment to the would-be "liberators" of the twentieth to learn that liberty, by whatever name, is not a gift to be bestowed or a species of largesse to be distributed from across the border or across the seas.

Goethe, perhaps Napoleon's greatest contemporary, at once scientist and mystic, sought an esoteric significance in the Napoleonic epic in its relation to world history, world trends: "The story of Napoleon produces on me an impression like that produced by the Revelation of Saint John the Divine. We all feel that there must be something more in it than meets the eye, but we do not know what." From the vantage point of the twentieth century, the perspective may be better: Napoleon enunciated the words Liberty, Equality, Fraternity, the principles of the democratic process, even where he did not put them into practice, even where they were rejected, and here perhaps is the "something more" for which Goethe strained his eyes—the something more than merely a spectacular exercise in military science. Napoleon's republican armies sowed the seeds of liberty, equality and fraternity along the wide swath they cut across all Europe and into Africa and Asia Minor—in Italy, Egypt, Syria, Prussia, Poland, Austria, Russia— where feudalism and autocracy might otherwise have prevented their dissemination for another hundred years.

Napoleon's republican Army of the East in the spring of 1799 appeared hopelessly marooned, cut off from France—"imprisoned in its own conquest," as the civilian Denon saw it. But Napoleon was not the man to submit meekly to any status quo. "Imagination rules the world," he said, using Bourrienne as a sounding board for his latest improvisation: If Admiral Nelson had clamped a blockade upon the Mediterranean, then he, General Bonaparte, would march along its littoral, "through Syria, to Damascus, Aleppo, Constantinople! I shall overthrow the Ottoman Empire, found a great new Eastern dominion to assure my place in the records of posterity. It may be that I shall return to Paris through Adrianople

—or even through Vienna, annihilating the house of Hapsburg en route." And he might have done it, might have put the stupendous project into execution, but for the stubborn resistance of Syria at the walls of Acre.

General Bonaparte reluctantly raised that lengthy, costly siege in May, in time to return to Cairo to put down an insurrection, and in time to meet and defeat a mighty Turkish invasion force in a landing attempt near Alexandria on July 25.

In retaliation for Bonaparte's bloody, brilliant victory that day on the shores of Abukir Bay, the English fleet commander extended him a malevolent courtesy, the gift of a sheaf of Continental newspapers. The first to reach Egypt in months, they brought him his first news of French disasters on the Continent: retreats to pre-Revolution borders; defeats at the hand of a powerful new coalition of Austria, England and Russia; Italy lost, Malta under blockade, and the Republic of France imperiled internally as well as externally. Political conflict, civil disorder, economic emergency— "the pear was ripe," in Bonaparte's metaphor, for Bonaparte's plucking. The Directory was rotten and ready to fall; the time had come for "the Caesarean solution," for plots hatched within the national legislative assemblies by Talleyrand and the brothers Bonaparte.

On August 18, 1799, Napoleon entrusted his army—and his mistress, Pauline Fourès—to General Kléber and embarked for France with some five hundred men and a handful of his military, scientific and personal staff: Eugène, Bourrienne, and General Berthier, of course, plus Roustam, the former Mameluke slave who, for the next fifteen years, would ride at his master's side on every battlefield and stretch out at night to his full six feet and more of barbaric splendor, as a human barricade before his master's door— loyal unto death, everyone said of Roustam (although not, as it proved, unto exile).

Napoleon's two frigates slipped out of Alexandria harbor during the night and in strictest secrecy, lest the English fleet be alerted. No word filtered through to France, none to Josephine. Had she heard of the sailing, she would not have known whether to be glad or sorry; she would not have known whether France would hail her husband as savior or traitor, and, if the former, whether he would share the triumph with her. With communications so long severed, she could no more guess at his intentions concerning the government than at those concerning their marriage.

Josephine was never noted for stability, for acumen or for circumspection, but now she appeared to have lost all sense of equilibrium and decorum. There was something distraught and bewildered about her actions and reactions during that summer and autumn of '99. Avoiding her usual society, she took cover at Malmaison with only Hortense, Madame de Krény and, of course, Charles to keep her company. There had been a series of slights and snubs, those pinpricks of society to remind her of the precariousness of her position—and, even more significantly, of Bonaparte's. Talleyrand, for example, had recently turned his back upon her as a dinner partner, directing his attentions to Madame Tallien on his other side. Madame Bonaparte had been left in silence to puzzle out the interpretation: whether Talleyrand's secret service had reported Bonaparte's death in action or his decision to repudiate his wife.

There is an echo of that unhappy summer in this passage from the memoirs of Claire de Rémusat, who, as Mademoiselle de Vergennes, had been Hortense's friend and playmate at suburban Croissy during the Revolution, and who was a bride of seventeen when her path crossed Madame Bonaparte's again in that last year of the century:

> It was at Malmaison that we met again, in the course of a visit my mother and I were making at the nearby château of a friend. Naturally expansive, and at times even somewhat indiscreet, Madame Bonaparte had no sooner been reunited with my mother than she indulged in a great number of confidences about her absent husband, about her brothers-in-law—a whole world of people utterly unknown to us. Bonaparte was considered well-nigh lost to France; his wife was neglected. My mother felt sorry for her, forlorn and isolated as she was, bereft even of her son; and we showed her some courtesies and attentions of which she was never to prove unmindful. [Gratitude was one of Josephine's cardinal virtues, praised too faintly here by Madame de Rémusat, who, along with her husband, would find it a fount of blessings over the next fifteen years.]

It was at Malmaison that Madame Bonaparte showed us the prodigious quantity of pearls, diamonds and cameos which at that time comprised her jewel collection, already as fabulous a treasure as any in the *Arabian Nights*, and later to be augmented further still. A vanquished but grateful Italy had contributed to these riches—especially the Pope, touched by the consideration of the conqueror in denying himself the pleasure of flying his flags on the walls of Rome. The salons of Malmaison were sumptuously decorated with paintings, statues and mosaics, further Italian loot; it is only fair, however, to state that all the generals who had taken part in that campaign displayed a similar booty.

Surrounded by all these treasures, Madame Bonaparte often lacked the cash to pay her day-to-day expenses, and, to extricate herself from this predicament, she resorted to selling her influence in high places, compromising herself by imprudent associations.

Prey to anxiety, despairing of her husband's return, on worse terms than ever with her brothers-in-law and furnishing them steadily with all too much concrete evidence to support their accusations against her, Madame Bonaparte was tempted to make a match between her daughter and the son of Director Reubell. But that young lady refused.

Hortense, a typical youthful nonconformist, insisted at this stage that she would marry only for love. Josephine forgave her her stubbornness when Reubell *père* was shortly ousted from the government.

In need of powerful patrons, as the estrangement between Barras and herself persisted, Josephine began in June, with her usual political flair, to cultivate the friendship of Louis-Jérôme Gohier, newest member of the Directory and its next President. It may be that the fifty-two-year-old judge (a dedicated revolutionary and an incorruptible republican), in responding so cordially to Madame Bonaparte's overtures, had in mind something more than friendship. Honest bourgeois that he was, he kept a secret record of his *bonnes fortunes*, his amorous conquests or seductions, and he may have hoped to inscribe the name of the glamorous Creole—already in her lifetime a symbol of erotic fantasy—in his little black book. Gohier came to call every afternoon at four when she was in residence in Paris, returning often to the Rue de la Victoire for her evening receptions. He enjoyed the privilege of bidding his friends to her table at Malmaison, and she that of inviting hers to his Directorial headquarters at the Luxembourg.

If Gohier could not compete with the dashing and youthful Charles for Josephine's favors, he could undermine Charles's influence by advising her, as he recalls in his memoirs, to "break off a liaison which compromises you in the eyes of the world." Having made an honest woman of his cook by marrying her, the President of the Directory felt justified in moralizing. "Then get a divorce from the general!" he quotes himself as saying when Madame Bonaparte tearfully refused to heed his advice to break with Charles. "You tell me that it is only friendship you feel for each other, you and Monsieur Charles. But when a friendship is so exclusive that it leads you to violate all the conventions of society, then I must say to you exactly what I would say if it were a case of love: Get a divorce! A friendship so imperious as to exact abandon of all other sentimental attachments should requite you for all else. Believe me when I tell you that if you continue thus you will live to regret it."

Divorce Bonaparte to marry Charles? A Charles nine years her junior, twenty-six to her thirty-five, younger even than her husband, who was six years her junior? A Charles who had already shown signs of being restive, a few months earlier? A Charles presently without position, without means of livelihood? Exchange the titles of Notre Dame des Victoires and Madame la Générale for a simple, unadorned "Madame Charles"? Or it might have been Charles himself who discouraged Josephine from following Gohier's suggestion of divorce. At a moment when rumors of an imminent coup d'état were flying, it would seem the height of folly to incur the wrath of the future dictator.

Josephine floundered, pathetic in her confusion as to whom to listen to, whom to trust, what to hope for—above all, how to know her own mind, her own heart. Highly suggestible as she was, her course of action, if it could be dignified by that term, seemed to depend on the identity and perspective of the last person with whom she had consulted, whether Charles or Gohier, whether

Madame de Krény or Madame Tallien. Now, at the end of September, it was Barras again to whom she turned, writing him beseechingly on the thirtieth:

> *Please be so kind as to let me know what day during the next décadi I may see you alone—if only for a quarter of an hour. The forenoon, toward lunchtime, would be the best for me. Since I have been living in the country, I have become such a rustic, so much of a recluse, that the great world frightens me. Besides, I am so unhappy that I prefer not to be an object of pity to others. I want to see only you, my dear Barras—you who love your friends even in adversity.*
>
> *So please tell me which day you will offer me luncheon. I will come in expressly from Malmaison and can be with you as early as nine in the morning.*
>
> *I must talk with you! I need your counsel. You owe it to the wife of Bonaparte as well as to our own friendship, yours and mine. . . .*

7

Barras's counsel to Bonaparte's wife was to work toward a reconciliation with her husband and to look for his return in the not too far distant future—in response to a secret summons from the ever fearful but presently desperate Directors.

Four days later, on October 4, Josephine wrote to the general. This letter, unfortunately, is missing; but a letter to Eugène dated the same day is extant and suggests the tenor of the other, apparently one of denial (that "eternal negative" of hers) and injured innocence rather than contrition. "I think constantly of you, my dear Eugène," she wrote, "and live for the moment when I shall be reunited with all that I hold dear in this world, especially if I find Bonaparte as he was when he left me—as he should never have ceased to be!"

Crisis

But five days later, on October 9, before the courier could embark for Egypt, Bonaparte and Eugène were disembarking on the French Riviera. Eugène, as soon as he set foot ashore, rushed off a note to his mother: "The general is sending this message to you at once by special courier. We are all well and thinking of you. . . ." The news of the landing reached Josephine by a method speedier than dispatch rider. She heard it the very next day, October 10, at a dinner party at President Gohier's, as he remembers:

Madame Bonaparte was dining with me that day when a telegraphic dispatch [meaning a semaphoric telegram, a sensational innovation of 1794] was delivered to me to announce the arrival of her husband at Fréjus. She could see that this news brought me greater astonishment than joy, and said:

"Monsieur le Président, have no fear that Bonaparte comes as an enemy of liberty. What is essential, however, is that you join forces with him to prevent certain dastardly subversive factions from gaining control over him. I am going to meet him. It is important for me to reach him ahead of his brothers, who have always hated me. Not that I have anything to fear," she added, turning toward my wife. "When Bonaparte learns that it is in your company, madame, that I have spent my time during his absence, he will be flattered as well as grateful for the cordial welcome given me in your home. . . ."

Josephine sped out of Paris at daybreak the very next morning, the eleventh, without so much as a maid and with only Hortense as tender buffer against the general's predictably righteous indignation. But, early as she set out, the Bonaparte brothers were ahead of her on the road to Lyons, the easterly route through the Burgundy countryside which she knew her husband loved.

"In every town and every hamlet as we drove along," in Hortense's words, "we saw arcs de triomphe going up; and whenever we stopped for a change of horses, people crowded about our carriage to ask if it was true that the Savior was on his way—for that was the name by which all France hailed the general at that hour. With foreign reverses and internal turmoil, with the exchequer depleted and the Directory impotent and in disrepute, the nation envisaged Bonaparte's return as a blessing from heaven. His passage all the way from Fréjus to Paris was one long triumph—a sign to him, as to his enemies, of what France expected of him."

Men lined the roads to catch a glimpse of him, standing throughout the night with torches to light his way back to the capital. A tingle of joy, relief and hope raced along the network of highroads and byroads. The wave of excitement and adulation must have affected Josephine as it had Hortense, recalling to her Madame de Montesson's dictum, "Never forget that you are married to an extraordinary man!" If she had forgotten it, or never fully realized it, she felt it now, going to this encounter with him more eagerly, more yearningly, than to any before in all the years of courtship and marriage.

"But it so happened that at Lyons" (Eugène takes up the story) "Bonaparte left his companions and changed to a lighter carriage to arrive the sooner in Paris. As a perverse fate would have it, my mother had taken the easterly Burgundy route while he took the westerly, through the Bourbonnais, with the unfortunate result that we arrived in Paris two days ahead of her. Time enough for her enemies! They turned it to their advantage, seizing on the opportunity of her absence to further injure her in her husband's estimation, to poison his mind, to turn him against her."

"They" were Letizia Bonaparte, the mother, and her daughters Pauline Leclerc and Elisa Bacciocchi—Caroline being still too young to join in the attack on the hateful "interloper," the "cloying sweet," "mealymouthed" Josephine, who had usurped their place at the fountainhead of Napoleon's bounty, diverting the golden stream away from Bonapartes to Beauharnais'.

Laure Junot, as always loyal to her compatriots the Bonapartes, censures Josephine for "having failed to conciliate her mother-in-law, who might have protected her against those who sought her downfall," but with this Napoleon takes issue, contending that if no entente cordiale was ever established between his wife and mother it was not for lack of trying on the part of his wife. Josephine's unfailing fund of small talk dried up on her tongue in the presence of that taciturn and humorless matriarch; Josephine's spontaneous warmth and geniality froze before that glacier of reserve and dignity. Madame Mère (as she would be officially listed in the imperial hierarchy) might forgive her totally amoral daughters their flagrant misconduct, but no such condonation was to be expected by a faithless and—worse than faithless—a childless daughter-in-law.

At this juncture, Josephine herself had furnished her enemies the ammunition to be used against her; whatever was lacking to consolidate the victory, they could manufacture. Notified on the morning of October 16 of Napoleon's arrival, his mother and sisters converged on the Rue de la Victoire.

The general, clattering into the courtyard at 6 A.M., rushed into the house, only to find it silent and shuttered. "The effect upon him of that homecoming," says Laure Junot, "was profound and terrible: the house empty, its mistress missing. His wife's absence he interpreted"—Madame Junot is here speaking the family point of view—"as an admission of her unworthiness to come into the presence of his mother and sisters, an admission of her fear to face the man she had wronged."

His first thought was that Josephine had eloped with Charles. So Pierre-François Réal, an old family friend and an early Bonapartist in the national legislature, says Napoleon told him, adding, "The warriors returning from Egypt have this in common with the warriors who returned from the siege of Troy: their wives demonstrate the same species of fidelity." Bonaparte was talking as freely as Josephine.

For possibly the first time in his life, he gave evidence of uncertainty and confusion, taking counsel of others. The second instance of indecision on his part—and these would appear to be almost the only two—would again concern Josephine. The only area in which his superior intellect could not function alone and forcefully, then or ever, was that in which Josephine moved; Napoleon's obsession with Josephine, his love and his passion for her were not susceptible to the analysis or the logic of which he was the master. He was disillusioned but not disenchanted. She still haunted his flesh.

He went immediately upon arrival, as was the duty of a returning general of the armies, to report to the Directory—to President Gohier and to Barras. After the official business was concluded, the talk came around to the unofficial, that of the Bonapartes' domestic issue, and both Gohier and Barras pleaded Josephine's cause—Gohier out of genuine interest in his beguiling friend, Barras (who was unlikely ever to act disinterestedly) out of a conviction that his own best check on this enigmatic, ruthlessly ambitious general was through the general's wife.

"You must be philosophical about the matter," Barras quotes himself as saying.

"Advice easier to give than to take," came the reply.

More shrewd than Gohier, Barras used a line that was less a defense of Josephine's indefensible conduct than a warning on the political consequences of divorce: "The law permits divorce, but society disapproves. Divorce is a black mark against the record of a man in public office; his public conscience is judged by his private life, his personal morals. The marital status is simply one more guarantee to be offered to society by a prominent political figure."

The next day the general went to see Josephine's friend Madame Hamelin, thinking perhaps that the one giddy Creole might be led into a positive incrimination of the other, but the frivolous Fortunée could not or would not do him the service of resolving the torment of his doubts. That same day, the octogenarian Marquis de Beauharnais, Josephine's former father-in-law, paid him a visit that must have affected Napoleon emotionally—else he would not have so clearly remembered it twenty years later, when, reminiscing with General Bertrand at St. Helena, he recalled, "The old man threw himself at my feet, saying, 'Whatever her faults, forget them. Do not cast dishonor on my white head, on a family which honors you.' "

Bourrienne too served as Josephine's advocate, and to his pleas were added those of the couple's friend the banker Jean-Pierre Collot, who would finance the coming coup d'état and later the Consulate regime in its early years. Bourrienne took down the dialogue in that famous shorthand of his, devised through the years to keep pace with Napoleon's lightning-fast stream of thought and rapid-fire dictation:

"Everything is over between her and me."
"What? You mean to leave her?"
"Is it not what she deserves?"

"I cannot answer that question, but I ask you another: Is this the proper time for it? Think of France! Her eyes are on you. France expects you to consecrate all your time and thought and energies to her safety. If she sees you embroiled in domestic squabbles, your grandeur will suffer; you will become instead just another comic husband out of a Molière farce. Overlook your wife's shortcomings for the moment; put them out of your mind. If you continue to be dissatisfied with the situation, you can send her packing later, at a time when mighty concerns are not demanding your attention. But now your duty is to affairs of state. After you have ensured the Republic from disaster, you may be justified in a divorce action, but not at this hour. Besides, you are too familiar with our moral climate not to realize how important it is for you not to make your political debut on the national scene in a role that verges on the ridiculous."

Bonaparte allowed Monsieur Collot to speak so uninterruptedly that he thought he had succeeded in putting over his point, when suddenly the general broke in with a shout: "No! My mind is made up—she shall never set foot in this house again! What do I care what people say? Tongues will wag for a day or two; on the third, it will be forgotten. In the light of the momentous events that are brewing, of what significance is another broken marriage? Mine will attract little notice. My wife will go to Malmaison. I'll stay here. The general public knows enough about what has gone on not to be deceived as to the reason for the separation."

Monsieur Collot tried in vain to bring about a moderation in his attitude. Bonaparte gave vent to a stream of abuse and invective.

"Such violence on your part," said Collot, "convinces me that you are still in love with her. She will make her appearance, make her excuses, you will forgive her, and peace will be restored."

"I forgive her? You should know me better than that! If I were not sure of myself, I would tear this heart out of my bosom and hurl it into the fire!" As he spoke, Bonaparte almost strangled on his rage, and he clutched at his breast as if to tear it open.

Bourrienne claimed that Collot's eventual fall from imperial favor could be traced back to that very episode; that Napoleon never forgave the financier for having been a witness to his rare display of weakness. "Napoleon had no fondness for those people who had acquired too intimate a knowledge of certain family secrets which later, as emperor, he would choose to conceal."

The scene between Collot and Bonaparte took place in the early evening of October 18. During the night, Josephine arrived.

It had been at Chalon-sur-Saône that she discovered the mischance that had befallen her: that her husband had gone on north from Lyons by the other road, that she had missed him. Travel-weary as she was, she ordered the horses turned around at once to retrace those more than two hundred miles back to Paris. When she arrived at the Rue de la Victoire the sentry swung open the gates for her carriage, but at the porter's lodge a mountain of trunks and boxes confronted her. They were her own; her closets had been ordered emptied, her wardrobe packed, her personal possessions gathered up and crated.

Josephine emerged from the carriage and embraced Eugène on the terrace, but left him abruptly to his reunion with his beloved and loving sister and ran up the stairs to the bedroom, which she found empty except for her maid. The latter, reading the query in her face, pointed to the room across the hall, the general's study.

The door was shut, locked, bolted against her.

"She called out to Bonaparte, beseeching him to open," Madame de Rémusat says, repeating the story of that climactic night as told her, she says, by Josephine herself. "Through the closed door, the general replied that it would never be opened to her again. Then she fell to her knees and wept, imploring his pardon in her name and that of her children. But silence was the only answer. The house was hushed about her, and the long hours of the night went by in that same deathly stillness and suspense, broken only by her sobs."

With the dawn, according to another source, Josephine at last abandoned hope and admitted defeat, difficult as it had been for her to accept the fact that, for the first time in the three and a half years since their marriage, her husband was actually proof against her tears, her entreaties, pledges and blandishments. Picking herself up hopelessly and wearily from the narrow back stairs on which she had lain prostrate, weeping, sobbing, beseeching, throughout the night, she had started down the steps in final retreat when her maid came up, leading Hortense and Eugène by the hand, and urged her mistress to make one last appeal, with the children to intercede for her.

"The children's pleas," again according to Madame de Rémusat, "shook Bonaparte in his iron resolve. With a grim visage, but with reddened eyes which betrayed that he too had been weeping, the general opened his arms to embrace Eugène. Josephine and Hortense clung to his knees. Shortly afterward, all was forgiven."

Where Madame de Rémusat gives Josephine's version of the night of reconciliation, Bourrienne gives Napoleon's—the version that Napoleon, "somewhat embarrassed," gave to Collot when the latter arrived the next morning for an early luncheon appointment with the general:

"Well, Collot," he said as soon as they were alone, "well, she is here. So much the better. And it's you who have done us a great service. Yet never think that I have forgiven her. I swear to you that I have not! I ordered her out of the house when she arrived—but what could I do, Collot? Just as she was leaving, going down the stairs in tears, I saw Hortense and Eugène go after her, sobbing too. I was not born with a heart in my bosom that would be able to endure the sight and sound of weeping. Eugène accompanied me to Egypt; I have come to look upon him as my adoptive son. He is so brave, such a fine young man! And Hortense is just about to make her debut in the world; everyone who knows her sings her praises. I admit, Collot, I was profoundly stirred. I could not bear the sobs of those two children. I asked myself, should they be made the victims of their mother's failings? I reached out, caught hold of Eugène's arm and drew him back to me. Then Hortense came back up the steps with her mother. I said nothing. What was there to say? One cannot be human without being heir to human weaknesses."

"You can rest assured that the children will compensate you for your generosity, General."

"I hope so. I hope so. For it has cost me dear, this night."

According to Madame de Rémusat, the general had already been assured his compensation by the children's mother: "In the course of the explanations made to the general by Madame Bonaparte, she succeeded in clearing herself of the venomous charges made against her by her brothers-in-law; and Bonaparte, eager to avenge her, sent for Lucien at seven o'clock the next morning. Napoleon instructed that his brother be shown upstairs and into the bedroom without so much as a word of forewarning. There Lucien was greeted by the sight of husband and wife in bed together, in a state of unmistakable, total reconciliation."

8

At the crucial moment, Josephine's magic had not failed her. But even so, before she had been thus reassured, she had suffered a night-long agony of doubt and fear. The devastating experience on the stairs outside the general's study door had shocked her out of her old indifference and her old confidence in her power over him. She would never again take her husband or his love for granted as she had in the Italian honeymoon days when she had boasted that he worshiped her as if she were a divinity. She had toppled her own pedestal; the worshiper had risen from his knees, come out of his state of ecstasy. Napoleon's surrender to her on that suspenseful night of October 18 had been conditional; the condition specified was her pledge of an immediate and final break with Hippolyte Charles.

Was the condition fulfilled? The answer appears to have been Yes. Or "Yes, but." Yes, but for two disconcerting scraps of paper that have fluttered along—one out of a dusty file in the Charles family archives, the other out of a private collector's hands and autograph auction rooms—to confuse the issue. The first is a little note in Josephine's hand addressed to Charles, undated—but evidently, to judge by the reference to "Consul Cambacérès," written in the first year of the Consulate, late 1799–1800:

I am sending you [Je vous envoie] *Consul Cambacérès' reply. I have only one regret—that you did not make this request of me a* month earlier. *Not that I have wasted a moment's time attending to it, for within the hour after your letter was delivered to me I sat down and wrote both to the Consul and to the Minister of Justice. I am all the more disappointed at having failed in this mission for you in that it would have given me great pleasure to prove to you by such a service that my sentiments remain the same, that nothing can ever bring about a change, that I am bound to you by the most tender and enduring friendship. The Consul has promised me that the very first such post to fall vacant will be given to your friend* [votre ami].

"Votre ami," "Je vous envoie"—the formal *vous* and *votre*, no longer the intimacy of the *tutoiement* between them: a highly significant change of relations indicated by a highly sensitive French grammar. This, then, is no billet-doux, but only a gracious assurance of the writer's eagerness to do a favor for a petitioner with an especial claim upon her friendship; thus, technically no violation of her pledges.

The second of the two telltale scraps of paper better serves the historian who would prove that Josephine did violate her pledges to her husband: a note from Josephine to confidante Madame de Krény, again undated, and one to which it is more difficult to assign a date (whether the winter, spring or summer of 1800), except to say that it must have been written subsequent to Napoleon's return from Egypt, as is evident from the reference to Malmaison, which was not acquired until after his departure for the East.

At seven o'clock in the evening, Bonaparte decided to go to Malmaison, and to go that very same night—a plan put promptly into execution. So here I am, my darling, confined to the country for I cannot tell how long, and so bored, so sad, I could die at the prospect. Malmaison, which has always held such delight for me before, this year seems a desert. I had to leave Paris so suddenly yesterday that I did not even have time to send word to the gardener, who had promised me some flowers. Since I am absolutely determined to write to him, please tell me how to frame my message—

because, you see, I don't know exactly what arrangements you had made with him. Above all, I want to express to him my disappointment, which, I can assure you, darling, is very keen.

Enigmatic, this letter, in the true sense of the word, and so intended to be; "gardener" and "flowers" are obviously code words used by the Creole intimates to convey their secrets. But whether they refer to Charles (and, if so, whether to a tryst or to a business appointment, since Josephine and he were still involved together in the Bodin affair) or to some one of Josephine's other numerous confidential business agents and associates* (in which case the promised "flowers" might mean a cash payment owing)—whether, then, they refer to a romantic or to a financial intrigue remains a mystery, and insoluble unless further evidence is unearthed, which now appears unlikely.

Until now, beyond this cryptic scrawl of Josephine's not one scintilla of evidence or one word of valid testimony by even hostile or suspicious contemporaries points to any breach of promise on Josephine's part after her husband's return from Egypt, in regard to Charles or to any other man.

Even so, there is enough in this short letter addressed to Madame de Krény to disconcert the biographer who would make out a case for Josephine's loyalty to her husband subsequent to their reconciliation: the statements that Malmaison had become a "desert" to her (the first and only time in her life that it was not her enchanted garden) and that she was bored and sad enough to die, "confined to the country"—with only Bonaparte. The biographer must remind himself that this may have been a passing mood, a *crise des nerfs*, or that it may indicate a period of readjustment or a reaction to shock—to the abrupt severance of bonds that were no less binding for having been illicit.

> As for Napoleon [this on the authority of Laure Junot], he never uttered Monsieur Charles's name, never allowed it to be uttered in his presence. He hated Charles, and I learned of some

---

* Even Rouget de Lisle, composer of the "Marseillaise" and an old—if platonic—admirer of Josephine's, became involved in one of her clandestine army-contracting schemes, to his eventual embarrassment and public humiliation.

incidents in connection with that story which have astonished me because I had not believed Napoleon capable of such profound emotion.

One day, for example, in Paris, while Napoleon was out walking with General Duroc (these incognito expeditions across his capital were the delight of the Emperor as they were of Harun al-Rashid), they went to look at the Pont Austerlitz, at that time under construction. Suddenly Duroc felt a pressure on his arm, as if his companion was about to fall, and he noticed that the Emperor's face had paled beyond even its normal pallor. Duroc was about to cry out to summon help when the Emperor silenced him: "There's nothing wrong with me. Be quiet!" A carriage had sped past and the passenger in the carriage had been Monsieur Charles, and Napoleon had caught sight of him—for the first time since the Italian campaign. Napoleon considered the man his enemy and hated him.

So that when the subject of Napoleon's despotism is raised, the case of Hippolyte Charles should be remembered. As first consul, as emperor, at the summit of his power, Napoleon never harassed his wife's former lover, never subjected him to surveillance by the ubiquitous imperial secret police. If Charles's financial affairs did not always prosper, it was through no interference on the part of the Emperor.

The two men were destined to meet once more, during the Hundred Days that led from Elba to Waterloo. It was a face-to-face encounter, in the throne room of the Tuileries: the Emperor back from his first exile; Charles, in a court costume of puce velvet, joining in the throng of the faithful come there to pay homage, and daring to hope that old scores might have been forgotten or considered settled. But not so. Not by Napoleon. In his final exile at St. Helena he still had only contempt for the man who had been "the type of little dandy who appeals to hussies."

Laure Junot kept in touch with Charles through her husband, whom Charles, she said, loved like a brother. And so he must have, to have made Junot, in 1802, a loan of thirty thousand francs. This loan, like Charles's purchase of a handsome Paris *hôtel* and an Île-de-France *château*, would indicate that the munitioneer's affairs were then still flourishing. "It was later that he suffered sharp reverses," again according to Madame Junot. "He never married, but, in 1812, fathered a daughter, for whom he fondly hoped to arrange a good marriage and appropriate dowry. The fact that his declining fortunes prevented consummation of this project deeply grieved him, for he was a good father, a good friend—the most noblehearted man imaginable."

As his fortunes continued to decline, Charles also disposed of his Paris properties and retired to his natal village of Romans, to the life of a country gentleman and breeder of saddle horses at his ancestral Château of Génissieux. There he died in 1837, twenty-three years after the death of Josephine, who had died an empress.

The secrets of the illicit romance of Madame Bonaparte and the dashing hussar died with him, carried by him to his grave. Charles had proved to be the most gallant of gentlemen. He did not kiss and tell, like Murat, Barras or Hoche. No one could ever quote him, no word ever passed his lips or his pen. As he lay dying, her impassioned love letters to him—all those he had been able to locate—were, on his instructions, gathered up by his niece and consigned to the flames in the fireplace that warmed his death chamber. So that when Hortense, seeking to destroy whatever incriminating evidence might have survived, requested that Charles's heirs surrender all letters of her mother's in their possession, his niece could reply in all honesty that these had already been destroyed.

Charles cast a shadow over the lives of Napoleon and Josephine, a substantial one. National events, however, were moving swiftly in late 1799; the Napoleonic epic was mounting to the climax of the eighteenth Brumaire. Josephine was about to be swept up to dizzying heights, and the panorama of her former life would dwindle and fade in the distance, the figure of Charles becoming as dwarfed and hazy as all the rest. Charles would be forgotten in the splendor of the pageant and the magnitude of the adventure into which she moved as her husband's consort.

But even before the pageant and the adventure had begun, even in October of 1799 upon the general's return from Egypt, there came a marked and salutary change in the Bonapartes' relations as man and wife, in Josephine's attitude toward the general who preceded the Emperor. In the past, their marriage had been on her terms; in the future, it would be on his, and, as is the case with so many women who are submissive by nature, Josephine found that she preferred it so, that this was the condition upon which she could yield up her heart.

BOOK TWO

Josephine in Love with Napoleon

I

The Marriage

Yes, oh, yes, that is my wish, too: to please you and to love you—or, rather, to adore you.

LETTER FROM JOSEPHINE TO NAPOLEON, NOVEMBER 1803

1

"THE STORMS of the early years once weathered and blown over, the Bonapartes' marriage proved a very happy one."

The judgment was made by Antoine Thibaudeau, who had occasion to observe the couple often in the weeks following the reconciliation, being one of an ever-increasing number of politicians who beat a path to the door of the house on the Rue de la Victoire. Talleyrand and politico-journalist Pierre-Louis Roederer made pilgrimage there, too; and in the dusk of a late-October evening, says the latter, they came upon a scene of blissful domesticity: the general and his Josephine at a table before the fire, "alone in the salon, playing at backgammon" (the general, a notoriously poor player, and a gleeful and self-avowed cheat, most often returned his ill-gotten gains to this or to any other skillful opponent).

Resuming life with her, within the warm circle of her embrace, basking in the soothing ambiance that was an emanation of her serene and gentle spirit, Napoleon may have reflected—as many another has done before and since—that if a man is not so fortunate as to take a wife endowed with both virtue and good disposition, then good disposition may be the quality to shed the brightest benediction on the backgammon, the breakfast and the dinner table. Life with Josephine was an unending source of delight and refreshment to his turbulent spirit; he would speak again and again of "the infinite delight" of it, as he did to Roederer, and of "all the charm she has brought to my private life," as he would tell Talleyrand.

The note of domestic bliss in the Bonaparte menage rang true, but the air of peace and quiet in the salon of the Rue de la Victoire house was deceptive. Behind the scenes, in the general's private study, a feverish activity went on: secret comings and goings at all hours of the day and night throughout the last weeks of October and the first week of November.

Napoleon, with his keen sense of the dramatic, closeted himself in his study, shunned the spotlight, lingered in the wings, deliberately kept his audience waiting—glued to the edge of their seats—for his rare appearances. "He had laid down a rule of conduct," Bourrienne explains, "from which he never deviated during the twenty-three days that passed between his arrival in Paris and the eighteenth Brumaire. He refused almost all invitations in order to avoid unwelcome advances and indiscreet questions or answers which might be compromising to him." He nursed his glory and refused to "wear it out" in public. So all official Paris came to him— the military, the ministers of state, the representatives of the two national legislative bodies, the Council of Ancients and the Council of Five Hundred, members of the national tribunals, even some of the Directors.

It was universally recognized, by the regime itself as well as by the people of France, that the present executive branch must be scrapped, and with it the constitution, a document sacred to republican minds, but demonstrably inept, unwieldy and impractical in application. The trick was to bring about a change in the document and in the form of government without, in the process, exposing the state to civil war; to enlist the support of the two irreconcilable factions of radical left and radical right without losing the delicate balance of power to either—to the Jacobins, pressing for a return to the Terror, or to the royalists, advocating a return to monarchy.

The man of authority, of national and international reputation, the strong man strong enough to bring off such a coup d'état successfully was clearly General Bonaparte, France's acclaimed hero and savior. But in addition to having the backing of the people, the intellectual elite and the Army, he would need to rally a modicum of support within the administration itself if any semblance of legality was to be preserved and if republican sentiment was not to be outraged. And there were, to be sure, other contenders for the key position, with Directors Barras and Sieyès and Generals Jean-Victor Moreau and Jean-Baptiste Bernadotte leading the list.

The political jugglery, the machinations, the jockeying for position, the bullying and cajolery, the conniving and intriguing went on behind the closed doors of the general's study. In the salon, where Josephine presided, all was serenity and platitude as usual. As usual, she graciously greeted and entertained her guests at the appointed reception hours, on her traditional afternoons and evenings at home.

In the crucial weeks that led up to the eighteenth Brumaire, Josephine's was a minor role, but she played it to perfection, which is perhaps a capsule version of the story of her life—that, and the fact that her role in history was consistently confined to that of hostess or of mistress; her scenes, played out exclusively in the salon or the boudoir.

In the vitally important prologue to the imperial drama, Josephine proved a genuine asset to her husband, as a score of contemporary memorialists, such as Thibaudeau, Roederer, General Charles de Montigny-Turpin, Barras, Gohier, Arnault, Bourrienne and General Count Philippe-Paul de Ségur, all testify. "Josephine was in the secret," Ségur makes clear. "Nothing was concealed from her. At every conference at which she was present, her discretion, her grace, her gentle manner, her cool composure, ready ingenuity and wit were of great service. She justified Bonaparte's renewed confidence in her." Josephine reconciled, at least temporarily, all the disparate, violently antagonistic and mutually suspicious elements of the body politic involved in the conspiracy, in transit through her salon. She smoothed ruffled feathers and soothed roily waters. While General Bonaparte stormed in and out, alternating between the irresistible smile that lightened his countenance and the fierce scowl that darkened it, Josephine stood by, tact incarnate, to supply the balm of banality to punctured pride and injured feelings; hers were the soft answer, the deft and gentle touch, the healing smile and the infectious ripple of laughter in relief of tension.

Montigny-Turpin describes just such a tense moment on one of his visits to Josephine's salon, where "a distinguished and elegant company had gathered, all talking horses and fashions, and with never a glimmer of suspicion as to the momentous subjects under discussion in the adjoining room"—until the moment when the inner door burst open and a voice was heard to shout, "You do not realize that you are dealing with madmen who will end up as outlaws of the state!" The voice was Barras's; and Josephine, recognizing it, slipped away from her guests to go to him, took his arm, calmed him and quietly escorted him out.

And Bourrienne tells of a nerve-racking dinner party at the Rue de la Victoire, with an ambitious, intransigent General Bernadotte vis-à-vis an imperial Bonaparte, and with Josephine and himself "in league, on the *qui vive*, conspiring to stave off any fresh outburst of angry words between the two powerful generals."

Old friend Arnault (who had missed the Egyptian campaign, having been sent on a mission out of Malta) takes up his pen to evoke another salon scene: "Josephine on her couch, sipping tea" between President of the Directory Gohier and Minister of Police Joseph Fouché. To Gohier's inquiry of "What's new?" Fouché's reply was, "Nothing at all, still the same old talk of a conspiracy."

"A conspiracy!" Josephine exclaimed in a tremulous, incredulous tone of voice.

"Yes, that's the rumor, although I'm not so easily taken in. If there were any truth to it, there would be evidence by now on the Place de la Révolution [traditional site of the guillotine] or on the Plaine de Grenelle [traditional site of public executions]." With which words Fouché burst into laughter.

The Marriage

"For shame, Citizen Fouché," Josephine reprimanded. "How can you laugh about such matters?"

"Do not be alarmed, Citizeness," Gohier broke in. "When the Minister speaks of such things in the presence of ladies, he furnishes proof that the rumors are without foundation. Follow the example of the government, madame, and slumber peacefully tonight."

Bonaparte was listening, smiling. . . .

Old Jacobin Fouché was a member of the conspiracy; Gohier was not, could not be inveigled into it by even his fascinating friend. What Josephine did succeed in doing, however, was to lull the President of the Directory into a false sense of security, effectively neutralizing him throughout the action.

"I don't know whether Gohier was one of my supporters," Napoleon would say to Gourgaud at St. Helena, "but there is no doubt that he was paying court to my wife at the time. When I had decided on the eighteenth as the date for the coup, I was eager to entice him in, and I wanted Josephine to get him to come, on any pretext whatsoever, on the morning of that day."

"Please come, my dear Gohier, both you and your wife, to breakfast with me at eight in the morning," Josephine wrote on the night of November 8, the eve of the eighteenth Brumaire. "Do not fail me. I must talk with you on matters of the utmost importance."

"Had he come," Napoleon told General Gourgaud later, "I would have forced him, willy-nilly, to ride with me that morning. As president of the Directory, his presence would have lent our cause tremendous prestige."

But Gohier had finally smelled a rat through the attar of roses. Or Madame Gohier had, and when she arrived at the Rue de la Victoire for that early breakfast engagement and saw the courtyard full of generals in full military regalia, astride their chargers, she could congratulate herself on having prevailed on her Jérôme to stay at home.

"What you see, madame, should enlighten you as to what is taking place," Josephine told her admirer's wife. "Use all your influence to bring your husband here, for Bonaparte is most desirous that the President become a member of the new government which he is about to inaugurate. I must warn you that at this very moment Talleyrand and [Admiral] Bruix are at Barras's to secure his resignation from the Directory, and it is unlikely that he will refuse."

Nor was he able to. Cursing, under his breath, both his ingrate protégé and his ex-mistress, Barras made his exit from the national capital and the national scene under military escort. Directors Sieyès and Ducos had early joined the ranks of the Brumairian conspirators. Director Moulin and President Gohier, the incorruptibles, were put under house arrest at the Luxembourg. "The Directory has ceased to exist!" Gohier was told by Bonaparte when he protested.

With the sixty-odd generals galloping after Bonaparte down the drive of the Rue de la Victoire house, "Josephine and I were left alone," Bourrienne notes in his firsthand version of the story. "She was consumed by anxiety. I assured her that every move in the plan had been so meticulously prepared that success was certain." (He spared her some nagging doubts of his own: "Success legitimized a bold adventure which the least misadventure might have converted into a crime against the state.")

By the time General Bonaparte had reached the Tuileries Palace, the seat of the legislature, the gates were opened wide to him as newly appointed commander in chief of the nation's capital, the official guardian of the Republic. The Council of Ancients, in early session, had already so decreed, at the same time declaring a state of national emergency and recommending removal of the two legislative bodies to the palace at suburban St.-Cloud.

But overnight an element of opposition developed in the Councils, and on November 9, at St.-Cloud, the "bold adventure" was suddenly in jeopardy. General Bonaparte's address to the Council of Ancients was not effective. Oratory was never his forte, but could he actually have said what he is quoted as saying, "I am the god of war and of fortune"? Or were his words instead, "I am accompanied by the gods of war and fortune"? (Which is the way Bourrienne heard them, just before he left the hall, on the general's instructions, "to go to send a messenger to Josephine to quiet her apprehensions and to assure her that everything promised to go well.")

That was before Bonaparte had entered the Council of Five Hundred. There not even his brother Lucien, taking the rostrum as president of the Council, could protect him from bodily attack and from the cries of "Down with Cromwell!" "Down with the dictator!" "Outlaw him, outlaw Bonaparte!" Thanks to a quartet of grenadiers, General Bonaparte escaped to the courtyard, where he remounted his black charger and dispatched General Murat at the head of a company of grenadiers to clear the Council chambers. The recalcitrant deputies bolted, scattering their red togas through the gardens and woods about the palace as they ran.

The deputies who remained issued a decree establishing an executive committee of three, a Consulate—a triumvirate in the ancient Roman concept—to administer the affairs of the nation. By three o'clock in the morning, the Consuls had been nominated and had taken the oath of office. The First Consul would, of course, be General Bonaparte; Sieyès and Ducos, former Directors, would be a poor second and third.

By three o'clock [Bourrienne here resumes the narrative] the logic of the bayonet had won the day, and I followed Bonaparte into his carriage to return to Paris. Physically and emotionally spent, preoccupied with the thought of the future opening up before him, the general did not speak a word during the drive. But when he had arrived at his house in the Rue de la Victoire and had entered the bedroom to bid a good morning to Josephine, who was in bed and in a state of keen anxiety at his prolonged absence—then we began, all three, to talk. Madame Bonaparte regained her calm, Bonaparte his wonted confidence—the events of the day, of course, forming the topic of our conversation.

Josephine, who was devoted to the Gohiers, brought up the Director's name, in kindly concern.

"What would you have me do, my dear?" Bonaparte asked her. "He's an honest man, but a fool. . . . I should, perhaps, deport him. But let's drop the subject for now."

Josephine would not drop it. She pleaded her friend's cause so well that he was deported no farther than the suburbs, so well that the First Consul eventually appointed Gohier consul general at Amsterdam and awarded him the Legion of Honor, so well that the onetime President of the Directory would write of Josephine after her death as "that gracious lady who has never ceased to reign over the hearts of Frenchmen and who, during the Egyptian campaign, had no household in France more loyal to her than mine—where, moreover, her name will never cease to be revered."

"It cannot be denied," Bourrienne admits, still speaking of the Brumaire coup d'état, "that France, with an almost unanimous voice, hailed Bonaparte's accession to the Consulate as a blessing of Providence." France, weary and spent after a decade of turmoil, terror and confusion, was, says Napoleon's biographer Emil Ludwig, "like an adventuress weary of errant amours" (like a Josephine) "turning back to the arms of a strong man who can master her."

When Bourrienne was finally dismissed that morning of November 10, 1799, from the bedchamber of France's new First Consul and First Lady, it was with a smile and a handclasp and the bantering, confident reminder, "By the way, Bourrienne, tomorrow we sleep at the Luxembourg."

2

"Everything had to be created," as Bourrienne said. The entire edifice of national law, administration, finance and education awaited rebuilding. Even the social structure had collapsed. The old order had changed, but it had yielded place to a new chaos, not a new order. After eleven years of revolution, everything awaited creation by Napoleon, and to this task he proceeded with stunning speed, efficiency and wisdom. His genius was not only military but political as well; he now furnished proof of his brilliant legislative, organizational and administrative powers.

It was his credo, as he stated it, that while "the sword and the spirit are the two mightiest forces in the world, the spirit is the mightiest of the two." To the spirit of the newly enunciated rights of man he now gave definitive form. He undertook, in 1800, to codify those rights for the first time for the Continent of Europe in that Civil Code which was to exert enduring influence on the legislation of the regions into which he would penetrate as conqueror: on the law of central and southern Germany, Prussia, Switzerland and Spain, and, through Spain, on even that of Central and South America. The Code Napoléon, as it came to be called, still serves today as the main body of Civil law (of noncommercial private law in the domains of property, inheritance and family) of this fifth French Republic, having survived two empires, two monarchies, four republics and two world wars. Surviving as well, basically intact, into this century are Napoleon's administrative layout of departments and prefectures, his organizational blueprint for the composition of government ministries, his system of public education, his Bank of France and his Legion of Honor.

Ten to eighteen hours a day scarcely sufficed for the colossal enterprise upon which Napoleon was launched, the creation of a modern state, but his every leisure hour was spent with Josephine in her apartments, to which he repaired three or four times daily by the private staircase which opened off his study.

In the drafty, shabby splendor of those Luxembourg apartments, Josephine found some cause for regret at leaving her cozy, comfortable, smartly redecorated little house on the Rue de la Victoire, her former informal, casual ways and days, and her former circle of friends. Admission to the Luxembourg was by card, and those oval pasteboards were to be denied to almost all of Josephine's former associates—all the motley, raffish Directoire crew, the adventurers and adventuresses, the speculators and profiteers along with their wives and/or mistresses, all the ladies of easy virtue and dubious reputation; even divorcees were to be denied entree to the new Consular society which was taking shape at the First Consul's direction. Josephine doubtless shed copious tears at dropping the name of her "little darling" Thérèse Tallien from the new guest list. (By then the beauteous Madame Tallien had deserted her lover Barras—for whom she had earlier deserted her husband—to take up residence with banker Ouvrard, to whom she would unblushingly present a love child every year in the course of the next four or five.) Of all Josephine's former intimates, only Madame de Krény survived the purge, and she only because her lover Denon was, in

Napoleon's words, "one of my Egyptians"; he was also Napoleon's candidate for the post of curator of the Louvre Museum, which would be crammed with European art treasures discriminatingly selected by Denon as he traveled in the rear guard of his imperial patron's invading armies.

One of the most astonishing facets of Napoleon's mind was his capacity for infinite detail and infinite scope and variety in his designs. Now, during the Consulate, he dictated fashion as well as society. Both were to be reformed; both, suddenly respectable. He had had enough of the gauzy, flimsy shifts and tunics of Greek and Roman goddesses; furthermore, the rage for sheer India muslins benefited the British trade, while the heavy, lustrous French silks and satins went begging. Napoleon resorted to a startling object lesson and to the power of the government-controlled press to publicize it, putting over the point to the ladies of the nation in a spring issue of *Les Variétés*:

> On the occasion of a recent reception at the Luxembourg, the First Consul ordered the fires stoked higher and higher, until one of the footmen observed that it was impossible to cram more logs into the fireplaces. "Very well, then," Bonaparte replied in a voice to resound throughout the gallery. "I wanted to be sure to get it warm enough, because the weather is cold and these ladies are practically naked."

A second editorial blast followed in the Consular news organ, *Le Moniteur*: "Bonaparte has voiced his displeasure at the sight of naked women in his salon. . . . The ladies today are dressing to please the First Consul."

Certainly this was true of his wife, who, the Countess de Chastenay was to recall, "trembled like a leaf" at his frown. But, though she complied with his edict, she must secretly have deplored it. Had not Madame Despaulx, Paris' oracle of fashion, declared that nudity was "the most elegant and the most dressy of all fashions," and had not nudity been vastly becoming to Madame Bonaparte?

Josephine's concessions in the fields of fashion and friendship were reciprocated by Napoleon with a concession of his own: he

Malmaison, seen from the garden side. A contemporary print. [BIB-
LIOTHÈQUE NATIONALE, PARIS]

Coronation Procession of NAPOLEONE the 1st Emperor of France, from the Church of Notre Dame, Decr. 2d 1804.

| blican ession | Puisant Continental Powers, Train-Bearers to the Emperor | Ladies of Honor. (without Petticoats) — Train Bearers to ye Empress ye the Empress Josephine. | His Imperial Majesty NAPOLEONE ye 1st | His Holiness Pope Pius VII conducted by his old Faithful Friend; Cardinal Feish. offering the Incense | Talleyrand-Perigord. — Prime Minister & King at Arms bearing the Emperor's Genealogy |

Cartoon of the Coronation by Gillray. [BRITISH MUSEUM, LONDON]

Le Sacre de Napoléon (detail), by David, the official painter of the Imperial Regime. David, an eyewitness of the Coronation from his place of honor in the tribune, worked on the vast painting for three years. He made individual portraits of every figure, gave detailed study to the costumes and accessories, and reconstituted the choir of Notre Dame in a pasteboard model complete even to the original lighting effects. See pages 278 ff. [MUSÉE DU LOUVRE, PARIS]

Divorce of Napoleon and Josephine. Engraving by Chasselat roman-
ticizing the last supper of Josephine and Napoleon at the Tuileries:
Count de Bausset lifts the Empress from the floor where she has fallen in a faint upon hearing the Emperor's decision to divorce her. See
page 332. [BIBLIOTHÈQUE NATIONALE, PARIS. PHOTOGRAPH BY GIRAUDON]

The Empress Marie Louise with the King of Rome. Painting by
Gérard, from the Château de Versailles. [BETTMANN ARCHIVE]

Josephine in 1802. Engraving, after the portrait by Gérard. [BIBLIOTHÈQUE NATIONALE, PARIS]

19th-century lithograph of the scene in Josephine's death chamber at Malmaison in 1814: her children, Eugène and Hortense, weeping beside her canopied bed; in the foreground, her friend Alexander, Czar of Russia. [PHOTOGRAPH BY GIRAUDON]

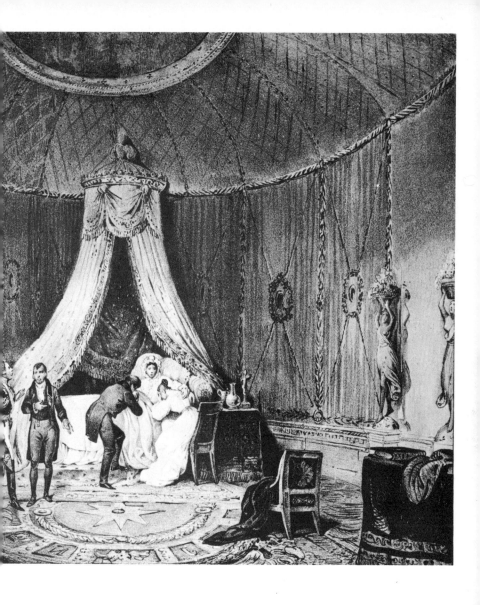

Aerial view of Malmaison as it appears today. [MUSÉE DE MALMAISON]

resolutely discarded his Egyptian-campaign mistress, refusing so much as to see Madame Fourès upon her return to France (he delegated General Géraud Duroc to arrange a generous financial settlement). "Napoleon was too newly reconciled with Josephine and too deeply immersed in serious and important labors to admit of any distraction," in the opinion of Laure Junot, whose (future) husband had sailed from Alexandria with the blond "Cleopatra." If the name of Hippolyte Charles ever came up between the Bonapartes after their reconciliation, Josephine had found a silencer: "She used the name of Pauline Fourès to great effect in any domestic altercation," says Madame Junot. Still, Josephine could not have been entirely resentful of the Egyptian liaison, which had been a contributing factor to Napoleon's decision against divorce; that childless liaison with Pauline Fourès had led him to suspect that he, rather than Josephine, might be responsible for the childless marriage. And Josephine would assiduously confirm him in that suspicion. All the same, she insisted that Pauline be banished—though to no great distance, as it developed, but merely beyond the city limits, to a pleasant house in a pleasant Paris suburb.

"Josephine would have given her husband no peace, no respite, had Madame Fourès been permitted to live in the capital." Could Madame Junot be speaking of Josephine? Of Josephine the gentlest of creatures, the model of wifely docility? Josephine was "always amiable," as Napoleon would tell her in a letter in 1807, "except when she is jealous—and then she becomes a female demon!" In only two areas did she, the most submissive of women, ever dare to oppose her husband, the most domineering and aggressive of men: she protested his infidelities and she persisted in her extravagances.

As swiftly and efficiently as the First Consul had dealt with France's disordered finances, he could never cope with Josephine's chronic insolvency, could never control her compulsive buying and her passionate collecting. "Josephine's mania for spending was almost the sole cause of her unhappiness," Bourrienne noted regretfully in 1800. "Her creditors were grumbling, and this brought about a highly unfavorable reaction in Paris."

When the grumbling reached Napoleon's ears, Bourrienne was instructed to extract an exact accounting of the state of her indebtedness from Josephine—who implored him not to press her.

"No, no!" she cried in a tone of terror. "No, I cannot admit to the full amount—it's too tremendous. He would make a terrible scene. I shall admit to only half of it."

"Madame," I replied, "your husband knows you owe a large sum, and is prepared to pay it. As for the scene, it will be just as terrible for half the amount as for the whole."

"No," she insisted. "I can never bring myself to tell him. I owe, as best I can determine, some 1,200,000 francs. You must not mention, however, more than 600,000—that's enough for the moment. I'll pay the rest gradually, out of my savings."

"Madame, it is my opinion that the Consul will be as outraged at the 600,000 as at the 1,200,000, so why not get it over with now, once and for all?"

"I dare not, he is so violent! I know him, Bourrienne, and I cannot stand up under his rages!"

Bonaparte suspected that his wife was not being completely honest in her estimate, but he confined himself to instructing me, "Take the 600,000 francs, pay off her creditors, and let me hear no more about it."

Madame Bonaparte gave me all of her bills. The overcharges were fantastic, due to the tradesmen's fear of delay in payment and of deductions to be demanded later.

Bourrienne was shocked at "one milliner's bill for thirty-eight costly hats in a single month," but concluded that "the same system of highway robbery prevailed throughout. Most of the creditors were well content to settle for fifty per cent of the figure of their original statements, their merchandise having yielded a handsome profit even at half price! . . . In the end, I was fortunate enough to settle all claims for 600,000 francs. Madame Bonaparte, unfortunately, soon relapsed into the same reckless squandering."

It was good friend Madame de Rémusat's interesting theory that "Napoleon secretly encouraged those close to him to go into debt, for the reason that their dependence on him increased in direct ratio to the increase in their indebtedness. On this score, his wife must have given him complete satisfaction. He never really wanted to clear up her financial involvements, because that would have deprived him of such fine opportunities to harry and discomfit her. . . . He enjoyed—and the words are his—'keeping people breathless,' that is to say anxious. He took a secret pleasure in exciting fear."

Laure Junot recalls a scene that tends to confirm Madame de Rémusat's theory. Visiting the Bonapartes one day, Laure heard Napoleon issue instructions to his wife to appear at her "dazzling best in jewelry and costume" upon a certain occasion. When she failed to reply, he pressed the point with a pointed "Do you hear me, Josephine?"

"Yes," Madame Bonaparte replied, "but then you will reproach me, or even go into a tantrum and refuse to approve payment of my purchases."

She pouted, but prettily, like a little girl, and with the utmost good humor. She looked at him so sweetly, approached him with such grace, the desire to please him shining so unmistakably bright in her eyes, that he must have had a heart of stone to have resisted her.

Napoleon, who loved his wife, drew her close and embraced her. "If I sometimes refuse to pay your bills, my darling, it is because you are so often imposed on by your tradesmen that I cannot conscientiously sanction the abuses. But there is no inconsistency in my urging you to look magnificent on state occasions. One interest must be weighed against the other, and I merely try to maintain the balance, equitably if strictly."

The state occasion he had in mind might have been the first formal reception at the Tuileries Palace.

By February of 1800, Napoleon had submitted the new constitution to the people and seen it endorsed by an overwhelming majority in the national referendum. Before the end of that month, the First Consul removed from the Luxembourg to the palace of the Bourbons—from which he had himself seen them evicted by the mob on that fatal August day only eight years earlier. He did not remove the sign at the Tuileries entrance gate which read: "August 10, 1792—Royalty in France is abolished and shall never be re-established"; but he ordered the renovation of the apartments of the ill-fated monarchs and the removal of the vandals' marks that defaced the walls, and he had the bloodstains scoured from the parquet floors where the Swiss Guards and the defending noblemen had fallen in the August massacre.

The First Consul occupied the suite of Louis XVI on the second story; Josephine, that of Marie Antoinette on the ground floor, directly below. "A bed of state—though not that of Louis XVI—was installed in the bedroom of the former monarch," relates Bourrienne, who had moved his desk from the Luxembourg to the Tuileries study, alongside that of the First Consul, "but I may as well make clear that Bonaparte seldom occupied that bed. He was quite simple in his tastes and in his private life, resorting to pomp and circumstance only as a means of impressing the general public. At the Luxembourg, at Malmaison and at the Tuileries during the early years, the First Consul always slept with his wife. Every night he went down to Josephine by a small interior staircase leading from a closet off his study, which had formerly served as the oratory of Marie de Médicis."

The rabbit warren of the Tuileries, with its complex of back staircases, its dark corridors and its endless series of high-ceilinged rooms, was vaster, darker and even more uncomfortable than the Luxembourg. "It's depressing," Roederer commented on his first visit to the First Consul. "Yes," the latter agreed, "like all grandeur."

It was even more depressing to Josephine. "I remember the sadness that overwhelmed my mother during our first days at the Tuileries," Hortense wrote in her memoirs. "She was obsessed with the thought of Marie Antoinette, saw her tragic figure everywhere. The palace was haunted for me too by the Poor Queen, for Madame Campan had told me so many harrowing stories of her royal mistress's last tragic hours there." (Hortense's teacher had been Marie Antoinette's first lady of the bedchamber.) "My mother upset me when she said, 'I know I shall not be happy here. The darkest presentiments came over me the moment I entered.'"

Having a flair for décor as for clothes ("the former discriminatingly selected as a backdrop for the latter, the color scheme of the one designed to harmonize with that of the other"), Josephine relieved the gloomy splendor with mirrors, color, and masses of her beloved flowers; the talented Madame Bernard was appointed palace florist, with a standing order for fresh bouquets to be delivered daily to fill the Sèvres urns and vases on every marble console. The Salon Jaune, the main reception room, went gay with yellow and leaf-brown satin and splashes of bright-red fringe. Josephine's inner sanctum of bath, boudoir and dressing room (where five hours out of her every twenty-four were spent) had been completely renovated, redecorated in the height of fashion, and lavishly mirrored for a lady who indulged in meditation—or, rather, reflection—only in front of a triple pier glass. For their bedroom she had chosen a color scheme of blue and white with a flurry of gold fringe, and an Egyptian motif in compliment to the conqueror of the East.

There Napoleon awaited her on the night of February 17, after the last of the guests attending the first of the Tuileries receptions had departed, after Josephine had dismissed her maids and emerged from her elaborate dressing-room ritual. (She was "as elegant at her bedtime toilette," he would reminisce to General Bertrand at St. Helena, "as for a public appearance—all charm and grace in bed as elsewhere.")

He pulled a stool up to the massive mahogany bed ornate with gilded bronze, set back in its alcove, and said with a smile (as Madame de Rémusat had the story "from his wife herself"), "Come, little Creole, step up into the bed of your masters!"

3

The period of Napoleon's love delirium was over, the crescendo of passion and rapture past, in this fourth year of their marriage. But a deep devotion and an infinite tenderness had come in their stead. Both husband and wife had made concessions and adjustments in the wake of the storms that had beset the early years.

Josephine was his perfect mate temperamentally as well as physically, melting as smoothly and adeptly into his moods as into his arms. She had become profoundly necessary to him. He turned to her for comfort, sympathy, diversion; above all, for relaxation from the terrible tensions that racked him. The human frame could not comfortably contain the ferment of his genius. His distress was manifest in his ceaseless pacing, in his rapid and jerky step, in the nervous twitch of his right shoulder, in the tic that pulled at his mouth, in his explosive rages. Tension was evident in the way he bolted his food and writhed with intestinal spasms; in the way he teetered backward and forward in his chair or hacked at its arms with his penknife; in the way he kicked at the logs in the fireplace, scorching his boots and scattering sparks across the Aubussons.

In an age whose pharmacopoeia boasted no synthetic tranquilizers, Napoleon sought relaxation for his taut nerves in a daily routine of scalding-hot baths (as often as twice or three times daily, or in the middle of the night, and for two hours at a time; the tub was kept filled and ready around the clock) amid clouds of steam so thick that Bourrienne could scarcely see to read the reports and dispatches to him. Napoleon sought relief, Madame de Rémusat notes, in "consciously induced revery in a darkened room, the sconces draped with gauze," and to the accompaniment of mood music in a monotony of theme and rendered *pianissimo;* or of faintly melancholy poetry read, preferably, by Josephine.

Above all, for surcease from that terrible tension, he turned to Josephine, to the unruffled pool of her serenity. The compound of her physical and emotional languor and the happy vacuum of her mind constituted the perfect anodyne to Napoleon's restless spirit. She was his nepenthe, his most effective tranquilizer. Laure Junot saw and even admitted it: "Josephine's hold over Napoleon was firmly established, and there was more to their relation than mere force of habit. It was her essentially bland personality, her gentle and tender nature, which, for a man like Napoleon, constantly agitated, harried by the intensity and immensity of his thoughts, provided an Eden, a sanctuary of repose."

It was Josephine he summoned, when he left his study at night, to come to read him to sleep in that mellifluous, melodic, deliciously soothing voice of hers; and she deserted all the guests in her salon and left her game of billiards, whist, or backgammon to rush to his bedside upon his summons. It was Josephine who diverted him at luncheon or at dinner with her frivolous prattle, her soufflé of scandal concocted expressly for his delectation.

"If he had so much as a few free moments between conferences or appointments, he came to spend them with Josephine, often rushing in unannounced across the terrace, at the Palace of St.-Cloud," according to Claire de Rémusat. If he found guests in Josephine's apartments, he glared and turned on his heel. He would leave the council table or his desk in bodily fatigue and mental stress and strain, and come clattering down his back staircase to seek out Josephine. He loved to visit her at the dressing table, charging in like a bull in a china shop, upsetting crystal perfume bottles, overturning trays of laces and feathers, and "turning her jewel cases topsy-turvy," as her first maid Mademoiselle Avrillon tells it; "hovering over her and giving her love pats (preferably on the shoulder) sharp enough to bring tears to her eyes, although her only reproach, in that soft, sweet drawl, was a mild 'Have done, now, Bonaparte, have done!' "

Josephine came to play a second important role in Napoleon's life and destiny, that of the ideal consort to the head of state, for her social talents complemented his political genius. She was the catalyst in the Consular court for those embittered, internecine political factions compelled by her husband into service in the Consular council chamber. Emerging from the Revolutionary strife *persona grata* to both parties, royalists and Jacobins, to the Old Regime and to the new, she was singularly qualified to reconcile the irreconcilable.

"Having attained to the Consulate, Bonaparte derived a vast advantage from the conciliatory and gracious qualities of his wife, who attracted to his court a great number of people who would otherwise have been offended or frightened off by his natural brusquerie," as Madame de Rémusat analyzed that formative era.

To which Bourrienne agreed: "Josephine's was the rare talent of putting people at their ease, making each person feel that he had been singled out for her especial welcome. By the magic of her cordiality, her consistently good humor, all was gaiety and relaxation in her company. With Bonaparte's entrance, a sudden change came over the room; every eye turned anxiously to read his mood in his expression—whether he was to be taciturn or talkative, gloomy or genial. His manner was imposing rather than pleasing; those who did not know him well were overcome with an involuntary sense of awe in his presence. He possessed all the attributes for being what society terms 'an agreeable man'—all save the desire to be one."

Again, on the international level—where it was essential that France regain her social prestige, as she had regained her military and political—Josephine was useful. With the success of the very first glittering reception she tendered the diplomatic corps in her Tuileries apartments, Napoleon was assured of realizing his ambition to make the French court once again the arbiter of elegance for all Europe, all the world. From that day on, it became standard procedure to usher the ambassadors and ministers from the Consular audience chamber to the salons of the wife of the First Consul, in the Versailles tradition of presentation to the Queen after presentation to the sovereign.

If the tradition of Versailles was to be revived, it was up to Josephine to show the way—with pointers from Madame Campan and Madame de Montesson. And even though Josephine had lived only on the fringes of that exalted world, she seemed instinctively to know her way through the labyrinth of royal etiquette. She would have to shape the Consular court out of Napoleon's crude, predominantly military entourage. Her Tuileries luncheon parties would serve as a finishing school for the unsophisticated young brides of her husband's young officers—among them Laure Junot, who remarked that under Josephine's tutelage "those timid girls acquired the confidence to take their place in a society superior to any they had known."

In addition, it was Napoleon's enlightened policy—his "policy of fusion," as he called it—to reintegrate the noble and aristocratic element into the classless new society, into the economic and cultural fabric of the new Republic, and to encourage the return of the *émigrés* to France by the promise of *la radiation*, the erasure of their names from the list of the proscribed "enemies of the Republic." To head this committee of mercy, he could have made no happier choice than Josephine, whom he encouraged to render publicly now a service she had been rendering privately for years.

The Marriage

Among the dossiers of the forty thousand expatriate families who would return to France under the Consulate and the Empire, there is scarcely a one which does not contain a note, a memorandum or a recommendation in the hand of Josephine.

"Noblemen with names too proud and memories too bitter to approach the First Consul directly besieged Madame Bonaparte instead with their petitions for *radiation* and for restoration of property confiscated by the state. She received them all with the utmost courtesy and seemed never to weary of listening to their tales of woe. She served as the original link between the French nobility and the Consular government." Madame de Rémusat's observation is echoed almost word for word by Napoleon. "Josephine served as my bond with a large and important segment of society," he told Las Cases at St. Helena. "My marriage . . . put me in touch with a whole party which was essential to the success of my policy of fusion."

From the burden of affairs of state and the constraint of state occasions at the Tuileries, Napoleon escaped to Malmaison—"looking forward as eagerly to his weekends there as a schoolboy to his holidays," in the words of Bourrienne, an indispensable member of the Consular entourage. As for Josephine, Malmaison was where she always longed to be, her enchanted ground, her intensely personal property. In the fleeting fifteen years in which she reigned in that bright and happy realm, she made it forever and indelibly her own. She is the immortal chatelaine of Malmaison, never to be exorcised; her warm and delicate touch pervades even the chill of the national monument it has become, her elegant and graceful hand is still discernible in the shapes of earth and water, wood and stone, bronze and marble which were its creation.

It was Napoleon, with his practical bent of mind, who extended the domain by hundreds of acres—farms and fields for revenue, forests for lumber or hunting preserves. But the lavish embellishments and the interminable, incalculably costly landscaping projects were the follies of Josephine: streams made to flow where rivulets had trickled; miles of garden path winding past pools and fountains, across stone and wooden bridges, beside flowering meadows and through grottoes adorned with marble gods and goddesses; the Temple of Love; the Lake of Cucufa; the menagerie; the

Swiss village with its herd of Swiss cows and its Swiss cowherd in picturesque Swiss costume; and those internationally renowned Malmaison hothouses with their brilliant exhibits of specimen trees and plants—rare and exotic blooms sent from the four corners of the earth in tribute to the earth's most celebrated florimanist, Madame Bonaparte.

"Nowhere, unless perhaps it was on the field of battle, have I ever seen Bonaparte as happy as in the gardens of Malmaison," was Bourrienne's curious reflection. It was a radiantly youthful and happy company that gathered there from Saturday to Monday during the radiantly bright and promising early years of the Consulate: Eugène and Hortense de Beauharnais, Jérôme and Caroline Bonaparte, all in their teens; the aides-de-camp in their twenties, dashing bachelors or recent grooms parading pretty young brides (like Junot with his Laure); all reveling in boisterous outdoor games—leapfrog and prisoners' base were the favorites—in which the First Consul joined exuberantly. "For Napoleon, one of the greatest delights of those recreational periods was to see us running beneath the leafy arches of the trees, all dressed in white [Junot's Laure among them]. Nothing else touched him like the sight of a graceful woman in a white gown. Josephine, well aware of this preference, almost always wore India muslin, filmy as a cloud. Indeed, in general, the white dress was a uniform for the women at Malmaison. . . . Napoleon loved that spot with a passion!"

In inclement weather the house party played at charades or trouped into the billiard room, where Josephine reigned as champion. On balmy spring and summer evenings the vogue was for dinner alfresco, on the broad green lawn onto which the French windows of the château's garden façade all opened. "And after dinner," Hortense reminisces fondly, "the First Consul always took my mother's arm, to lead her away from the others for a long stroll through the gardens." Hortense and Bourrienne shone as the brightest stars of the amateur theatrical company, whose performances became so popular that the First Consul replaced the original makeshift theater with a permanent structure seating two hundred, a separate building adjoining the Long Gallery, which was already a treasury of Italian and Egyptian art. From the Little Gallery, music sounded through Malmaison for dancing or for listening—with Hortense, who was a singer, a pianist and a composer, again the most accomplished artist. Josephine's great golden-eagle harp dominated the music room. Her repertoire may have been limited to a single melody, as Méneval caviled, but even he admitted that she was a vision of grace and loveliness when she took her place at that instrument.

Or on the dance floor, to which the First Consul led her to open the formal balls. A gasp of delight went up the night she appeared in her "rose-petal gown": hundreds of fresh rose petals of palest pink, scattered and tacked to cover and perfume every fold of the gleaming white satin—an ephemeral creation to make the enduring reputation of *couturier* Leroy. Those Sunday-night balls were the highlight of the summer season during the first years of the Consulate. A stream of carriages from Paris poured into the Malmaison courtyard, a hubbub of distinguished guests into the entrance hall, with its stately columns, its black-and-white checkered marble floor and its exotic aviary.

These were the halcyon days at Malmaison. "Malmaison was a delicious spot," in Hortense's recollection, while the Tuileries was "dismal," and Hortense begged to be permitted to stay on at Madame Campan's in St.-Germain instead of returning with the family to Paris.

When Josephine made tearful lament at the thought of her daughter's defection, her husband affected jealousy:

> He pulled my mother to his lap [as Hortense sketches the tableau], holding her fast in his arms, accusing her, in a tone half serious, half teasing, of "loving your children more than you do me."
>
> "Not so," my mother replied. "You cannot doubt my devotion, but without my children around me my happiness is incomplete."
>
> "What can be lacking to it," the Consul inquired, "with a husband who loves only you (and a pretty good husband, as husbands go) and with children who afford you only pleasure? Come, now, admit that you're a very lucky woman!"
>
> "You're right, it's true—I am," my mother conceded, all smiles, whereas a moment before she had been all tears.

4

And Josephine would indeed have considered herself very lucky at this period, had not the Bonapartes persevered so relentlessly in their troublemaking.

Josephine hoped, though vainly, to secure at least two allies in the Bonaparte camp when she encouraged the romance between Caroline and General Murat. Unlike Hortense, young Caroline burned to marry; but then, she was passionately in love with that boisterous, flamboyantly handsome, ferocious warrior. Murat's ego was exceeded only by his libido, but Napoleon might have spared himself anxiety on that account: his little sister, for all her fair and delicate beauty—her complexion, says Laure Junot, was "like white satin seen through rose-colored glasses"—was a true Bonaparte, lusty, insatiable. Napoleon objected, too, on the ground that Caroline might aspire to a more brilliant alliance, but it was Bourrienne's opinion that Bonaparte's objection stemmed primarily from an old resentment, dating back to the Italian campaign, to Murat's bragging reference to his flirtation with Madame Bonaparte; and that when Bonaparte finally consented to the match, it was upon the reasoning that his wife could have no further romantic interest in a man whose suit for another woman's hand she forwarded.

Josephine, then, could congratulate herself on her influence with her husband when the Murat wedding was celebrated in March of 1800. Until, that is, she saw the gift Napoleon presented to the bride: a magnificent diamond necklace belonging to Josephine. By an entirely feminine logic, she felt justified in replacing her diamonds with pearls, a superb collection once the pride of the last Queen of France. The price of 250,000 francs was staggering to a woman so recently insolvent, and to finance the purchase she resorted to the ugly old expedient of clandestine trafficking in army contracts.

But with the Marie Antoinette pearls "in her jewel case for more than a fortnight," Josephine had still not screwed up her courage to wear them in public and brave her husband's inquisition, and she turned to Bourrienne for help:

"There's to be a large party here tomorrow, Bourrienne," she said to me, "and I simply must wear my pearls. I beg you, don't leave my side—then, if my husband asks where I got the necklace, you can back me up in my statement that it's one I've had for ages. . . ."

Nothing escaped Napoleon's eagle eye, and everything happened as Josephine had foreseen. "How lovely you look tonight!" the First Consul exclaimed at first sight of her. "But aren't you wearing a new ornament? I don't think I have seen those pearls before."

"Good heavens, Bonaparte, it is the necklace given me by the Cisalpine Republic years ago. Ask Bourrienne, he will tell you."

"Well, then, Bourrienne, do you remember having seen these pearls before?"

"Yes, General, I remember having seen them," I could say without violating truth, since Josephine had previously shown them to me.

If Josephine sometime violated truth—"prevaricated," as Napoleon objected—then "it was a trait which she had acquired from her husband," Madame de Rémusat countered. "It was he who taught her to practice deceit, as well as to mistrust other people's motives."

But the necklace affair was forgotten in May, in the midst of military preparations. Napoleon was smarting under the steady Austrian advances in Italy and the gradual loss of his earlier conquests there. "My power depends on my glory, and my glory on my victories," he told Bourrienne.

Crossing the Alps in early May of 1800, in a logistical maneuver as original and daring as Hannibal's two thousand years before, Napoleon wound up his whirlwind thirty-day campaign with the resounding victory of Marengo. From the battlefield he addressed the vanquished Hapsburg in a tone amazingly pacifistic and conciliatory for the pen of a victor: "Let us give our generation peace and tranquillity." Furthermore, he seemed sincere, to judge by the generosity of his terms, although in the very next breath he was telling Bourrienne, "Were I to die tomorrow, ten centuries hence all my accomplishments would not take up so much as half a page in a world history."

France made a triumph of his homecoming. In Paris, in the

courtyard of the Tuileries, voices rang out in endless *vivats*—"acclamations as sweet in my ears as the sound of Josephine's voice," he said happily to Bourrienne. And yet, in Milan, he had just taken himself a mistress. La Grassini, *prima donna assoluta* of La Scala, had raised her glorious voice again to hail the Liberator, as she had in 1796, and this time Napoleon, no longer an ardent and dedicated bridegroom, no longer resisted either the appeal of the voice or that of the woman. Bourrienne, upon a summons to the general's bedside the morning after the gala performance, was presented to the famous star and charged with the arrangements for her transportation to Paris and her installation in a pleasant residence on the Rue de la Victoire.

Via the whispering gallery of the Tuileries, the news was not long in reaching Josephine. Her reaction was frantic. In the throes of her first acute attack of jealousy, that malady which in time would prove to be chronic, she sent off a pathetic appeal to her confidante Madame de Krény:

Darling, I am miserably unhappy. Every day I go through another terrible scene with Bonaparte. They seem to come about over nothing. I just can't go on living like this. In an attempt to find out what could have accounted for it all, I learned that a week ago La Grassini arrived in Paris. Obviously it is she who has caused me all this anguish. As far as I'm concerned, I assure you, darling, that I have not been guilty of the slightest fault. I would tell you frankly if I had. Would you please send your Julie to try to discover where that woman is living, and whether he goes there to her or she comes here to him?

It was a sordid method to which Josephine resorted—setting her friend's Julie or her own maids and lackeys to spy on her husband —but it was a sordid situation with which she had to deal. As time went on, a whole procession of singers, actresses and outright adventuresses would be smuggled into the Tuileries Palace by the panderers—the valet Constant, future "Grand Marshal of the Palace" Duroc, brother-in-law General Murat, Foreign Minister Talleyrand—to meet the master of France in a special suite reserved for assignations and kept prepared with fresh flower arrangements on order daily from the palace florist, as for the state apartments.

Josephine had not long to anguish over *l'affaire* Grassini. That temperamental and tempestuous diva was not one to suffer long or patiently Bonaparte's highhanded methods and his cavalier treatment of women—his brief and random visits, under cover of darkness. Within a matter of months she had flown the police-patrolled love nest on the Rue de la Victoire to elope with a fellow artist and countryman and ostensibly a more gallant lover, the violinist Rode. La Grassini had been among the first to learn that the life of a mistress to Napoleon was anything but glamorous.

Napoleon's sexual appetites were as "terrible" as those of "the terrible Bourbons," his predecessors on the throne of France, but he vowed never to follow their precedent of taking "official" mistresses, of glorifying and flaunting his women in the public eye. There was to be no Montespan, no Pompadour, no Du Barry in Napoleon's career; no mistress of Napoleon's could ever dispose of a vestige of political power or influence, or look forward to any prominence at court or any prestige—only to a series of furtive assignations and a generous financial settlement.

As the year 1800 rolled on, Josephine's alarms were to be excited by other, graver causes: continuing attempts on her husband's life and growing talk of the need for the designation of a successor —either an appointee or a natural heir—to save the nation from civil war in the event of the First Consul's assassination or his death on the field of battle. She shuddered at the thought that he was the target of both Jacobins and royalists, seeking to profit in a political vacuum, in anarchy. All through the summer and autumn came reports to disconcert her: a conspiracy to attack the First Consul in his opera box, thwarted by the police at the eleventh hour; ambushes narrowly avoided on the road to Malmaison; the contents of Napoleon's snuffbox poisoned. And in December she was shaken literally as well as figuratively by the "infernal machine" that exploded minutes after Napoleon, en route to the Opéra in his carriage, passed the street corner where it had been planted. Josephine, in a second carriage with Hortense and Caroline, arrived on the scene only moments after the explosion, which killed seven persons less fortunate in their timing and wounded twenty-five. Fearing that Napoleon had been caught in the blast, she "screamed and fainted dead away," by Hortense's account. Revived and reassured by an officer of Napoleon's staff that her husband had arrived safely at the Opéra, Josephine struggled to recover her composure before joining him, but in vain; her fright was evident in her face, white under her rouge, her features drawn. Napoleon, however, being no stranger to the experience of hostile fire, needed only the sight of his wife and family entering the box to regain his usual icy calm. Calmly sending for a libretto, he settled back to listen to the Paris première of Haydn's oratorio *The Creation*.

With the fear that spread through the nation at the news of Napoleon's brush with death, attention focused on a pamphlet entitled *A Parallel Between Caesar, Cromwell and Bonaparte*, recently authored and published, though anonymously, by Napoleon's brother Lucien, and advocating that the office of first consul be made not only permanent but hereditary, in order to preserve the stability of the government in the face of just such a threat as the "December Bomb Plot." Hereditary office implied an heir, and Napoleon, after five years of marriage to Josephine, was still without one. The issue of succession, raised by both Lucien and Joseph Bonaparte, was a provocation to divorce.

The talk of succession, hereditary office and supreme power was troubling Josephine, as Bourrienne could see, the morning she came unannounced to Napoleon's study, interrupting him at his dictation:

. . . she came quietly [on her heel-less silken slippers], approached him in her gentle, beguiling way and settled herself on his knee, caressing him and brushing her finger tips softly across his cheek and through his hair.

Her words came in a tender rush: "Bonaparte, I implore you, don't go making yourself a king. It's that horrid Lucien who puts you up to such schemes. Please, oh, please, don't listen to him."

Bonaparte was not angry; he even smiled when he replied, "You must be out of your mind, my poor Josephine. Where are you hearing such wild tales as these? From your dowager friends in the Faubourg St.-Germain? But off with you, now. You are interrupting me at my work, and I must get back to it."

Napoleon's remark about the Faubourg St.-Germain, the old aristocratic quarter of Paris, was in reference to Josephine's renewed contact with the nobility in her many missions on behalf of *émigrés*, which had won her the title of "Angel of Mercy" in royalist circles.

It is small wonder that the head of the royalist party, the Bourbon pretender the Count de Provence (Louis XVI's eldest surviving brother, the future Louis XVIII), directed his agents to enlist Madame Bonaparte's sympathy and her influence with her husband to aid the cause of the Bourbon restoration. A direct approach—by letter—had already been made by the royalists to the First Consul, and, to judge by the many months which elapsed before he made reply, it would seem that he gave it thought. The offer was handsome: a duchy, the hereditary office of high constable of France and the top ministerial position for General Bonaparte from a "grateful monarch."

It cannot be surprising, then, that Josephine saw in the proposal a solution to her personal dilemma and to the national one—perhaps in that very order, since she is accused of having thought exclusively of herself. With the Bourbons re-established on the throne, the issue of succession and of an heir would cease to constitute a threat to the security of the nation—and to her marriage. As for her husband, his genius might find its golden opportunity for expression in a legitimate monarchy; she could have had no great confidence in the recently established Consulate, which was perhaps merely another of the ephemeral, hybrid executive forms improvised by the Revolution. As concerns her role in the legitimist intrigues at this time, it must be remembered, too, that she was an aristocrat by birth, a royalist by sentiment and tradition.

When an emissary from the Count de Provence hinted that his royal master would go so far as to erect a statue to France's greatest general in the Place du Carrousel ("the figure of Bonaparte, atop a lofty column, shown crowning the Bourbon monarch"), Josephine hopefully relayed the message to her husband.

"Very flattering indeed," Bonaparte commented sardonically. "But beware of the statue's pedestal—it may well contain my corpse."

5

With the state of the nation at apogee in 1801-1802, the First Consul could scarcely be expected to turn back the clock of revolution, turn back a triumphant France to her old masters—a France at peace with herself and the world for the first time in ten years, with prestige abroad and order at home, increasingly prosperous, proud, grateful, confident in her destiny as a republic and in her chief executive. Napoleon had given France victories; now he gave her treaties: with the United States of America, with Spain, Portugal, Holland, Turkey, Bavaria, Prussia, Russia, Austria, England.

Even a treaty with Rome, with the new Pope, Pius VII. Predominantly Catholic France was at peace again with the Church, in accordance with the will of the majority—and with no coercion of the minority: a Napoleon who respected the tradition of the Mussulman would respect that of Protestant and Jew.

The signing of the Concordat of 1801 served as a reminder to Josephine that her marriage to Napoleon still lacked the sanction of the Church; that, in the eyes of a Catholic France, its head of state was living in a state of sin, of concubinage. And yet a signal public tribute was paid to the First Consul's lady that same year. In January of 1801, as one of the festivities attendant on the promulgation of the Civil Code, the Legislative Body tendered Madame Bonaparte a banquet, at which the tables were laid with banks of jonquils and jasmine imported from the south in a compliment to the noted flower lover. Josephine was radiant in shimmering white satin covered by whorls of pearl-tipped white toucan feathers, with a headdress of pearls and feathers and with a parure of Oriental rubies at her throat, ears and wrists. When she made her entrance into the hall, the orchestra greeted her with strains from Gluck's *Iphigénie:*—"*Que d'attraits, que de majesté!*" ("What charms, what majesty!").

A proud and gratifying moment, as it would have been a proud and gratifying year for Josephine had not Lucien been up to his old political machinations and conspiracies against his sister-in-law. This time, from Madrid, where he had been sent on an ambassadorial mission, he submitted a proposal from the Queen of Spain to the First Consul: the hand of the thirteen-year-old Infanta Isabel in marriage. The First Consul promptly revealed the contents of the confidential dispatch to Josephine. (It was a curious and unpleasant habit of Napoleon's to divulge the confidences made him by his brothers and sisters to his wife, even those—or especially those—inimical to her interests.)

Napoleon's reaction to the matter of the Spanish Infanta, "Were I in a position to consider a marital alliance with a royal European house, it would certainly not be with one crumbling into ruins," brought Josephine cold comfort, implying as it did that he might consider other, more tempting alliances. On the other hand, he was displeased by Lucien's clumsy meddling in his private and public life; he mistrusted his brothers' motives. Napoleon was familiar with the Bonaparte family's theory that, while Josephine was probably barren, he himself was probably impotent. Their advice to him to divorce his wife and take another in order to provide a direct heir was a subterfuge. When his sisters and brothers incited him to seize supreme power, it was in the secret hope that they or their children would inherit it. This he knew, and he let them know he knew it. His outbursts of resentment and bitterness over the whole miserable business were directed now against Josephine, now against his brothers and sisters. "After me, the deluge!" Lucien quotes him as shouting. "You can all fight it out over my grave, like the heirs of Alexander."

Josephine, mild, soft-spoken, slow to anger, reluctant to controversy, shrank from the increasingly acrimonious family parleys and the eternal harping on the question of sterility. When she pointed one day in self-defense, as she had so often, to Hortense and Eugène as the living, breathing proof of her fecundity in her first marriage, Elisa Bonaparte Bacciocchi snapped back at her shrewishly with the words, "But you must remember, sister, that you were a great deal younger then than now." Napoleon, coming upon Josephine in tears and demanding to know the reason, rebuked Elisa, saying, "Tactless as you are, even you should know that there are times when the truth is best left unspoken!"—a defense of his wife little calculated to please her.

Little was left unspoken among the Bonapartes; they called a spade a spade. Their conversations on what might have been considered a delicate subject showed less and less restraint, and not only in the bosom of the family but also in the presence of rank outsiders.

"I have no children [Lucien again quotes Napoleon]. You say, you and Joseph and the others, that I am impotent. As for Josephine, it is my opinion that at her age, despite her eagerness to oblige, she will have no more children—not even if she is willing to have them by another man."

I had heard my brother express himself along these lines before [Lucien continues], half in jest, half in earnest, and without the slightest embarrassment, in the presence of Josephine—in the presence of even such others as Murat, Davout, Lannes and Savary. Once, I remember, I followed up his line of reasoning, although addressing my words to Josephine: "Come, then, sister, prove to the Consul that he is mistaken by promptly giving us a little Caesarion!" Josephine laughed and seemed rather grateful to me for my suggestion and its implication.

Josephine's version of the incident, as told to Bourrienne, carries no hint of laughter or of gratitude to a malicious Lucien:

"What a man, what a wicked man, that Lucien!" she cried out in tears and despair. "If you only knew, Bourrienne, the shameful proposition he dared to make to me! 'You are going to Plombières,' Lucien said, 'and you must have a child by another man, since your husband is unable to father one.' You can imagine, Bourrienne, what indignation I expressed at such counsel. 'Well,' Lucien went on, 'if you will not or cannot have a child yourself, then Bonaparte must try to father one by another woman, and you must agree to adopt it, for the succession must be assured. It is in your own best interests to comply, as you should realize.' 'What, monsieur,' I exclaimed, 'do you think the nation would accept a bastard? Lucien, Lucien, you will bring about your brother's ruin! I hope you do not suspect me of giving so much as a thought to your infamous suggestion.' 'Very well, then,' Lucien replied, 'there is no more to be said on the subject, except that you have my deepest sympathy.' "

The Marriage

Was Lucien's "infamous suggestion" so indignantly and resolutely rejected as Josephine implies? Napoleon, at St. Helena, would indicate that Josephine urged resort to that very expedient. And Madame de Rémusat insists that her friend the illustrious Dr. Corvisart, the imperial physician, told her that he had been approached by the couple, and sounded out as to whether he would be willing to help them pass off a possible byblow of Napoleon's as his child by his lawfully wedded wife and consort, Josephine, but had refused to co-operate in the perpetration of such a hoax. Bourrienne, who recommended Corvisart to the Bonapartes in the first place, claims that the only fraud to which the honest doctor ever lent himself was that of encouraging Josephine to hope that either his medicines or the mineral springs of Plombières could lead to the conception of a child.

Undaunted by the failure of her previous visit, Josephine set out again hopefully for Plombières in July of 1801, with Hortense as companion and her mother-in-law as chaperone; Madame Mère's presence was a safeguard against malicious gossip by the family that she had taken Lucien's wicked suggestion to take a lover. En route, she made a pilgrimage to the monastery of Luxeuil, renowned for its sixth-century relics and its miraculous cures in stubborn cases of sterility. At the age of thirty-eight, after five years of childless marriage, it was a miracle she needed.*

She would not, however, put her entire reliance on a miracle. Josephine had evolved a more practical solution to the problem that plagued her: the project of a marriage—Hortense's to Louis Bonaparte.

Louis, who had come as a boy to France under Napoleon's tender care and tutelage, was the brother closest to his heart. Louis was the brother most likely to be designated as successor in the event Napoleon had no issue of his own. Lucien was far brainier, but erratic, unpredictable and undependable. Joseph was mentally uninspired and temperamentally incapable of sustained or

---

* In the opinion of modern medical science, Josephine's barrenness during the early years of her marriage to Napoleon, before she was thirty-five years old, was less probably the result of a premature menopause than that of a venereal infection; barrenness is often the sole symptom of gonorrhea in the female.

vigorous action. Jérôme, at seventeen, already gave promise of becoming the "little Heliogabalus" he would appear in the eyes of his future subjects in his future kingdom of Westphalia. With Hortense married to Louis, Josephine could look forward to being, if not the mother of her husband's successor, then that successor's mother-in-law or grandmother. Of all the members of the Bonaparte clan, Louis was the one least openly hostile to the Beauharnais', and he had already evinced an interest in lovely young Hortense. He would avow it openly at a ball given by Josephine upon her return to Malmaison in the early autumn.

Hortense at first put up a show of resistance, as she had done in every instance of her mother's matchmaking during the course of the past two years. At eighteen, her head still full of romantic notions, she was still reluctant at the thought of matrimony. But Josephine now felt justified in forcing the issue; she herself had been a wife and mother at her daughter's age, and certainly in the early nineteenth century family-arranged marriages were still traditional. The alliance held out a promise of compatibility, in age and in tastes; both Hortense and Louis were dilettantes in the arts, she with her painting and her music, Louis with his writing, for he fancied himself a poet and novelist. Josephine could not foresee that the frail, introspective young man would become a morbid neurotic, an invalid in mind and body (with syphilitic complications), prey to melancholia, to a persecution complex and to a devastating jealousy. Louis later claimed that he had been maneuvered into the formal proposal of marriage to Hortense by Josephine and Napoleon at a ball at Malmaison. But Napoleon, Lucien and Joseph are all three on record with the opinion that Louis was in love with Hortense.

Josephine's success in bringing off the match in the face of the formidable Bonaparte opposition was a miracle in its own genre. "The marriage between Louis Bonaparte and Hortense was the result of Josephine's intriguing," Bourrienne concluded, and his was the perfect vantage point from which to observe her *modus operandi*. It was Bourrienne's impression that "the influence exerted in the boudoir was more potent, at that time, than any in the council chamber," and that "Josephine brought the First Consul around to approval of the match by her great talents of persuasion,

her repeated entreaties and her caresses—in short, by all those subtle resources of hers which she knew so well how to apply." (Was
Josephine as much of an intrigante as Bourrienne credits her with
being? "She did not lack finesse," was playwright Arnault's opinion. "She baffled all the calculations, all the maneuvers of her ad-
versaries," was the accolade from Metternich. And as Talleyrand,
in one of his famous epigrams, said when asked whether Josephine
had been a woman of intelligence, "No one ever managed so brilliantly as she without it.")

Hortense requested eight days in which to reach her decision, in
which Bourrienne collaborated. "You must know that there are constant intrigues afoot to persuade the First Consul to divorce your
mother," Hortense says that Bourrienne warned her. "Only your
marriage to Louis can strengthen and reaffirm those bonds on
which your mother's happiness depends." "And so I learned for the
first time," Hortense concludes, "that it was in my power to con-
tribute to my mother's security and peace of mind. My consent
once given, I grew calm. All the anguish I had earlier experienced
seemed to transfer itself to my mother. She never stopped crying."

Until, presumably, the hour of the wedding on January 4, 1802.
The civil ceremony in the Tuileries was followed by a nuptial
Mass at Josephine's and Napoleon's honeymoon house on the
Rue de la Victoire, a gift, now, to the newlyweds. The Murats,
married earlier without benefit of clergy, knelt beside the Louis
Bonapartes to receive Cardinal Caprara's blessing. Surely Josephine
must have tried to induce Napoleon to do the same; just as surely,
Napoleon must have refused her. But he did invite her to ac-
company him the next day on a state visit to Lyons upon the occasion of his investiture as president of the newly named Italian
Republic (formerly the Cisalpine), allowing her to share in the
wave of acclaim that swept over him.

The news of Hortense's pregnancy in the early honeymoon
months did not bring the rejoicing that might have been expected. Not to her husband, at any rate. To his warped mind, it
came as corroboration of the vicious charge leveled against his wife
by the Bonapartes: that the expected child had been sired by
Louis's brother, Hortense's stepfather—Napoleon. Lucien, as he
coolly admits in his memoirs, had planted that hideous seed of

doubt in Louis's mind before the wedding, with the warning that the date was being advanced and Hortense rushed to the altar "in a state of emergency." Louis savagely informed his bride, "If the birth of the child comes one day ahead of the prescribed term of days, I shall never see you again as long as I live!"

The charge that illicit relations existed between Napoleon and Hortense is refuted by every contemporary whose testimony carries authority, even by those otherwise unlikely to champion Napoleon's morality. Bourrienne, writing after his rupture with Napoleon and his dismissal in 1802 on charges of "massive peculation," issues a categorical denial: "During the three years I lived in such intimate association with the family, I was never witness to a word or action which might have aroused the slightest suspicion in my mind of any culpable intimacy between the First Consul and his stepdaughter. Napoleon cherished no sentiment beyond a paternal tenderness for Hortense, and she regarded him with a respectful awe." Likewise Napoleon's valet Constant, from his observer's post within the circumference of the family circle, insisted: "Napoleon would never have been guilty of such an illicit relation, if for no other reason than his dread of public scandal. I can affirm on my word of honor that no such infamous desire ever stirred his heart."

Madame de Rémusat, writing at a period when disenchantment had set in with regard to her former hero, adds her testimony to that of the other intimates of the Bonaparte family: "As little respect as Napoleon had for women in general, he held Hortense in veneration. The manner in which he spoke of her and his attitude toward her gave the lie to the calumny which victimized her. In her presence Napoleon guarded his tongue and kept his conversation respectable. He often applied to Hortense to arbitrate in disputes between his wife and himself, and he accepted criticism from his stepdaughter as he would have from no one else. 'Hortense,' I have heard him say more than once, 'forces me to believe in virtue.'"

In that very month of May 1802 which announced Hortense's pregnancy, the Council of State formally proposed that Napoleon's tenure of office as first consul be extended to life, and that he be granted a privilege enjoyed by the Caesars of ancient Rome, that of designating his successor. A plebiscite, scheduled for August, would ostensibly afford the nation the opportunity to signify its approval or disapproval of the Council's proposal. The result was a foregone conclusion: there were few No votes in the balloting. Josephine's sterility had become an affair of state. But there was comfort in the thought that the child to be born to Hortense and Louis promised to be the heir designate, and Josephine wrote that summer to her mother, "I am to be a grandmother soon, and I am elated at the prospect."

6

This did not mean, however, that Josephine had yet abandoned all hope of herself becoming a mother. Shortly after her thirty-ninth birthday she set out, for the third time, for the springs of Plombières, to follow a strict regimen of mineral waters, baths, tonics and potions prescribed by Dr. Corvisart. Her husband was as eager and as hopeful as she. A child of hers and his would be the ideal solution to the problem of succession; Josephine was the perfect consort, wife and companion. He wrote to her at Plombières: "I love you as I did the first day of loving, because you are dear and sweet and tender and agreeable beyond all compare."

Not that his expression of affection for his wife was any indication of his continence during her absence. And there was always some kind friend in Josephine's entourage to report on her husband's dalliances. Within ten days of her departure, word reached Josephine in Plombières that Louise Rolandeau, star of the Opéra-Comique, was being summoned with suspicious regularity to sing at Malmaison, where the First Consul spent the summer weekends with Hortense as official hostess.

"My mother wrote to upbraid me," Hortense notes, "for not having put a stop to the actress's visits—as if I had any control over that situation. My mother left Plombières suddenly, and I have

often heard the Consul reproach her for having yielded to an uncontrollable jealousy which caused her to interrupt a course of
treatment upon which such high hopes depended."

For a moment, it seemed that those high hopes had been justified. One morning shortly after Josephine's return, as Bourrienne
tells it, "the First Consul came rushing into the study where I was
working, and announced to me, in a transport of joy beyond my
power to describe, 'At last, at last, it's happened! My wife's menses
have been restored!'" But, as Dr. Corvisart had forewarned Bourrienne, the phenomenon constituted no genuine promise of fertility.

On August 15, 1802, Napoleon Bonaparte was proclaimed consul
for life, and Paris celebrated the occasion with city-wide illumina-
tions and with concerts and fireworks—including Napoleon's star,
"thirty feet in height, gleaming above the towers of Notre Dame
throughout the night," Bourrienne recalls; and the state apartments of the Tuileries took on a gala air. But "Josephine's melancholy presented a striking contrast to the prevailing gaiety. She had
to receive a host of dignitaries and officials on that evening, and
did it with her customary grace despite the profound depression
that weighed down her spirits. She knew that every step the First
Consul took toward the throne was a step away from her."

That next step—the throne—was what she most feared. She ve-
hemently disclaimed to Bourrienne any ambition to become a
queen or an empress: "All I want," she said, "is to continue to be
the wife of the First Consul." Madame de Rémusat, with strong
political convictions of her own, would deplore the fact that Josephine had none; that she was "indifferent to the national destiny;
her reactions to political developments were purely personal; her
only concern was with their effect on her."

But Josephine struggled grimly, persistently, and audaciously at
this point, against the rising tide of monarchical sentiment. She
told Roederer, one of its strongest proponents and Lucien's hench-
man, "Bonaparte's real enemies are those who feed his ambition
with talk of dynasty, divorce and remarriage." And even to Thibaudeau, a member of the Council of State, she expressed her concern
at the ultimate consolidation of power in her husband's hands: "I
disapprove of the projects under consideration, and I have said so

to Bonaparte. He seems to listen to me, but then the flatterers soon change his mind again. The new powers to be granted him will increase the number of his enemies. His generals are already crying that they did not overthrow the Bourbons to set up the Bonapartes in their stead."

Bourrienne has exaggerated Josephine's influence over Napoleon. Hortense was more realistic when she said, "My mother had influence over her husband only in unimportant matters." Josephine could not have hoped to dissuade Napoleon from following that "star" of his to which he referred over and over again.

A quasi-royal tone had asserted itself by the end of 1802: Napoleon had adopted the royal practice of using his Christian name only, without benefit of patronymic; four prefects had been appointed to do the honors of the palace for the First Consul, and four ladies of the palace to do them for the consort; and the royal Palace of St.-Cloud, in the Paris suburbs, was reopened and restored to its former glory to serve as the First Consul's second official, or summer, residence. But its marble staircases, its gilded and frescoed galleries, and its thousand-acre park with fountains playing spectacularly and cascades descending majestically could not console Josephine for having had to desert Malmaison, too small now to accommodate the swelling ranks of the Consular entourage, both military and civilian. "I was not born to such grandeur," she wrote plaintively to Hortense.

At St.-Cloud, an Old-Regime courtier would have thought himself back at the court of the Louis'. Mass was celebrated on Sundays, with Napoleon standing erect where Louis XVI had knelt and Josephine kneeling before the altar—a pose which even that paragon of grace Marie Antoinette could not have assumed more gracefully. The First Consul and his consort dined alone, except on those specified occasions when members of the immediate family or high government officials were invited to join them. Royal protocol prevailed in the audience chamber: foreign dignitaries, distinguished guests and visitors formed two circles, the gentlemen behind the ladies, and the latter were presented by two prefects of the palace to the First Consul as he made the rounds. He would acknowledge each presentation with one or two gruff, perfunctory questions as to the length of the lady's stay in Paris or the climate or population of her native city; the formula was varied only occasionally by an outrageous question such as whether she nursed her own children. Josephine, following her husband around the circle with two other prefects, acquitted herself of her duties far more winningly, her remarks giving proof of her prodigious memory for facts and faces and of her genuine interest in people. Her courtesy was more than the ultimate refinement of the social amenities; it was a courtesy of the heart, an expression of her natural sensitivity and her consideration for other people and their feelings, and it communicated itself unmistakably as such.

The First Consul's tour of Normandy in October, accompanied by his wife and escorted by the Consular Guard and by red-coated hussars and mounted grenadiers, was a royal progress. The cities of Rouen, Le Havre and Dieppe offered the Bonapartes the feudal tributes formerly paid to the kings and queens of France, cheering this couple as those kings and queens had rarely been. As for Josephine, wherever she appeared the sight of her, the sound of her voice and the warmth of her greeting delighted the eye, the ear and the heart. At Dieppe, where the young girls waited on her to present a floral tribute, Madame Bonaparte in turn presented a bracelet to the little spokesman of the band. When the child ingenuously held out her other arm, Josephine smilingly unfastened a bracelet of her own to meet the droll emergency. From that day on, she made a practice of wearing on her person the jewelry she was to present to others—knowing that the gift may be immeasurably enhanced in the giving; the recipient was made to feel that Josephine had given a part of herself, a souvenir as well as a gift.

October saw the birth of Hortense's and Louis's child. October 15, to be precise—a date that satisfied Louis and his requirement of "the prescribed term of days," with, fortunately, days to spare. To the intense satisfaction of both Napoleon and Josephine, the child was a boy. Christened Napoléon-Charles, he became the First Consul's great favorite.

But not even this handsome and well-loved child could save the Louis Bonapartes' marriage. It had foundered on the rock of Louis's hatred of the Beauharnais'; it had been infected by the miasma of Louis's morbid, totally unjustified suspicion of his wife.

Jealousy tormented him, and he tormented and humiliated her, opening her letters, hiring maids to spy upon her, locking her in her bedroom and posting a sentry under her window. Her young Tascher cousin, one of many brought over from Martinique by Josephine for education and placement, was denied entree to the house. Even Eugène, his sister's mainstay and comfort in all the tribulations of her life, came under suspicion and was made unwelcome. And: "My husband forbade me under any circumstance whatsoever to spend a night under the same roof with my mother," Hortense admits in her memoirs. On their wedding night, her husband had recited a list of her mother's former lovers. "You are the daughter of an immoral woman," he had told her. "You are now a Bonaparte, and our interests should be yours; those of your family are no longer your concern."

Although Napoleon could discern the disaster of the marriage, he was grateful to Hortense for her Spartan silence. Once he made a bitter jest: "What a pair your husband and my wife would have made—he spying through the door, she through the window." Under her husband's tyranny and maltreatment, his grand and petty persecution, Hortense would lose her health, her youthful radiance and her spirit, to become—as Claire de Rémusat saw her—"the unhappiest woman of our time."

7

The winter season of 1802-1803 was the most glittering and most festive the capital had enjoyed in a decade. Paris, the perennial mecca, attracted a host of visitors from all parts of the Continent and the British Isles, all curious to appraise the effects of revolution on the City of Light and on the nation.

Napoleon, who had already promised himself (aloud, to Bourrienne) to make Paris the most beautiful city in the world, was well on the way to doing it. The plans for the Rue de Rivoli were his, as well as those for the beautification of the district between the Tuileries and the boulevards, for new quais and bridges for the Seine, for the Vendôme Column, for the Arch of Triumph of the Carrousel and that of the Champs-Elysées, for the colonnade and the new façade of the Louvre. The Louvre's galleries were opened, in 1802, as a museum (the Musée Napoléon) of French, Italian and Egyptian art, while its central courtyard served as the scene of the National Industries Exhibit.

Josephine and the Murats put in an appearance as official patrons of the first masked opera ball since the day the Bastille had fallen. The Comédie-Française and the Théâtre Français were in their heyday, with Napoleon's close friend Talma as the brightest male star; and that season Mademoiselle Georges, an actress with the face and form of a Greek goddess, appropriately made her debut as Clytemnestre.

"All Paris, and especially the Palace of the Tuileries, was given over, that winter, to gaiety and pleasure," says Madame de Rémusat, recalling her first year as lady-of-the-palace to her long-time friend and benefactress, Madame Bonaparte.

In the Bonapartes' private apartments all seemed peace and serenity, until suddenly the First Consul's fancy for a beautiful young actress of the Théâtre Français, Mademoiselle Georges, troubled the waters and gave rise to stormy scenes. . . . Madame Bonaparte learned quickly enough, through her household espionage system, that Mademoiselle Georges had made several secret visits to the small apartment in a remote wing of the palace, a discovery that caused her great distress. She shed more tears than seemed warranted by such a passing fancy, and I urged her to calm and moderation. For I had quickly perceived that if the First Consul loved his wife, it was because her normal sweetness and gentleness provided him repose, and that she would lose her hold over him if she began to agitate him.

It was then that she imparted to me some notions about her husband that I had not heard up to then; her agitated state made me think, however, that there might be some exaggeration in her bitter complaints. To hear her tell it, he had no moral principles whatsoever, and he concealed his vicious inclinations only for fear they would damage his reputation; if he were permitted, however, to follow his bent without restraint, he would gradually abandon himself to the most shameful excesses. Had he not seduced his own sisters, one after the other? Did he not consider himself especially privileged to satisfy all his lusts?

It seems incredible that Josephine could have made such a charge about her husband and his sisters to one of her ladies. And yet, considering her extreme and morbid jealousy and the satyrlike tendencies of her husband, who certainly gave her cause for seeing potential rivals all around her—in the court, in her household and later in her own family, if not in his—it is quite probable that she did voice this "notion" to Claire. Even her daughter, Hortense, admits that Josephine, in her jealous frenzies, talked indiscreetly about Napoleon to her attendants, calling him a "seducer" and "the most immoral of men." As for the nature of the accusation, which is so shocking to twentieth-century ears, one must remember that all of the people concerned were products of the eighteenth century, a period more lax than ours in its attitude toward such subjects. The Bonapartes themselves were not apt to be shocked by an accusation of illicit or incestuous relations. When General Murat took offense at a rumor involving his wife and her brother Lucien, the latter could broach the subject quite matter-of-factly to brother Joseph, writing: "Madame Murat has never stayed here with me. Her husband is a fool whom she should reprimand by not writing to him for a month." And in 1814 there was a great deal of talk about a letter written by Pauline from Elba (where she had gone to share Napoleon's exile—the only one of his brothers and sisters to do so) in which she referred in the boldest terms to her incestuous relations with him.

In any case, there is no doubt as to the truth of Josephine's statement that her husband considered himself "especially privileged" to have extramarital affairs. According to Claire de Rémusat, he was surprised and outraged that Josephine should object to these "necessary" distractions. "I am not a man like other men," he would tell her. "The laws of morality and of society are not applicable to me. I have the right to answer all your objections with an eternal *I*." "When Madame Bonaparte wept or complained at such declarations," says Claire, "he turned on her with a violence I do not choose to record."

She did record other details of the Bonapartes' domestic habits that winter, such as the fact that Napoleon, who still slept every night in his wife's bedroom, now often went first to Mademoiselle Georges after his evening working hours and did not come downstairs to Josephine's apartments until very late. And she describes what happened one night when, at Josephine's request, she stayed to keep her unhappy mistress company in her salon:

It was, by then, one o'clock in the morning, and a profound silence reigned over the Tuileries. Suddenly Madame Bonaparte rose to her feet and said, "I cannot endure it another moment. Mademoiselle Georges must be up there with him. I am going to surprise them together."

Shocked at this sudden decision, I did my best to dissuade her, but in vain.

"Follow me," she said. "We'll go upstairs together."

I tried to show her that, while her participation in such a mission would be indelicate enough, mine would be intolerable. She would not listen, but reproached me for deserting her in an emergency and pressed me so hard that, despite my repugnance, I yielded to her entreaties, consoling myself with the thought that precautions must surely have been taken on the floor above to preclude the possibility of any such surprise as was being contemplated.

There we were, then, Madame Bonaparte and I—she, in extreme agitation, leading the way, I behind her, carrying a lighted taper—tiptoeing silently and slowly up the dark, winding inner stairs that led to the First Consul's apartments.

Halfway up, a noise, muffled but distinct, reached our ears, stopping us in our tracks. Madame Bonaparte turned to me and said, "It must be Roustam, Bonaparte's Mameluke, who guards his door. That devil is capable of slitting both our throats."

At those words, I was seized by such a fright—ridiculous as it may now seem—that I waited to hear no more, but went flying down the steps, back to the salon, the candle still in my hand— forgetting completely that I had abandoned Madame Bonaparte to total darkness. She joined me a few moments later, astonished at my sudden flight. But when she caught sight of my face and the terror written on it she burst out laughing, and I with her, and we renounced our enterprise.

The Marriage

But the conjugal strife continued, and soon Madame de Rémusat found herself drawn in by both sides, first as confidant and later
as arbitrator:

One day, to avoid a dinner tête-à-tête with his wife, the First
Consul invited me to make the third at table. Madame Bonaparte was in a highly emotional state. He had just announced to
her that he would thenceforward occupy a separate bedroom.
The question he called upon me to arbitrate was the strangest
one imaginable: whether a husband was obliged to yield to the
whim of a wife who insisted that a married couple spend every
night together, in the same bed.

I was not only unprepared to answer, but I well knew that
Madame Bonaparte would never forgive me if I did not decide in
her favor. I tried to beg off, but Bonaparte—who took a perverse
pleasure in embarrassing people—pressed me so hard for a reply
that I found no way out of the predicament save to say that I
could no more define the point to which a wife should limit her
exigencies than I could that to which a husband should go in
complying with them. I was therefore obliged, I explained, to
confine myself to a single observation: that any change in the
Consul's way of life was certain to provoke unwelcome comment,
for the slightest variation in the palace routine always set the
household buzzing.

Bonaparte burst out laughing, pinched my ear [his favorite
—and painful—expression of approval] and exclaimed, "You
women! You are all in league together."

Not that he was in any wise discouraged from carrying out his
resolution. From that time forward, he maintained separate sleeping quarters. On the other hand, this did not mean that he did
not, from time to time, return to terms of fondest intimacy with
his wife. Indeed, it was my observation, the first year I spent at
court, that these rather superficial altercations were invariably
followed by reconciliations, and by an ardor and an intimacy
more pronounced than ever.

Madame Bonaparte, once she had achieved a more reasonable
frame of mind, took my oft-repeated advice to ignore these passing fancies of her husband's, to disdain competition unworthy of
her notice. "It would be time enough to distress yourself," I told
her, "were the First Consul to choose a favorite from among the

ladies of your court. Then you would have cause for tears, **and I** for concern."

Claire de Rémusat could not guess, she says, that her prediction was to be only too well realized, particularly with regard to herself.

As she had also predicted, word of the First Consul's change in sleeping habits promptly echoed through the palace, from the boudoir to the state apartments, from the kitchen basements to the service attics; but it as promptly lost its interest when no material change was indicated in either the marital or the official status of Madame Bonaparte.

On the contrary, her position appeared to have been enhanced when, in June of 1803, the announcement came that she was to accompany the First Consul to Belgium on a forty-eight-day state visit—resplendent as never before, glittering for the first time in the French crown jewels, which had been hidden from sight since the day in 1791 when Marie Antoinette had surrendered them to the National Convention.

At an hour when Anglo-French relations were rapidly deteriorating toward war, the enthusiasm of the Channel ports and the border provinces was to be stimulated by a glimpse of the French hero and chief of state. The break in diplomatic relations had come in May; England's refusal to evacuate Malta had constituted a breach of treaty terms. With northern Italy, Belgium and Holland under French dominion, and the other states fawning or trembling before Bonaparte, the threat of a Continental economic blockade caused sharp alarm in England. Despite her mastery of the seas, Britain considered the balance of power on the Continent imperiled, and she would begin to rally the forces of Europe to counteract the French hegemony.

Key cities such as Brussels, Antwerp and Ghent were, of course, included on Napoleon's itinerary, and there, as throughout all of Belgium and northern France, an ovation greeted him and Madame Bonaparte: cheering masses everywhere, a rain of flowers upon their path, triumphal arches at every mile, galas, banquets, Te Deums, oral as well as floral tributes. "Madame Bonaparte charmed everyone wherever she appeared on this official journey," wrote Madame de Rémusat, who traveled in her retinue. "When

I visited those regions fifteen years afterward, I discovered that the memory of her graciousness and kindness was still fresh in men's minds."

Napoleon too had come under the spell of the charm so universally radiated by Josephine in the course of the Belgian journey. Even so, another domestic storm blew up after their return to Paris —again over Mademoiselle Georges. The scene in which it culminated was one of broadest palace farce. Napoleon, in "Georgina's" arms in the Tuileries rendezvous apartment, had been seized by one of the attacks which gave rise, erroneously, to the report of epilepsy. The actress, succumbing to panic, had roused the whole palace with her screams. Napoleon regained consciousness to discover valets, sentries and aides-de-camp peering in the door, and at his bedside his wife, wearing a negligee which had been thrown hastily over her nightdress, standing beside his mistress, who was clad in nothing but a chemise. Georgina paid for having lost her head by losing her lover.

Josephine, mollified and reassured, dried her tears to enjoy another of those halcyon marital interludes. This one was interrupted only by Napoleon's departure from Paris in November for an inspection of the military and naval forces assembling on the Channel coast for an invasion of England. The letter Napoleon wrote to her from Boulogne, telling her how indispensable she was to him in many ways, has been lost; but her reply survives, one of the few of her letters to him that is still extant. It is as poignant and graceful an expression of love as any in history or literature:

All my cares have vanished in reading your wonderful and touching letter, your expression of your feeling for me. How deeply grateful I am for the time you took to write at such length to your Josephine. If you could only know how deeply, you would feel rewarded for the effort and gratified at the power you have to bring so rapturous a delight to the woman you love. A letter is the portrait of the soul, and I clasp this one of yours to my heart. It does me so much good, I shall treasure it forever. It shall be my consolation when you are away from me, my guide when you are near. For I want always to be, in your eyes, as you desire me— your "sweet and tender Josephine," her life devoted solely to your happiness. Whether you are touched with joy or sorrow, may it be upon the breast of your devoted wife that you seek solace or felicitation. There is no emotion which you might experience that I would not share with you.

These, then, are my desires and fondest hopes, all of which reduce themselves to the one hope and desire of my life—to please you and make you happy.

Adieu, Bonaparte. I shall never forget the last sentence of your letter. I have taken it to heart. How deeply it is graven there! With what transports of joy, what ecstasy, mine has responded! Yes, oh, yes, that is my wish, too: to please you and to love you—or, rather, to adore you.

8

Josephine would no doubt have pridefully shared that "wonderful and touching letter" from her husband with her friend Claire de Rémusat, as she had all those of the Italian campaign (this was one of her most unseemly and most irritating practices); but Claire had been called to Boulogne by the sudden illness of her husband, whose duties as prefect of the palace required his attendance on the Consul at headquarters. During those autumn weeks of 1803 while Bonaparte was about his military duties, Josephine found another source of pride and pleasure in contemplation of the four white swans gliding on the garden pool beneath her Tuileries windows. They were a recent gift from the city of Amiens and a pretty compliment to her, for the swan, the bird whose mating is for life, a symbol of eternal love, was her personal symbol of grace and majesty—embroidered in Empire tapestries, woven into carpets, carved on thrones, chairs, tables and beds, most notably the great gilded swan bed at Malmaison in which she was to die.

Madame de Rémusat, the only woman to appear at the encampment, was shown every courtesy by General Bonaparte. Too many courtesies, perhaps; those daily invitations to lunch and to dine with him succeeded in compromising her reputation with the mili-

tary clique, which refused to believe that such tête-à-têtes between their libidinous commander and a pretty twenty-three-year-
old female were exclusively devoted to discussions of literature, art
and political philosophy, as the lady herself insisted.

An intellectual, Madame de Rémusat could "recognize Napoleon's genius, his mastery of the science of power, his formidable
mind which encompassed every subject at once"; and at that time,
when she considered "his glory still unsullied," she was still wor-
shipful of the hero. "With such awesome faculties as he displayed,
he might have become—if only his goal had been the good of
humanity—the greatest man who ever lived, instead of merely the
most extraordinary." A *savante* though she might be, and as Napoleon had publicly labeled her (which was enough to damn her in
the eyes of that court), young Claire could also recognize that here
was "an extremely attractive man, one who enjoyed great success
with women." Napoleon usually disdained to converse seriously
with females, but this one drank in his words. "I never truly understood the Revolution," he told her, "but it suited my purposes. The
tenet of equality, which was to favor my rise, won me over to it.
'Equality,' there's the catchword! 'Liberty' is only a pretext. Liberty is necessary to only a privileged few endowed with faculties
superior to the common man. And this is why liberty may, with im-
punity, be restricted. The principle of equality, on the other hand,
satisfies the masses."

"Napoleon had discovered," Claire continues, "that France's secret weakness was vanity, that it was difficult to prevent Frenchmen from ranging themselves on the side of glory. He revived the
system of honors and distinctions, but on a democratic basis, in the
sense that any and every man might aspire to them. And the avidity
with which men sought the titles, badges and crosses he distributed
proved that he had not been mistaken. Both the French tempera-
ment and France's geographical position on the Continent were,
in his opinion, incompatible with the laggard processes of representative government."

If any personal note crept into these conversations ("mono-
logues" is Claire's word for them), it was on the subject of Napoleon's jealous wife, who "distressed herself far more than necessary," he told Claire. "Josephine is always afraid that I will really

fall in love. She fails to comprehend that love is not for me. For what is love, after all, but a passion which casts all the rest of the universe aside, to concentrate wholly, solely and exclusively on the object of its desire? Surely I am not the type of man to deliver myself over to such exclusivity of objective. So why should she distress herself over these innocuous diversions of mine which in no way involve my affections? And that's the point," he concluded rather pointedly, "on which her friends should seek to convince her."

But Claire, upon her return to Paris, found that she was no longer numbered among Madame Bonaparte's friends; gossip about those tête-à-têtes with the First Consul had preceded her:

> I found my patroness cool and distant. My own clear conscience and my single-minded devotion to my husband had prevented me from even conceiving of the notion that my innocent relations with the First Consul might arouse suspicion, might be subject to another interpretation. It was my first unhappy experience as an object of unjust judgments in this world, and one day, when I sensed the hurt most keenly, tears welled to my eyes and words to my lips. "Ah, madame," I cried involuntarily, "can it be I whom you suspect?"
>
> Whereupon Madame Bonaparte—who was essentially a kind and tender woman and susceptible to emotional appeal, even though fleetingly—put her arms about me, took me back to her heart and restored me to her confidence. Not that she really understood me—her soul was incapable of understanding the righteous indignation of mine; and so, without actually concerning herself as to whether the nature of my relations with her husband at Boulogne had been such as they had been described to her, she was satisfied with the evidence that they had been merely transitory—were to have no sequel. She later admitted to me that she had reproached her husband for the assiduity of his attentions to me, while he apparently had amused himself by leaving her to her nagging doubts.

Of all the arguments to which Josephine had resorted in her desperate effort to dissuade her husband from abandoning the custom of a joint bedroom, none had seemed so pitiful to Claire as the reminder that his wife's presence in his bed constituted a safeguard to his personal security—"that she was a very light sleeper and therefore, in the event of a nocturnal surprise attack, could be relied upon to give the alarm."

Alarms came thick and fast in the early months of 1804; Paris appeared to be in a state of siege: the gates of the city closed, the river approaches patrolled by gendarmes' barges, the Tuileries and St.-Cloud under strictest security measures: the guard doubled and redoubled, the passwords and countersigns changed in the middle of the night.

The newspapers broke the story of the Cadoudal conspiracy in February: Under the leadership of the fanatic, dedicated legitimist Georges Cadoudal, the conspirators had gathered and stood poised to attack the First Consul in his carriage en route to St.-Cloud, assassinate him (abduct him, they would later plead) and then proclaim the Bourbon pretender as King Louis XVIII. This royal exile and his followers had grown desperate at the First Consul's rejection of their bid for a Bourbon restoration; and a now openly hostile England, fearful of a prosperous, vigorous, aggressive French nation under Bonaparte, did not hesitate to aid and abet the royalists' plots, nor to subsidize their armies.

The French secret police were on the traces of the conspirators early in the winter; by mid-February two disaffected generals, Pichegru and Moreau, and a long list of aristocratic émigrés, including two members of the exalted Polignac family, had been arrested. The redoubtable Cadoudal was finally captured on March 9 in a bloody ambush on the Place de l'Odéon, and the trials began.

Interrogation of the prisoners revealed that an illustrious ringleader was still at large, a mysterious figure who had appeared from time to time in Paris incognito at the conspirators' secret meetings. He was a Bourbon prince, according to report, and was now at the border awaiting word of the First Consul's assassination to lead the royalist armies across the Rhine into Alsace. This prince of the blood, again according to report, was the thirty-two-year-old Duke d'Enghien, last of the great Condé line. On March 10, Napoleon and the Council of State issued orders for a raid over the border into the duchy of Baden to capture the Duke, who was at Ettenheim, across the Rhine from Strasbourg, and bring him back to Paris for trial.

The situation was critical; the Bourbon pretender later openly admitted that he kept sixty hired assassins in Paris. And some decisive action was clearly needed to put an end to the series of assassination plots hatched in the past three years by the royalists. Napoleon's line of action in the Enghien case was to be one of the most controversial in his entire career. He himself was still thinking about it at St. Helena and referring to it in conversation with his biographers and in his last will and testament—in which he declared that, confronted by the same situation, he would make the same decision. Technically speaking, the trial of Enghien—an avowed enemy of the Republic and a leader of armed forces—by a duly constituted military tribunal might have been construed to be within the framework of justice. But the world, especially the royalist world, which included all the rest of Europe, expressed outrage at the entire procedure and would agree with the words of Minister of Police Fouché, who later (much later) labeled it "worse than a crime—a blunder" (and later still, in his memoirs, went to great pains to establish his claim to the epigram, so often attributed to Talleyrand).

Claire de Rémusat, a royalist at heart, was of course horror-struck at the news of the Duke d'Enghien's arrest, which was revealed to her in confidence by Madame Bonaparte as the two were driving out of Paris on March 18 for a weekend at Malmaison.

> "My God, madame," I cried, "what will they do with him?"
> "Why, he will be court-martialed," she replied. . . . "I have done all I could to make Bonaparte promise me that the Prince will not be sentenced to death, but I am very much afraid that a decision has already been made." . . .
> I hastened to point out to her some of the aspects of the case which might not have occurred to her: the special significance of the Condé name in French history, the old fears and hatreds which would be resuscitated—and terror along with these. I succeeded in giving her such a fright that she promised me that night, as we parted to go to our rooms, to do all in her power to avert the deed, to repeat her pleas to the First Consul.

It was one of the nights he went to her, to her room, as he so often did in times of mental or physical stress and strain. ("Whenever he suffered the slightest indisposition," Josephine's treasure of a maid, Mademoiselle Avrillon, points out, "when any problem arose to trouble him, she was, so to speak, at his feet, and at such times he could not get along without her.")

The next morning, however [Claire de Rémusat continues], Madame Bonaparte admitted to defeat [having been silenced by her husband's dictum, "Women should not interfere in affairs of state"].

That day dragged on in gloom. Madame Bonaparte, who loved her trees and flowers, went out into the garden to supervise the transplanting of a cypress, throwing on several clods of earth with her own hand so that she could honestly claim to have planted it.

"How appropriate a tree to the occasion," I moaned.

My profound distress troubled her. Superficial and volatile, she was capable of strong but not sustained emotion. Convinced that the Duke's death had been resolved—and, furthermore, supremely confident in the infallibility of Bonaparte's judgment—she would have preferred to turn away from vain regret. She did not like to dwell on unpleasant subjects, but I held her to this one all day. I sobbed and entreated, and, though she knew Bonaparte better than I did, she finally agreed to make one last attempt.

And she did. According to Lucien, she told Napoleon, "Just remember, Bonaparte, if you insist on having your prisoner executed, you may wind up on the guillotine just like my first husband, and I along with you this time." But, as she told Claire on the morning of the twentieth, after another night spent with Bonaparte, her pleas had been in vain. "The Duke d'Enghien arrives today and will be tried tonight at Vincennes. Bonaparte has forbidden me to bring up the subject again."

There was, that day of March 20, constant coming and going between Paris and Malmaison, carriages in and out of the courtyard, bearing the highest officials of the government for conferences in the study. At dinner that night, the presence of little Napoléon-Charles, now a year and a half old, furnished welcome comic relief to mounting tension. Napoleon, who doted on the child as much as did his grandmother, set him in the center of the table and laughed uproariously at the havoc to glassware and china. He was still laughing later when he played with his namesake on the floor in the salon, but Madame de Rémusat thought his gaiety forced, tasteless and immoderate.

Claire's anguish was visible on her face, but when Napoleon asked the reason for her pallor she sidestepped by murmuring that she had forgotten her rouge. She continues:

> "Such a thing would never happen to my Josephine!" he laughed. "She knows that there is nothing more becoming to the ladies than rouge—and tears."
>
> With which words, he approached his wife and began to caress her with more license than decorum. . . .
>
> That night, that terrible night, Napoleon spent alone in his own apartments. At midnight, at Vincennes, on the outskirts of Paris, the Duke d'Enghien was brought before a military tribunal; at daybreak that morning of the twenty-first, he fell before a firing squad in the moat before the ancient fortress.

Napoleon's valet Constant saw Madame Bonaparte rush in, weeping, to her husband at an early hour of the morning; saw Napoleon take her in his arms and lead her gently back to her apartments. "You don't want to see me assassinated, do you?" he asked her. "The Bourbons must be taught a lesson; they cannot be allowed to continue to hunt me down like a wild beast. . . . But come, now, you are a child when it comes to politics. Try to rest."

The day brought another confluence of visitors from Paris. Their faces were grim and set, Claire de Rémusat thought—"all except the military ones." That night Napoleon had Louis de Fontanes, president of the Legislative Body and his good friend from the Académie Française, read aloud from letters which had been seized upon the person of the English ambassador to Bavaria, and which gave clear evidence of England's role in the Cadoudal conspiracy. After which, Claire says, Napoleon broke out with:

"There's incontrovertible proof for you. These people all want to sow disorder in France and kill the Revolution in my person. . . . If I have shed blood, it is because I had to. I may have to again. But never in anger; only because bloodletting is one of the specific remedies of political medicine. I am the Man of State. I am the French Revolution! And I repeat: I shall uphold it."

9

The very next week, Napoleon braved the Paris public, testing opinion by a visit to the Opéra. But, Claire de Rémusat noted, on this night he waited, contrary to custom, for Madame Bonaparte to reach their box before he entered it. "She was pale and he trembling; his eyes seemed to question us as to what sort of reception we thought awaited him. Finally, with the air of a soldier marching straight into an enemy battery, he went out and took his seat. An ovation greeted him, as it always did; either the sight of the man had produced its usual effect or the police had taken the precaution of hand-picking the audience. I had been dreadfully afraid that he would not be applauded, and yet when I saw that he was I felt a swift pang at my heart."

The tide of public opinion ran so high, in reaction to the panic over the Cadoudal conspiracy, that within a matter of weeks the Senate had unanimously proclaimed Napoleon Bonaparte "emperor of the Republic"—a title Napoleon preferred to that of king, finding it "even grander, more nebulous, more stirring to the imagination," according to Claire de Rémusat. The title represented "a combination of the Roman Republic and the Empire of Charlemagne, which went to Napoleon's head," in Talleyrand's opinion (although, as one member of the Tribunate pointed out, the original significance of the Latin word *imperator* had been nothing more than "victorious general"). The proposition of dynasty, of a succession hereditary in the Bonaparte family, would be confirmed later that summer—with the usual suspicious near-unanimity—in a national plebiscite.

On May 18 the Senate filed in solemn delegation into the Gallery of Apollo in the Palace of St.-Cloud to hail Napoleon I, Emperor of the French, as well as his Empress, Josephine, to whom its president, Cambacérès, addressed these words: "The Senate has another agreeable duty to perform, that of offering its homage to your Imperial Majesty, and of expressing the gratitude of the French people for those good works which you never tire of doing—for your accessibility to the unfortunate, for your influence exercised in

their behalf, for your tact and amiable delicacy which make gratitude doubly sweet and the benefit doubly precious."

"The Empress Josephine responded to the president of the Senate with that natural grace and geniality by which she rose to meet
every occasion, no matter how exalted," Claire de Rémusat observed. "That day of May 18 had dawned bright and hot, but at the
moment of the senators' arrival the skies suddenly darkened and
thunder rumbled; those black and menacing clouds gathering over
the Palace of St.-Cloud seemed to me an evil omen. The Emperor,
however, was gay and serene, responding to the new title as calmly
as if it had been his all his life. . . . And the new Empress lost
none of her easy grace and affability. . . . The new prerogatives
of rank sowed discord, however, in the rest of that formerly tranquil court—above all, in the Bonaparte family."

Joseph and Louis had been decreed princes of the Empire, so
their wives automatically became princesses, but Caroline Murat
and Elisa Bacciocchi went into a tantrum at being denied equal
rank—which earned them Napoleon's famous quip, "One would
think, to hear you, that I had just despoiled you of the heritage of
our late father the King." He relented, of course, after Caroline's
spell of the vapors, and accorded both sisters the title "Imperial
Highness." Pauline already had her title of *principessa*, having married the Italian Prince Camillo Borghese after the death of her first
husband, General Leclerc, a casualty in the disastrous Santo Domingo expedition of 1802.

But it was his brothers with whom Napoleon had his bitterest
quarrels over the succession. The Senate decree had stipulated that
the succession was to go to Napoleon's direct and legitimate issue;
failing which, to that of Joseph or of Louis. The catch was in the
provision by which Napoleon was granted the privilege of adopting
one of his nephews, who would then be directly designated as his
heir. Joseph had no sons, only daughters. It was Napoléon-Charles,
the son of Louis and Hortense, upon whom Napoleon had set his
heart (and Josephine, of course, hers) as adoptive son and heir ap-
parent.

At the very mention of the word *adoption*, however, Louis
turned upon them in one of his wildest rages. "How have I deserved to be disinherited?" he demanded of Napoleon. "What will

be my position when this child, having become yours, considers himself next in line to you, thus outranking me? No, I shall never give my consent to the adoption. Rather than bow before my son, I shall leave France and take him with me. Then we shall see whether, in the face of world opinion, you would dare to wrest a child from its father!"

The names of Lucien and Jérôme had been struck from the hierarchy. Napoleon's hopes of arranging royal alliances for these two members of his family had been frustrated by their recent injudicious and unsanctioned marriages. Young Jérôme had married an American girl, Elizabeth Patterson of Baltimore, with whom he had fallen in love on a tour of naval duty in the Atlantic. Lucien's defiance had delivered the more telling blow to Napoleon's projects: widowed in 1802, he had disobeyed Napoleon's express prohibition and secretly married the beauteous Madame Alexandrine Jouberthon, who had borne him a child before the death of her first husband, from whom she had been separated.

Claire de Rémusat happened to be at St.-Cloud in attendance on the Empress that spring night in 1804 when Napoleon emerged like a thundercloud from a midnight conference with Lucien and announced to his wife, "It's all over! I've come to a final rupture with Lucien, and ordered him from my presence!"

When Josephine tried to calm him, he took her in his arms and told her she was a kind and forgiving woman to plead Lucien's cause. And then, "with his head on her shoulder and his hand upon her hair," says Madame de Rémusat, "that elegant coiffure of hers making a strange contrast to his sad, grim visage," he went on to tell her that his brother had been impervious to threats and pleas alike, rejecting his every proposal. "It is hard," he said, "to meet in one's own family with such resistance to one's greatest interests. Very well, then, I shall suffice to myself—and you, Josephine, will console me for all the rest."

Lucien, the firebrand, departed his brother's realm for Rome, accompanied not only by his wife but also by his mother, who took that means of expressing her sympathy with her younger son and her challenge to the Emperor's authority—a challenge to be flung in his face by all the rest of the Bonaparte family.

In times of family dissension such as this, Napoleon's dependence on Josephine increased and his devotion to her intensified. He could not but be struck by the contrast between the ambitious, vindictive Bonapartes and the unpretentious, amenable Beauharnais': Josephine, "no more rancorous than a dove" (as he told Lucien), making few or no demands upon him for herself or for her children; Hortense, uninterested in rank and honors, submissive, uncomplaining in even the cruel trials of her disastrous marriage; Eugène, "doing his duty wherever he was assigned to it, currently as a simple colonel of the Chasseurs" (as Claire de Rémusat says), "gay, unassuming, forthright in his manner, avoiding involvement in intrigue—so much so that he disarmed all calumniators," including even the Bonapartes.

Thus, the Bonaparte family's fervid campaign to persuade Napoleon to divorce his wife before the coronation was, to say the least, ill-timed. "The question of divorce came up again at this period," Hortense relates. "A family council was convened, but the virulence of the Emperor's brothers was so pronounced, in the midst of what had been intended as a discussion of topics of general interest, that the Emperor could not fail to recognize his family's relentless animosity toward the Empress."

One can hear Napoleon's counterarguments in his words to Roederer, himself an advocate of the family's point of view: "It might be to my interest to seek a divorce, but I have always been a man of justice, so how can I be expected to put aside a good wife just because I have become greater than I was when she married me? Had I been imprisoned or exiled, she would have shared my fate. How can I abandon her now? No, I have not the strength to bring myself to it. I am a man and have a man's heart; I was not whelped by a tigress. Furthermore, my existence would be unbearable without some happiness and relaxation in my private life."

Instead, Napoleon promptly proceeded to appoint a corps of honor attendants for his Empress: twelve ladies in waiting instead of the previous four, and as lady of honor Madame de La Rochefoucauld, a distant cousin of Josephine's first husband. Madame de La Rochefoucauld, who bore one of the proudest names in France, would only now, at the proclamation of the Empire, condescend to meet Napoleon face to face, being one of the great number of Old-Regime aristocrats who had hitherto "divided the Tuileries into two separate and distinct regions, petitioning Madame Bonaparte for favors in her ground-floor apartments while sedulously avoiding any recognition of the power which inhabited the second story," as Claire de Rémusat put it.

The nobility reminded Claire of cats who become attached to a house rather than to a master; aristocrats were drawn back to the Tuileries whether a Bourbon or a Bonaparte was in residence. Napoleon subscribed to the same theory, although he phrased it in a different way. Sitting one night that summer in his wife's salon with the Rémusats ("in one of his amiable and expansive moods, straddling his chair, his chin resting on the chair back") he said to Claire's husband, "I'll wager, Monsieur de Rémusat, that you are a hundred times more comfortable now, addressing me as 'Sire' and being addressed by me as 'Monsieur' instead of 'Citizen.' . . . You French love monarchy and all its trappings. The stern, stark republican ways would not long have pleased you. Now I have brought the Revolution to a close at last—and smoothly, I flatter myself—forever silencing both royalists and Jacobins."

"If Napoleon's reign had opened a long parenthesis in the Revolution," Claire reflected, "he was convinced that the parenthesis would be closed with his death. 'My successor,' he said, 'will have to keep step with the liberal theories of the century—but in a modified form, relieved of their original harshness. That will be my legacy to him.'

"And were we not his accomplices in his seizure of power," Claire questioned herself and her generation, "subscribing as we did to his theory that he should take advantage—both for his security and ours—of that supreme authority inherent in him, which alone seemed capable of suspending the Revolution without destroying it?" Claire did give mild expression to the wish that, upon his accession to the throne, Napoleon had presented to France a constitution that defined the sovereign powers and guaranteed the popular rights, but she was not one of those ardent liberal intellectuals of her time to whom the return to absolutism in France constituted a shocking reversal of the world trend. She was not a Madame de Staël, who spouted her indignation in the spoken and printed word; not a Lord Byron, who volubly expressed his disillusionment in the man he had originally heralded as a champion of liberty; not a Beethoven, who rescinded the dedication of his *Eroica* to Napoleon.

Yet it was in the Revolutionary tradition that the newly proclaimed Emperor chose Bastille Day for the inaugural ceremonies of the order of the Legion of Honor, distributing on July 14, 1804, the first of those prized crosses to members of the Army, the government and the court.

"The Empress, thanks to her exquisite taste and the infinite attention she gave to her attire, looked young and lovely in the midst of the young and lovely ladies of her court, who were in attendance on her for the first time in public," according to Claire (she herself having been among that number). "In radiant sunlight, Empress Josephine made her appearance in a cloud of pale-pink tulle sparkling with silver stars, an extremely low-cut gown, as was the fashion, and an arrangement of diamond wheat-ears in her hair. This splendorous and scintillating costume, the elegance of her bearing, the charm of her smile and the sweetness of her expression made such an impression that I heard many people remark that day that she outshone her entire entourage."

10

Shortly after these ceremonies, the Emperor was off for another inspection of the military and naval bases on the Channel coast and for a final decision on the feasibility of the projected invasion of England. His decision would be in the negative, as it had been in 1798, and for the same reason—the superiority of the British fleet over the French.

And the Empress was off in another direction, to another watering resort, this time to Aix-la-Chapelle (an appropriate choice for the consort of the nineteenth-century Charlemagne) for another "cure," this time under the personal supervision of Dr. Corvisart, the imperial physician—a final and valiant effort for a woman who had just celebrated her forty-first birthday. She traveled in imperial pomp, with a suite of a hundred or more, including a master of the horse, chamberlains, ushers, lackeys, chefs and maids.

One of the Empress's ladies in waiting on that journey was a recent appointee of the Emperor's, a Madame de Vaudey, an Old-Regime aristocrat and a young and piquant beauty. And when the Emperor arrived unexpectedly in Aix from Boulogne, his wife realized with a sinking heart that Madame de Vaudey was the magnet which had drawn him there ahead of schedule. Josephine's state of nerves expressed itself, as usual, in excruciating migraine headaches, which plagued her constantly on the subsequent state journey east to the Rhine, across the river to Coblenz and down to Mainz; but when she begged off from so much as a single entertainment offered the French imperial party by the German princes, her husband literally dragged her from her bed.

She returned to Paris ahead of him in early October to be with Hortense at the time of the birth of the Louis Bonapartes' second child; the infant, a second son—double insurance for the imperial succession—would be named Napoléon-Louis. There Josephine's health improved rapidly when she learned that Madame de Vaudey's withdrawal from the court had been demanded by the Emperor, who had found her gambling and extravagances excessive.

On the Emperor's return, however, it was obvious to the entire court, including Josephine, that he had found a new romantic interest, one more serious than the last. Josephine's suspicions lighted on one and then another of the ladies of her court, among them Laure Junot (whose memoirs contain a provocative account of the curious attentions paid her one summer by Napoleon, in a series of predawn visits to her bedroom at Malmaison*) and Aglaë Ney, one of Hortense's friends and former schoolmates, niece of Madame Campan and wife of the famous marshal. But she finally established that the object of her husband's affections was Adèle Duchâtel, a young noblewoman of remarkable beauty, ambition and

* Madame Junot claims to have tactfully discouraged Napoleon's overly ardent interest by the stratagem of persuading her husband, then governor of Paris, to spend the next night with her at Malmaison, so that in the morning the First Consul would be confronted with an unexpected second head upon the pillow.

arrogance, a rival far more formidable than any of the others. For some reason—possibly out of respect for her husband, who became a high-ranking government official and lived to an advanced age— a mystery was made of the lady's name for generations; she is referred to in contemporary memoirs as "Madame X" and has been openly identified only within this century.

These periodic passions of the Emperor's—of which Josephine's tear-stained face and jangled nerves were the first and clearest indication—were called by the court his "rutting seasons." He himself was no more delicate in his references to his lustful phases. "Love is a singular passion, turning men into beasts," he told Montholon at St. Helena. "I come into season like a dog."

When Josephine, in her distress, turned to her usual confidante, Madame de Rémusat urged her to discretion. Claire knew that Napoleon had been ominously silent on the subject of Josephine's role in the forthcoming coronation. Joseph Bonaparte had strongly advised that she be only a spectator, since her consecration as empress would only further complicate the repudiation which he and all the Bonapartes insisted was inevitable. But, Claire laments, Josephine was "too passionate a woman" to be cautious, and at this critical moment she played directly into the Bonapartes' hands:

In vain I implored her to avoid furnishing the Emperor the pretext of a quarrel, of which his family was certain to make capital. Against my advice, she watched and waited for the occasion to prove what she thus far only suspected.

At St.-Cloud the Emperor's suite opened onto the gardens, and he had recently arranged a small apartment on the floor above to which he had access by a small secret staircase—a mysterious retreat the purpose of which the Empress was not long in guessing. One morning when a group of ladies of the court had gathered in her salon, she saw Madame X suddenly slip out the door, and she rose to follow. . . . I tried to stop the Empress, but she was beside herself and rushed out, leaving me on pins and needles. A half hour later she returned, scarcely able to control herself, and called me into her boudoir. . . .

"All is lost!" she cried. "What I have feared is true. I went upstairs; the door of the apartment was locked, but through the keyhole I could hear their voices, Bonaparte's and that woman's.

The Marriage

I knocked and rattled the door handle, calling out my name. They were long enough in opening it, and when they did their disheveled state and that of the room made the situation all too clear. I know that I should have controlled myself, but I couldn't —I broke out in reproaches. Madame X wept, but Bonaparte became so enraged that I barely managed to escape in time to avoid his violence. I am still trembling, and I know that he will follow me here and make a dreadful scene." . . .

A few moments later a terrible racket issued from the Empress's inner apartments, and I knew that it was the Emperor making the scene his wife had dreaded. Later she sent for me and told me, through her tears, that Bonaparte, after most cruelly threatening and blaspheming her and even smashing furniture in his rage, had informed her that she should prepare to leave the palace; that, weary of her jealous surveillance, he had decided to shake off the yoke and to follow the dictates of his dynastic interests by marrying a woman capable of giving him and the nation a successor. She told me, too, that Bonaparte had summoned Eugène de Beauharnais to St.-Cloud to arrange for his mother's departure. She knew that her situation was desperate, and she asked me to go to Paris to tell her daughter what had happened.

I went, as instructed, next morning, to Madame Louis Bonaparte, who had already had the news from her brother. . . . I found her less perturbed than I had expected.

"I cannot intervene in any way," she told me. "My husband has expressly forbidden it. My mother has been imprudent. She will lose a crown—but at least she will have peace and respite. Ah, believe me, there are women more to be pitied than she."

She spoke these words with a sadness which left no doubt of her meaning, but, since she never parted her lips on the subject of her own tragic marriage, I dared make no reply to indicate that I had understood her implication.

"Besides," she concluded, "if there is any chance at all of a reconciliation between the Emperor and his wife, that chance lies in the empire she exercises over him by reason of her sweet and gentle nature and her tears. It would be fatal for anyone to interfere. The two of them must be left absolutely alone to work it out themselves, and I urge you to stay away yourself . . ."

Following her advice, I allowed two days to pass, and only on the third did I return to St.-Cloud to seek out my Empress, whose fate profoundly troubled me.

The worst of her ordeal was over. Her tears and her submissiveness had indeed disarmed Bonaparte. It was no longer a question of his anger or the cause of it—their reconciliation was complete; but he had thrown his wife into a fresh alarm by pointing out to her how vitally necessary a divorce had become in the light of his imperial position. "I lack the courage to make the decision," he had told her, "and if you display too great an affliction, if you refuse to act except in obedience to my command, I know I shall never be able to bring myself to issue it. I must tell you, however, that I do ardently wish that you yourself could withdraw in the national interest, and so spare me the pain of forcing the issue."

The Emperor wept as he spoke, the Empress said.

Claire thought—but did not say it aloud to Josephine—that if such a plea had been made to her she would have found it in her soul to sacrifice her personal happiness to the national good. But Josephine never pretended to be as noble as Madame de Rémusat envisioned herself. What she told her husband was that whereas she stood ready to obey if he demanded a divorce, she herself would never take the initiative.

"So, with an adroit and tender sweetness, taking the attitude of an unresisting victim," says Claire, "she succeeded in parrying the blow the jealous Bonapartes had aimed against her. Sad, complaisant, completely submissive, but shrewd enough to take advantage of her empire over her husband, she reduced him to a state of agitation and uncertainty from which he could not extricate himself.

"Finally, pushed and harassed too far by his scheming family and resentful of their premature air of triumph, . . . he suddenly announced to his wife that the Pope was on his way from Rome to Paris and would crown them both. She was to proceed immediately to make her preparations for the coronation, which was to take place on December 2."

II

The Crown

As for me, . . . all my ambitions are limited to the one—possession of his heart.

LETTER FROM JOSEPHINE TO EUGÈNE, SEPTEMBER 1, 1807

1

"IT IS IMPOSSIBLE to imagine the excitement, the gaiety and the revelry that prevailed in Paris at the time!" Laure Junot exclaims. "The streets were thronged from morning to night with a joyous, hustling, bustling multitude—some rushing to try to secure tickets for the ceremony, others to engage windows along the route of the procession, from which to watch it pass."

"The Empress," Claire de Rémusat reminisces, "called in the greatest artists and artisans of the day to confer with her on the design of the official costume for the court ladies as well as of her own: the long mantle to cover our dresses, the gold- or silver-embroidered lace or tulle ruff, called a *chérusque*, rising high from the shoulders to frame the neck and face. . . . At this point, we ladies of the court suddenly discovered a sad lack in our education: that of making a proper obeisance. And as suddenly we called in Despréaux, the dancing master to the former Queen, to give us a course in approaching and curtseying before a throne. Next came rehearsals of the intricate coronation ritual, with the court painter

277

David to direct the principal figures in their movements, designing the living tableau of the rite as he would later put it on canvas. . . . It still seems a dream, one of Oriental splendor straight out of *The Arabian Nights.*"

The Pope arrived on Sunday, November 24. To the gentle, white-haired, white-robed Pius VII, who addressed her so kindly as "my daughter," the Empress responded with a reverent affection and abiding devotion. And she found occasion, alone with him, to confess her distress at the irregularity of her marital status. It is not surprising that Pius insisted on a religious marriage; His Holiness could scarcely be expected to anoint and consecrate as emperor and empress a man and woman living in sin. Nor is it surprising that Napoleon acceded to the demand; he could not run the risk of the Pope's refusal to go through with a ceremony which had been heralded throughout Europe and the world.

In the greatest secrecy two days before the coronation, according to Claire de Rémusat, an altar was prepared in the Emperor's study, and, with two aides-de-camp as witnesses, Cardinal Fesch, Napoleon's uncle, performed the midnight ceremony—the ceremony so ardently desired by Josephine for the past four years. As softly, as mildly, as quietly as she went about it, how often she managed to have her way with this autocrat of autocrats.

"Before daybreak on the second of December"—Madame Junot speaking again—"all Paris was awake and stirring, hundreds never having gone to bed."

"At nine o'clock"—Madame de Rémusat takes up the narrative —"the great golden coach, drawn by eight bay horses and surmounted by a crown and four spread-winged imperial eagles, passed through the gates of the Tuileries, the Emperor and Empress seated on its white velvet cushions. She, resplendent in diamonds, wore a diamond bandeau in her hair—which was arranged in a Louis XIV coiffure, a mass of ringlets—and a gown and court cape of white satin embroidered in gold and silver, . . . carrying all this with her customary style, and looking not a day over twenty-five. The Emperor was brilliant, too—in crimson velvet, which would be exchanged for the imperial vestments upon arrival at the sacristy. There the great ermine cloak would be placed upon his shoulders, the Caesar's golden laurel crown upon his head."

"Who that saw Notre Dame on that memorable day can ever forget it?" Laure Junot asks. "The walls were hung with glowing tapestries and adorned with flowers; the vaulted ceiling re-echoed the chant of the priests and the voices of the choir. All the representatives of France were assembled: the military in their bright-hued uniforms, senators and tribunes in plumed hats, the clergy in ecclesiastical habiliments, the young and beautiful women glittering in jewels and arrayed in style and elegance to be seen only in Paris. On his arrival at Notre Dame, Napoleon ascended the steps to the throne in front of the high altar. . . . The Pope anointed his hands and brow with the triple unction and gave the benediction. But at the moment when the Holy Father reached for the crown of Charlemagne to take it from the altar, Napoleon seized it in his own hands and placed it upon his own head. He was strikingly handsome at that moment." ("His profile was like that of a Greek or Roman coin," Madame de Rémusat commented, not for the first time.)

"Then," Laure Junot continues, "it was Josephine's turn to descend from the throne and advance toward the altar, followed by her retinue of court ladies, her scarlet velvet train borne [under protest] by the Princesses Caroline, Pauline and Elisa. One of Josephine's chief beauties, in addition to her exquisite figure, was the graceful tilt of her neck, the elegant carriage of her head; indeed, her entire bearing was conspicuous for grace and dignity. And I could read in Napoleon's countenance the confirmation of my observation. He looked with an air of proud satisfaction at his Empress as she advanced toward him and the altar; and when she knelt down, when the tears she could not repress fell upon her clasped hands raised to heaven—or, rather to Napoleon—both he and she appeared to enjoy one of those fleeting moments of pure felicity unique in a lifetime."

There was, at that moment, in Josephine's aspect something of the awe and wonder and adoration of a Leda, a Danaë, a Europa—an earthling snatched up in the arms of an Olympian, transported, ravished, apotheosized. It was the sublime moment of the rite, caught by David and immortalized on canvas.

"The Emperor performed every action of that complicated ritual with remarkable grace," Madame Junot continues, "but his manner of crowning Josephine was the most striking. After receiving the small crown surmounted by the cross, he had to place it on his own head first and then to transfer it to that of the Empress. When the moment arrived for her coronation, his manner was almost sportive. He took great pains to arrange this little crown over Josephine's tiara of diamonds, putting it on, taking it off and finally putting it on again, as if to promise her that she should wear it gracefully and lightly.

"After the Empress had risen from her knees to move back to the throne," Claire de Rémusat again takes up the story, "the three Bonaparte princesses allowed the full weight of her ermine-lined velvet train to fall against her, with the result that the Empress almost staggered as she mounted the steps of the dais. The Emperor's eagle eye caught the byplay, and he hissed a low but effective warning, so that his sisters quickly picked up the Empress's train again. . . . The *vivats* rang out in full diapason from organ and choir. . . .

"The imperial cortege did not arrive back at the Tuileries until after dark on that December evening, its way illumined by torches. The Emperor, in a gay and charming mood, insisted that the Empress keep on her little crown, even though they dined in their private apartments tête-à-tête. He lavished compliments on her for the grace with which she wore it."

They were more than ever alone now, he and she, on a lonely eminence. Josphine would be the only one left in the world to *tutoyer* him and call him Bonaparte; all the rest of the world breathed a respectful "Sire"—including even his mother, save on those rare occasions when she lapsed into "Nabulione" or "*mio figlio.*" There was one other exception, a trained parrot of Josephine's which was given to shrieking "Bonaparte!" but that gaudy and impertinent bird was soon banished to the servants' quarters, a gift to Mademoiselle Avrillon.

In that solitary splendor in which Napoleon and Josephine found themselves, they inevitably drew closer. His dependence on her increased, as did his tenderness for her as his companion and indispensable confidante. In Bourrienne's opinion, it was now "only through Josephine that the truth was ever to reach the Emperor."

The coronation was followed by a genuine *rapprochement.* Napoleon could take pride in Josephine as his consort, in her success as a sovereign. "I have had the honor," Laure Junot would write, chary as she was with praise of Josephine, "of being presented to many 'real princesses'—to use the Faubourg-St.-Germain expression—but I never saw one who presented so perfect a personification of elegance and majesty as the Empress Josephine."

And if aspersions have been cast on Josephine's intellectual capacity and her powers of mental application, they are refuted by the aptitude she displayed in the strenuous curriculum assigned her at that period by her tutor, the Abbé Halna: a course in the history and traditions of the nations and courts of Europe, including the genealogies of all the royal houses. No French queen before her was ever more knowledgeable on those subjects, as was remarked throughout the Continent. Never once, in her own or in any foreign court, in any gathering of crowned heads or statesmen or in any public ceremony, did she ever falter or fumble over protocol, ever commit a social or a diplomatic blunder. She had, furthermore, acquired the art of the diplomatic banality: "Her every word in public was studiedly insignificant." "Keep silent," Napoleon had enjoined his wife, "for whatever you say will be thought to have come from me." He recommended that she abstain from talking politics, and she followed the recommendation to the letter. As Mademoiselle Avrillon expressed it, "If she was inclined to indiscretion concerning her private affairs, she preserved steadfast silence on public ones."

In the weeks following the coronation, the Bonapartes squirmed to see "the Beauharnais" and her children at the pinnacle of honor. Eugène was named vice-arch-chancellor of the Empire, publicly and warmly commended by the Emperor as "one of the pillars of our throne, one of the staunchest defenders of our realm." And Hortense's second son, Napoléon-Louis, was held over the baptismal font by the Pope himself; while the first, Napoléon-Charles, now a handsome fellow of three, enjoyed the Emperor's conspicuous favor —to the fury of the parents of the other nieces and nephews. Napoleon dandled his first namesake on his knee at table, feeding him from his plate, giving him coffee or wine from his cup. He even unstrapped his sword of state at the child's request and laughed to see the boy strutting and stumbling with the great scabbard strapped about his neck. (Josephine commissioned the artist Baron Gérard to paint the lad in that pose which so amused the Emperor.)

Festivity followed festivity throughout December. At the banquet tendered the sovereigns at the City Hall, the city of Paris' gift was a flattery to the vanity of the woman as well as to the pride of the Empress: a magnificent vermeil toilet case, the masterpiece of that master of Parisian goldsmiths, Germain, which was to be her cachet and her especial treasure, occupying the place of honor in her boudoir and accompanying her on all her travels.

In December, too, in an imposing ceremony on the Champ de Mars, Napoleon distributed his famous eagle standards to certain select regiments of the Grand Army, with Josephine beside him on the dais. She is missing, however, from David's picture of that event, *The Distribution of the Eagles*, for the reason that Napoleon instructed the artist, later, to paint her out of the scene, on the theory that history might be altered by a brushstroke. It was on the same theory that David later on his *Coronation* canvas painted in the figure of the Emperor's mother, Madame Mère, who had been still sulking in Rome with Lucien when the coronation took place.

Sometime in the early spring of 1805, Napoleon gave his wife the dubious honor of breaking the news to his mistress that their relations were to be severed. As he told Josephine, he thought he had detected symptoms of overweening ambition in Adèle Duchâtel, and he had no intention of playing Louis XIV to her Montespan. "He gave his wife a detailed account of the whole affair, in its every phase and with the most indecent openness," Madame de Rémusat tells us. "In her interview with her former rival, the Empress confined herself to pointing out what risk Madame Duchâtel had run of open disgrace and of dismissal from the court, and gently cautioned the lady to greater discretion in the future. But Madame Duchâtel brazenly denied that she had merited any censure or needed any advice, and she continued to perform her duties at the court with her wonted hauteur, and this in the face of the Emperor's marked disdain and discourtesy. "The Empress, it should be said in justice to her" (and Claire de Rémusat was nothing if not rigorously just), "was not in the least vindictive; once she saw that she had nothing more to fear, all was forgiven and forgotten. She became her usual bland and indulgent self, as the Emperor suddenly returned to terms of the fondest intimacy with her."

So Laure Junot saw them that spring at St.-Cloud, in the Blue Salon:

> Josephine was a vision in "misty-white *mousseline de l'Inde,*
> with a narrow lamé border like a rivulet of gold around the hemline of the pleated skirt, a gold-and-black enameled lion's head at each shoulder and another as clasp for the golden belt. Her coiffure was like that of an antique cameo, curls spilling out of a golden circlet, and she wore a golden serpent for a necklace, with matching earrings and bracelets. If there was a striking simplicity in her costume, it was simplicity of the most artful kind; if it was tremendously becoming, it was because Josephine always adapted the mode to her person—one explanation for her reputation as the most elegant of women.
>
> It was clear that the Emperor was as struck as I by her charming ensemble, for he went to her as he entered the room, kissed her on the shoulder and the brow, and led her to the mirror over the mantel so that he might see her from all sides at the same time.
>
> "Now, now, Josephine, I think I should be jealous. You must have some conquest in mind. Why are you so beautiful today?"
>
> "I know that you love to see me in white, and so I put on a white gown, that's all."
>
> "Very well, then, if it was to please me, you have indeed succeeded." Whereupon he kissed her again.

The news that the Emperor had resumed his nocturnal visits to his wife could not long be kept secret at the Palace of St.-Cloud, where, as his valet Constant describes the processional,

> to go from his apartments to hers, he had to walk the length of an entire corridor and up a flight of stairs—he wearing his dressing gown and Madras headcloth, I marching ahead to light his way, with a candelabra in my hand.
>
> When I went into their bedroom between seven and eight in the morning, it was seldom that I did not find the august pair awake. The Emperor usually requested and drank some tea, or a tisane of orange leaves, and then arose at once.

"Must you go already?" the Empress would ask, smiling fondly. "Stay a little longer!"

"But I thought you were going back to sleep," he would laugh and tease, as he tucked the covers back around her, patting her cheek and shoulder, kissing her goodbye.

Then: "I am late rising this morning," the Empress would say to her ladies in waiting, rubbing her delicate little hands together almost gleefully. "But then, you see, Bonaparte has spent the night with me!"

"She always wanted to sleep with me," Napoleon told General Bertrand at St. Helena. "She was well aware of the fact that a woman's influence over a man derives primarily from the sexual relation."

2

In May of 1805, Josephine became queen of Italy as well as empress of France. She was, however, an honored spectator rather than an active participant in the coronation ceremony in the Gothic gloom and glory of Milan's Duomo, where the iron crown of the Lombard kings was placed on Napoleon's head and Eugène de Beauharnais was proclaimed his viceroy.

When Josephine wept at news of her son's promotion, Napoleon could not tell whether it was in joy or sorrow. "If you are weeping because Eugène is to stay on here in Italy, it doesn't make sense," Mademoiselle Avrillon quotes Napoleon as saying to his wife in the dressing room at Milan. "And if separation from your children costs you such anguish, can you imagine how I must feel? Your emotion brings me cruel realization of my deprivation in having no children of my own." Whereat her tears fell faster than before. Josephine had laid herself wide open to that most fearsome of all reproaches.

He, in turn, laid himself open to hers, in another amorous adventure—this time with a Mademoiselle de Lacoste, officially designated on the imperial household payroll as a "reader," though neither she nor any other so designated was ever heard to read. (To some observers, Josephine's retinue appeared a harem collected expressly for the sultan's delectation.) Perhaps Napoleon was stirred by tender memories of honeymoon days in Milan, memories of his "sweet and incomparable Josephine" as a bride, for he put up little or no resistance to her demands that the "reader" be dismissed—as was accomplished, in this instance, with more consideration than usual, according to Mademoiselle Avrillon: the young lady, who is described as blond and an orphan, was given proper escort back to Paris, where an advantageous marriage was subsequently arranged for her by the Emperor.

"The Emperor often sacrificed these passing fancies to his wife's jealousy" (again according to her maid), "on which occasions he often told her more about them than she really cared to know, cataloguing not only their evident attractions but their hidden imperfections. When these moods of confession were upon him, he often went on to name other ladies of the court of whom the Empress had been totally unsuspicious but whose favors, he made clear, had not been denied him."

Mademoiselle de Lacoste was replaced at Genoa by Carlotta Gazzani, one of the "most ravishingly beautiful creatures" Mademoiselle Avrillon had ever seen. The Genoese "reader" was to prove so unassuming in her brief hour as a favorite, so respectful and considerate of her lover's wife, that she would become the Empress's protégée after being discarded as the Emperor's mistress.

Genoa feted the new sovereigns in a fashion so splendid as to impress the Empress's usually blasé maid as "a gala unique in all my experience of imperial travel": a fairyland of lights and music conjured up on the bay; piers and rafts bedecked with trees and flowers to make a floating garden; banquet tables and dance pavilions on the surface of the water; thousands of boats in the harbor, their multicolored lanterns "twinkling in the night like the famous Italian fireflies."

That very body of water that twinkled like fireflies was, in great measure, responsible for the international crisis brewing. The annexation of the port of Genoa by the French Emperor constituted a breach of the Treaty of Lunéville, and Austria, Russia, and England aligned themselves in a new coalition against France. The creation of the kingdom of Italy, with its crown on Napoleon's head, touched off the conflict, and it was in Genoa that the Emperor learned that Austria, without a formal declaration of war, had invaded Bavaria and was advancing toward the Rhine.

"Such was the Emperor's haste to return to the capital," Mademoiselle Avrillon says, "that the Empress had great difficulty in persuading him to allow her to accompany him on the journey. When he yielded, it was only on the condition that she promise to have none of her headaches—as if she had control over such a thing!" Furthermore, she had to agree to the condition of a nonstop trip from Turin to Paris.

The Empress's maid and the Emperor's valet, riding in the second carriage of the convoy, burdened down with the imperial luggage and the imperial jewel cases, soon lost sight of the lead coach, and they never could catch up again. What consternation for Avrillon in the thought of her mistress without her vermeil toilet case and its cosmetics, without so much as a change of linens—she who was accustomed to three changes daily. And what despair for Constant at the thought of his master without his *nécessaire*, his prized kit of toilet articles—flacons of eau de cologne, special razors and special manicure scissors, of which Napoleon, who was extremely vain of his fine hands, required a dozen or more. But the Emperor, up ahead on the road leading through the Alpine passes, had, says Constant, insisted on "such a breakneck rate of speed that at every relay station, while the lathered horses were removed from their traces to make way for fresh ones, buckets of water had to be poured over the smoking-hot carriage wheels."

If Mademoiselle Avrillon, at the journey's end, collapsed into bed with her "feet and legs puffed and swollen from the long days and nights of jolting in a carriage," Josephine could have fared little better. Travel with Napoleon was arduous, and yet, with all his galloping back and forth across the Continent, over thousands of miles, Josephine never willingly stayed behind, never willingly parted from him.

If she parted from him to go to Plombières for the month of August, it was because she needed to recuperate from the exertions of the Italian expedition. She would not, in any case, have been permitted to accompany him to the Channel coast, where he had gone on another inspection tour of the armies gathered, ostensibly, for the invasion of England. This was, perhaps, in the nature of a feint, and by September those regiments were marching eastward toward the Rhine.

By September 24 the Emperor himself was speeding from Paris to Strasbourg, a fifty-eight-hour nonstop trip on which Josephine insisted on accompanying him. He settled her in the Alsatian capital, in the episcopal palace of the Rohan princes, before he departed on October 1 to assume command of his troops in the whirlwind campaign which was to accomplish the rout of the Austrian Army within a single month.

He wrote to Josephine almost daily, from every bivouac: not the impassioned, delirious love letters of the Italian campaign, but letters that breathed a warm affection, an abiding devotion, letters expressive of his need to have her near him, his hope of reunion with her—his closest, surest friend, his best and happiest, most indispensable companion. As one of those letters reads: "Everything in this world must come to an end: beauty, wit, sentiment, the sun itself; but that which has no term is the happiness I find with you— the ineffable goodness and sweetness of my Josephine."

His letters from Austria carried reports of his victories interspersed with reports on his health and spirits, the intimate details of his everyday life which were her especial province. As from Augsburg on October 12: "The enemy is beaten, has lost his head. From all indications, this promises to be the most successful and most brilliant campaign I have ever waged. . . . I am well, but the weather is dreadful. I change uniforms twice a day when it rains. I love and embrace you."

And from the battlefield of Ulm on October 9: "I have destroyed the Austrian Army by a series of simple marches, taken sixty thousand prisoners, one hundred twenty cannon, ninety enemy standards and more than thirty generals. Now I shall turn upon the Russians. They are as good as lost already."

On November 3 Napoleon led his triumphant Grande Armée into Vienna, and he lost no time in writing to his Josephine to tell her that she could shortly proceed to Munich, where he would come to join her. She was to stop at Stuttgart and Baden en route, visiting the various Rhenish courts. "Be civil, but accept their homage as your due," the conqueror coached his wife by letter. "The Electress of Württemberg is the daughter of the King of England, and a nice enough woman. You are to treat her with courtesy, but nothing more. . . . My armies are beyond the Danube in pursuit of the Russians. . . . I am feeling more fatigue than I should, so I have stayed in today to rest. . . . I hope we shall be together again before the end of the month. A thousand kisses."

In accordance with his instructions but to the regret of all Strasbourg, Josephine set out from that city on November 28, heading west on a royal but exhausting progress across southern Germany toward her appointed rendezvous with her husband in Bavaria. The blare of the brass bands, the salvos of the cannon and the clamor of the cathedral bells along the way were enough to start up her migraines, but her winning smile lighted her eyes and lips as every city gate swung open. It was that charm and radiance and cordiality, even more than the largesse scattered by her hand, that made her a legend in the region, so that a hundred years after her passage the peasants of the Black Forest still told their children the tale they had heard from their fathers about the French Empress who had appeared among them "like a fairy queen, glittering in pearls and diamonds, in a cloak the color of dawn and a gown the color of sunlight."

Josephine's conquest of Germany in the name of Paris fashion was to prove more enduring than Napoleon's in the name of French military and political might. It was Josephine who came (with a hundred glamorous costume changes), who was seen and who conquered. "I win battles, Josephine wins hearts," Napoleon said to Méneval when told of the enthusiasm and admiration his wife had evoked all along her path.

One of his greatest battles and most resounding victories was fought and won on December 2, as he wrote to Josephine the very next morning: "I have conquered the Russian and Austrian armies under the joint command of the two emperors. The Emperor Alexander is withdrawing into Russia, three fourths of his army destroyed. The battle of Austerlitz is one of the greatest I have ever fought. We have taken . . . thirty thousand prisoners in all. More than twenty thousand dead—a horrible spectacle. Now I have concluded a truce . . . Very dear to me will be the moment which sees me reunited to you. I yearn to embrace you." As he would, on the last day of the year 1805, when he drove into the palace of the Bavarian Elector Maximilian in Munich and found Josephine waiting for him on the threshold.

With the new year of 1806, Bavaria—which later that year would join with Württemberg, Saxony, Westphalia and Baden to form the Confederation of the Rhine, a French protectorate—became a kingdom and the Elector Maximilian a king, thanks to Napoleon the kingmaker. The newly created King expressed his gratitude by bestowing the hand of his daughter Amalie Augusta on Eugène de Beauharnais, despite the fact that she had been promised to the Crown Prince of Baden.

As Josephine had written to her son in Italy, "No one could be prettier than this princess." Augusta had not only beauty but wit, character and the most beatific disposition. So that this prince and princess, who were wed on January 13, lived happily ever after— even after Waterloo; their marriage was to prove the one exception to the rule of unhappy royal alliances arranged by Napoleon for various members of his family and Josephine's in the course of the next few years.

Hortense's husband arbitrarily forbade her to attend her brother's nuptial celebrations. Caroline Murat came instead, protesting all the way from Paris to Munich, snarling that Napoleon himself rather than Eugène should have wed the young (and, to be hoped, prolific) Bavarian Princess. Caroline, like all the Bonapartes, smarted under the elevation of the Beauharnais'. As a preliminary to the wedding, the Emperor had formally adopted Eugène as his son, created him a prince of France and promised him the crown of Italy as his inheritance. Now Josephine's son as well as her grandson stood, by imperial decree, in the line of succession.

Josephine's cup was overflowing. Never had her future and that of her children seemed so bright, never could she have felt so certain of having exorcised the grim specter of divorce which had haunted her for the past five years. Nothing seemed missing to her happiness. Eugène even acceded to her whim, the night before the wedding, and shaved off the luxuriant mustache which it had taken him months to grow and which he had considered so dashing.

3

Honors continued to be heaped upon the Beauharnais'. Back in Paris, at the end of January, a marriage was arranged by Napoleon for a niece of Josephine's by marriage, seventeen-year-old Stéphanie de Beauharnais, with Crown Prince Charles Frederick of Baden—who was in need of consolation after his fiancée, Augusta of Bavaria, had been lost to Eugène.

Josephine was flattered at first by this second royal alliance for her family within three months. But pretty, pert Stéphanie lost her head when the Emperor—who formally adopted her as his daughter and created her a princess of France to adjust her rank to that of her exalted bridegroom—began to show her attentions which could be construed as neither avuncular nor paternal.

"As the wedding date approached, the Emperor did not trouble to conceal his penchant for the impudent blond beauty, and, by now intoxicated by power, he showed positive impatience when the Crown Prince of Baden dared take exception to such goings-on before his very eyes." This much Claire de Rémusat could have observed with her own eyes, but only the Empress could have told her the rest: that "she had spoken seriously to her niece and tried to point out to the girl what dishonor she risked if she did not resist the Emperor's efforts to seduce her. The girl admitted that these efforts had been very vigorous, and finally promised to conduct herself with greater reserve in the future."

Josephine must have drawn a sigh of relief on April 7 to see giddy Stéphanie to the altar. The wedding, in the chapel of the Tuileries, was no less beautiful a pageant for all the ugly undercurrents. The Empress, in gold-encrusted tulle, led the procession on the arm of the bridegroom, followed by her twenty-four glittering ladies of the palace, with garlands in their hair and bouquets on their arms, trailing silk and satin trains and escorted on either side by a double file of little pages, eighty strong, each boy carrying a golden taper. (The pace for such processionals was set by Josephine's lovely, languorous step; in one of the rare instances of her defiance of her husband's orders, she refused pointblank to quicken the gait to the martial "on the double" Napoleon tried to enforce.) Behind the Empress's luminous, pastel cortege came the military contingent, uniformed in bright green, vivid blue and sharp red; then the high officers of the Empire—ministers, marshals, princes, beribboned and bemedaled; and finally the Emperor, in a Spanish costume, giving his hand to a bride in silver-starred and silver-trained white tulle, diamonds and orange blossoms. (One wonders who was the gifted impresario for these court extravaganzas; perhaps the master painter David, the brilliant stage manager of the coronation.) After the ceremony the Emperor and Empress, with the bride and groom, made their appearance on the balcony over the Tuileries gardens, to acknowledge the cheers of the multitude and to watch the spectacular display of fireworks sent up from the Place de la Concorde by Maestro Ruggieri.

To the Bonaparte sisters, disgruntled at being outranked not only by their sister-in-law but by her niece as well, their brother offered consolation prizes: the Italian principality of Piombino-Lucca to Elisa and her husband, the grand duchy of Berg to Caroline and Murat. Pauline appeared content as a mere Princess Borghese, although she had long since parted company with the Prince; she cared less about titles and appanages than the others, obsessed as she was with her beautiful body—alternately taking rest cures and lovers. The throne of Naples, recently vacated by a Bourbon, seemed to satisfy Joseph, until he learned that Louis and Hortense—another hated Beauharnais—were to have that of Holland.

A throne was the last thing Hortense wanted. It was, she says, "the cruelest ordeal of all those fate had laid up for me," for it took her away from her mother and away from Paris, to a gloomy palace at Rotterdam in the gloomy lowlands fog, putting her more than ever at the mercy of her husband, who would show her none and who would find his spiritual home in the gloom. As for Josephine, theoretically she preened herself at the thought of Hortense as a full-fledged queen; but faced with the actual fact of being parted from her daughter and her two little grandsons, she grieved herself into a state of collapse. "I was utterly stricken at your sister's departure," she wrote to Eugène in Italy. "I experienced the same grief which struck me when you went away. I have been too upset and too ill to write you sooner."

In the winter of 1806, Caroline Murat congratulated herself for having hit upon the perfect scheme to even the score with Josephine and at the same time win high favor with Napoleon. It was Caroline's theory that her brother's ability to procreate must be definitely proved before he would divorce Josephine; such proof had been thus far impossible to establish in view of Napoleon's inconclusive commerce with light-heeled actresses and singers, outright adventuresses and married women. Caroline now proposed to conduct an experiment under proper scientific conditions: to furnish him with a young, healthy and, of course, appealing female, who would be immured, under rigid surveillance, in a pavilion on the Murats' estate at Neuilly. The sleek little guinea pig selected by Madame Murat could not wait to step into the palatial experimental cage. She was Éléonore Denuelle de la Plaigne, seductive, dark-eyed and dark-haired, an alumna of Madame Campan's select finishing school, like the Emperor's sister, Caroline, and like her, unscrupulous. Barely eighteen, but just sufficiently sophisticated at the end of a two-month honeymoon (rudely interrupted by the arrest of her husband on charges of forgery), she was just the tender morsel to tempt the jaded imperial palate.

Josephine's personal secret service was not long in reporting this new development in the Emperor's love life, but "the Empress had at last learned resignation," Madame de Rémusat rejoiced to see. "Either that, or she no longer had the strength to make useless scenes. At any rate, only her air of sadness revealed her secret sorrowing." Perhaps Napoleon was right in giving the credit to her children, as he did when he said to Roederer, "Hortense and her brother take my side, even against their mother, when she raises a fuss over a woman or some such damned nonsense. 'You are making a mistake,' they tell her. 'You should remember that he is a young man and needs distraction from his problems. Remember how good he is to all of us.'" Hortense, in recent months, then, could compliment her mother; and she did, in a letter to Eugène in Milan: "Maman is behaving very well. She no longer makes jealous scenes, which is a great improvement."

"With the Emperor, she was invariably, unalterably, unfailingly sweet, adapting herself to his every mood, every whim, with a complaisance such as I have never seen in anybody else in the world. If

I have made this statement before, I do not mind repeating it." (It is Mademoiselle Avrillon who here repeats herself.) Josephine studied her husband's moods, watched for his slightest change in tone or expression, offered him the only things he any longer required of her: in public, her talents as a consort, her co-operation in that grueling schedule of state and official functions; in private, for the quiet hours, the bland balm of her personality. In the evening, after completing her elaborate late-afternoon costume change, she sat patiently waiting for him to come to dinner, often until the clocks struck eight or nine, even midnight, while he worked on in his study, in conference or at dictation, oblivious to time and to hunger. The Emperor's chefs, turning spits on which chickens roasted by the dozens from six o'clock on, might grumble, but the Emperor's wife might not.

She knew that her husband was confronted by international problems that spring and summer of 1806. His implacable enemy, England, could not long tolerate the Continental System, the economic blockade which Napoleon was preparing to establish and enforce with the co-operation of his satellite states. England could, by now, read Napoleon's mind: his vast design of a league of European nations—a United States of Europe—under French hegemony. Napoleon's sponsorship of the Confederation of the Rhine was interpreted by England as the opening gambit. Now Prussia, Russia and Saxony threatened to join with England in another coalition against France unless French troops were withdrawn from beyond the Rhine.

A hostile Bourrienne quotes Napoleon as saying, "A newly created government must needs dazzle and astonish. My power would decline if I did not give it a base of more fame, new victories." But Napoleon's letters to King Frederick William III of Prussia at this crucial hour are anything but aggressive; he urges a peaceful negotiation to settle their differences. "I hold unalterably to the terms of our alliance," he wrote. "But if your answer indicates that you repudiate it and put your trust solely in the power of arms, then indeed I shall be compelled to take them up."

Josephine may have reacted with less alarm to the news of the outbreak of war in September than to that of Éléonore Denuelle's pregnancy.

4

As the Emperor made ready for another breakneck, nonstop journey to the Rhineland, he prevailed on Josephine to travel separately, at a more leisurely pace, and to join him later at Mainz. But at the last moment, on the evening of September 24, she won her point, and when his carriage sped out of St.-Cloud she was in it, with only one maid and the bedrock minimum of luggage; the trunkloads of clothes, the jewel chests, the vermeil toilet case, the rosewood Sèvres *bidet* and Mademoiselle Avrillon were to follow later.

On October 1, after only three days with her at Mainz, Napoleon was on his way northeast to Saxony to meet the advancing Prussian forces.

Their parting seemed "highly emotional" to Monsieur de Rému-sat, who, with Talleyrand, found himself a witness in Napoleon's study. "The Emperor held his wife for the longest time in his arms, as if unwilling to release her. Still clinging to her, he extended his hand to Monsieur de Talleyrand and encircled them both in his embrace, with the words 'It is painful indeed to leave those one loves best in the world.' [If "loves" was a strong word to be applied to the Minister of Foreign Affairs, the latter was undoubtedly at that time in the Emperor's highest favor.] Then, repeating his words, the Emperor gave way to tears; a sort of nervous spasm seized him, and he went into convulsions which brought on severe vomiting."

He left Josephine in a state of deepest depression. She was concerned about his health; she was sorely troubled about the developments in the house on the Rue de la Victoire where, she knew, he had installed Éléonore Denuelle to await the birth of their child; she was even worried, for once, about the campaign, for there was defeatist talk in her own salon, from her own lady of honor, Madame de La Rochefoucauld, who harped on the legendary might of the Prussian military machine and predicted that France was about to meet its most redoubtable opposition.

"Pay her no attention. She is a stupid fool, as you should know by now," was Napoleon's blunt reply to Josephine's letter of complaint about her subversive honor attendant. "You should make it clear that you are offended, and forbid her to make talk in your salon which might reach the ears of the public and create a bad impression. Your mistake is being too nice to people who are unworthy of it." There it was: the defect of the virtue, the reverse of the medal. Josephine was too nice, too kind, too long-suffering— "too generally cordial," as Laure Junot objected. It might have been said of Josephine, as of Browning's "Last Duchess," that she smiled "too much the same smile" for everyone, indiscriminately. She had not *hubris* enough, she lacked Napoleon's self-assurance and arrogance, his conviction that he had been "born on the eighteenth Brumaire," as he phrased it. "If her position and her grandeur did not turn her head," Claire de Rémusat said, "neither did it elevate her or give her stature." She was never sufficiently imposing, and she could never enforce discipline among her retinue.

Morale, like Josephine's spirits, was very low at her court at Mainz. Not even Princess Stéphanie, coming from Baden, and Hortense and her two little sons from Holland, could greatly cheer the Empress. And certainly not the divertisements offered by the princes, the grand dukes and the margraves of the Frankfurt region. (Even Josephine's maid was bored: "Just imagine a series of galas, fetes, pageants, theatrical performances and fireworks, and you have a picture of all of those imperial tours.") At night, after the whist scores had been settled, Josephine sat playing her interminable games of patience, her endless variations of solitaire, all a form of fortunetelling to which she was addicted.

One midnight in mid-October, when she had succeeded in working out the great patience, the little patience and the windmill one after the other, she exclaimed jubilantly to her ladies in waiting, "This means we are soon to have good news from the battle front—some incredibly great victory!"

Even as she spoke, a footman threw open the double doors to announce a messenger from the Emperor. It was his premier page, mudspattered from head to toe, who knelt and held out a letter on his hat brim, to present it to the Empress. Napoleon had written from Jena on the night of October 14: "My dear Josephine, we have met the Prussian army and it no longer exists. I am well, and press you to my heart."

"Now, then!" Josephine exulted, after reading the victory bulletin aloud to the assembled company. "Now will you at last begin to believe in my cards and my predictions?!"

By October 25 the French army was in Berlin and Napoleon was at Sans Souci, the Potsdam palace of Frederick the Great, whose disciple he was in the art of war—sitting reverently at the great Frederick's desk and appropriating Frederick's sword and alarm clock as the most precious trophies of the campaign. Perhaps out of reverence for this fabled warrior's line, Napoleon forbore from deposing the Hohenzollerns in the person of Frederick William III. Napoleon felt sorry for the King— "How unhappy those princes can be who permit their wives to interfere in affairs of state"—and blamed the warlike Queen Louise ("a woman with beautiful features but little brain") "for all the suffering she has brought upon her country," or so he stated it in the official bulletin for French consumption. Josephine must have reproached him for this public discourtesy to a woman, since he wrote to her in reply: "You seem displeased at my speaking ill of women. It is true that I detest intrigantes. I am accustomed to women who are gentle, sweet and captivating. That's the kind of woman I like. But that's your fault, not mine—it is you who have spoiled me for the others."

Victory followed upon victory; yet Josephine's black mood persisted. "I don't know why you should be weeping—I am feeling marvelously fit and well, and you have had news of my successes," Napoleon wrote to her in October from Berlin. And again on the first of November: "Talleyrand has arrived here, and tells me that you do nothing but cry. What can be the matter with you? You have your daughter and grandchildren with you and good news from me—everything to make you content and happy."

Nothing could content her or make her happy—nothing short of being reunited with him and resuming the pattern of their married life. She read the danger in the breaking of the habit of their life together. During the next two months, by every courier, she begged to be allowed to join him; by every courier, he encouraged her to think she could, yet put her off, as in November: "I am distressed to hear that you are so unhappy at Mainz. If the trip were not so difficult, you could come at least this far [to Berlin]. I shall wait to hear what you think of the idea." On November 22: "I am upset to learn that you are so sad . . . I shall decide within the next few days whether to have you come here or go back to Paris. You can hold yourself in readiness." But no, she could not count on his meeting her in France. "I still have too much unfinished business here."

Unfinished business with the will-o'-the-wisp Russian army, yet to be defeated. "Things go well, the Russians are in flight, but I must make a foray into Poland. After that, I'll call you to Berlin."

Was she clairvoyant, did she really have a dream about a Polish enchantress, about a romance that would begin in the plains of Poland—a really serious love affair such as she had so long dreaded? Apparently she had, to judge by Napoleon's letters of December 2 and 3 from Posen: "You told me of your dream, yet you add that you were not really jealous. It is my observation that those who are most afraid protest the loudest that they are not. Thus you convict yourself of being jealous. I am flattered. Though, of course, you are being silly. Here in the wastes of Poland, one gives little thought to beauties. . . . Besides, there is only one woman for me. Do you know her? I would draw her portrait for you, but I don't want you to become conceited. . . . The winter nights are long, all alone! Goodbye, my well-beloved."

Other letters written that month are in the same vein: "I can see that that little Creole head of yours is in a spin, and I am reminded of the verse that runs: 'A woman's desire is a consuming flame.' Calm yourself. As I have written you, I am still in Poland, but just as soon as winter quarters are established you can come— although a final decision must still be postponed for several days. . . . The heated tone of your letter of November 27 proves to me that pretty ladies brook no obstacle across their path. . . . You must wait, however, until conditions are favorable." And finally, from Pultusk: "Your recent letters have really made me laugh. You overestimate the fascination of the Polish ladies."

Those last lines were written on New Year's Eve. By a strange coincidence, it would be on the next day, January 1, 1807, that he would first lay eyes on the most fascinating Polish lady of all,

Countess Marie Walewska, as, with snowflakes glittering in her fair hair and on the dark furs enveloping her, she stood on the roadside at Bloni on the approaches of Warsaw, one of the vast throng waiting for a glimpse of the man reputed to be the champion of the freedom of the peoples, the man the Poles envisioned as the liberator of a dismembered, anguished Poland. (Were not his enemies the enemies of Poland—Prussia, Russia, Austria? Had he not let it be known that he was considering re-establishing an independent Polish kingdom?)

That night, however, the last night of the old year, news of an event of great significance reached the Emperor at Pultusk, when a courier cantered up to headquarters and delivered a letter from Caroline Murat announcing a birth in Paris: a "male child"—so reads the registry of the Second Arrondissement—born on December 13 and registered two days later as "Léon, the son of Éléonore Denuelle, a spinster [sic] of independent means, and an absent and unknown father . . ."

Napoleon's grave doubts had been resolved by a son of his own loins. He could, then, hope—with a young and fruitful wife—to beget an heir of his own. He need no longer depend on the sons of other men, the sons of his brothers.

His doubts, that is to say, had been nearly resolved, but not wholly; a residual doubt still remained to nag at his mind. Rumors had reached him via the grapevine of his secret police that his sister's experiment had been something less than ideally scientific; that her own uncontrollably lusty husband, General Murat, had forced the supposedly impregnable pavilion on the Murat estate ahead of even General Bonaparte. He would get to the truth on his return to Paris. Even so, he would begin drawing up a list of the matrimonially eligible princesses of Europe.

Meanwhile, in Warsaw, where a veritable tidal wave of enthusiasm and adoration broke over him, he had only one command for the Polish representatives obsequiously consulting his pleasure: to identify and find his Polish countess with the snowflakes in her hair.

Prince Józef Poniatowski, a general in Napoleon's army, led a delegation to the mansion of Count Walewski to persuade that septuagenarian's eighteen-year-old wife to attend the ball being given in the hero's honor, and to induce her to reply to the Emperor's fervent letters: "Why has your enthusiasm suddenly waned? Oh, do not deny a measure of joy, of surcease, to a poor heart ready to adore you! Why is it so difficult to secure a reply? You owe me two." Then three, then four: "There are moments when fame palls, weighs heavily on the spirit, and it is from this I suffer now. . . . Oh, come, come to me! All your hopes shall be fulfilled. Think how much dearer your country will be to me if you take pity on my heart.—N."

The "raging" Poniatowski camped on her doorstep, "arguing, pleading, even threatening," according to her account. It required all his persuasions, plus a joint appeal by the leaders of the Polish nobility, to coerce Marie Walewska to "the final surrender"—although Poniatowski's account shows her somewhat less obdurate than does her own. Hers, of course, was written to justify herself in the eyes of her descendants—or to justify herself to herself. For her conscience was to torment her all her life for the dishonor she had brought upon the honorable name of her "fond and kind" husband (who, in joining his voice to those of the other fanatic Polish patriots, seems never clearly to have understood the proposal being made to his wife).

This was no light woman, although she may have been bedazzled by the glory of this impetuous lover. Yes, she admits, she had gone rushing out to hail him "in a mad, patriotic exaltation," but "it was the statue of Genius, the figure of the Savior of Poland, that I had worshiped from afar. Close up, the man terrified me! That extraordinary man! He was like a volcano. The passion that dominated him was ambition, but those of love were nonetheless violent, transitory as they were."

By Napoleon's account to General Gourgaud, "She did not struggle overmuch"—words to be interpreted at will, perhaps as a literal confirmation of her statement that she "fainted dead away at the moment of the consummation of the sacrifice." "The dove could not escape the swooping eagle," she quotes him as saying to her. Ironically enough, statues might have been erected to Marie Walewska in the public squares of Warsaw as a Polish Joan of Arc, had her lover only kept his promises to her to liberate her country;

but he did not, and so she rates merely a full-page portrait and a chapter to herself in the Napoleonic legend.

Napoleon may have spoken coarsely to General Gourgaud at St. Helena in 1816, at the news of the Polish countess's death, but in the autumn of 1807 he spoke tenderly. "Her soul is as lovely as her face," he told his brother Lucien in a moment of brief reunion in Italy in November. Rarely did Napoleon concern himself about his mistresses' souls. It was only to Marie, out of all the long list of his inamoratas, that he displayed any genuine tenderness, only with her that he was emotionally involved. And if his love for her was "transitory," to use her adjective, still it was the most enduring of all his extramarital relations. What is significant is that Marie was, temperamentally, a facsimile of Josephine. She was his kind of woman, the "gentle, sweet and captivating" kind he had described to Josephine when he wrote that she had spoiled him for any other. Like Josephine, Marie was docile, making no demands upon him save for her country. The "renaissance of Poland" was her only desire, she was to write. "Not all the other treasures of the world" (which he tried to heap on her) "could content me or restore me in my own estimation."

Having become Napoleon's mistress—and in full view of all Warsaw, which was agape at "the romance of the century"—Marie Walewska would not return to her husband's roof when, on January 31, her imperial lover was called away to the French outposts in pursuit of the elusive Russians. She secluded herself at her mother's estate in the country, "there to await the Emperor's summons" and a reunion for which she was now as eager as he.

Josephine, in Mainz, waited for the same summons. Hers was not to come. With the very first week of January, with the beginning of *l'affaire* Walewska, Napoleon had abandoned all thought of having Josephine come to join him, and his letters that month all urged her to do the same:

January 1: I am touched by your pleas, but there is simply too vast a distance to be traversed between Mainz and Warsaw. The winter is too cold, the roads too poor, too insecure. I am more disappointed than you that we are not spending these long winter nights together [sic], but I cannot permit you to expose yourself to such fatigues and dangers. . . . Go back to Paris, where your presence is needed.

January 3: You must give up the idea of a three-hundred-league journey at this season, through the mud, across enemy territory, on the heels of the armies. . . . Paris claims you. Go there; it is my desire.

January 8: Go back to Paris for the winter. Go liven up the capital! Be gay and happy. I laugh at your fears about my being under fire, but I am distressed at the melancholy tone of your letters and at the reports that reach me about you.

Later that month: I love you very much, but if you continue weeping all the time I shall consider you without courage and without character, and you know how I detest cowards. . . . An empress should show more spirit!

Still later: I had a good laugh over the letter in which you said that you had taken a husband in order to be with him! I always thought . . . that woman was made for man, and man for country, family, glory, honor. Pardon my ignorance. One always learns something new from you beautiful females.

Finally, in an undated letter written after he had departed Warsaw to join his army:

Josephine, your heart and your instincts are excellent, infallible. I cannot say as much for your head or your logic. Now, enough of this quarrel. I want you to believe me when I tell you that it costs me dearly to forgo the pleasure of having you join me. Say to yourself, "It is proof of how precious I am to him." However, I want you to obey me, not moping and weeping, but with good heart, good will, good spirits. Go back to Paris now. It is my will.

Hoping for a reprieve, pleading illness, Josephine had put off her departure from Mainz again and again, until she could do so no longer. On January 26 she yielded to that final imperative, that final expression of "my will," and returned to Paris.

On February 9, he wrote to her from the battlefield of Eylau, in East Prussia, to announce another "memorable day": "A great victory yesterday [over the Russians], although it cost me many brave men. . . . Only two lines tonight, in my fatigue, to tell you that I am well and that I love you." And a few days later he advised her: "Because of the bad weather, the army will have to go into winter quarters."

To go back on the offensive, he would have to wait until the spring. He waited—though not alone—from April 1 to the end of May, in a fortified Prussian castle. While the thaws of that spring of 1807 were coming, the Emperor and his Polish sweetheart lived out their romance at Schloss Finckenstein.

5

The news was not long in reaching Josephine.

"I found the Empress, upon her return," Claire de Rémusat notes, "very upset over what she had learned, from several Polish ladies then resident in Paris, on the subject of a liaison between the Emperor and a young compatriot of theirs. The Empress's attachment to her husband was always greatly complicated by her fear of divorce, which of all her sentiments was the most compelling. She tried occasionally to slip some oblique reference to this new affair into her letters to him, but to these she received no direct reply."

The tenor of these replies may be judged by these excerpts:

As usual, you immediately lose that little Creole head of yours and begin to agonize. . . . Whatever makes you think you are going to die? You are in good health and have no reasonable ground for worry. . . . Pay no heed to malicious gossip. Never doubt my sentiments; on that score, you may be completely at ease. . . . I have taken up quarters in a very fine château with many fireplaces, and, since I often arise during the night, I find the sight of the flaming logs extremely pleasant.

And in May:

I do not know with which ladies I am supposed to be in correspondence. . . . I love only my little Josephine, sweet, sulky and capricious, who, even when she quarrels, does so with grace—as she does everything. For she is always amiable, except when she is jealous—and then she becomes a female demon.

As for the disquietude that gripped Paris that winter over the military stalemate and the prolonged campaign, Napoleon had a sharp rebuke for Josephine and her contribution to poor morale: "Yes, I 'know how to do something else besides making war,' as you put it. I too yearn to return to Paris, to you, to a peaceful life, but duty comes first, and all my life I have sacrificed personal pleasures and happiness to my destiny." Then, with a curt "Now let's drop the subject," he went into a detailed list of do's and don'ts to regulate Josephine's way of life in the capital:

You are to stay in Paris for the month of April and go to St.-Cloud on May 1. You may go to Malmaison for the weekends, but remember never to receive ambassadors or strangers there, where you live informally. . . . I am pleased to hear of the fetes given in your honor and of the resumption of your formal weekly receptions. I was glad to note that you had attended the Opéra, and you may go occasionally to one of the four principal theaters— provided you use the imperial box . . . But you must not go to the small houses or [vaudevilles] or sit in private loges. It is unsuitable to your rank . . . Grandeur has its price—an Empress cannot live like a private citizen. . . . Live exactly as you do when I am there. You are to dine only with persons who have been invited to dine with me; your own guest list is to remain the same. Any infraction of these rules would seriously displease me. And, finally, do not allow yourself to be taken advantage of by people whom I do not receive and who would not be permitted in your apartments if I were there.

And that meant Thérèse Tallien, Josephine's good friend of Directoire days, who, after her divorce from Tallien and her years-long affair with banker Ouvrard, had married into one of the most distinguished families of France. The Prince de Caraman-Chimay could forgive the beautiful Thérèse her notorious past, but the Emperor could not, and he rejected all her petitions for entree to the court. Could it have been that this former intimate of Barras was too poignant a reminder to the Emperor of his wife's former relations with the exiled Director? At any rate, Thérèse was made the subject of an individual imperial decree:

My dear Josephine, I absolutely forbid you to see Madame T—— on any pretext whatsoever. I shall accept no excuse. If you care about my esteem and want to please me, never transgress this order. From what I hear, she must come to your apartment surreptitiously and spend the night. Give orders to the porter that she is to be denied admittance. Some renegade, I know, has married her—with her litter of eight bastards—but I find her more despicable than ever. She used to be a nice enough trollop; she has become a horrible, infamous woman.

"The Empress forced herself to conform to the Emperor's wishes, dutifully issuing and accepting invitations to a round of gala functions," Claire de Rémusat writes of this period. "The larger the imperial court grew, the stricter the ceremonial and the more impersonal and monotonous the life there became; and as the Emperor's despotism increased, so did the fear and the silence among the courtiers. All former intimacies with him ceased. We seemed, all of us, on an eternal dress parade, our sole function being to surround the throne with the appropriate pomp and splendor, in line with the Emperor's theory that luxury and glory were unfailingly intoxicating to the French. His wife came gradually to the same state of dependence as all the rest—shut out, like all the rest, from his ever loftier, ever more ambitious projects. She lived quietly, always kind and pleasant, but detached, indifferent, languid, idle. If she was not a pleasure seeker, neither did she seek escape from boredom. She manifested the same affability to everyone, little or no real friendship to anyone."

She could not call her life her own; she lived in a grandiose void. Alone in Paris as she was, her husband, children and grandchildren* far away in foreign lands, no wonder the Empress's happiest hours were those spent in her mirrored, marbled and frescoed dressing room and bathroom—floating in her delicately perfumed bath, or luxuriating under the expert ministrations of pedicurist, manicurist and masseuse, or seated at her vermeil toilet case, lighted by its matching pair of gold-and-crystal girandoles, with all its fascinating cosmetic paraphernalia spread out before her: crystal perfume flacons, gold and silver boxes, jars, cases, combs, brushes, scissors. Only there, perhaps, in her gilded triple mirror, could she find reassurance of her grace and beauty, reassurance of vitality, of the very fact of her existence.

Her only real confidantes were her staff of six handmaidens of the toilette—four maids, one chief wardrobe mistress and Malvina, another faithful mulatto from Martinique—whom she consulted thrice daily on the serious business of her life, the cultivation of her attractions. It was to them that she read the letters from her children, even from her husband, often entrusting the precious packets to Mademoiselle Avrillon for safekeeping (along with her jewel chest) in those palaces overrun with attendants where an empress could count on little privacy.

Only the two maids on duty each day shared her beauty secrets: the application of hair tints, facial masks, emollients and astringents, rouges, powders and chalky skin whiteners. Only after the intricate, hour-long ritual of *maquillage* had been completed and after a frilly peignoir had been slipped over her lacy batiste chemise, only then were the ladies of the palace invited in to watch the coiffeur at his work. In the morning Josephine's resident hairdresser, Herbault, presided; in the late afternoon the celebrated Duplan, whose pay was said to exceed that of a brigadier general, came to the palace to create the elaborate flowered, feathered or jeweled evening coiffures.

While the master artist effected his latest inspiration, the wardrobe mistress and her assistants brought in the great baskets of as-

---

* Eugène's and Augusta's first child, a girl, had been born that spring in Milan, and had been named by the Emperor in honor of the Empress: Joséphine-Maximilienne, Princess of Bologna.

sorted slippers, hose, gloves, petticoats, redingotes and dresses for the Empress's final selection. No easy task, this last, out of a wardrobe collection that at times contained as many as 676 dresses (not to mention 49 *grands habits de cour*, special costumes for special occasions such as weddings and state functions), 252 hats or headdresses, 60 cashmere shawls, 785 pairs of slippers, 413 pairs of hose (no pair worn more than once) and 498 embroidered or lace-trimmed chemises (certainly an adequate supply, even considering that Josephine made three complete lingerie changes daily). With staggering statistics such as these confirmed in the official wardrobe inventory of 1809, it can come as no surprise that, along with the ritual of the toilette, the selection and purchase of these garments and accessories constituted Josephine's greatest pleasure and principal interest in life. ("It was fortunate for the Empress," Claire de Rémusat remarks, perhaps maliciously, "that she could always find distraction from her problems in the selection and modeling of some dazzling new creation.")

Not that her acquisitive mania was confined to wearing apparel. "The truth was," Mademoiselle Avrillon admits, "she had an uncontrollable passion for everything beautiful. One couldn't even say that she had a special penchant for this or that, one kind of thing more than another. Everything beautiful, artistic, in good taste caught her fancy, and she simply had to have it—whatever it was, whatever it cost. Often she bought extremely expensive objects for which she had no use whatsoever, merely for the pleasure of acquiring them. No one in the world, I might add here, had such exquisitely refined taste as she; but then, those artists and artisans who vied with one another to display their wares before her were all masters in their specialties, so all were accepted. To make it worse, she could never summon up the courage to turn away a tradesman without making a purchase of some kind."

"She bought everything, and without ever asking the price," Claire de Rémusat tells us, "and most of the time immediately forgot what she had purchased. The waiting rooms off her private apartments were always crowded with merchants and merchandise of every sort and description. Her husband would have liked to prevent these people from gaining access to her, but in this field even Napoleon admitted to defeat."

He managed to enforce, if briefly, a rule forbidding tradesmen to come to the Empress unsolicited; but, as Mademoiselle Avrillon relates, even this taboo was shortly violated: "Mademoiselle [sic] Despeaux, the most fashionable modiste of the day, sat waiting one day in the Empress's anteroom beside a mountain of hatboxes when the Emperor happened to pass by on his way to his wife's dressing room. He burst in, flailing his arms and shouting, 'I demand to know who sent for that woman!' . . . I resisted the impulse to decamp in terror with the rest of the staff, for I did not want to desert my Empress, who was caught helpless, with the coiffeur working on her hair and the pedicurist on her feet. . . ."

The Emperor issued orders for the milliner's arrest . . . and only the prompt action of General Duroc, Grand Marshal of the Palace, saved her from being hauled away to prison.

The Empress sent immediately to Paris to inquire after Mademoiselle Despeaux's health, for the poor woman had been frightened out of her wits. . . .

On such occasions as these, the Empress, groaning in silence, met the Emperor's tantrums with an unshakable sweetness and gentleness. . . . But in his behalf it is only fair to say that those rages of his were of short duration; he never harbored resentments. . . . A day or two later, he joined his wife in laughing over the "Despeaux incident."

He did not laugh, however, over the Empress's uncontrollable extravagances and constantly recurring debts; in her compulsive spending sprees, not even his usually dread imperative could restrain her. "Then, sad to say," says Mademoiselle Avrillon, "when the hour of reckoning sounded, the expenditures had always exceeded the Empress's allowance. Then she had to turn to the Emperor to liquidate her debts, and though he always ended up by doing so, it was only after the most violent scenes. The Emperor raged, the Empress wept; a reconciliation invariably followed, but these altercations were so shattering to her nerves that she invariably made a resolve never again to allow herself to become so involved. But, just as invariably, her acquisitive mania won out once more over her resolve, and she was soon back at it again, running up bills with all the tradesmen of the capital. Her extravagance was the principal basis for her husband's complaints." ("She was

in never-ending financial straits," Napoleon told General de Caulaincourt in 1812. "She waylaid me in ambushes of tears, in which
I granted her what I should have refused her.")

Josephine's annual allowance for "toilette"—clothing and personal adornment—was, at this period, 360,000 francs, a figure
which would be raised to 450,000 in 1809. To this, each year,
were added supplemental grants for extraordinary expenses such
as a special trousseau for a foreign journey or an especially splendid
costume for an especially splendid occasion, like the wedding of
Jérôme Bonaparte to Princess Catherine of Württemberg in August of this year of 1807. Then, almost yearly, Napoleon settled
Josephine's outstanding indebtedness—to the tune of 391,000
francs in this same year and of 650,000 francs the year before, with
an average of better than half a million francs a year paid out for
debts during the years 1804-1810. Thus, one arrives at the staggering annual average of 1,100,000 francs for the Empress's personal
expenditures. "Not all the revenues of all the provinces of France
could have satisfied her extravagances," had been the Marquis de
Sade's dictum on Josephine as early as the days of the Directory.

In all fairness to this madly extravagant, inveterately profligate
woman, it should be pointed out that many of Josephine's private philanthropies came out of the toilette allowance; she had a
special allowance for charities, of course, but, with all the demands
upon her from family and friends in addition to her public charities, she was often obliged to dip into this personal account. Often
Malmaison expenses also came out of the toilette fund—which is
not to imply, however, that such expenditures were not an extravagance. "The Empress could have built a tremendous palace
for what she poured into improvements for that relatively simple
country estate," Mademoiselle Avrillon says. "Why, I once saw
her pay three thousand francs for a single tulip bulb from Holland."

Costs for jewelry were also chargeable to that same allowance.
Josephine had all the crown jewels of France at her disposal, in
addition to her fabulous personal collection (which had outgrown
the jewel chest of that former "Queen of Diamonds" Marie Antoinette), but each year found her sending stones to be reset, having rings made over into pins and pins into bracelets, ordering

new mountings for old, trading one set for another, exchanging rubies for emeralds or diamonds for pearls, and incurring considerable expense in each transaction. Throughout her years as empress, a shimmering stream passed endlessly through her fingers.

6

A cruel blow struck Josephine suddenly that spring of 1807, jolting her out of her lethargy and her vague melancholy: the death of her eldest grandchild, her own and Napoleon's favorite, the four-and-a-half-year-old Napoléon-Charles, who succumbed to a brief but fatal attack of croup on May 4 at The Hague. The news came to Josephine by letter from King Louis, along with the advice that Hortense was in a serious state of shock. Josephine dared not go beyond the city limits of Paris, much less cross the frontiers of France, without express permission from her husband; in his absence, she waited for formal authorization from the imperial Council of State before setting out for the Château of Laeken, near Brussels, where Louis was bringing Hortense to meet her.

A death and a birth within six months of each other, the death of Napoleon's heir designate in the spring of 1807 and the birth of Léon Denuelle in the winter of 1806 (about which the Empress had, inevitably, learned): here were two new and cogent reasons for divorce, as Josephine could not fail to recognize.

Napoleon, still in hibernation at Finckenstein, his mind fastened upon his spring campaign against the Russians, his heart upon his Polish mistress, was inclined to be philosophical about the family tragedy; and, although he wrote to his wife frequently and solicitously in May, he exhorted her to adopt a like frame of mind: "You can imagine what grief I suffer at the news about poor little Napoléon, and I wish I could be with you, but even grief must have its limits, and one must seek diligently for consolation. . . . I note that you are being unreasonable about this loss of ours. . . . Try to calm yourself, unless you wish to add to my distress. . . . I am indeed disturbed at your report that Hortense continues in that state of stupor. She simply must get hold of herself and show more courage. . . . You may stay on at Laeken for two weeks or so, since this will not only please the Belgians but serve as a distraction for you."

But Josephine and Hortense would be returning before then to France, as is indicated by Napoleon's letter of June 2 from Danzig: "I am advised of your return to Malmaison, though I have had no letters recently from you. I am very displeased with Hortense, who has not written me so much as a line. Why have you not succeeded in consoling and distracting her? Weeping with her will not accomplish the purpose. Please take care of yourself for my sake, so that I do not return to find you utterly woebegone."

Dr. Corvisart prescribed a trip to the Pyrenees for Hortense. Louis, shattered by grief and contrite at the sight of his wife's alarming mental and physical condition, not only agreed, but later joined her there. Their brief reconciliation, to which Josephine had constantly urged her daughter, was to result in the birth of their third child—a third son, Charles-Louis-Napoléon, the future Emperor Napoleon III.

On May 31 Napoleon had left Marie Walewska at Finckenstein to join his armies north of Berlin. His only disappointment in their two-month idyl of love was in the fact that his mistress still showed no sign of pregnancy. Marie was only eighteen; she had already borne a child to seventy-year-old Walewski. Napoleon's new-found confidence in his virility was again shaken. How embarrassing it would be to take a young and royal bride, only to see the new marriage go childless; it would make him the laughingstock of all Europe.

The only "children" of whom he could be certain were his soldiers. On June 14 he and they caught up with the Russians at Friedland, and on the fifteenth the Emperor's favorite courier, Moustache, was sent racing back to France, to Josephine, with the news.

She was at St.-Cloud, playing her eternal games of patience, that midnight when Moustache dashed into the palace courtyard. At the sound of the clatter of hoofs and the cries of "*Holà!*" she went running down the marble-columned staircase, her courtiers behind her, to meet the rider, whose horse fell dead from exhaustion even as he dismounted to hand her the Emperor's letter.

Napoleon had written: "Only a line, my dear, for I am very weary after many days' bivouacking. My children have this day worthily celebrated the anniversary of the battle of Marengo. The entire Russian army is in flight. Friedland is a victory worthy of her sister victories Marengo, Austerlitz and Jena, a name to become equally famous and glorious among my people. You may give out this news as official notice, if it arrives before the army bulletin. The cannon may be fired."

And Josephine, having exultantly given out the news by reading the letter aloud, slipped a magnificent diamond ring from her finger as a fitting reward to the messenger from Friedland.

But even that signal victory failed to dissipate her persistent malaise, her indefinable, lingering melancholy, as Napoleon noted critically in his letter dated July 6: "I have received your letter of June 25, and I am hurt to see that you are thoroughly egotistical, that you appear uninterested in my military successes. I too am most eager for our reunion, but that must wait on the will of destiny."

He was on his way to the River Niemen, where, in a tent on a raft opposite the town of Tilsit, he and the Czar of Russia were to meet to begin peace negotiations and divide the world between them.

In their fortnight together, their friendship took on the form of a mutual-admiration society. "I am delighted with the Emperor Alexander," Napoleon wrote to Josephine on June 25. "He is a fine, handsome young emperor, with more wit than is generally ascribed to him." Napoleon himself was irresistible when he set out to charm anyone, as Claire de Rémusat, Laure Junot, Bourrienne and a host of others all attest. Alexander was visibly impressed with the victor of Friedland, whose peace terms to the conquered Russians were magnanimous: no territorial demands and no demand for reparations, merely a proposal for the division of the Continent into two spheres of influence mutually agreeable to the two great powers, with a proviso assuring the co-operation of Russia in the enforcement of the Continental blockade against England. And, yes, one other request, though this was no part of the treaty proper: a request that the hand of one of the Russian Emperor's sisters be given in marriage to the Emperor of the French.

The Prussian sovereigns were dealt with less amiably at Tilsit; Prussia was reduced to a second-rate power, despite the advocacy of its beautiful Queen. "The Queen of Prussia is truly enchanting," Napoleon wrote to Josephine on July 8, "and she is playing the coquette with me. But you need not be jealous—all her appeals run off my back like water off a waxed cloth. It would cost me too dear to be gallant in this instance."

He was carving a sizable slice out of Prussia to be served up, in the form of a new kingdom of Westphalia, as a wedding portion for brother Jérôme Bonaparte. Even so, Queen Louise of Prussia had found Napoleon extremely attractive. "His head is shapely," she wrote, "his lineaments are those of a thinker, his whole appearance reminds one of a Roman emperor."

From Dresden, on his way home, Napoleon announced to Josephine: "I am here with the King of Saxony" (looking over that monarch's daughter, who, at thirty, was too old and too homely to appeal to him as a matrimonial candidate, even were he to consider so politically insignificant an alliance), "and thus I am half-way home to you. I shall be extremely happy to see you again. One of these fine nights, very soon now, I shall come hurtling into St.-Cloud like a jealous husband, so I warn you, be careful!" This timeworn warning about surprising her in the arms of a lover was his favorite cliché nowadays, used over and over again in his letters to her—now that he was no longer jealous of her, now that he knew she gave him no cause to be.

He "hurtled" into the palace on July 27, after a ten-month absence; and the reunion with Josephine appeared, at least at first, a very happy one.

7

Flushed from his recent triumphs, bluff, jovial, Napoleon even teased his Empress good-humoredly about the attentions paid her by the handsome, intelligent young Crown Prince Frederick Louis of Mecklenburg-Schwerin, one of the German princes who came to Paris for Jérôme Bonaparte's wedding in August and stayed on to work out terms for the entry of their principalities into the Confederation of the Rhine.

Claire de Rémusat is at pains to make clear that her patroness did not provoke such attentions, that her conduct at this period was above reproach. "I saw her always almost totally preoccupied with her position," says Madame de Rémusat (who in the period of which she is now writing was herself preoccupied with position, having recently become a countess), "and trembling lest she displease her husband. Certainly she showed no trace of coquettishness; her manner was entirely decorous, even restrained." What had attracted the Prince was the Empress's "consistently good nature, her sweet face, her exquisite figure and the elegance of her person." When people noticed signs of his romantic interest in Josephine, Claire tells us, "she laughed and seemed amused."

Amused and perhaps flattered, at forty-five, to have an admirer in his late twenties. And certainly it was a moment at which she needed some diversion, saddened as she was by a second death in the family, that of her mother in far-off Martinique (for whom Napoleon had required her to sorrow in silence, because an official announcement would have plunged the court into formal mourning at a most inopportune time).

Napoleon laughed, too, about Prince Frederick Louis's penchant for Josephine, Claire de Rémusat observed. As well he might, since it served to distract her attention from her husband's gallivanting at the Château of Fontainebleau, where the court had gone for the autumn hunting season. Napoleon may or may not—opinions differ—have made a conquest of Zoë de Barral, one of the beauties in Pauline Borghese's suite. (Princess Borghese is quoted as having tried to overcome her reluctance with the remark, "But

no one is supposed to refuse His Majesty *anything!*") If Madame
de Barral proved stubborn, Napoleon could always turn to Carlotta Gazzani, Josephine's beautiful Genoese "reader," whose apartment at the château had been assigned with a view to convenience
of access from his own.

Josephine no longer uttered the faintest protest. As she wrote
her son: "I do everything in my power to please the Emperor. No
more jealousy, no more scenes—and you can believe me when I
tell you this, my dear Eugène. . . ."

And in another letter, dated September 1:

I have positive proof that Prince Murat made every effort while
the Emperor was with the army to force a decision on divorce.
. . . Unhappily, the Emperor is so great that no one dares any
longer to tell him the truth; he is surrounded by flatterers from
morning to night. As for me, you know that all my ambitions are
limited to the one—possession of his heart. If these people should
succeed in separating him from me, it is not the rank I should regret. A profound solitude would then be what would suit me best.
. . . Still, I have no complaint to make about him, and I like to
believe that I can count on his sense of justice and his affection
for me.

Eugène wrote in reply from Milan, later in September:

Yes, there has been a great deal of talk about divorce again
lately; I have heard it both from Paris and from Munich. But I am
very well satisfied with the interview you had with the Emperor, if
you have reported it accurately. . . .

If His Majesty continues to harass you about the necessity of
having children, tell him that it is not fair for him to persist in reproaching you on that score. If he believes that his happiness and
that of France require him to have heirs, then he must act accordingly. He should treat with you appropriately, provide you a sufficient dower and permit you to live with your children in Italy.
Then the Emperor would be free to contract the marriage which
he considers a national as well as a personal necessity. We will be
no less devoted to him—even though circumstances oblige him to

detach himself from our family. If the Emperor wants children of his own, this is the only course open to him. Any other would be reprehensible, and history would ferret it out. He has worked too hard for history to leave a single page which might be reproached him by posterity.

Could it have been that Napoleon was again suggesting to Josephine the hoax considered at the time of the coronation, the idea of passing off some illegitimate child of his as their legitimate issue? If he was, nothing came of it.

Another highly emotional scene between the Emperor and the Empress was reported by her later to Claire de Rémusat, who reported it in her memoirs:

In an interview with his wife one day that fall, the Emperor asked her whether she would not assist him in "making the sacrifice" of a separation by herself taking the initiative.

Too familiar with her husband's willful character to facilitate matters for him by an imprudent word, the Empress replied:

"You are the master of my fate and shall decide it. When you command me to leave the Tuileries, I shall instantly obey. But I am your wife, I was consecrated as empress by the Pope; and if you divorce me, all France shall know that it is by your decision, that I have only obeyed—and in profoundest sorrow." This response, spoken in a calm and dignified tone, did not offend the Emperor, but instead moved him deeply; and, as often happened during these interviews, he gave way to tears. "In her flights of imagination," Claire de Rémusat reveals, "the Empress let slip a word now and then on the subject of her fears for her personal security, saying, 'If it comes to the point where I represent a serious inconvenience to his policies, who knows what he might be capable of doing to rid himself of me?' "

Napoleon was no stranger to his wife's suspicions. Lucien reports him as saying later that year, "Just imagine, that woman cries every time she has indigestion, thinking she has been poisoned by those who favor my remarriage."

The word *poison* had come up among the Bonapartes even earlier. One of brother Joseph's arguments in favor of divorce prior to the coronation had been that suspicion would fall on Napoleon's head should Josephine later die under mysterious circumstances. "Who would believe that you had not done what was so obviously in your best interest?" he had said. "Make the break and leave her now for clear-cut political reasons, and don't run the risk of having it appear that you had to resort to crime to rid yourself of her later."

The sinister Minister of Police, Fouché, formerly Josephine's good friend but currently in league with the Murats, expressed himself brutally in Bourrienne's hearing: "The Empress's death would certainly be convenient, solving many difficulties." No wonder a panicky Josephine ran to the Rémusats with the letter that reached her in late September or October, over Fouché's signature, urging her to retire from her marriage and the throne of her own free will and accord, for the sake of the national good and because it was the will of the people.

Acting on the advice of the Rémusats (and they on the advice of Talleyrand), Josephine replied to Fouché, says Claire, that whenever the subject of divorce was to be broached to her, it should be done without an intermediary. Furthermore, she showed Fouché's letter to the Emperor,

who affected astonishment and displeasure, promised to reprimand the Minister of Police for his misplaced zeal and even offered to dismiss him if that should be her pleasure. . . . Still in the throes of indecision, Bonaparte lavished caresses on his wife and assured her, "The important thing is that you and I both know that his advice will be rejected. You know I could not live without you."

Not only did he keep repeating those words to her over and over again, but he also resumed his habit of paying her nocturnal visits—visits far more frequent than at any time in the recent past. Genuinely upset, he clasped her in his arms, wept and vowed undying devotion. . . . And yet he continued to betray severe mental and emotional strain, . . . referring again and again to the danger to the Empire and to the dynasty in the absence of a direct heir. He said that he did not know how to resolve the problem. Clearly he was torn by a conflict of emotions.

He unburdened himself to Monsieur de Talleyrand, who revealed to me some portion of their conversations. "Were I to divorce my wife," the Emperor said, "I would be giving up all the charm she has brought to my private life. I would have to start all over again to learn and to accommodate myself to the tastes and habits of a new and possibly very young wife. This one adjusts herself to mine and understands me perfectly. Then, too, I would be displaying ingratitude for all she has done for me. I am not actually beloved by my people. Divorce from a beloved Empress would not enhance my popularity. . . ."

He said much the same thing to the Count de Champagny, who had succeeded Talleyrand as minister of foreign affairs in August: "Were I to have the misfortune to lose Josephine, reasons of state would compel me to remarry; but I would only be marrying a womb. Josephine alone would have been my choice as life companion."

"For my part," Claire de Rémusat exclaims, "I was astonished that a woman disenchanted with her husband, devoured by sinister suspicions, somewhat indifferent to glory, would cling so tenaciously to so precarious a royal position. . . . Her daughter, especially since the death of her child, did not seem disposed to any great understanding of her mother's problems; her only reply to the Empress's laments was, 'How could anyone regret a throne?' "

For comfort and sympathy Josephine turned to Eugène. "I hope soon to see you in Milan," she wrote to her son from Fontainebleau in October, knowing that the Emperor was planning a trip to Italy. But in November, shortly before his departure, Napoleon advised her that she was not to accompany him. "It has been a long time, my dear son, since any of my wishes have been consulted," she wrote Eugène in disappointment.

In the course of his visit to Milan, Napoleon accorded Eugène the title of prince of Venice and further confirmed the inheritance of the kingdom of Italy to his Viceroy, unless—and here was a newly significant proviso—unless he, the Emperor, were to have a direct heir of his own.

Another of Napoleon's purposes in crossing the Alps that winter of 1807-1808 was to inspect another possible bride, Eugène's sister-in-law Princess Charlotte of Bavaria, who failed, however, to capture his fancy. Now he narrowed the field of princesses down to two: a grand duchess of Russia and an archduchess of Austria—the only two alliances representative of true political value. Napoleon's confidence in his virility had been restored by a visit to Éléonore Denuelle, upon his return to Paris from Tilsit in July. Although she had been forced to a confession that General Murat had indeed preceded General Bonaparte in her bed, still the infant Léon's resemblance to the Bonapartes was so striking as to leave no doubt as to his paternity.

The third and perhaps most compelling reason for Napoleon's Italian journey in November was to induce Lucien—the most capable of all his brothers, the most desirable ally in the Emperor's ambitious projects—to return to the fold. The inducement offered was the throne of Portugal, from which the Braganzas had been ousted within recent weeks by French troops under the command of General Junot.* Or, if Lucien preferred, the throne of Spain promised shortly to be available, as a result of the current conflict raging between the Spanish King, Charles IV, and his rebel son, Ferdinand, Prince of Asturias. The only price for the choice of thrones, as the proposition was presented by the Emperor to Lucien, was Lucien's repudiation of his wife. Lucien considered the price too high; it was Napoleon's final offer, and the two brothers parted again in bitterness, not to meet again until Napoleon's return from exile in Elba.

Despite all these vast designs churning in his brain, Napoleon found time to study detailed reports on Josephine's social activities in Paris, where, says Claire de Rémusat,

> she was the cynosure of a hundred eyes; a hundred tongues reported on whatever she said or did. The German princes came nightly to the Tuileries to play cards or to listen to music. The Empress seemed to converse more frequently with the Crown Prince of Mecklenburg-Schwerin than with the others; people commented, though laughingly, as I have already stated, and actually attached so little importance to it as to tease the Empress openly.
>
> There were some, however, who took the matter seriously enough to write to the Emperor. Accustomed as he was to indulging himself freely in his own fancies, he yet showed himself

* Junot's title, duke d'Abrantès, commemorated his victory at the Portuguese town of Abrantes.

severe in regard to those of others. During his absence in Italy, a highly successful *vaudeville* had opened at one of the small Paris theaters, and everyone wanted to see it, including the Empress, who asked Monsieur de Rémusat to reserve a private, grilled box and went there incognito, dressed unostentatiously and riding in a carriage unmarked by any imperial insignia, in the company of one or two of her ladies and several German princes, including the one from Mecklenburg-Schwerin. A report of this innocuous little outing promptly went off to Milan, whence the Emperor thundered back at the Empress by letter, and upon his return he called her severely to task for failing to maintain her dignity. I even remember that in his displeasure he reminded her that the last Queen of France had severely damaged her reputation by just such frivolities.

The Emperor's "displeasure" was so acute that he instructed Talleyrand to take proper measures to hasten the Prince's departure from Paris—he was to be gone within two days' time, to be exact. And Napoleon was later to tell General Bertrand, at St. Helena, that Josephine's indiscreet remarks to Frederick Louis on the subject of her husband's impotence had been repeated by the Prince to the Dowager Empress of Russia, the mother of his deceased first wife, and had thus proved prejudicial to Napoleon's suit for the hand of a Russian grand duchess.

The Emperor had returned to France early in the new year of 1808, and Josephine wrote to Eugène in February:

You will not be surprised to learn that I have had many sources of concern. . . . [Not the least of them was the arrival of the Countess Walewska in Paris.] The rumors which circulated during the Emperor's absence have not died down since his return, and no effort is being made to silence them. . . . I can only put my hope in Providence and in the Emperor. My only defense is to live in such a way as to leave myself open to no reproach. I no longer go out, I have no pleasures. People are astonished that I can endure such a life as I am leading, accustomed as I have been to greater independence of action and to a large society. I console myself with the thought that it represents my submission to the Emperor's wishes. My influence, my credit is ever on the wane, while that of *others waxes. . . . Ah, my dear Eugène, how unhappy a seat is the throne! My own—and those of my children—I would forswear tomorrow, and without a pang. The Emperor's heart is all I care about. Should I lose it, I would have little regret for all the rest.*

8

The time of losing the Emperor's heart seemed close at hand for Josephine, as Claire de Rémusat remembered:

One morning that spring [of 1808], Monsieur de Talleyrand emerged from the Emperor's study and told Monsieur de Rémusat that His Majesty had now apparently reached a final decision on divorce. I was profoundly saddened when my husband reported these words to me. . . .

A formal reception and a theatrical performance had been scheduled for that night at the Tuileries . . . The state apartments were crowded with princes, ambassadors and courtiers, all waiting long past the appointed hour, when word came that the play was to begin without Their Majesties; a slight indisposition on the part of the Emperor was offered in explanation. At the conclusion of the performance, Monsieur de Talleyrand and Monsieur de Rémusat went to the Emperor's private apartments to inquire after him, only to learn that at eight o'clock in the evening His Majesty had closed and bolted his doors and retired to his bed—with his wife.

"That devil of a man," Monsieur de Talleyrand exclaimed to my husband as they left the palace, "yielding to his impulses, unable to decide what he wants to do! Why can he not make up his mind, so that we may know what line to take with him on this issue?"

The Empress saw Monsieur de Rémusat next morning and told him that on the previous evening, after a silent dinner with her husband, she had gone to her boudoir to dress for the reception, when a messenger summoned her to the Emperor's apartments, where she found him suffering from severe stomach spasms and in a dreadful state of nerves. At sight of her, he was unable to repress his tears, and, without regard to her formal and elegant attire, drew her down upon the bed beside him, clasping her in his arms and repeating over and over again, "My poor Josephine, I shall never be able to live without you!" To which she had replied, "Sire, calm yourself, make up your mind what you want to do, and let us put an end to these devastating scenes."

But her words only added to his agitation, and his condition became so acute that she urged him to cancel his scheduled appearance and go to bed. To win his consent, nothing would do but that she must, that very instant, step out of her elaborate costume and share his couch, which, the Empress said, he literally bathed with his tears, repeating again and again, "I am surrounded by people who torment me and make my life a hell!"

It was a night of love interspersed with intervals of restless sleep. Later the Emperor regained control of himself, and he was never again to betray such turbulent emotion.

Thus it was that the Empress vacillated between hope and fear. She did not entirely trust these pathetic scenes her husband played out for her; she claimed that he passed too quickly from protestations of devotion to quarrels on the score of flirtations of which he accused her, or some other pretext. She thought that what he wanted was, by constant torment, to disgust her with him, to exhaust her strength and patience and to bring her to a state of collapse or perhaps something even worse—for, as I have already said, her imagination knew no bounds. What is certain is that, either through cold calculation or in consequence of his own inner turmoil, he upset her mentally, physically and emotionally to the point where she was truly on the verge of collapse.

One joins Claire de Rémusat in wonder that Josephine could have so long stood up against such pressure—this docile, submissive, passive, pliant woman, pitting her puny will against that of "the most willful and despotic of men." But hers was a curious strength, with the proverbial tensile strength of the vine, sending out a thousand delicate tendrils to wind about and inextricably engage his heart. Thus she clung until it was too late for Napoleon to achieve the greatest goal he had set himself, the founding of a dynasty. (One wonders what the denouement of the Napoleonic epic might have been had Josephine been other than she was, had she not put up so amazingly stubborn a resistance to divorce—holding, resisting until it was too late. One wonders how it might all have come out had she yielded in time for Napoleon to beget an heir who would have been old enough in 1814, at the time of the first abdication, or in 1815, at the time of the second, to have been entrusted with the crown. The majority of the nation was certainly not disposed to welcome a Bourbon restoration. The Czar, most influential among the Coalition monarchs, showed every disposition to accede to the will of the French people, and might have done so, had they expressed themselves in favor of a young Bonaparte monarch under the guidance of a competent regency—as the French people might have done had the King of Rome been ten or eleven, instead of an infant of three.)

The Spanish crisis in April of 1808 demanded Napoleon's undivided attention, providing a reprieve, a breathing spell, for Josephine. Civil war had broken out when Charles IV had been forced to abdicate in favor of his son, presently enthroned as Ferdinand VII. Seizing upon the excuse of anarchy, Napoleon had dispatched troops to Spain under Murat, and then imperiously hailed the royal rivals, father and son, to a conference near the border, at Bayonne, where he settled the dispute between them by deposing both.

Thus Napoleon could call the tune, that spring of 1808, for a game of musical thrones: establishing brother Joseph Bonaparte upon the throne of Spain, sending sister Caroline and her Murat to take over that of Naples, just vacated by Joseph. The Spanish Bourbons, father and son, having lost out completely, were sent to sit out the game behind the walls of various French châteaux and Italian *palazzi*.

Talleyrand recognized that French control of the Iberian Peninsula would ensure total Continental blockade against England, but he deplored Napoleon's first resort to unprovoked aggression and outright usurpation—not out of any moral scruple, to be sure, but out of political acumen: Talleyrand foresaw the fatal involvements inherent in the occupation of that rugged peninsula, the fierce and bloody resistance to be offered to Napoleon's version of liberation. The proud and stubborn Spaniards, loyal to their priests, even to their decadent Bourbons, would make their own revolution in their own good time and wanted no part of this watered-down, imported Gallic variety; they would co-operate with English forces under Sir Arthur Wellesley, Viscount (later Duke of) Wellington, by carrying on endless guerrilla warfare against the French interloper.

Josephine was overjoyed at Napoleon's invitation to accompany him to Bayonne, where, at the Château of Marrac, she acted as hostess to Spain's trinity: the King, the Queen, and the "Prince of the Peace," Manuel de Godoy, who was indispensable to both, being chief minister to Charles IV and lover to María Luisa. Josephine was her usual tactful self, talking fashions with the Queen to keep off politics. For María Luisa to admire anything Josephine wore was for Josephine to snatch it off and make her royal guest a gift of it, even of magnificent jewels. The Empress of the French went so far as to share her master coiffeur with the Queen of Spain —although if that other master, the court painter Goya, could not beautify María Luisa with his brush, Duplan could have had little more success with his brushes, combs and curling irons. The Queen, forever coquetting with Godoy, was "grotesque, yellow as a mummy, making herself ridiculous, at sixty, in her short-sleeved, décolleté gowns," Napoleon was heard to comment. The King, gouty and cantankerous, was indifferent to his hosts and to his crown; he preferred timepieces to people, pinning dozens of watches to his valets' livery to ensure the "ambulation" necessary to his vast collection. His habit of whistling for his confessor as for a dog must have been disconcerting.

The house party at Marrac, then, was certainly no gay one. Even the accommodations were poor. Mademoiselle Avrillon, the maid, complains of the cramped quarters and of the "epidemic of flies which made it positively dangerous to yawn." But Josephine was undismayed. "I am near the Emperor!" she exulted by letter to Eugène. "And every day he seems more amiable."

There was, to be sure, one fly in the ointment: an eighteen-year-old Irish beauty, a Demoiselle Virginie Guillebaut, who proved a disturbing influence at Bayonne. But it was apparently Josephine herself who brought her there (as another "reader" in her retinue), "as if some secret demon forced her always to do what she would later regret." The episode puzzled Napoleon, or so he told General Gourgaud at St. Helena: "I am not certain what Josephine had in mind with regard to that girl and me." And there are those who claim that Josephine, in those desperate latter years, took Madame du Barry as a model and pandered to her husband's appetite for those "*jolis boutons de rose*"—pretty rosebuds—for which he expressed preference in one of his letters to his wife from Poland. Beautiful as this one was ("beautiful as an angel," in Napoleon's words), she was shortly sent packing, in disgrace, with only a lowly chambermaid to escort her back to Paris in the diligence.

"Reader" Madame Gazzani was at the Château de Marrac, too, but her heyday was over, and Josephine seems to have had the field to herself. She and Napoleon drove about a countryside new to both, most frequently along the Bay of Biscay: Napoleon, gay as a boy, playing the gallant, pulling Josephine from the carriage to frolic on the beaches; Josephine, making light of the loss of her little satin slippers, running hand in hand with him across the shimmering sands in her cobwebby stockings. The calendar said July, but it was the Indian summer of their love.

Not even the arduous three-week journey back to Paris, driving at night to escape the dust and the blazing August sun, could discourage Josephine in her rapture at being with the Emperor. Fighting down fatigue and the pain of headache, she stepped smilingly out of their carriage in the morning to greet and to be greeted by the welcoming committees of towns and hamlets along their path; visited city halls, cathedrals, hospitals; thanked the mayors and the citizenry for gifts and accepted their thanks for her own; presided radiantly at luncheons, banquets, theaters, galas, balls— then back into her carriage again for another jolting night on the road.

Back in St.-Cloud, however, she took to her bed, as she told Eugène in a letter dated September 22, the day Napoleon left for Germany to meet Alexander of Russia. "You know to what stress and strain I have been subjected," she wrote. "I have paid for it with excruciating headaches. But the Emperor proved his attachment by the concern he manifested, getting up as often as four times a night to come to see how I was feeling. For the last six months he has been simply perfect to me. Thus when I saw him leave this morning it was with sadness at the parting, but with no disquietude as concerns our relations." Josephine was still in her fool's paradise, not knowing that Napoleon, at Erfurt, would press for a final decision concerning his marriage to a sister of the Czar.

The latter refused, however, to commit himself either to the marriage contract or the political treaty which Napoleon was now urging to formalize the agreements made between them the year before. Napoleon needed reassurance that Russia would contain a restive and resentful Austria while he turned south again to Spain, to come to grips with Wellington, who had already routed Junot from Portugal.

If the Czar was vague and evasive, yet he seemed as cordial as ever, or so Napoleon described him to Josephine in a letter written in mid-October. "I am well pleased with Alexander," he told her, "as he should be with me. If he were a woman, I think I would have him for a sweetheart. . . . I will be home with you soon now, and hope to find you plump and glowing with health and vigor."

Napoleon was living in a fool's paradise of his own, flattering himself that his impressionable Russian friend and ally could resist him no more successfully at Erfurt than at Tilsit. But then, Napoleon did not suspect that his Grand Chamberlain, Talleyrand, had begun his treasonous game of intrigue with both Russia and Austria, encouraging Russia to maintain neutrality and Austria to make her move in central Europe while Napoleon and a quarter of a million men of the French Army were engaged in Spain. Not that Napoleon actually trusted Talleyrand, but he did not consider him capable of outright treachery to France.

9

Within ten days of Napoleon's return from Germany to Paris, he sped south again, toward Madrid.

His wife, at St.-Cloud, had the company of her daughter and her two grandsons, the four-year-old Napoléon-Louis and the infant Charles-Louis-Napoléon, born that past April. (Hortense and her husband had finally agreed—an experience unique in their marriage—to live apart.) Yet Josephine fell into a state of deep despondency, prey to dark presentiments. The Spanish war was unpopular; Paris was nervous at Austria's bellicose gestures, fearful of war on two fronts.

Josephine made so bold as to express her personal fears as well as those of the nation in a letter to her husband, as is indicated in his reply:

I note, my dear, that you are in a black mood of depression. Austria will not make war on me; if she should, I have 150,000 men in Germany and as many again along the Rhine, in addition to 400,000 Germans ready to take up arms on our side. Nor will Russia desert us. People in Paris are crazy! Things are going splendidly here. I will be back in Paris as soon as I deem it expedient. So watch out —one of these fine days, or in the middle of the night, when least expected, there I'll be!

Things were not "going splendidly" there, in Spain, but the Emperor could not stay on to achieve a decisive victory: reports of Austrian troop movements were disconcerting. Even more so were those of a conspiracy in Paris: Murat plotting to snatch control from the weak hands of the Bonaparte heirs in the event of Napoleon's death in Spain, and Talleyrand and Fouché reconciling their lifelong differences to conspire with him. It was in order to surprise not Josephine but the conspirators that Napoleon appeared unexpectedly in Paris on January 23.

Both Fouché and Talleyrand were publicly rebuked, before the Council of State, and the latter was stripped of his office as grand chamberlain, although Napoleon could not dispense with the services of either of these two most dangerous but most brilliant and effective of his agents.

On April 12, 1809, Austria invaded Bavaria and invested Munich. On April 13, Napoleon flashed out of Paris toward the Rhine. Intending to travel fast and alone, he had "tried to slip out of the palace at one o'clock in the morning without the knowledge of the Empress, who wanted to go everywhere with him," according to the valet Constant. "He was impatient, like so many husbands, of his wife's cumbersome baggage as well as her multitudinous retinue. But the Empress heard the sounds of departure in the courtyard, sprang out of bed, slipped on the first garments at hand, ran out and down the steps stockingless, in bedroom slippers, and, crying like a child, threw herself into his carriage. As nearly always happened at the sight of his wife's tears, the Emperor weakened. She perceived it, and was already crouching on the floor of the carriage. She was so lightly garbed that His Majesty threw his pelisse about her shoulders, and then issued orders for her luggage to be sent on to her."

They were off on another sixty-hour nonstop trip, the carriage wheels smoking and the horses lathered—destination Strasbourg, where Napoleon lingered only long enough to install Josephine in the Rohan Palace and to take one of his steaming tubs before he set out for the Bavarian front.

Within three weeks, Vienna fell and Napoleon settled himself in the palace of the Hapsburgs at Schönbrunn. But it was not Josephine whom he summoned to join him there. It was Marie Walewska.

Josephine seems to have sensed by then that her plight was hopeless, or perhaps she was too exhausted to struggle further. The year before, she had cajoled and implored to be allowed to come to him. This year she made not so much as a single plea, but confined herself to requesting permission to go with Hortense and the grandchildren to the springs of Plombières.

Permission was forthcoming, but the Emperor's letters were few and brief during the Austrian campaign of 1809. He wrote to reassure her about a spent cannon ball that had grazed his ankle at Ratisbon (puncturing the legend of his invulnerability, if not the leather of his boot): "It scarcely bruised me, striking the tendon of Achilles. There is no cause for you to be so alarmed." From Ebersdorf on May 27 he had complimentary things to say about her son: "Eugène joined me with his army and perfectly fulfilled the mission assigned him. You well know my sentiments for Josephine; they are unvarying." And on July 7 he could write to her of a decisive victory over the Austrians: Wagram, a battle name to be chiseled beside the other glorious names on the Arc de Triomphe, now under erection at the head of the Champs-Elysées.

A truce was signed on July 13, but Austria shilly-shallied on terms for the formal peace treaty, emboldened by reports of French reverses on other fronts: Wellington's defeat of King Joseph at

Talavera, an English landing in force on Belgian shores, the British fleet's capture of Martinique, Santo Domingo, Senegal. Napoleon waited less impatiently than might have been expected—but then, he waited at Schönbrunn, in the arms of Countess Walewska.

On August 15, on the occasion of his fortieth birthday, Marie gave him of all gifts the one he most desired: the promise of a child that he could know to be, beyond the shadow of a doubt, his own. Nothing short of a consultation with Dr. Corvisart could satisfy him; the imperial physician was summoned from Paris to Vienna to verify the pregnancy and prescribe the regimen for the expectant mother. Marie would have liked to await the birth of their child in Paris, but the Emperor was to insist that she avail herself of the privilege so chivalrously extended her by her aged husband: of being delivered at the family estate of Walewice so that the child might be recognized as a legitimate Walewski instead of going through life as a bastard of Napoleon's.

The news of La Walewska's pregnancy reached Josephine soon enough at Malmaison, where she had arrived on August 18, going there direct from the Vosges Mountains—bypassing the capital, as if shrinking from view. There, under the only roof she could truly call her own, she had taken cover, with only her grandchildren to keep her company. Of late she had not even written to her husband, as if hesitant to intrude, even by letter, upon his idyl of love, his hour of fulfillment.

He had sent her floral tributes, some eight hundred rare shrubs, blooms and plants from the Hapsburg hothouses at Schönbrunn for hers at Malmaison, but his letters had been few, curt, distracted, or self-consciously flippant, as: "I have not heard from you in many days. The delights of Malmaison, the beautiful conservatories and lovely gardens, cause you to forget the absent." And he agreed to her purchase of a long-coveted adjoining estate to round out the properties, "since the acquisition will serve you as a diversion—but only on the condition that you promise not to tear down the château to make another of your famous grottoes."

If Josephine could spare a thought from her personal problems, it was, says Mademoiselle Avrillon, a sorrowful one for her revered friend Pius VII, recently stripped of sovereignty in Rome, deposed, and held in captivity at Savona. Josephine was superstitious enough, if not sufficiently ardent in religion, to be sorely troubled by the bull of excommunication that the Pope had laid upon her husband (which act had accounted for Napoleon's swift retaliation). On October 14 the peace with Austria was finally signed, and on October 22 Napoleon wrote to Josephine from Munich, en route back to France after a six months' absence: "I am happy at the thought of seeing you and impatiently await the moment . . . I am leaving within the hour and should arrive at Fontainebleau on the twenty-sixth or twenty-seventh. You may go there to await my arrival . . ."

She was late at the rendezvous by several hours, not having dreamed that he could arrive as early as the early morning of the twenty-sixth. It was probably the first time in ten years that she had kept him waiting, but he seized upon the excuse to vent his wrath upon her in a scene described by her maid as "frightful." Josephine recognized it for the pretext it was—for when she went to her apartments she discovered that the communicating door to his had been walled up. Perhaps she could even find some crumb of comfort in this tacit admission that he could not trust himself to lock his heart against her and had thus been obliged to resort to sealing off the doors. Past experience had taught him the danger of parleying with her in the bedroom; from this time on, he would confine their interviews to the salon or the dining room, and then only in the presence of a third party whenever possible.

Even now, when he had finally and firmly resolved upon divorce, he could not bring himself to the point of telling her. He had solemnly promised her, as he later admitted at St. Helena, that it would be he and he alone who would apprise her of the decision when and if it came. Nevertheless, he had that very morning asked Arch-chancellor Cambacérès to undertake the mission—and been refused, as he would shortly be refused by Hortense and by the Count de Lavallette, Josephine's nephew by marriage.

Cambacérès, Josephine's fast friend, continued to oppose the idea of divorce, but he now stood alone among the Emperor's advisers in doing so. Even Talleyrand had by this time come over to Fouché's way of thinking in the matter. The advantages to France in a marital alliance with Austria or Russia were unmistakably clear, and another recent attempt on Napoleon's life, this time in

Vienna, had underscored the necessity of an assured succession. The Council of State agreed that divorce should be the first step in the procedure; once the Emperor of France was free to choose a bride, the royal house so honored could not long delay assent. Josephine stood condemned for reasons of state.

"So now we have come to the epoch when the Empress's agony begins; her destiny must needs play itself out," writes Mademoiselle Avrillon, agonizing with her mistress. "I could see all too clearly that the Emperor was no longer the same toward her, venting his displeasure even on those friends of hers who dared to show her their devotion and their sympathy. I witnessed the end of the intimacy which had so long reigned between Their Majesties. The Emperor showed embarrassment, even fear, at being alone with his wife; she, on her side, lost her confidence and trembled at their every encounter. It was a heartbreaking spectacle. Convinced as she was of the inevitability of the denouement, still she clung till the very end to some faint ray of hope, plying with subtle questions every imperial minister or high dignitary who visited her, though none of these would speak out."

One of them was Napoleon's secretary Méneval, who wrote later: "The Empress's obsession with her fate accounted for her endless applications to me for information. My role became so embarrassing that, to escape her inquiries, I had no choice but to avoid her altogether. She dared not put the burning question directly to the Emperor in those brief moments he accorded her. This situation was too charged with tension to be long endurable. The constraint that His Majesty had brought about in their daily contact was a torture to them both."

The situation became intolerable to Hortense too. "All tenderness on the Emperor's part, all consideration for my mother, had vanished. . . . He became unjust, tormenting," she writes. "Witness as I was to my mother's tears and to the indignities which set them flowing, both my heart and my pride rebelled. I actually found myself wishing for the end, for the final act of separation. Family security and even my children's interests faded into insignificance in the light of such humiliations."

Hortense especially resented the fact that the Emperor complicated the domestic crisis by an amorous dalliance with "a Piedmontese lady," a member of his sister Pauline Borghese's entourage. As Mademoiselle Avrillon diagnosed the situation, the Princess Borghese, like Caroline Murat, made a practice of surrounding herself with the type of beautiful and obliging female known to attract her brother, such as the one in question, whom the maid describes as a twenty-five-year-old blond countess named Christine de Mathis. "During that fatal sojourn at Fontainebleau, Princess Borghese was hostess nightly at parties in her apartment from which the Empress was pointedly excluded—soirees which did not begin, indeed, until after the Empress had retired. Still, from her windows Her Majesty could see the lights in her sister-in-law's salon, and God knows how many sleepless nights she spent peering across the shadows of the courtyard. I often ask myself which caused her the greatest anguish, the blow itself when it finally came or the cruelly protracted preliminaries."

But it was, actually, as Méneval had said, a torture to them both, to Napoleon as well as to Josephine. His anger was with himself, not with her; his impatience was with his own weakness in his dealings with her—his only weakness, as this was almost the unique instance, in his entire career, of his failing to deal swiftly, efficiently and ruthlessly with any obstacle that blocked his path.

And so the days at Fontainebleau dragged on into mid-November. And when the court returned to Paris he still had not steeled himself to break the news to her.

On November 22, however, he commissioned General Louis de Caulaincourt to go to the Court of St. Petersburg to make formal application for the hand of the fourteen-year-old Grand Duchess Anna.

On November 27, he sent a semaphore message to Italy to summon Eugène to Paris.

III

Divorce

Bonaparte, you promised never to abandon me. . . . I have only you in all the world. You are my only friend!

LETTER FROM JOSEPHINE TO NAPOLEON, SEPTEMBER 23, 1810

1

BACK IN PARIS, at the Tuileries, Josephine spent her evenings in her salon, on the edge of her chair, "her heart in her throat as she waited, jumping at every sound, listening for a knock on the door at the foot of the little staircase which led from her boudoir to the Emperor's study, the knock that was his signal to summon her to his apartment." The knock never came.

They dined together alone, but these solitary dinners were limited to fifteen minutes. At dinner on November 30, Napoleon cut the fifteen minutes to ten, the longest ten of Josephine's life. Count de Bausset, the palace prefect in attendance, was the sole and discomfited witness of the scene, which he recalled in his memoirs:

> Josephine's large white hat shadowed her face, but I thought I could discern the trace of tears. She was the very image of sorrow and despair. . . . They scarcely touched the dishes set before them, and the only words spoken were a question that the Em-

peror addressed to me: "What's the weather?" Even as he spoke, he rose from the table. The Empress followed slowly.

Coffee was served, . . . but His Majesty himself took the cup from the tray [breaking with the practice whereby the Empress poured his coffee, sugaring and tasting it before handing the cup to him] . . . and then gave a signal to the lackey to withdraw.

I made my exit quickly, too, and was waiting in the adjoining salon when suddenly I heard the Empress cry out loudly. . . . I was standing at the door when the Emperor flung it open, saying, "Come in, Bausset, and close the door behind you." . . .

The Empress was lying on the floor, crying and moaning piteously. "No! No!" she cried over and over again. "No, I shall never survive it!" . . .

"Do you think you can carry Her Majesty to her apartments?" the Emperor asked me. I replied that I thought I could, and lifted her from the floor (she seemed to have fainted, overcome by her acute attack of nerves); meanwhile the Emperor picked up a candlestick and opened the door into a dark corridor leading to the back stairway which he indicated he wished to use. At the very first step, however, I could see that it was too narrow and too winding for me to descend with the Empress a dead weight in my arms; whereupon the Emperor called a guard to precede us with the light while he himself helped me with his wife, grasping her under the knees.

Halfway down the stairs, I came close to tripping over my sword and involuntarily clutched at Her Majesty to prevent a fall; I was holding her about the waist, with her head resting on my right shoulder. Suddenly I heard her whisper in my ear, "You are holding me too tightly!" At which point I realized that if she had lost consciousness it had been only temporarily, and that I need have no further alarm as to her condition.

At length we made the descent and deposited our precious burden on an ottoman in the bedroom. The Emperor immediately pulled the bell rope to summon the Empress's attendants.

Throughout this distressing episode, I had been occupied with Josephine and had had no opportunity to observe Napoleon, but now I saw that his agitation and distress were acute. Tears welled in his eyes. Panting from exertion and emotion, he enlightened me as to the situation with these words, which were interrupted by pauses and gasps for breath: "The national welfare has caused me to do violence to my heart. . . . Divorce has become a political necessity. . . . But I have been all the more affected tonight for the reason that the Empress's reaction took me by surprise. . . . Her daughter was to have prepared her for this three days ago. . . ."

He must indeed have been beside himself thus to have taken me into his confidence.

(Indeed he must, if he knew Bausset as the "hypocrite and eavesdropper" Mademoiselle Ducrest accuses him of being.)

Returning to his own apartments, the Emperor issued instructions for both Dr. Corvisart and Hortense to go to Josephine. Hortense, who found her mother in tears, takes up the story:

"It is for the best," I told her. "We will all of us go away and you will have that long-desired tranquillity at last."

"But what will become of you and Eugène?"

"We will go with you. I know my brother will feel as I do. For the first time in our lives, far from the world and the court, in some peaceful retreat, we will live a real family life and know our first real happiness."

My determination and my plans for the future seemed to calm my mother. When I left her, she seemed resigned to her fate.

Later the Emperor summoned Hortense to come to him.

"My decision is irrevocable," he told me brusquely, rapping out the words. "Nothing can make me change my mind, neither tears nor entreaties."

"You are the master here, Sire," I replied coldly and calmly, determined to betray no sign of weakness. "You will meet with no opposition to your purposes. Yet you should not be surprised at my mother's tears. After thirteen years of marriage, it would have been stranger still if she had shed none. She will show herself submissive, I am sure, and when we leave you we will take with us the remembrance of your kindness."

His expression changed even as I spoke. Tears coming to his eyes and a sob into his voice, he cried, "What? You are all going to abandon me? You no longer love me? Had it been merely a question of my personal happiness, I would have sacrificed that. But the happiness and the welfare of France are at stake. You should feel sorry for me, for I am about to renounce all that is dearest to me in this world! . . ."

Then it was my turn to be moved, to see not the monarch but an unhappy man. "Take courage, Sire," I said. "We will need it, too, to give up being your children. But I promise you that if we leave you it will be only so as not to stand in the way of your plans." . . .

"But you must not leave me. The interests of your children— a mother's first obligation—should be enough to hold you here."

"Sire, I have an obligation to my mother, who will need me. It will be a sacrifice to leave you, but we must."

The palace seethed with rumors and whispers, but the news of the imperial divorce was to be withheld from the general public for at least another fortnight. A caravan of German kings, grand dukes, dukes and princes was on its way to Paris at that very moment to join with the Emperor in celebration of the victories of the recent Austrian campaign. The Empress must gulp down her tears, rouge her cheeks against their pallor and go through the paces of a dozen ceremonials, galas, banquets and balls, facing the inquisition of a thousand prying eyes.

On December 3, at the Te Deum at Notre Dame, the imperial crown was still in place on Josephine's brow, but, significantly, she did not ride to the ceremony in the Emperor's carriage. And at the city of Paris' banquet and ball in honor of Their Majesties on December 4 the Emperor escorted the Queen of Naples, leaving Josephine to make her entrance and find her way to the dais almost unattended, with only a single official to escort her. Laure Junot, (now Duchess d'Abrantès), loyal Bonaparte partisan though she was, melted with sympathy for the Empress, who, she says, "seated herself quickly, her legs almost giving way beneath her. She must have wanted to sink through the floor, yet somehow she managed a smile."

Commenting on Napoleon's motives, Laure Junot writes: "As often as he defied public opinion, he yet attached great importance to it and was disturbed by its murmurs. He had chosen this occasion to test it and to prepare the general public for the divorce which was to come." If this was a trial balloon, then it indicated that public opinion was offended, for the Empress was beloved, says Madame Junot—beloved especially by the common people and the middle class, who seemed to feel that, in losing Josephine, they were losing their guardian angel, their lucky star. To the popular mind, she would always be "Notre Dame des Victoires" and "La Bonne Joséphine."

The court itself had cause to regret her going. The usually cynical Talleyrand told Madame de Rémusat, "There is no one in the palace who will not live to rue the day she leaves. She is gentle, sweet and kind, and she knows the art of calming the Emperor. She understands everyone's problems here and has been a refuge to us all on a thousand occasions. When you see some foreign princess arrive to take her place, you will see discord between the Emperor and the courtiers. We will all be the losers by it." Even the actress Mademoiselle Georges, Napoleon's former mistress, joined the chorus of lament: "This divorce—what a misfortune for France and for the Emperor!"

Eugène arrived on December 5. When he was told the news by Hortense, who had gone to meet him en route, his first question was, "Has our mother the courage to endure this ordeal?" His sister's reply was a reassuring Yes. Later, she says,

> Eugène, whom my mother had not seen since their parting in Munich, when his future had seemed so bright with promise, came into her apartment with the Emperor. It was a painful reunion. . . .
>
> The Emperor repeated to Eugène what he had already said to me, and assured us that the entire proceedings were to be handled with good will on every side, in utter congeniality; that the Empress was to lose neither her position nor his affection. Still, my brother continued to insist that the break should be complete. "My sister and I would find ourselves in a false and embarrassing position were we to remain at court," he said.
>
> The Emperor accused us of mistrust. "I need you," he declared. "Nor is it your mother's wish that you should separate yourselves and your children from me. Were you to leave me, it might well appear that your mother had been repudiated perhaps for some just cause. Whereas, as I foresee it, her position is to be

one of dignity and honor—retaining her rank, remaining close to me. Here is proof to posterity that the divorce is purely a political one, one to which she herself agrees and by which she will win even greater respect, esteem and gratitude from the nation for which she sacrifices herself."

Such arguments as these were unanswerable, and Eugène and I could not but resign ourselves to their wishes, my mother's as well as the Emperor's.

There remained only the final settlement. Eugène's request that the Emperor meet with him and his mother "in a frank and friendly discussion of the terms" was granted on December 7. "Politics has no heart, only a head," the Emperor said, still explaining the cruel necessity. When, at this meeting, he offered Josephine a principality in Italy, with Rome as her official residence and capital city, she went into hysterics, reminding him of his solemn promise that she was to be permitted to stay in France—preferably in Paris, close to him. She had no desire for principalities or kingdoms for herself, only for her children and grandchildren—the crown of Italy, perhaps, outright to Eugène? But Eugène vetoed the suggestion before the Emperor could reply; Josephine's son refused to turn the altar of his mother's sacrifice into a bargaining table.

The provisions of the separation would seem to have been generous: an allowance of three million francs a year, the château and vast estates and revenues of Malmaison, the Élysée Palace in Paris (today the official residence of the President of the French Republic), and the rank of queen and empress, "crowned and anointed," carrying with it all the honors, privileges and distinctions hitherto enjoyed: the title of "Majesty," the right to use the imperial coat of arms, to clothe her servants in the imperial livery, to have her carriage drawn by eight horses (as was the Emperor's) and to retain her honor household substantially as before. Her debts, which totaled nearly two million francs, were to be paid by cash advanced out of future revenues.

That night after the conference, at the banquet and theatrical performance scheduled at the Tuileries, Napoleon stood alone to receive his royal guests. Josephine had succumbed, stricken by one of her severest migraines. She struggled to her feet again for the night of December 14 to do the honors at a Tuileries reception, and an observer such as Stanislas de Girardin was "struck by the flawless propriety of her demeanor in the presence of a court fully aware that she was making her last appearance, that within a few hours she was to step down from that throne and depart that palace, perhaps never to re-enter it."

For the function scheduled for December 15, invitations went out as to a ball. Addressed to all the high officers of the Crown and of the Empire, and signed by the Grand Chamberlain, they read: "I have the honor to advise Your Excellency that the Emperor requires your presence tonight at nine o'clock in the throne room of the Palace of the Tuileries." The function was the formal and official ceremony of imperial divorce.

While these guests, in full court regalia, waited in the throne room, the imperial family filed into the grand salon and took their seats, followed by Arch-chancellor Cambacérès and Count Regnault de Saint-Jean-d'Angély, secretary of state to the imperial family. "The Bonapartes gloated," says Hortense. "Try as they might not to show it, they betrayed their joy by their air of satisfaction and triumph." Josephine, as she made her entrance and looked into those basilisk eyes, may have thought—in paraphrase of the Psalmist—"Thou preparest a table before mine enemies in my presence."

She sat at it while the Emperor rose and spoke. The words were his own; a dry, platitudinous text had been prepared for him, but he had discarded it.

"God alone knows what this resolve has cost my heart," he said after announcing his decision. "I have found courage for it only in the conviction that it serves the best interests of France. Far from having any complaint to register, I have only gratitude to express for the devotion and tenderness of my well-beloved wife. She has embellished thirteen years of my life; the memory thereof will remain forever engraved upon my heart. She has been crowned by my hand. It is my wish that she retain the full rank and title of empress; above all, that she never doubt my sentiments for her, but consider me always as her best and dearest friend . . ." The account printed in *Le Moniteur* next day noted, "The Emperor wept."

338

When it was Josephine's turn, she began: "With the permission of my dear and august husband, I wish to declare that, devoid now of all hope of bearing children who could satisfy the requirements of his dynastic interests and the welfare of France, I proudly offer him the greatest proof of attachment and devotion ever given a husband on this earth . . ." Here she faltered, choking on her sobs, and sank into her chair.

Regnault finished reading for her: "Everything I possess has come to me through his bounty. It is his hand that crowned me, and as long as I sat upon the throne the French people vouchsafed me abundant proof of their love and affection. It is in recognition of these sentiments that I consent to the dissolution of a marriage which is an obstacle to the national good, in that it deprives France of the happiness of being someday governed by the descendant of the man whom Providence raised up to remedy the evils of a terrible revolution and to re-establish the altar, the throne and the social order of France. . . . We both, he and I, stand transmuted, glorified by the sacrifice we make on the altar of the national good."

But the ordeal was still not over—not until the official record of the proceedings had been presented by Cambacérès for the signatures of the Emperor, the Empress and the ten members of the family assembled. Then, at last, Josephine could go.

"The Emperor," says Hortense, "kissed her, took her by the hand and led her to her apartments."

2

At eleven o'clock on the morning of the following day, December 16, 1809, the proposal for the dissolution of the civil marriage bonds of the imperial couple was presented for approval to the Senate by none other than Eugène, in his official capacity of senator and vice-arch-chancellor. The archives had been consulted for precedent, but much of the technique was improvised by Napoleon to clothe this singular case with all possible dignity and semblance of legal formality.

Annulment of the religious marriage bonds presented knottier problems. Such annulment, in the case of Catholic sovereigns, came traditionally under papal jurisdiction, but the current Pope, a prisoner of the Emperor of France, could scarcely be expected to oblige his jailer. Even the dubiously competent ecclesiastical court convoked by Cambacérès in Paris declined to consider the argument that Napoleon's consent to the religious marriage ceremony had been obtained "under duress," those prelates judging it patently absurd "that the man before whom all Europe trembled could have been constrained into marriage like some juvenile." When the bishops begrudgingly conceded the nullity of the marriage ceremony, it was on the technicality that no curé of the parish had been called as witness.

On that morning of the sixteenth, Napoleon went to bid Josephine goodbye. He was careful not to go alone, however, taking Méneval along as chaperon. "We found the Empress alone, plunged in melancholy reflection," the Emperor's secretary notes. "At the sound of our voices, she rose to meet us and threw her arms around the Emperor's neck. He in turn clasped her to his breast, covering her with kisses. Overcome by emotion, she fell into a faint, and I hurried to ring for aid. The Emperor, having assured himself that she was regaining consciousness, gave her limp form over into my arms and hurried away. The maids who answered the summons took her from me and settled her on a divan."

Among them was Mademoiselle Avrillon, who continues the story:

> I remained for many hours with the Empress that last day at the Tuileries, helping to pack her personal possessions for our removal to Malmaison. All of us on her staff had been up since early morning making preparations for departure.
>
> Consternation was general throughout the palace; tears were in every eye. How could it have been otherwise, when the Empress had always been so kind to everyone? Who among the Emperor's servitors did not consider her their protector? It was to the Empress that everyone turned for a favor, a special dispensation, an indulgence, a reprieve. All were agreed that it was she

whom we had to thank for moderating the Emperor's irascibilities.

Her children did not leave her side during those cruel hours. Prince Eugène, a model of filial piety to a model mother, made a valiant effort to keep calm and, affecting a gaiety he was far from feeling, told droll stories to make us smile. And Queen Hortense lavished the fondest attentions on her mother, seeking to bring her consolation.

"I felt that I must help her keep up her courage to the end," Hortense writes. "I reminded her of the unhappy Queen who had preceded her in that palace and who had departed it for the guillotine, and I pointed out the difference in her own case, all the consolations remaining to her. . . .

"Her apartments were filled with ladies of the palace, weeping at the parting."

The departure was set for two o'clock [Mademoiselle Avrillon goes on]. The fatal moment had come, and we were leaving the Tuileries forever. . . . The household staff, myself included, followed immediately behind Her Majesty. The carriages were waiting in the courtyard. The Emperor was holding a military review that afternoon, so that the approaches to the palace as well as the courtyard were thronged with onlookers, some come out of simple curiosity to see the military maneuvers and others out of affection and sympathy for the Empress. The Parisians loved her for her graciousness, her kindness, her benefactions . . . This divorce may have had the approval of the Emperor's family, of certain ambitious courtiers and perhaps even of his enemies, but certainly not that of France.

If there was any element of comic relief in this tragic moving-day scene, it might be said that I provided it, with my menagerie. Not only the Empress's parrot in its cage went into the carriage with me, but also her favorite dogs—a pair of miniature German wolfhounds—and a basketful of their newborn puppies. . . .

That first day and night—above all, that night—at Malmaison were painful, with the Empress plunged in deep despair. I stayed with her most of the night, and, since she could not sleep, we passed the hours of darkness talking. She was still dizzied by her fall and certainly she deplored her fate, but in terms so gentle and in such a spirit of resignation that anything said to the contrary may be taken for pure fiction. Even that first night, when the shock was still so fresh, she spoke of the Emperor with the same respect and affection as in the past. She suffered as a woman from the blow to her feminine vanity and pride, but she met misfortune with her own brand of heroism. . . . There, at her beloved Malmaison, she would seek consolation in the frequent visits of her children and in the affection of those persons who had followed her into her retreat.

Of these there were unfortunately too few. The Emperor was obliged to instruct the Grand Chamberlain to send out notice to the Empress's honor attendants that they were expected to take up their duties with her at the Château of Malmaison.

Claire de Rémusat, however, came unprompted. Though she was somewhat self-righteous about the sacrifice it cost her to do her duty by her friend, Claire's sympathy for Josephine is evident in her letters to her husband, then the prefect in attendance upon the Emperor at the Trianon Palace at Versailles—where Napoleon, to escape the hushed and haunted galleries of the Tuileries, had gone, accompanied by his mother and sisters, a few hours after Josephine's departure. "I made the Empress go for a walk this morning," Claire wrote. "I wanted to try to weary her body as a means of bringing repose to her mind. . . . 'Sometimes,' she told me, 'I have the feeling that I am dead, and that the only sign of life remaining to me is the nebulous sensation that I no longer exist. . . .' She is so gentle and so affectionate in her sorrow that it breaks my heart to see her. Never a word that is *de trop*, never a word of bitterness or complaint, escapes her lips. She is truly as sweet as an angel."

Josephine's spirits rallied on the second day, the seventeenth, at the word that the Emperor was driving over to Malmaison from nearby Trianon. This first visit set the pattern for all those to come, a pattern that is described by Mademoiselle Avrillon: "His visits were always announced in advance, and there was something ceremonious and constrained about them. He came always accompanied by two high-ranking staff officers. As soon as his carriage came into sight, the Empress went out into the courtyard to await his arrival.

There was no embrace. The Emperor gave the Empress his arm or, more often, his hand and led her for a stroll through the gardens. Sometimes they sat down on a bench and remained there talking for quite a while, but it was easy to see that the Emperor made a point of staying in full view of the château windows. During those tête-à-têtes the two officers who had accompanied His Majesty joined Her Majesty's ladies in the salon. When the Emperor gave the signal for departure, the Empress walked with him to his carriage."

Her Majesty's ladies, "all consumed with curiosity," says Georgette Ducrest, who later was one of them, "would peer out from behind the window curtains, trying to read in Josephine's expressive face and Napoleon's lively gestures the subject of their conversations." If the ladies' curiosity was frustrated at this first meeting of the couple since the divorce, a letter written by the Emperor to Josephine that very night, upon his return to Trianon, gives us the gist of the words they had exchanged:

My dear, I found you weaker than you should be. You have exhibited great courage up to this point; you must call upon it again now to sustain you. You must not allow yourself to sink into a fatal melancholy. You must take care of your health, which is precious to me. . . . You cannot doubt my unwavering and tender friendship, so you should realize that I cannot be happy if you are not—that I can have no peace of mind unless I know that you have.
Good night, my dear. Sleep well. Remember that is my wish.

It was also his wish that she be paid the same homage and respect as heretofore, as he made clear to his bewildered courtiers by means of the pointed question, "Have you been to Malmaison to pay your respects to the Empress?" The majority had needed precisely such clarification of the almighty Emperor's attitude before venturing to offer their sympathy to his discarded wife.

Laure Junot, despite her Bonaparte affiliations as an official member of Madame Mère's honor household, had needed no such prodding; she had been profoundly affected by the divorce, she says, and had gone the very next day to Malmaison, as had a number of Josephine's other friends. She describes the scene:

The drawing room, the billiard room and the gallery were all crowded with company. The Empress never appeared to greater advantage than she did then, seated at the right of the fireplace, beneath that wonderful Girodet painting, simply dressed, a voluminous hood partially concealing the tears which welled up in her eyes whenever anyone came who particularly reminded her of the halcyon days at Malmaison, those of the Consulate [as, for instance, Laure]. Her tears rolled gently down her cheeks, causing none of that contortion of the features which is inimical to beauty. . . . She even managed a smile for each new arrival.

When she saw me, she stretched out her hand and drew me toward her. "I could kiss you," she said, "for coming on this day of mourning. . . ."

She seemed to me, at that hour, deserving of the respect of the entire universe. . . . She regretted all she had lost, but in justice to her it should be said that what she regretted above all else was the loss of her husband.

Consciously or unconsciously, Josephine presented her pathetic and appealing tableau of majestic heartbreak to a responsive audience. She wept her stream of artistic tears for a stream of distinguished guests, including the Kings of Bavaria and Württemberg, whom Napoleon likewise encouraged to pay her court.

But it was the Emperor's visits for which she lived, and for his letters, his messages, his messengers. He came again in person on December 18 and wrote the next day: "I was heartsick at sight of you yesterday . . . Write and tell me what you are doing today." He sent General René Savary to deliver the letter and to bring him a report, which occasioned another letter: "Savary tells me that you are still weeping. That is awful. . . . I will come back to see you when you can assure me that you are in a more cheerful frame of mind. . . . I too am sad today, and need to know that you are more composed. Sleep well . . ."

Two letters came from him on the twenty-first, others on the twenty-second and the twenty-third. Madame de Rémusat decided that he was overdoing it, and she somewhat officiously suggested that her husband give the Emperor a hint that his letters were too poignant and that when they were delivered in the late afternoon or evening they "caused the Empress the most frightful nights."

Divorce

Napoleon came to Malmaison on Christmas Eve, and on Christmas Day Josephine and her daughter dined with him and his sister Caroline at Trianon. "The Empress came home so elated, so happy, that one might have thought no divorce had ever taken place," Mademoiselle Avrillon remarks. "This was to prove, however, the last time Their Majesties met in intimacy."

On the twenty-seventh, His Majesty returned to Paris. "I hated coming back to the Tuileries," he wrote to Josephine that evening. "This great palace echoes with emptiness, and I feel terribly alone, isolated. . . . I am dining all alone tonight." (Almost as if he were reproaching her for having deserted him. No wonder she dissolved "like Niobe, all tears.") "The page I sent to Malmaison this morning tells me he saw you weeping. You promised me that you would stop. . . . I want very much to come to see you, but you will have to show more self-control."

Madame de Rémusat's hints notwithstanding, he continued to write daily, assuring her, for example: "It was wonderful to see you yesterday [January 6]. The visit made me realize what charms your company holds for me." And: "Sometimes I am susceptible to weakness, too, and suffer terribly."

"The most ardent and devoted husband could not have showered more attentions on a cherished wife than did the Emperor on the Empress," Mademoiselle Avrillon writes of this period. He sent wild game for her table after his every hunting expedition. His pages shuttled back and forth between Paris and Malmaison, delivering his messages to her, returning hers to him. He spent an entire day working with the Minister of Finance to straighten out her tangled financial affairs, writing later:

I arranged yesterday with Estève for an additional one hundred thousand francs for extra expenses at Malmaison for this year of 1810. Now you can plant everything you want. . . . At the same time, I instructed Estève to pay two hundred thousand francs owing on the Julien property, as well as the amount due on your parure of rubies—after it has been appraised by the intendant, for I mean to stop these jewelers from robbing you. That makes a total of four hundred thousand francs it's costing me. . . . In addition, there should be five or six thousand francs in my money box at

345

*Malmaison, and this you may apply toward the purchase of your
silver and linens. I also ordered a handsome porcelain table service for you . . .*

But the visits slackened now that he was back in the capital. "If
I do not come today, I will come after Mass tomorrow." Or: "A
review of troops is scheduled for today. If it is over by three o'clock,
I shall come to see you. If not, tomorrow." Then: "I hope to get to
Malmaison within the week." Josephine knew that he had played
host at a hunting party at Versailles and attended a ball at the
Ministry of Foreign Affairs. Was he already adjusting himself to
life without her, to a life in which she had no share?

Suddenly she showed signs of restlessness at Malmaison. Her attendants too were beginning to murmur. "Spirits would have to be
far blither than they are to make this place agreeable at this time
of the year, with the moan of the wind and the constant rain,"
Claire de Rémusat wrote to her husband. Josephine's own letters
now hinted to the Emperor that it was high time for the Murats to
go home to Naples and turn over the Élysée Palace to its rightful
owner.

"Audenarde, whom I sent to see you this morning, tells me you
are no longer satisfied at Malmaison," Napoleon wrote in reply.
"And yet that spot should be full of memories, a reminder of our
unchanging sentiments—at least, on my side they are. . . . I have
taken care of matters for you here and have given orders that all
your effects be taken to the Élysée. . . ." And again (on January
30): "It will give me great pleasure to know that you are close by,
at the Élysée, and so to see you more often, for you know how
much I love you." The Murats being obviously loath to leave
Paris, he simply could not evict them, but he reproached Josephine
for listening to rumors that she was to be kept out of the capital,
perhaps even exiled. "You obviously put more faith in the ridiculous rumors that circulate in a big city than in what I tell you. As I
told Eugène, people should not be allowed to upset you with tales
such as these. I have had your things moved to the Élysée. You will
be able to come in to Paris any day now. Please trust me."

3

While she waited at Malmaison, Josephine engaged in an exceedingly curious undertaking: matchmaking for her former husband.

From Paris the wife of Prince von Metternich—the new Austrian Foreign Minister, formerly Austria's ambassador to France—reported a strange interview with the former Empress of the French in a letter to her husband in Vienna:

I have the most extraordinary thing to tell you! . . . I went to Malmaison yesterday . . . and the Empress said to me, "There is a certain project which occupies my attention to the exclusion of all else; its success will assure me that my recent sacrifice has not been in vain: It is my hope to arrange the marriage of the Emperor to your Archduchess [Marie Louise]. I spoke to him about it yesterday, and, while he told me that his choice had not yet been settled, it is my belief that it would be if he were given assurance that his offer would meet with acceptance in Austria."

She went on to tell me that the Emperor was coming to see her again that day, and that she would afterward be able to give me some more positive assurance. "We must try to arrange this between us," were her parting words.

I have just this moment received a message from the Queen of Holland, setting another appointment for tomorrow. We shall have to wait and see what the Empress has to tell me then.

Metternich's reply to his wife, dated January 27, expressed enthusiasm. "The Empress," he wrote, "has recently given proof of a strength of character which must augment the veneration in which she is held in France and in all of Europe. . . . I consider this matter of the Emperor's marriage of supreme importance to Continental affairs." The letter ended with the comment that it was ardently to be hoped that the Empress would persevere in the negotiation she had initiated. It would be Josephine whom Metternich would later choose as his intermediary to relay to the Emperor the decision of the Austrian Cabinet.

Undoubtedly it was Josephine's hope, in sponsoring the Austrian alliance, that the Archduchess Marie Louise would consider herself the Empress's protégée and respond accordingly, with gratitude and consideration. Could Josephine—and Napoleon—have hoped for even more, for an imperial *ménage à trois*: the ex-Empress and ex-wife, worldly-wise and tolerant, initiating the new Empress and bride into both her conjugal and her imperial duties? Later developments tend to prove that both Napoleon and Josephine had precisely some such idea in mind. Even as early as at the time of the divorce, the archives had been consulted to determine the order of precedence governing the court appearances of an ex-sovereign, and it had been established that the former Empress was to yield precedence to the reigning Empress, but to her alone, and that in the throne room the reigning Empress was to be seated at the Emperor's right and the former Empress at his left, the position presently occupied by Madame Mère. If it was not intended that the former Empress should appear at court, why go to such pains to establish the ritual?

On February 3 Josephine's wish was granted and she made her long-desired move from Malmaison to the capital—where she was doomed to disappointment and frustration. At the Élysée, in the heart of the city, she found herself in social quarantine, her isolation more pronounced than in the suburbs. She read in the court circular published in the *Moniteur* and the *Publiciste*—the daily calendar of brilliant entertainments and festivities—about a ball last night at the Austrian Embassy, one tonight at the Princess Borghese's, one tomorrow at the Arch-chancellery, from which she was excluded. Her ladies of the palace moped, giving her to feel that she should be grateful to them for resisting such functions to keep her company in the silent salons of the Élysée, yawning over a table of whist or nodding to the measures of sedate chamber music.

To the livelier strains of a full orchestra, the Emperor was dancing every dance, gay as he had not been in years, even asking Hortense for lessons in the waltz, presumably for the benefit of a nineteen-year-old archduchess. He came dutifully to visit Josephine, the very day of her arrival. But his visits were sporadic and brief; he was shaking off the pall of his sadness and seemed reluctant to come back under hers. The Emperor—and all the Emperor's court—had turned to face the rising sun. Nothing is so stale as last winter's sorrow when a spring wedding is in the offing.

On February 7 the marriage contract with Austria was signed, with Eugène acting as marriage broker for his mother's ex-husband "in the name of the Emperor and with the approval of the Empress, my mother" (his words to the Austrian ambassador). For fickle Paris, the fifty-day wonder of imperial divorce was over. The new topics of conversation were the forthcoming festivities, the appointment of the new Empress's honor attendants, the amount of her allowance (four million francs, to Josephine's three), the jewels and the *corbeille* (the groom's contribution to the trousseau) being convoyed to Vienna by General Berthier. The proxy wedding was to take place in Vienna on March 11; the bridal cortege was expected in Compiègne on March 27.

Perhaps at a hint from Vienna, Josephine was to be invited to quit Paris, even the Île-de-France, for a princely domain in Normandy, near Évreux, thirteen posting stations and sixty-odd miles away, bestowed upon her by the Emperor on March 12—as he advised by letter of that date, saying, "My friend, I hope you will be pleased by this fresh proof of my desire to be agreeable—this gift to you of the Château of Navarre. Go, take possession of your new domain. You may leave on March 25 and spend the month of April there." It was tantamount to banishment.

Accompanied by a token entourage of honor attendants, Josephine obediently "took possession" of her new duchy on April 2, the same day upon which her successor made her triumphal entry into the capital and repeated her marriage vows in the presence of eight thousand guests in the chapel of the Tuileries.

Both Hortense and Eugène were members of the imperial family party assembled at the Château of Compiègne to greet the bride upon her arrival on March 27. Did either of them report to their mother on the impetuosity of the bridegroom, who consummated the marriage that very night, a full week in advance of the official Tuileries marriage ceremony? Did Josephine's son or daughter repeat to her the bridegroom's enthusiastic morning-after comment, "Marry a German girl; they make the best wives in the world —good, sweet, naïve and fresh as roses"?

Naïve as this one was—having never in all her nineteen years spent so much as a moment alone in the company of any man save her Emperor father, Francis I, having never been permitted so much as a pet, neither dog nor cat nor pony, of the opposite sex —still, to the Emperor's relief, "she giggled her way straight through" their wedding night. Napoleon must have exerted himself to charm and reassure this buxom, blond, blue-eyed, Hapsburg princess, who had twice in the past four years been chased out of her Schönbrunn Palace by this very "Ogre" ("Der Krampus," in her native tongue), this "Hunnish invader" now jumping into her bed.

From Navarre, on April 3, Josephine wrote to her daughter at Compiègne: "All the citizens of Évreux turned out to give me a gala welcome, but it somehow struck me that they might have been extending me their condolences for no longer being anybody." As for Navarre, "it could be made into a lovely retreat, but only at tremendous cost. The château is uninhabitable, in need of total renovation. The persons with me have only one small room each, with windows and doors that will not close. My own apartments are small and uncomfortable; the woodwork is rotting." Mademoiselle Avrillon would complain even more bitterly than her mistress of the damp and the cold, of the impossibility of heating that "crumbling pile," of the lack of furnishings, of "camping out, as it were." Long abandoned, empty, moldering, Navarre was a relic of better days, of former glories and splendors—like its proprietor.

"The park is magnificent," Josephine's first letter to Hortense went on to say, "lying in a valley between forest-clad hills, but there is too much water"—lakes, pools and an elaborate series of canals—"making the place damp and unhealthy. . . . At this season, I far prefer Malmaison, primarily for reasons of health . . . and hope to return there in three or four weeks. . . . I invited all the members of my honor service to join me at Navarre, but most of them have not been able to come."

Shameful to say, six out of Josephine's seven chamberlains transferred to Marie Louise's service, and almost as many of her ladies of the palace. Shameful to say, *"chère cousine"* Madame de La Rochefoucauld had been the first to hand in her resignation. Madame la Maréchale Ney, Hortense's schoolmate and Josephine's own protégée, had been the second; yielding to her husband's demand, she had applied for an appointment with the new Empress instead—and had obtained it thanks to the good offices of the old. Even Madame de Rémusat was conspicuous by her absence; with the best will in the world, Claire simply "could not make it all the way to Navarre without a sleeping carriage." Who wanted to bury himself or herself in that provincial backwater, far from Paris, far from the imperial court, the fountainhead of grace and favor?

The dignified, elegant, levelheaded Countess d'Arberg, a Belgian noblewoman, would prove the happiest of choices as the former Empress's new lady of honor, and other ladies of the palace and other chamberlains would be signed on to replace the deserters, but even so the defections in the honor household came as straws to break a camel's back. Another was added by *couturier* Leroy, who was too busy with Marie Louise's trousseau to give his customary attention to Josephine, to whom he owed his reputation. The last straw was laid on by Napoleon, with his raid on Josephine's domestic staff: without so much as a by-your-leave, he summoned her first mistress of the wardrobe and her master coiffeur and hired them away from the old Empress for the new. Hortense's talented hairdresser, Charbonnier, could never really console Josephine for the loss of Duplan, much as she appreciated her daughter's gesture in relinquishing him. Thank heaven for Mademoiselle Avrillon and the other three faithful maids. Thank heaven for Madame Gazzani, the "reader"—for whom Josephine had interceded in 1809 when Napoleon had threatened to dismiss her. ("No, let me keep her," she had said. "She and I will weep together.")

Josephine had cause to weep with her daughter too, that spring of 1810, for the Emperor suddenly decreed that Hortense must return to her husband, to sit with him on the shaky throne of Holland. "As long as I have anything, I will share it with you so that you may be the mistress of your own fate," Josephine wrote to the unhappy Queen on April 4. She found a second cause to weep in the blight to her son's career; Napoleon's award of the grand duchy of Frankfurt to Eugène could only be taken as an indication that the kingdom of Italy was destined for the Emperor's first legitimate son of his own.

The skies wept to keep Josephine company that dark month of April. "She found herself in strange surroundings. Navarre smelled of exile"—at least, to Mademoiselle Avrillon. "The order to remove herself from Paris and its vicinity struck the Empress as a second divorce. Only another woman can put herself in the Empress's place or understand the anguish she suffered. There was Marie Louise, close by the Emperor's side; would he give so much as another thought to Josephine?"

Paris wondered, too. Madame de Rémusat, taking alarm at the rumors, wrote to her husband, who was at Compiègne with the imperial honeymoon party: "All sorts of tales are going around here about what is going on there at court—mostly malicious ones to the effect that the new Empress is cold and haughty and that the Other is to be reduced in rank to a mere duchess of Navarre or relegated to the duchy of Berg [across the Rhine], even that Malmaison is to be bought back from her because our new sovereign has expressed displeasure at the Old One's living so close by! I await your return to know the truth."

It was Josephine who needed desperately to know the truth. As she had heard not a word from the Emperor since his remarriage, she delegated Eugène to put certain questions to him on her behalf. When a favorable reply was returned to her, again through Eugène, Josephine was emboldened to write directly to her former husband —or, rather, it might seem, to His Majesty, the Emperor of France, for it was the letter not of a first wife and first love but of a respectful subject to her sovereign, a letter sonorous with "Majestys" and "Sires:"

SIRE:

Through my son, I have received assurance that Your Majesty consents to my return to Malmaison and graciously accords me the advances requested for the repairs necessary to make Navarre habitable. This double favor, Sire, dissipates to a great extent the anxieties, even fears, inspired in me by Your Majesty's long silence. I feared that I had been entirely banished from Your Majesty's memory. I see that I have not. Today, therefore, I am less unhappy—even happy, or as happy as it is possible for me ever to be again.

I shall go at the end of the month to Malmaison, since Your Majesty finds no objection. But I do want you to know, Sire, that I would not so soon have taken advantage of the liberty you accord me in this regard had the Château of Navarre not so urgently required repairs, for reasons of health, my own as well as that of my attendants.

It is my plan to stay at Malmaison for only a very brief period. I shall shortly absent myself to go to a watering resort. But Your Majesty may be sure that even such time as I am in residence at Malmaison I shall live as if I were a thousand leagues away from Paris. I have made a great sacrifice, Sire, and every day brings me to fuller realization of its extent. Even so, the sacrifice shall be wholehearted on my part. Your Majesty, in your happiness, shall never be troubled by any expression of my regret.

I pray constantly for Your Majesty's happiness. Perhaps I even include a prayer that I may see you again, but Your Majesty may be confident that I shall always respect your new situation, and respect it in silence—putting my trust in the sentiments you formerly bore me, and so requiring no new proof. I rely on your sense of justice and your heart. I confine myself to asking only one favor: that you yourself deign to find some means of vouchsafing to me and to those about me a token of the fact that I still retain a small place in your memory and a great place in your esteem and friendship. Whatever form of expression this may take, it will sweeten my grief without, it seems to me, compromising that which is most important in the world to me—Your Majesty's happiness.

With what a deft touch she plucked at his heartstrings and twanged at his memories! His first impulse was to raise her from her knees, this woman he had so long held within the circle of his arms. Eugène, arriving at Navarre for a brief visit with his mother, brought this reply from Napoleon:

My friend, I have received your letter of April 19. I find the style objectionable. I am always the same. My kind never changes. . . .

I had not written to you for the reason that you had not written to me, and I wanted to do what seemed best to you.

It gives me pleasure to know that you are going to Malmaison and that you will be happy there. Remember that I will be happy to have news of you and to send you mine. I shall say no more until you have had time to compare your letter to this one of mine. After that, I leave it to you to decide which is the better friend, you or I.

Goodbye, keep well and try to be just to both yourself and me.

"Thou" and "thee," he said to her, using the intimate *tutoie-ment* she had not dared to use, dispensing with "Majestys," setting the tone—one of familiarity and intimacy—for their future communion.

Her masterpiece of a reply she entrusted to Eugène to hand to the Emperor:

A thousand and a thousand tender thanks for not having forgotten me! My son has just brought me your letter. How eagerly, how ardently I took it up! Yet I spent hours reading it, for there was not a word which did not blur my eyes with tears—but tears of happiness, these. I have found my heart again, found it whole again, as it will now always be. There are sentiments as strong as life itself, which end only with the end of life.

I am distressed to learn that my letter of the nineteenth displeased you. I cannot remember exactly how I expressed myself, but I do remember what painful emotion dictated it. It was despair at not having had any word from you. I wrote to you before my departure from Malmaison, and how many times since then have I wanted to write again! But I understood the reasons for your silence and hesitated to importune you with a letter. Yours is a balm to my soul. Be happy—happy as you so well deserve to be! It is my full heart which speaks. You have just given me a share of happiness of my own, a share profoundly appreciated. Nothing in the world means as much to me as your remembrance of me.

Goodbye, my friend. I send you thanks as tender as my undying love.

Again the virtuoso touch, striking the very chord to set his heart and memory vibrating. She would not spoil the effect by going into practical matters. She would leave it to Eugène to take up the bothersome financial arrangements and to secure the Emperor's permission for her projected itinerary: a brief visit at Malmaison, a three months' cure at Aix-les-Bains, Italy for the autumn, the winter with her son's family at Milan, a return to Malmaison and Navarre in the spring of 1811. The plan as submitted to Napoleon was ostensibly her own, made of her own free will. As such, he approved it.

With a state visit to Belgium on schedule for him and his new Empress, the month of May provided a most opportune time for Josephine's Malmaison sojourn. With what joy she made her entrance into those grounds, her personal Champs-Élysées, at tulip time! All Paris flocked out to welcome her, comparing "La Vieille," the Old One, with "La Nouvelle," inevitably to the detriment of the latter—who, they said, was stiff-necked and unresponsive ("haughty, cold," as Claire de Rémusat remarked), a Hapsburg looking down her long Hapsburg nose at the revolutionary element of the court and of the administration, an Austrian indisposed to trouble her thick head or tongue with the names of the French nobility.

Not only friends and courtiers thronged the gates of Malmaison, but *couturières* and milliners and jewelers, all the purveyors of the fashion capital, spreading their wares before the hungry eyes of their perennial prize customer.

The Emperor found time to write her from Belgium:

My friend, I have received your letter. Eugène [on tour with the imperial party] will give you news of my trip and of the Empress. Stop listening to the Paris gossip. You should know me better than that. You show a lack of confidence in me, and I resent it. I am in good health, and the only thing lacking to me is the assurance that you are well and happy. If I do not soon receive it, I shall scold you severely. My sentiments for you will remain unchanged so long as I live. . . . I am very eager to see you again, and if you are still at Malmaison when I return to St.-Cloud on May 30, I will come to pay you a visit. . . .

Josephine put off her departure day after day to await that promised visit, which was paid her finally on June 13, as she wrote in a flurry of excitement to Hortense on the fourteenth:

Yesterday was a great day for me. The Emperor came to see me. His visit made me happy, although it started up all the familiar heart pangs again. Even so, that is a price I am willing to pay over and over again for the pleasure of seeing him. While he was with me, I found courage to hold back the tears. After he had gone, I could no longer restrain them and sank into a most unhappy mood. But he was most kind and amiable toward me, as he usually is, and I hope that he could read in my heart all the tenderness and devotion for him with which it is filled.

4

Josephine's letter followed Hortense from Amsterdam to Plombières, where she had gone in flight from her warder-husband, this time on doctor's orders.

The diagnosis of tuberculosis and melancholia naturally alarmed her mother. "Your tone of despondency afflicts me," Josephine wrote. "How can you talk of giving up, when so many bonds hold you fast to life? How can you talk of leaving me, now when I need you most, now when I am alone, abandoned, among strangers, bereft of all my family?"

Josephine hoped Hortense would join her at Aix-les-Bains, on the shores of Lake Bourget, to which she herself traveled incognito under the name of Madame d'Arberg, with only two ladies in waiting, one chamberlain and one equerry in her entourage. She kept to the shadows, "sedulously avoided calling attention to herself, declining all official recognition, referring to the Emperor only at appropriate moments and in appropriate terms," and was "a model of tact, diplomacy and dignity"; so Madame de Rémusat saw her in July, at the height of the season, when she finally found it convenient to rejoin her patroness.

The little party led the quietest of lives, as Claire described it to her husband: "The thermal baths, the waters and the toilette take up most of the morning, until lunch at noon; then for five or six hours we gather in the Empress's salon to chat, to sketch, to do needlework. At six o'clock we dress for a carriage drive; at eight we dine, going afterward to the casino for some music. At that rate the days slip by, one indistinguishable from another."

The calm of Aix was shattered the first week in July by a bombshell of news exploding by letter from the Emperor: "The King of Holland has just abdicated . . . and left Amsterdam. . . . I have re-united Holland with France. But these developments have one fortunate consequence—they free the Queen. That unfortunate girl can now come back to Paris with her sons. And this should make her supremely happy. . . . I look forward to seeing you in the autumn. Never doubt my friendship; I never change."

Josephine knew of the clash of wills that had come between Napoleon and his brother over the latter's conscientious objection to the Continental System as prejudicial to the best interests of his subjects, and his refusal to close Dutch ports to English traffic. Napoleon's threat of armed invasion was met by Louis's of armed resistance and of flooding the country by opening the dikes. Clearly, the King of Holland could not long stand up to the Emperor of France, and abdication was inevitable.

For Josephine, the significant point of the Emperor's letter was that Hortense was free. Free of her marriage as well as the throne, free to respond at last to the man she had long loved: the debonair and handsome Colonel Charles de Flahaut (who had been acknowledged as son and heir by the Count de Flahaut, although he had been sired by Talleyrand—on authority as incontrovertible as that of the Countess de Flahaut, Charles's mother).

Josephine was grateful to see Hortense smile again, to see her health and spirits revive in the mountain air of Aix, where she arrived in late July and where Flahaut came to dream midsummerdays dreams with her under the indulgent eye of her mother. "The happiest month of all my life," Hortense would say of it in retrospect. Understandably, Josephine regarded Charles de Flahaut as a son. Even critical contemporaries regarded the Hortense-Flahaut romance less as an affair than as a morganatic marriage.

Early in September Josephine went to stay at Sècheron, a small lake resort on the outskirts of Geneva. By then, some six months after the imperial wedding, rumor had the Empress Marie Louise pregnant, and Josephine wrote to Hortense: "I thought I should let the Emperor know what interest I take in the Empress's condition, and have just written to him on the subject. I hope that this will show him that he can speak to me of it with as much confidence as I have devotion for him."

On the fourteenth, Napoleon replied to Josephine from St.-Cloud: "Yes, the Empress is in her fourth month of pregnancy. She is feeling well and is very much attached to me. . . . Never doubt my interest in you or my sentiments for you."

The Empress Marie Louise may have been "feeling well" enough, but disturbing reports were circulating to the effect that she was exercising the prerogatives of pregnancy by giving way to whims and fancies, by making extraordinary demands on her solicitous and indulgent husband. One such report reached Josephine via Claire de Rémusat, who was back in Paris, having successfully extricated herself from the obligation of accompanying the Empress on a chilly autumnal tour of Switzerland:

The Empress Marie Louise seems to have a very easily excitable imagination, or perhaps first love makes her fearful and suspicious. . . . Proof is furnished by an incident described to me by the Grand Marshal [General Duroc, the Emperor's most frequent attendant]: The Emperor, driving one day with the Empress in the vicinity of Malmaison, offered to show her that fair domain in your absence. She made no open protest; but her eyes filled with tears, and the symptoms of distress were so unmistakable that the Emperor called off the visit.

You will remember, Madame, having told me how much you regretted that the Emperor did not succeed, at the time of his remarriage, in effecting the meeting between two persons whom he had hoped to bring together for the reason that both were dear to him. You have told me since that it was his hope that a pregnancy might provide that opportunity, on the theory that the prospects of motherhood would reassure the Empress as to her claims upon his heart.

But, Madame, unless I am greatly mistaken in my observations, the time is not yet come. . . . The Empress Marie Louise's disposition to jealousy at this particular hour could only be further stimulated by your presence in the region. Were your personal charms less striking, your role today might be less difficult. . . . The Grand Marshal seems to share this opinion. Of course, he dared not express himself openly, but he spoke to me in convincing words of the Emperor's attachment to you—which must, of itself, impose on him the severest circumspection.

As for you yourself, Madame, what would you do here in France in the midst of the national rejoicing which the birth of this eagerly awaited child will set off? You would not relish finding yourself in oblivion—at best, an object of pity. . . . In sum, your position would gradually become untenable, to the point where a total removal from the scene might present itself as the only remedy. You might have to leave Paris, Malmaison . . . ; even Navarre might come to be considered insufficiently remote. . . .

It is thus my conclusion that there remains yet one more sacrifice for you to make . . . and that it would be worthy of your noble character to forestall developments by writing to the Emperor to announce your courageous resolution. By sparing him the embarrassment of having to make the recommendation himself, you will establish new claims on his gratitude . . . and reassure a young wife whom time and motherhood should render calmer.

Whether written on hints from higher up relayed through Duroc, as this devious letter indicates, or on orders direct from the Emperor, as Rémusat family tradition has it, Claire's myriad pages of flattery, apology and innuendo spelled out a single dread word to Josephine: exile. And sent her into a panic.

She had only exchanged one specter for another. If her earlier years had been haunted by the specter of divorce, the specter of exile had risen to haunt her later years. Although it had been Josephine herself who had originally elected to spend a year away from Paris and to winter in Italy, now she feared that if she ever crossed the Italian border she might never be permitted to recross it back into France. Now the only thing she wanted was to go directly home—if she still had a home.

There was panic in her pen when she took it up to address herself to the Emperor. There were no "Majestys" now, no "Sires" on this page; now, in a cry from the heart, it was the old familiar name she used, the name by which she had addressed him throughout thirteen years of wedlock, the name she had whispered to him on their pillow; now it was "Bonaparte":

Bonaparte, you promised never to abandon me. Now I find myself in a position in which I need your counsel. I have only you in all the world. You are my only friend!

Talk to me straightforwardly. May I return to Paris or must I stay away? Naturally I would rather be near you, above all if there is any hope of seeing you; but if that hope is denied me, what would be my role this winter? Need I prolong my absence another seven or eight months? Circumstances will become more favorable for me before then, I hope, since the Empress will have acquired new titles to your love.

. . . If you advised me to stay away, I would lease or buy a small property on the lake [of Geneva]—at Lausanne or Vevey, if that should suit me, and if you approve. I would go to Italy, too, to see my children. I would spend the rest of the autumn traveling through Switzerland, for I am in need of constant distraction, and the only way I find it is to keep on the move. Then next summer perhaps I would return to the waters of Aix, which benefited my health. That would make a whole year of absence—a year I would be able to get through only in the hope of seeing you again at the end of it, only in the thought of winning your approbation by my conduct.

So please decide what I should do, and if you cannot write to me yourself, then ask the Queen [Hortense, who was returning to the court on Napoleon's orders] to let me know your decision. Ah, I implore you, do not refuse to guide me! Counsel your poor Josephine. It will be a proof of friendship, one to console her for all her sacrifices.

Josephine's thinking was as distracted as her letter. She fluttered like a bird in a net, thrashing frantically in a restraint she could feel rather than see. She wrote to Eugène in Milan. She sent Deschamps, her secretary, to Paris to question Claire de Rémusat face to face—whether she must really stay away. She sent Deschamps to Hortense with messages too confidential to be entrusted to paper. At Fontainebleau, where the court now was, Hortense had a private audience with the Emperor about Josephine's plans.

I could see at once how tremendously relieved he would be if my mother were to volunteer to stay in Italy with my brother [she recalls in her memoirs].

"I must think of my wife's happiness," he said to me. "Things have not turned out as I had hoped they would. She [Marie Louise] resents the privileges and honors accorded to your mother and the influence your mother is known to exercise over me. . . . Despite all this, I shall never agree to constrain the Empress Josephine in any way. I shall never forget the sacrifices she has made for me. If she should wish to establish herself at Rome, I would appoint her as governor. If at Brussels, she might preside over a brilliant court of her own and, at the same time, do a service for that country [Belgium]. However, it seems to me that in Italy, near her son and grandchildren, she would be better off than anywhere else, and most suitably settled. . . ."

Hortense, as well as Eugène, realized that some such sovereign position as the Emperor here proposed was the only one compatible with the dignity of the ex-Empress, and that the responsibilities of such a role were the only solution to her barren and blighted life. It was now clear, however, that Josephine could never be brought round to that point of view, that she would "die of grief" —as she wrote to Hortense in October—if she were forced to live outside France.

While she waited for word from Paris, she wandered distractedly from Geneva to Neuchâtel to Interlaken to Bern, dragging her reluctant retinue and her own heavy heart up and down the Alpine passes, in charabancs and on muleback, to take in all the renowned attractions.

"Not a word from you in the three weeks since we parted!" she wailed to Hortense. "What can your silence mean? For pity's sake, dear Hortense, let me know where I stand."

Then, at last, a letter from the Emperor:

Hortense will have told you what I think. Go see your son this winter, then return to the waters at Aix next year or, if you prefer, spend the spring at Navarre. I would advise you to go to Navarre immediately if I were not afraid you would be bored there. It is my opinion that there are only two places suitable for you for the winter . . . either Milan or Navarre. After that, I will approve anything you want to do, for I want never to constrain you in any way. . . . Try to make yourself content and don't go all to pieces over this.

But, of course, she did. The Emperor was still not speaking "straightforwardly" to her. If he conceded Navarre as an alternative to Italy, it was obviously in the hope that it was Italy she would choose. So, what should she do now? She bombarded Hortense with questions, messages, letters, among them this:

Before making definite plans for Navarre, I still need one final word from you to make absolutely certain the Emperor approves my wintering there. I find great drawbacks to the Italian visit. Were it only a question of spending two or three months there, I would gladly go to see my son, but to stay longer—that is impossible. Why, I am sure that most of my attendants would resign at the very prospect, and that would be awful.

"What a red-letter day that was for us in the Empress's party," Mademoiselle Avrillon voices their sentiments, "the day the courier rode into Sècheron bringing authorization to spend the winter at Navarre! As soon as Her Majesty gave us the news that we could go home, back to France, the entire household was seized by a delirium of joy. Without exaggeration, you would have taken us all for crazy people."

5

With permission for Navarre in hand, Josephine now begged for "just twenty-four hours at Malmaison." And with the Emperor and Empress still out of the city, at Fontainebleau, she stretched the hours into days, the days into a week and more. After all, there was her winter wardrobe to be selected, and there was Leroy, dancing attendance on her as in the good old days, whispering that Napoleon's second Empress lacked the flair, lacked the figure, lacked the elegance—failed utterly to do Leroy's creations justice and offered no such inspiration for his talents as had Josephine.

And, whether with Josephine's knowledge or without, Malmaison became a rallying point for the malcontents, for the opposition; the ranks of Josephine's friends were swelled by Napoleon's enemies. Such as Bourrienne, the Emperor's former secretary, still Josephine's fast friend; one of the few to whom, by his account, she could reveal her disillusionment.

"I have run the full gamut of misfortune," Bourrienne has her saying. "He has discarded and abandoned me. The hollow title of empress he preserved to me only to make the indignities more poignant. I never had any illusions as to my fate. After all, is there anyone or anything he would not sacrifice to his ambition? He has done it all with a cruelty which not even you could imagine. I would be better off a thousand leagues away!"

That last sentence taxes the credulity of the reader who has had access to the Empress's correspondence of the preceding months. But whether or not the evidence of an embittered Bourrienne is to be trusted, it is almost with a sense of relief that one listens to some such vigorous, natural, long-expected outburst from those tightly sealed lips of Josephine's. That "angelic sweetness" described over and over again by Claire de Rémusat, that spirit of resignation and abnegation, confirmed by maid Avrillon, valet Constant, Laure Junot, Georgette Ducrest and all the rest, come to seem either superhuman or subnormal. Could Josephine (could any woman?) have been as noble as all that—or as spineless? Still, Bourrienne's testimony leads squarely to a basic question: What was Josephine's true feeling about Napoleon after the divorce? If she had ever loved him, did she love him still?

In direct contradiction to Bourrienne comes Georgette Ducrest (who, as an impecunious young émigrée, had been presented to Josephine in Switzerland, whose pretty singing voice and pretty face and figure had won her an invitation to join the Empress's household, and whose somewhat maudlin memoirs, written after the Empress's death, would preserve the authoress from starvation during the Restoration): "The Empress's adoration of the Emperor amounted to a cult. His Malmaison apartments were preserved exactly as they were the day he left them. There was his uncurtained Roman bed, there were his guns and swords hanging on the wall; even several pieces of his clothing were to be seen scattered about on the furniture. On his desk was his world map and the pen with which he wrote the laws of Europe; on the table, a history book lay open at the page he had been reading. One expected to see him enter any moment into that room which he had forever abandoned. Josephine seldom granted permission for a visit to that sanctuary. No one but she could touch or dust what she called her 'relics.' "

The Emperor, preparing to return from Fontainebleau to Paris in mid-November of 1810, sent Arch-chancellor Cambacérès to Malmaison to remind Josephine that she had overstayed her leave, and she promised to start for Normandy no later than the sixteenth. But it proved to be the twenty-second before she could actually collect herself, her retinue and her luggage, including the mountain of cartons stacked up in her recent shopping spree.

It was more than the shroud of fog, more than the melancholy rain, which dampened the enthusiasm of the welcome extended the former Empress on her return to Évreux. An imperial decree expressly prohibited the garrison of cuirassiers from furnishing an honor escort, as had been done for her arrival the preceding March, and this time neither the citizenry nor the National Guard had been alerted to her coming; only a handful of municipal police accompanied her carriage as it rolled through the gates of Navarre. No church bells chimed, no cannon boomed to herald a sovereign's return to her domains; it was rather the homecoming of a prominent private citizen back from her travels.

But Josephine could dispense with carillons and salvos; these had too often, in the days of glory, started up her migraines. Actually, the sight of Navarre was good to her eyes. Isolated, lonely, drafty pile that it was, its foundations rested on French soil and so it was to be preferred to any *palazzo* in sun-warmed Italy. And her architects had, by now, effected satisfactory structural improvements and additions, and her decorators had furnished the dark and dreary rooms comfortably if not splendorously. Thanks to the new heating system, there was no longer need to shiver in the damp and the cold, even if, as Claire de Rémusat commented, "only a royal proprietor could afford the maintenance of those mammoth furnaces."

With the specter of exile exorcised, at least temporarily, Josephine could settle down almost gratefully to "that simple country life I lead here," as she described it by letter to Hortense. "In the morning I go out for a promenade on foot or in the carriage . . . when it doesn't rain. In the evening I play a game of backgammon with the bishop of Évreux, a delightful companion despite his seventy-five years."

And Claire de Rémusat could advise her husband:

> I am quite reconciled to the idea of spending the winter in the country. The Empress has surrounded herself with a very representative group, a company as easygoing, mild and agreeable as she is herself. We are always together, for, as you know, the Empress dislikes to be alone.
>
> Time passes astonishingly fast, though we do nothing much of anything; there is very little serious conversation or discussion. But we do the same thing at the same hour every day, so that it becomes difficult to know whether it is yesterday or tomorrow. . . . Luncheon is at eleven; then we come, we go, we sing, do needlework or drawing, or play checkers. At two o'clock one of the chamberlains reads aloud, usually some trashy novel to which we listen more or less attentively and, moreover, seldom finish.

The literary fare at Josephine's court, bluestocking Claire notwithstanding, was not limited exclusively to "trashy novels"; the supervisor of the Paris Printing Bureau was under orders to send down all the new and interesting publications, such as Chateaubriand's travel adventures, *Itinéraire de Paris à Jérusalem* (just off the presses that winter of 1810-1811), which, as Georgette Ducrest remembered, stimulated such interest among the Navarre coterie that "we had no sooner come to the end of the book than we turned back and started all over again."

As Claire de Rémusat completed the outline of the daily schedule for her husband: "At four o'clock we are free to go our separate ways; at six we dress for dinner. After dinner, card games, a concert, tea, . . . and so to bed by midnight." While Georgette Ducrest, speaking for the younger set, makes mention of their livelier diversions: "adjourning after dinner to sing and dance in a salon adjoining the cardroom," the gay youthful voices and laughter "rejoicing and cheering the Empress, who declined to allow her lady of honor to call us to order."

Josephine delighted in matchmaking for her ingénues, spending a small fortune on their dowries, trousseaux and wedding parties. And, incurable romantic that she was, she looked with a more indulgent eye than the Countess d'Arberg on the flirtations that developed among her adult honor attendants. Monsieur de Pourtalès may have lost his heart in the velvety depths of Madame Gazzani's night-dark eyes, but he was a perfect gentleman who kept his head, and not a breath of scandal escaped the gateway of Navarre to reach the Emperor's ears in the Tuileries. As for Josephine's own conduct, no breath of scandal involving her was even breathed by anyone who knew her intimately at this period; if, in the century and a half since her death, two of her chamberlains, the Count de Viel-Castel and the Count Turpin de Crissé, have been suggested as her lovers, no conclusive evidence can be found to support the suggestion.

"Peace of mind is a substitute for happiness," Josephine sighed to Claire de Rémusat that winter of 1810. Claire passed this along to her husband with the comment, "The Empress seems to be in a very good frame of mind."

"How great a boon is tranquillity," Josephine wrote to Eugène. "Only ambition could detract from it, and fortunately I am not susceptible to that passion." To Hortense she phrased it: "I only cry occasionally now."

"No longer being empress seems to agree with me," Josephine

told Marshal Oudinot and his wife. "The crown had literally as well as figuratively hurt her head," according to Georgette Ducrest; "even though she wore an inner band of velvet under it, the heavy crown . . . invariably left a cruel mark upon her brow." With the release from the strenuous round of official duties, with the relaxation of the tensions of the past six years, Josephine's psychogenetic ailments vanished, the migraines along with the nervous stomach spasms. Dr. Corvisart had always recognized them as such and had prescribed silvered and gilded breadcrumb pills.

Josephine's slender figure was not quite so slender now. "I hear you are as plump as a good Normandy farm wife," the Emperor teased by letter; while Mademoiselle Avrillon noted with a sense of shock that whalebones had to be added to those wisps of lace and batiste which had heretofore served her mistress as stays.

With the end of that fateful year of 1810, Josephine sent the Emperor greetings for the equally fateful one of 1811. He wrote promptly to thank her for her good wishes, adding: "It gives me pleasure to know that you are now content. Keep well. I am well, and hoping that my child will be a boy. I shall let you know immediately."

But it was by the din of the bells and cannon of Évreux on the night of March 20 that she learned of the birth of the long and eagerly awaited successor to the throne of imperial France. The first twenty-one salvos could have been for a daughter, but the twenty-second to the one hundred and first proclaimed a son and heir to a nation delirious with joy. (At last Napoleon had the answer to his query, "To whom shall I leave all this?") Josephine dispatched a messenger that same night to Paris to carry her congratulations to the Emperor, and issued invitations to the entire region for a glittering ball at Navarre.

"No one can read, of course, in the closed book of a woman's heart," Mademoiselle Avrillon says, "but the Empress manifested the most lively and apparently the most genuine delight at the news. I could detect no affectation and no mental reservations in the satisfaction she expressed. 'In this blessing to the nation, I reap the reward of my sacrifice,' were her words to me. And it was with a sort of pride that she showed me the letter written in the Emperor's own hand in announcement of the great event." (In the tradition of *noblesse oblige*, nothing less than a magnificent diamond decoration was appropriate as the reward from the Empress to the page who had ridden six hours at the gallop to bring her the Emperor's message from Paris.)

"I thank you for your letter," the Emperor had written. "My son is big and sturdy. I hope he will develop well. He has my chest, my mouth and my eyes. I hope he will fulfill his destiny. I am well pleased with Eugène. He has never in any way disappointed me." This reference to her son along with his struck Josephine as "a delicacy of sentiment worthy of the man who, when he chooses, can be the most irresistible, most winning man in all this world."

In a second example of tact and consideration rare with Napoleon, he sent Josephine's son to Navarre to give her a firsthand report of the suspenseful night of the accouchement.

Eugène's visits constituted the highlights of the winter season. The blithe, jaunty, handsome Viceroy of Italy would breeze in, rousing Navarre from the doldrums, distributing princely prizes to the winners of his dancing, fishing and billiards contests, and smiles (and sometimes kisses) to the losers (as to Georgette Ducrest). An "avowed enemy of etiquette," says Georgette, he encouraged his mother in her tendency to let down the bars in that remote, provincial backwater of Évreux. With the discard of court costume and court ceremonial, personal familiarities developed, the sense of hierarchy diminished.

It may have been Josephine's lady of honor or her daughter, both sticklers for etiquette, who reported to Paris on the loss of decorum and of imperial prestige; then again, it may have been "that unidentifiable 'informer' appointed by Napoleon to Josephine's retinue," as she is said to have suspected. In any case, orders were issued from the capital: Get back into court harness. No more drives through Évreux Forest without the specified fourteen uniformed horsemen, officer and trumpeter as escort to Her Majesty's carriage. An honor guard of twenty-five cuirassiers from the local garrison could be expected to report for duty at Navarre.

A second sharp reprimand from the Emperor stemmed from the old familiar source: Josephine's extravagance, her mounting debts, currently in the neighborhood of a million francs.

Divorce

Poor Monsieur Pierlot was to be pitied. An eminently capable and respectable banker assigned by Napoleon as Josephine's intendant, he allowed his own affairs to go to rack and ruin in the process of untangling and regulating hers. What chance did he ever have of controlling that disordered, spendthrift household? If he cut down on the domestic staff's coffee ration or issue of bed linen, one complaint by Mademoiselle Avrillon to Josephine and the order was countermanded. No less exalted a personage than the Prince of Monaco, Josephine's first equerry, submitted feed bills for sixty horses when there were never more than fifty in her stables.

But, to do Josephine justice, certain statistics should be cited: a payroll of 170 servants, including one footman behind every chair at table; scores of pensioners dependent on her bounty—old retainers, retired members of her domestic staff, her honor household, friends, cousins, cousins of cousins; public as well as private philanthropies; costly repairs to Navarre and Malmaison. And dowries! Half a million francs in one year alone to finance her matchmaking—dowries for her young protégées, for Tascher and Beauharnais relations, for maids (as for Mademoiselle Avrillon in 1812).

"Put your affairs in order!" Napoleon thundered by letter in 1811. "Interest yourself in financial matters and stop handing out your money to anyone and everyone who asks you for it. . . . Just think what a poor opinion I would have of you if I were to hear that you are in debt, with three million francs a year in revenue." She should spend not more than a million and a half a year and put an equal amount aside, he told her.

He had softened by the time he wrote a second letter on the subject: "I was angry with you for accumulating debts. I want you to stop it . . . If you want to please me, let me hear that you have built up a large reserve to provide for your grandchildren, to dower your granddaughters. That thought should give you an incentive." He added: "Never doubt my friendship for you, and don't distress yourself about this." What had softened him was a report from Count Mollien, the Minister of Finance, that Josephine had wept when, at Napoleon's request, he had given her a talking-to about economizing. Napoleon's heart had melted at the tears he had not even seen her shed. "But you didn't have to make her cry," he had rebuked his minister.

If she cried, she still did not economize. Her debts were to soar to the sum of four million francs before the next three years were out.

6

His cup overflowing with happiness at the birth of his little son, whom he created King of Rome, Napoleon's impulse was to grant Josephine the privilege of spending spring at Malmaison, which was one mammoth bouquet, colorful and fragrant, on her arrival, April 24. Her retinue was as elated as she at the "return to civilization," within easy distance for modistes and jewelers, for "all the high dignitaries of the Empire, senators, generals, marshals, princes, dukes, foreign sovereigns" in such a glitter of gold braid and jeweled orders that even a debutante in court circles, such as Georgette Ducrest, grew blasé at the sight within a few weeks of her arrival.

"With time and leisure," Claire de Rémusat observed, "the Empress will substitute new interests of her own for her memories." Two great and abiding interests to which she could turn with delight and zeal were not new, had been hers for years: her gardens and her gallery.

Josephine's gardening, more unusual in her generation than in this one, was more than affectation, more than a becoming pose self-consciously assumed. She worked at it as a science; botanists found her highly knowledgeable; she supervised her gardeners. Her passion for flowers spread through Europe with the seed packets and cuttings she sent out so generously—for the asking—to amateurs and professionals. Thanks to Josephine, French public parks as well as private gardens burst into new bloom. Her experimental gardens exercised a definite influence on French horticulture; through her efforts, some 180 species of flowers blossomed for the first time in French soil between 1804 and 1814, among them camellia, mimosa, purple magnolia, rhododendron, geranium, phlox, dahlia, hibiscus (her tastes running to the brilliantly colored, exotic flora of her native islands).

That minx Mademoiselle Ducrest would "yawn and perish of ennui" at the daily tour of the hothouses, with its standard lecture by the Empress to guests "who proclaimed themselves utterly fascinated by that 'fascinating science' and awestruck at 'Her Majesty's prodigious memory for all those botanical names.' " Mademoiselle Ducrest was flippant, too, on the subject of the gallery tours: "stopping in front of every picture, just as one had yesterday and the day before, listening to the explanations one already knew by heart, waiting politely for the more or less enlightened comment of the visitor."

Josephine had cause for pride in that fabulous collection of more than two hundred canvases. Among the 110 from Italy (loot of the campaign of 1796-1797) were paintings by Correggio, Giorgione, Ghirlandaio, Perugino, Giovanni Bellini, Paolo Veronese, Carlo Dolci, Guido Reni and no fewer than four each by Andrea del Sarto, Titian and Leonardo da Vinci. Of the group of canvases by Dutch, Flemish and German painters, a number had come as tribute to the Empress from their native lands, but at least half had been acquired by purchase out of private funds at the time of her state visit to Belgium in 1803. These included examples of the work of Cuyp, Dürer, de Hoogh, Teniers, Van Dyck and Holbein, not to forget three Rubenses and four Rembrandts. Of the Spanish school, only three, but those three were Murillos, gifts of the King of Spain. French artists were represented by Philippe de Champaigne, Claude Lorrain, Claude-Joseph Vernet, Poussin, Vanloo, Nattier. As for the contemporaries, Carle Vernet, Gros and David had all been commissioned as illustrators of the Napoleonic epic; Prud'hon and Jean-Baptiste Isabey, friends of Josephine's since Directoire days, were included, of course, as were Gérard, her first choice as her own personal portraitist, and Guérin, a miniaturist without peer.

Sitting for portraits should perhaps be listed as the third of Josephine's consuming interests. She made a career of having portraits of herself painted—portraits for her own and Napoleon's walls and, above all, for gifts to kings and concierges, to duchesses and chambermaids, to Robespierre's sister and the Czar of Russia, to Mademoiselle Avrillon and the Duchess de Montesson. Louis-Bertin

Pérant alone had delivered fifty of his "cameo" miniatures; Isabey received twenty-five commissions in all; Josephine's accounts showed forty portraits purchased in the years 1812-1814.

With the date for the public baptism of the King of Rome set for June 9, 1811, Josephine was encouraged to remove herself to Navarre for the summer. Perhaps the suggestion was made to spare her the sight and sound of rejoicing at the christening of the child she had failed to bear. More probably it was at the instigation of an enduringly hostile Marie Louise, as Josephine interpreted it in a letter to Eugène:

> *It seems that the Empress Marie Louise has no desire to see me. On that point we are in perfect accord, for I would have consented to meet her only to please the Emperor. But it appears that she regards me with something less than benevolence, and this I do not understand, because she can know me only through the sacrifice I made for her. I desire, as does she, the Emperor's happiness; this mutually shared sentiment, if nothing else, should dispose her to be friendly toward me.*

As a sign of the Emperor's favor, however, Josephine's daughter had been designated to share with Madame Mère the honor of serving as godmother to his child, to hold the royal infant over the baptismal font at Notre Dame. At the conclusion of the ceremony and the attendant festivities at the Hôtel de Ville, Hortense drew a great sigh of relief. The following morning, accompanied only by one devoted friend, she left for Aix-les-Bains. It is subject for astonishment that no one had suspected that the former Queen of Holland was almost six months pregnant.

She traveled incognito from Aix in September to her mother's house at Prégny, on the Lake of Geneva, for her rendezvous with Charles de Flahaut. In some Swiss village, at some Swiss inn, on September 15 or 16, their son was born. Dear and loyal Eugène was discreet enough to be let in on the secret arrangements, if Josephine was not. (Hortense "adored her mother, but understood her perfectly, realizing that she could not confide in her," Claire de Rémusat says. What secret could Josephine have ever kept from Mademoiselle Avrillon?)

The child's birth was registered in Paris in October; he was listed as Charles-Auguste-Joseph-Louis Demorny, son of Auguste-Jean-Hyacinthe Demorny—an old soldier and a pensioner of Josephine's—and his wife. (The boy was brought up and educated in Paris under the fond eye of his paternal grandmother and was eventually adopted by Charles de Flahaut. And on December 2, 1851, when Hortense's son Charles-Louis-Napoléon rode into Paris to establish the Second Empire, his half brother the Duke de Morny rode at his side—a prominent figure in the parade, as he would be in the regime.)

Late in that same eventful summer of 1811, on September 3, Josephine was permitted to return from Navarre to Malmaison (to take up permanent residence there, as it developed). Perhaps Marie Louise, in a growing sense of security, had relented, although not to the point of sanctioning her husband's visits to her predecessor —so that these had to be made surreptitiously by the Emperor— and certainly never to the point of permitting her son, the King of Rome, to be taken for a visit to "that woman at Malmaison."

The royal governess, the Countess de Montesquiou, was to write later that she learned from the Emperor, in deepest secrecy, of Josephine's longing to see the heir to the French Empire.

"But that would distress the Empress [Marie Louise] so much that I cannot bring myself to give you the necessary instructions" [Napoleon added, as Madame de Montesquiou recorded the conversation].

"Let me see to it, Sire. Just give your approval to what I intend to do."

"Very well, but be careful how you go about it."

The very next day [Madame de Montesquiou continues] I sent Monsieur de Canisy [the infant King's first equerry] to Malmaison to tell the Empress Josephine that . . . we would be going for a drive to Bagatelle [a small château in the Bois de Boulogne] the following Sunday, at half past two. . . . To keep our plan a secret, I had arranged with Monsieur de Canisy that as we got into the carriage I should say to him that I left the choice of a route entirely to him. . . . When we drew up in the courtyard of Bagatelle, Monsieur de Canisy, a look of surprise on his face, came and told me that the Empress Josephine was there.

I replied: "Now that we are here, we cannot go without seeing her. That would be unseemly."

She was in the little room at the back. . . . She went down on her knees before the child, burst into tears and kissed his hand, saying:

"Sweet child, one day you will know the extent of the sacrifice I made for you. I rely on your governess to help you to appreciate it."

After spending an hour with the child and myself, she asked if she could see the people who were then in attendance on the young King. She was as gracious as she always was, and spoke so kindly to the nurse that as we were getting into the carriage later the woman said:

"My, but that one's got a kind heart! She's said more to me in a quarter of an hour than the other one has in six months."

Eighteen years later, in his gilded cage of Schönbrunn, orphaned by Napoleon's exile and death and by the dereliction of Marie Louise, the ill-fated youth who as an infant had been embraced by Josephine at Bagatelle would pay tribute to his father's first wife. "If Josephine had been my mother," he was to say to his friend Anton Prokesch von Osten, "my father would never have been sent to St. Helena and I would not be languishing here in Vienna."

IV

Till Death Do Us Part

Never forget him who has never forgotten you and never will forget you.

LETTER FROM NAPOLEON TO JOSEPHINE, APRIL 16, 1814

1

LATER in that same spring of 1812, just when Josephine was complaining by letter to Eugène, "The Emperor seems to have forgotten me completely," he paid one of his now rare visits to Malmaison, "sitting two whole hours with her on the circular bench under the tulip tree."

Possibly he was explaining his reasons for the campaign he was about to launch against Russia—if these were comprehensible to any mind but his own, in any terms save those of his own sense of destiny. "I realized that the invisible Providence whose power and dominion I recognize would decide this issue as it has decided so many others," he explained himself in one of the last of his numerous conciliatory messages to that other mystic, his onetime friend the Czar. According to the explanation he gave Fouché, it was his old imperishable dream of a United States of Europe which was impelling him; he still had to fulfill his mission to "fuse all the nations into one," with "a European legal code, a European court

375

of appeals, a unified coinage and a common system of weights and measures." But as Claire de Rémusat saw it, "Napoleon would have preferred peace, if peace had served to enhance his power. As it was, he felt that he had to bedazzle us by an extraordinary and ever-changing spectacle—hence those interminable wars."

In more concrete terms, Napoleon may have explained to Josephine, under the tulip tree, that his peace proposals over the past few years had been consistently rejected by England, who was encouraged in her defiance by the knowledge that a quarter of a million of his troops and the best of his generals were still tied down in "that ulcer of a war" in Spain and were retreating steadily now before Wellington's advances. If England's economy had suffered by the Continental System, so had France's. So had Russia's, and now the impressionable, unstable, moody young Czar refused any longer to co-operate in it. Alexander, furthermore, suspected that Napoleon planned to re-establish an independent kingdom of Poland. When word came that Alexander had signed a secret treaty with the King of Prussia, Napoleon had ordered mobilization.

Eugène was summoned to Paris in April and was offered the regency of France during the Emperor's absence, in clear preference to all the Bonapartes. While Josephine appreciated the compliment paid her son, she understood his declining it in favor of active combat as a corps commander. Eugène would depend on his mother to go to Milan that summer to be with his wife at the time of the birth of their fourth child.

Eugène, Napoleon and the Grand Army (half of which were reluctant allied conscripts—Germans, Dutch, Swiss, Poles, and Danes) were deep inside East Prussia and the Grand Duchy of Warsaw by early June. From Danzig, on June 8, a brief but cordial message went to Josephine from the supreme commander: "I will always receive news of you, my friend, with greatest interest. . . . Never doubt my interest in you. I will take care of all those matters as you asked me to."

The last letter from him written to her during the Russian campaign was dated June 20, from Gumbinnen, East Prussia, near the Niemen. He wrote: "I see no objection to your going to Milan to be with the Vicereine. . . . I am well, and so is Eugène. He acquits himself extremely well." (Eugène was a zealous and valiant officer if not a brilliant one, taking down Napoleon's orders on paper and consulting them in the thick of battle.)

In mid-July, while the French army, having crossed the Niemen, plunged ever farther east, Josephine went south on an arduous twelve-day journey into Italy, at long last to see her son's family. "You can imagine with what delight I make their acquaintance," she wrote to Hortense, and she lapsed into the hyperbole typical of a grandmother: four-year-old Eugénie-Hortense was "a beauty"; three-year-old Joséphine-Maximilienne, "with her bright and sensitive face," gave "promise of being very pretty"; two-year-old Auguste-Charles was "a veritable infant Hercules." Less typical of a mother-in-law, Josephine found Augusta "utterly charming." "She adores Eugène, which delights my heart. We have had three letters from him, the last dated the thirteenth [of June]. He is well and is still in pursuit of the Russians, without, however, catching up with them."

Retreat was the Russians' haphazardly conceived but devastatingly successful strategy: to avoid all major engagements, to withdraw ever farther east, drawing the French legions across those barren, hostile steppes, those burned and empty fields and towns and villages, so that when Napoleon marched into Moscow on September 14, 1812, he marched into smoke, ashes and desolation.

If Eugène's letter to Milan written September 8 on the road to Moscow and telling of "a great victory over the Russians" brought rejoicing to his family, then they rejoiced over a hollow, costly victory—it was the one at Borodino—and rejoiced for the last time. Eugène had commanded the left, he wrote, and he added in a postscript to his mother: "I cannot thank you enough for your attentions and kindnesses to my little family. You are adored at Milan, as everywhere. They write me the most charming things about you. Everyone who has met you has fallen under your spell."

She was no longer in Milan when the letter arrived, and his message had to be forwarded to her. Did Milan remind her of honeymoon days when the most spellbound of all had been her husband? Did she make a sentimental journey to their honeymoon suites at the Palazzo Serbelloni and the Castello Mombello, where General Bonaparte had worshiped her as a divinity and had pleaded for her favors—favors granted more graciously to a little captain of hussars? (Hippolyte Charles would be forty now, and Josephine may or may not have kept track of him in his retirement.) It may have been that too many memories rose up to haunt her in Milan, or merely that she grew restless, as she always did at any distance from France. At any rate, early in September, a month after Augusta was safely delivered of a third daughter, Josephine left for Aix.

Soon, still restless, she moved on from Aix to her little house at Prégny, only to find herself restless there as well. For, although "the view of the Lake of Geneva and Mont Blanc is superb," as she wrote Hortense on September 30, she was filled with dark forebodings about the Russian campaign and was "profoundly disturbed at the lack of news from Eugène, the lack of news in the papers, and the delays in the publication of army bulletins."

Even Malmaison failed to cheer her when she arrived there on October 23. The capital was in a state of nerves to match her own, having been the scene, only the night before, of the most fantastic of conspiracies: a former army officer, one General Claude-François de Malet, had escaped from an insane asylum and, brandishing forged orders and announcing that the Emperor was dead, had managed to seize power in Paris and to hold it for several hours before the deception was discovered and he was captured.

That a plot out of a comic-opera libretto came so close to overthrowing the central government was symptomatic of the state of morale in France. The magnitude of the Russian catastrophe had not yet been revealed, but Paris guessed—as did Josephine, whether or not she was as clairvoyant as Mademoiselle Avrillon deemed her. Although, of course, she could not have known in October that the terrible retreat from Moscow had begun.

Napoleon had waited a full month in that city, but the truce proposals he had expected from Alexander never came. Instead there came the early snows.

It was only later that Josephine learned that the Old Guard had trudged west with her name on their frostbitten lips—her old name, "Notre Dame des Victoires" or her more recent one, "La Vieille." Superstitious veterans of Italy and Egypt, with wolves and Cossacks snapping at their heels, muttered that, whereas La Vieille had always brought their general luck, the Emperor's first campaign since his marriage to the Austrian had resulted in his first real defeat.

Common disaster brought the Austrian's first kindly gesture to Josephine. From Malmaison, in October, Josephine expressed her gratitude by letter to Hortense in Paris:

You restore me to life by your assurance that the Empress has shown you a letter from the Emperor. She is kind indeed to have shared the news with you, and I am infinitely grateful for the friendship she manifests. But I must admit that I am still prey to cruel anxiety. Why does Eugène not write? To allay my fears, I try to tell myself that the Emperor has forbidden letters out of Russia. The proof is in the fact that no one receives any. I am very sad.

The first week in December, the hitherto elusive Russian armies lay in wait at the icy Berezina to complete the decimation of the Grand Army. (Decimation was the *mot juste*: out of about half a million men who had marched into Russia, approximately fifty thousand would limp out.) Once across the Berezina, Napoleon decided that Paris was where he was most needed. "The French are like women," he told General Armand de Caulaincourt in the sleigh en route to Warsaw. "You cannot stay away from them too long."

He had appointed Murat to lead the straggling columns west into Germany, but his brother-in-law, among the first to betray him, deserted to go rushing home to Naples in a desperate effort to save his tottering throne. In January the command was given to Eugène, with this accolade from the Emperor by letter from Paris: "My son. . . . I only wish I had entrusted it [the Grand Army] to you when I left. I believe you would have brought it out with greater consideration and spared me such enormous losses."

(Josephine's first reaction, a purely maternal one, came out in a great gasp of relief by letter to Hortense: "Thank God my son is still alive!")

With the *Moniteur's* publication of the twenty-ninth army bulletin, announcing the destruction of the Grand Army, the nation rocked under the blow.

"We were the more frightened for the reason that twenty years of uninterrupted successes had led us to believe such reverses impossible," Mademoiselle Avrillon recalls. "For me and for those other persons devoted to the Empress, the effect of those bulletins from Moscow is beyond description. At the very mention of the Emperor's name, painful emotion was written on her face and tears trembled on her lashes. And it was not only the disastrous news from Russia. All too familiar with the character of courtiers, the Empress saw clearly what was going on about her, in her own household: persons who had only yesterday protested undying loyalty to the Empire fell silent today, testing the wind and looking around for a likely port in the storm. But when a courier rode into Malmaison to announce the arrival of the Emperor safe and sound in Paris—instead of his death in Russia, as had been expected momentarily—then these same courtiers suddenly expressed their loyalty more volubly, more vociferously than ever before." At which Josephine should not have been surprised; her honor household was composed primarily of *ancien-régime* noblemen and noblewomen, royalists at heart—not an honest republican or Bonapartist among them.

Arriving at midnight on December 18-19 at the Tuileries, Napoleon had not considered it too late to send off a courier to Josephine. Soon, as soon as he could, he went in person to Malmaison to reassure her about himself and her son. If Josephine wept after he left, as she usually did, it would have been with cause. This would prove to have been their final parting.

With his strong, firm hand gathering up the reins of government, morale and hope revived in France. Attentive as usual to detail, the Emperor commanded the imperial family to enliven the capital's winter season by a round of galas and balls; these festivities in the wake of the Russian disaster were labeled by the cynical Parisians "the Balls of the Wooden Legs," as those at the end of the Reign of Terror had been called "Victims' Balls."

Josephine, as might have been expected, did her bit in the way of entertaining. She was the most celebrated hostess of her age, and her invitations to Malmaison were eagerly sought after in the capital, especially by its gourmets. The Malmaison cuisine surpassed that of the Tuileries, thanks to Josephine's Neapolitan chef, Ruccieri, a specialist in ices, importer or originator of the *biscuit glacé*, and maestro of the buffet table (which was as artfully composed as a still life, the Malmaison hothouses supplying exotic tropical compotes of pineapple, banana and mango, as well as decorative dwarf fruit trees to provide the guests the privilege of plucking their own cherries, plums and apricots in mid-December). Georgette Ducrest complained that the very excellence of the cuisine discouraged conversation; for example, "Cardinal Maury, the celebrated wit, was invariably a disappointment to the company in that his mouth was always too full of *gâteaux* [pastries] to scintillate at repartee."

On January 1, bedecked and bejeweled, Hortense joined the other courtiers in the throne room of the Tuileries to wish Their Majesties a happy new year; later she drove out to Malmaison to wish the same to her mother. If Josephine was as superstitious as legend has her, she may have needed special cheering over the fact that this new year of 1813 began on a Friday. The year just out had been unlucky enough; to make matters worse, 1813 would bring her fiftieth birthday.

Worse still, the first two months of that year would pass without so much as a glimpse of Eugène, still in Germany, regrouping the fragments of the shattered army. Hortense was as disappointed as her mother at his continued absence, but she found consolation in a visit from her lover. Charles de Flahaut arrived in Paris in February, unscathed despite having been in the thick of the Russian fighting. A hero of the Berezina crossing, he had received a hero's reward: the rank of general and an appointment to the Emperor's personal staff.

But Charles's days in Paris with Hortense were limited; he was shortly dispatched to Germany to deliver to Eugène the Emperor's orders regarding measures of co-operation with the new army being raised in France. An army of raw young recruits, this one; the 1814 conscripts had been called up a year ahead of schedule, and those of 1815 were to be drafted before winter. "The Grim Reaper," a voice in the Legislative Body would dare to mutter of Napoleon. "For the last two years, our young men have been mowed down thrice annually."

As for the year 1813, France was faced with war on two fronts: Wellington's forces, which had wrested most of Spain from the French, now pressed hard at the remaining northern provinces, while the armies of a new coalition of Russia, Prussia and Sweden were massing beyond the Elbe.

Napoleon's proclamation naming the Empress Marie Louise as regent heralded his departure for the German theater of war on April 15. The early news from the front, in May and June, was encouraging: the battles of Lützen, Bautzen and Dresden were announced as signal victories. In fact, they signified nothing, and the two-month armistice that followed would serve only to give the other side time to connive and consolidate.

Josephine's spirits somehow failed to rise with the nation's, although if she had premonitions of disaster she kept all trace of them out of her letters to Eugène. "Life here at Malmaison goes on much the same," she wrote. "My time is taken up with my plants and my gallery." "Nothing, apparently, could induce a change in her habits or an interruption of the pattern of her life," says Mademoiselle Avrillon, "but some sort of emotional disorder had come over her. Her morale had broken under the fears which were inspired by her tender affection for the Emperor and her keen concern with everything which affected him."

"We speak often of the Emperor when we are alone together," Claire de Rémusat wrote to her husband from Malmaison. "The Empress likes to talk about him, to persuade herself that she still means something to him."

Josephine had occasion to talk to her heart's content about the Emperor with none other than Countess Walewska, a frequent visitor to Malmaison that summer along with her three-year-old Alexandre, the child sired by Napoleon in Vienna. It may be that Madame Gazzani joined Josephine and Marie to compare notes on the man whose favors they had all once enjoyed. (If Josephine seems to have relished collecting her ex-husband's ex-mistresses, she must also have relished the gossip that he was no more faithful to Marie Louise than he had been to her.)

Another of Josephine's visitors at Malmaison that summer of 1813 was the Princess de Caraman-Chimay, the former Madame Tallien; her *chère petite* Thérèse, a mother ten times over—with three legitimate children by the Prince, two by Tallien, one by her first husband, Fontenay, and that "litter of bastards" to which Napoleon had referred—was now fat and fortyish and showed few traces of her once fabled beauty. Josephine and Thérèse had ample material for conversation, could talk for hours to catch up on all the years that had passed since the Directory when they had been together in the Luxembourg as co-hostesses and co-mistresses to Barras. If there was any compensation for divorce, Josephine found it in the privilege of again receiving dear old friends upon whom the Emperor had forced her to close her doors.

By all odds, however, the favorite visitors that last summer at Malmaison were the two little princes, her grandsons, eight-year-old Napoléon-Louis and five-year-old Charles-Louis-Napoléon.

They brighten up the entire scene [the doting grandmother reported to Hortense, who was at Aix for another thermal cure]. How happy you have made me by leaving them with me here at Malmaison! They are charming, and in the best of health, their little cheeks all pink and white. The more I am with them, the more I love them. Your study program for them is being meticulously followed. When their week's work has been satisfactory, I have them to lunch and to dine with me on Sunday. But I promise you, I am not spoiling them.

On which point she was to be flatly contradicted by "little Oui-Oui," as she called the younger, who told his mother, "You indulge us when we are good, but Grand-maman spoils us all the time"—as she did, with constant gifts: with the most lavish assortment of toys she could find to buy in Paris or order from Germany (such as a pair of tiny golden hens that laid tiny silver eggs), with sweets and Neapolitan ices, with carriage drives and fishing expeditions, with daily visits to the Malmaison menagerie. The kangaroos, the ostriches, the storks and most of the monkeys had been sent to the Paris zoo in one of Josephine's random and erratic gestures of economizing, but, even so, rare birds and beasts enough remained to delight the children: gazelles, flying squirrels, imperial eagles and the trained orangutan that slept in a bed, wearing chemise and camisole, and ate at table in a fashionable long redingote, politely plying knife and fork.

Josephine's happy interlude with her grandsons came to a close at the end of August, when she regretfully relinquished them to their returning mother.

By then the interlude of truce was over, too, and Napoleon's father-in-law, the Emperor Francis of Austria, had joined the coalition against France, bringing the enemy's superiority to an ominous two to one. Two months later Eugène's father-in-law, Maximilian of Bavaria, also joined the ranks of France's foes. And after the crushing French defeat in the Battle of Leipzig on October 16-18, so did virtually all of the remaining princes of the Confederation of the Rhine. The French army, reeling from the defeat at Leipzig, retreated west, behind the Rhine. In the gloom of the Götterdämmerung, Napoleon was losing all control of events. Even as his enemies multiplied, the ranks of his best generals were reduced. Duroc, his inseparable companion, had fallen at Bautzen; Junot, the earliest of his followers, the first of his aides-de-camp, had gone mad and had leaped to his death from a rooftop; Murat, with the full sanction of his wife, the Emperor's own sister, was secretly treating with England and Austria to avoid losing his crown (as had already happened to Joseph and Jérôme); Marmont, Napoleon's companion in Italy, war-weary or embittered by a fancied slight, was to turn against him at the gates of Paris.

Almost alone among staff, friends and family, Josephine's son stood fast, refusing a kingdom in Italy offered him by his father-in-law on the condition that he join the Coalition. "I'll never be a king at that price," he wrote Augusta, who agreed with his stand; she recommended her children to her father's protection, but severed communications with Munich as her husband prepared to defend Italy in the name of France and the French Emperor.

Even as he did, the Emperor—in Paris, on November 14—made a grim pronouncement to the Senate: "The Grand Empire no longer exists. It is France that we must now defend."

He was working with his Council of State and chiefs of staff around the clock and could not go in person to Malmaison, but he sent Méneval there one day in late November 1813, some two weeks after his return from Leipzig, according to Mademoiselle Avrillon. "With all the solicitude of a mother, a sister or a wife, Her Majesty questioned him [Méneval] as to the truth of the rumor that the Emperor had returned in deep despair. He admitted that the first days were indeed terrible, but he went on to assure her that the Emperor was now working relentlessly to save the nation from invasion, and that His Majesty sent word for her not to be frightened."

Napoleon, at that time, could have settled with the Coalition for the frontiers of 1797, France's "natural boundaries," the Rhine, the Alps and the Pyrenees. But he would not, and on December 21 France's enemies began to cross the Rhine.

"That crusade of all the peoples of the north in league against us finally set foot on French soil, inviolate through so many years of victory," Hortense agonizes. "Never before had such panic seized the capital. 'The enemy in France!' people cried. 'What has happened to our armies? . . . What can the Emperor be thinking of?' "

Knowing her mother's anxiety in isolated Malmaison, Hortense went there almost daily, and sent messengers on the days she could not go in person, to report on everything that transpired at the Tuileries, including Marie Louise's curious and pathetic remark, "I bring bad luck wherever I go. . . . Since childhood, my life has been spent in flight." (From Schönbrunn Palace in 1805 and 1809 to escape the armies of her present husband, shortly now from the Tuileries to escape those of her father.)

And surely Hortense went to Malmaison on the night of January 23 to describe the scene she had witnessed in the Tuileries that morning: "The National Guard [of Paris] had assembled in the Hall of the Marshals. The Emperor, with the King of Rome in his arms and his wife and the rest of us [the imperial family] around him, announced his immediate departure for headquarters and expressed the confidence he reposed in the National Guard, to whom he would now entrust the defense of the capital and all those dearest to him."

It was the campaign of France he had gone to fight, and for three months, in defense of French soil, he waged the most valiant, the most inspired and perhaps the most technically brilliant campaign of his career—certainly the most desperate and most hopeless, for it was against overwhelming odds.

"How [Mademoiselle Avrillon asks] to describe the anguish in the Empress's heart during those desolate days—the heart of an ardent Frenchwoman, the heart of a wife more than ever inconsolable over the divorce that separated her from her husband in his hour of greatest need? Isolated at Malmaison, she suffered in spirit if not in flesh through every one of those savage engagements in which her former husband was involved. I can still hear her accent of distress, her endless, frantic, staccato questions addressed to every living soul, even the lowliest and most insignificant, who came out from Paris: 'What is the Emperor doing? Where is Bonaparte now? Where is the enemy? What are people saying? Is there still hope? Still courage?' "

She had word from the Emperor himself in early February, and she sent her reply at once. Both letters are lost, and the fact that the exchange took place is established only through a letter of Hortense's to Eugène in which she mentioned that she was enclosing copies of both messages and commented, "I don't understand a word of this." It is useless to wish that these letters might come to light, since Josephine's own children could not solve the riddle of what these two were saying to each other in that crucial hour. The letters may have related to the destruction of Napoleon's papers at Malmaison. Napoleon instructed Joseph to burn all those in his study at the Tuileries—in which conflagration his collection of letters from Josephine may have been destroyed, if indeed he had saved them until then.

Another curious message came to Josephine from the Emperor in the first week of February, from Nogent-sur-Seine. This letter is missing, too, but its contents may be surmised by means of a letter from Josephine to Eugène, dated the ninth:

Do not lose an instant, my dear Eugène, no matter what the obstacles. Redouble your efforts to comply with the Emperor's orders. He has just written to me on the subject. His intention is for you to withdraw into the Alps, leaving only Italian troops to hold Mantua and other Italian cities. His letter ends with the words, "France above all! France has need of all her sons." So come, come quickly, my son. . . . I can assure you that every moment is precious. Make haste!

How curious and how pitiful that Napoleon should have felt obliged to resort to such roundabout methods to secure compliance with an order, that he should have gone through this lieutenant's mother instead of the conventional military channels. Eugène took offense at the implication of disloyalty. "I do not feel that I have merited this," he wrote to his commander. "My devotion to Your Majesty and to my native land are motives strong enough; resort to any other was unnecessary." With five days each way required for a messenger to travel between France and Italy, the Emperor's original orders to Eugène apparently had not arrived in time for the Viceroy to bring his troops to participate in the campaign of France.

That campaign, by March, was drawing to its inevitable calamitous conclusion. Napoleon had led his valorous French troops to incredible victories; then, hopelessly outnumbered, encircled and outflanked, they retreated toward beleaguered Paris. A peace conference at Châtillon-sur-Seine had been fruitless; the Coalition's peace terms, a France shrunken to its 1791 borders, were unacceptable to the Emperor. "I could save my throne, but I would not have it at the price of France's humiliation," he had told Foreign Minister Caulaincourt, who represented him at Châtillon.

From the towers of Notre Dame, from the Butte Montmartre, enemy columns could be discerned converging on Paris. Yet Josephine was writing to Hortense on March 26: "This must be one of the Emperor's maneuvers which we cannot understand. He is not the man to allow himself to be taken by surprise. He will come at the moment when he is least expected and save the capital."

But when he came on the night of March 30, with a small troop and five of his still loyal generals, to the Cour de France (a posting station at Juvisy ten miles south of Paris on the road to Fontainebleau), it was to learn that Marshal Marmont had withdrawn his support and that Paris had capitulated after a few hours of sporadic and unco-ordinated resistance, after brief skirmishing beyond the city gates—just as Talleyrand had assured the Czar of Russia that it would.

2

If Hortense was shocked at the roar of the cannon ("Until then I had heard them fired only at victory celebrations"), she was stunned at the decision of the Regency Council (headed by a doltish Austrian Marie Louise, a bungling Joseph, and including a treacherous Talleyrand) that the capital was to be abandoned; the Empress, the King of Rome and the Bonaparte family were all heading south for Blois.

No one at the Tuileries had given a thought to the former Empress at Malmaison ("with a guard of only sixteen men—and these, disabled war veterans"). On March 28, when Hortense saw the travel preparations under way at the Tuileries, she sent a message to her mother to set out instantly for Navarre.

"That whole night was spent packing," Mademoiselle Avrillon recalls. "Her Majesty took with her whatever was possible to take of her most valuable possessions: all her horses and carriages and, of course, her jewels; her diamonds and pearls I sewed into the lining of the quilted skirt she was to wear on the journey. Everything else had to be abandoned—her countless treasures, *objets d'art*, statuary, paintings, gardens, all of which were now subject to pillage by the Cossacks. . . . Sad and trying a journey as it was, with Her Majesty in mortal anxiety over the fate of the Emperor and of her children, she was yet calm and resigned. But we had no news en route, and the night of her arrival at Navarre she could not close her eyes. So I remained with her, and we tried to hasten the hours till dawn by talking."

"Only news from you can console me," Josephine wrote to Hortense on March 31. The National Guard of Évreux had offered her a detachment for Navarre, but she had not yet accepted; her own safety was a matter of indifference to her, she said.

I have never lacked courage to meet the many perilous situations in which I have found myself during my life, and I should always be able to meet reverses of fortune with equanimity, but what I cannot endure is this separation from my children, this uncertainty as to their fate. I haven't stopped weeping in two days. Send me news of yourself and your children—and of Eugène and his family, if you hear from them. Let me know where you are going. One report has you at Chartres. . . .

Hortense was, however, on her way to Navarre, bringing both her children—in defiance of orders from her husband, Louis, that she and they join the imperial family at Blois. Josephine drew her first sigh of relief when they arrived on April 1, having come safely through the perils of Cossack-infested Rambouillet Forest.

"Neither my mother nor I had as yet received any word of what was going on at Paris," Hortense writes in her memoirs. "Finally a valet who had escaped from the city brought us the news, reporting that he had witnessed the entry of the Allies and heard talk of the restoration of the Bourbons."

And so it was. On March 31 the Coalition troops and sovereigns, led by the Czar Alexander, had marched into Paris, "the first time," as Chateaubriand lamented, "that aliens had ever come save to admire and to enjoy the benefits of our civilization in that city which had been preserved inviolate throughout twelve centuries." And it was Talleyrand, as president of the provisional government, who persuaded the Allied monarchs to reject Napoleon's proposal that he abdicate in favor of his son the King of Rome, and to support instead a Bourbon restoration in the person of the Count de Provence, Louis XVIII, eldest surviving brother of Louis XVI. The Emperor, at Fontainebleau, repudiated by the French Senate—which declared him deposed—with most of his army gone and his generals turning against him, had no choice but to agree to abdicate, which he did on April 6.

In the subsequent Treaty of Fontainebleau, which was ratified by the representatives of all the hostile powers, Napoleon stipulated that the Empress Josephine retain possession of all her properties and be allotted an annual revenue of one million francs. Nor were Josephine's children forgotten by Napoleon in his moment of defeat: a revenue of 400,000 francs a year was guaranteed for Hortense, while another treaty article provided that Eugène be assured "an appropriate establishment outside France."

If, on April 12, the night before he signed the treaty, Napoleon made a vain attempt to take his life—vain because apparently the cachet of poison he wore always in a locket about his neck had lost its potency—he sent a message to Josephine through Caulaincourt: "Tell her that my thoughts were of her before I departed this world."

It was not Caulaincourt, however, who reached her first at Navarre with the reports from Fontainebleau, but a functionary of the Council of State named Adolphe de Maussion. As Hortense tells the story, Josephine came in tears to her daughter's room in the middle of the night and threw herself upon Hortense's bed, crying, "Oh, that poor Napoleon! He is to be sent to the island of Elba! How dreadful for him! Were it not for his wife, I would go to join him in his exile." "I saw how much she still loved him," Hortense says, "and I thought bitterly of the courage it had taken for her to have separated herself from him. As Monsieur de Maussion gave us the details of the national disaster, it was above all the fate of the Emperor which my mother lamented."

Indignation was added to her grief when they began to receive newspapers filled with what Hortense calls "outrageous slanders against the Emperor." On April 9 Josephine wrote to Eugène in Italy:

How heartbroken I am at the way they have treated the Emperor! What dastardly things they print! And what ingratitude on the part of those whom he showered with honors! But it is all over now. He has abdicated. This releases you from all your pledges of allegiance. Anything more you might try to do for him now would be in vain. Now you are free and must act in the best interests of your family.

Hortense, having "suffered too much in the midst of grandeurs" to cling to them, could face with relative calm what she termed a mere "change of dynasty." If the imperial family were the only sufferers and France was spared from turmoil, then the misfortune was less terrible than she had anticipated. It was rather "the sight of members of the Empress's own entourage rushing to be among the first to welcome the conquerors and the aliens" that made her "blush for the national honor."

Josephine was left at Navarre with a mere handful of her honor attendants, all foreigners—the lady of honor, Countess d'Arberg, who was Belgian, a Polish lady in waiting and two Swiss. Madame de Rémusat had been "among the first" to welcome the new monarch and had had the effrontery to wear the Bourbons' white cockade in the Empress's own salon, to the Empress's express displeasure. Having worked hand in glove with her dear friend Talleyrand in the anti-Bonaparte, pro-Bourbon conspiracy, Claire and her husband were assured a royal welcome at the court of Louis XVIII and his younger brother, the Count d'Artois, the future Charles X.

The latter's son Charles Ferdinand de Bourbon, Duke de Berry, en route from England to Paris via Cherbourg, sent Monsieur de Mesnard, one of his gentlemen, to Navarre to express to Josephine his respect and admiration and to offer her an honor guard to escort her back to Paris. But Josephine had already departed Navarre, that day of April 15, and was on her way back to Malmaison upon the cordial invitation of an even more powerful patron, the Czar of Russia.

Through his minister Count Karl Robert Nesselrode and one of his generals, Prince Leopold of Saxe-Coburg, the Emperor Alexander had sent message upon message to Josephine and Hortense, urging their prompt return to the capital, assuring them of his great esteem and good will, and expressing his eagerness to call upon them in person and "to extend them his protection as concerned their personal safety, their position and their fortunes."

Hortense realized that the Czar was "making a clear distinction between the Beauharnais' and the Bonapartes," but, she wrote to Mademoiselle Cochelet, "it is all very well for my mother to stay on in France in view of the fact that divorce has freed her from that family, but my children and I still bear a name which cannot be tolerated here after the return of the Bourbons." She would sell her only remaining treasure, her diamonds, and go to Martinique, where her mother still had property. But she would go first to Rambouillet to express her allegiance to Marie Louise (who had arrived there with the King of Rome on April 12) and to offer her services.

At Rambouillet she was stung by Marie Louise's rebuff, "I am expecting a visit from my father and would like to see him alone.

Besides, since he does not know you, I'm afraid he would be too constrained in front of you." The Empress's question "Do you think my father will make me go to the island of Elba?" clarified the situation for Hortense, and she made her final bow to the woman who had succeeded her mother as Napoleon's wife and consort. What a contrast to her mother's impulse to share the fallen titan's exile—if Hortense's quotation of Josephine's words may be relied upon.

Napoleon wrote to Josephine from Fontainebleau, before his departure, the last of the 265 letters of his to her which have survived:

I wrote to you on the eighth of this month, but it may be that you did not receive the letter. There was fighting still going on, and it may have been intercepted. Now, however, communications have been re-established. . . .

I shall not repeat what I wrote you then. At that time I was still deploring my fate; today I congratulate myself upon it. A tremendous weight has been lifted from my mind and spirits. My fall is great, but at least it may serve a useful purpose, according to some reports.

In the retreat into which I am going, I shall substitute the pen for the sword. The story of my reign will make a curious one. Thus far, the world has seen me only in profile; I shall now reveal myself to history full face. How many things I have to tell! How many men are yet to be seen in their true colors! I have heaped honors upon thousands of ingrates, and how have they repaid me in my recent misfortune? They have all betrayed me—yes, all of them. With only one exception—that good Eugène, a worthy son to both you and me. May he find happiness under a king who will appreciate his natural sentiments and his high sense of honor.

Adieu, my dear Josephine. Resign yourself, as I have done, and never forget him who has never forgotten you and never will forget you. . . . I shall await news of you at Elba. My health is not good.

3

April 16, the date of Napoleon's letter, was also the date of Josephine's arrival at Malmaison—where the gardens were celebrating
the rites of spring as though this were a year like any other.

A Russian guard had been posted at Malmaison within hours of
the Czar's arrival in Paris, and now Josephine could assure herself that all her treasures were intact, including her gallery, her hothouses and her gardens; even her precious pair of black cygnets,
hatched out a week or so before her flight to Navarre, floated
serene and unruffled on the lake beneath her windows. (Impossible at Malmaison to believe in a national debacle.)

Mademoiselle Avrillon had to rush to unpack her mistress's costume and help her to change from her travel dress and complete
the elaborate ritual of her toilette in time to receive the Czar of
All the Russias when he drove into the courtyard shortly after
noon. He found the Empress as full of charm as he had expected,
and she found him as handsome, kind and intelligent as Napoleon
had described him in the days when those two had planned to divide the world between them.

Hortense, arriving from Rambouillet at one o'clock, was alarmed
to find the courtyard teeming with Cossacks, but was reassured on
learning that her mother was walking in the gardens with the
Emperor Alexander. When she joined them there with her children, Josephine was overjoyed to see her.

"Here are my daughter and her sons. I recommend them to your
protection," Josephine said to the Czar.

Alexander offered Hortense his arm, which her mother had relinquished, and Hortense was in the awkward position of having to
walk arm in arm with the man whom she considered the enemy
and conqueror of her country. She could find little to say to him,
even when he caressed her children, urging, "Only tell me what it
would please you best to have me do for them. Let me serve as
their chargé d'affaires."

Later, Josephine chided her for the chill reserve she had shown

393

toward their protector. Josephine's daughter wished that they had no need to ask favors of anyone.

But, of course, they had to. Only the powerful Czar could prevail upon the Bourbons to honor the Treaty of Fontainebleau, to guarantee Josephine and Hortense their pensions and properties, and confirm the titles of duchess de Navarre for the mother and duchess de Saint-Leu for the daughter. For Eugène Josephine had higher hopes, and she summoned him from Italy to meet with Alexander and talk about a principality or a duchy in Italy or Germany, or, failing that, a marshal's baton or the post of constable of France.

How, then, not respond graciously to a gracious Alexander, their only friend and hope? Especially when he requested not only Josephine's portrait (which she gave—a portrait painted on a Sèvres teacup) but also a copy of the book of ballads that Hortense had published, illustrated by her own hand. For if Alexander was enchanted with Josephine, he was enamored of Hortense.

He came to see them every day or evening. There was, in fact, a crush of crowned and coroneted heads at Malmaison throughout the weeks that followed: the Czar and Grand Dukes Constantine, Nicholas and Michael of Russia; King Frederick William III of Prussia and his son and namesake, the Crown Prince; Charles Frederick of Baden, now Grand Duke; Josephine's former admirer Frederick Louis of Mecklenburg-Schwerin. (The last-named had made her a formal proposal of marriage shortly after her divorce, and Napoleon, looking on the alliance as appropriate, had counseled Josephine to accept. But her sense of historical perspective, if nothing else, had led her to refuse him, firmly though gently; it would have been an anticlimax for an ex-Queen of Italy, ex-Empress of the French and ex-wife of a colossus of history like Napoleon Bonaparte to end her days as the consort of a German princeling.)

Historians have reproached Josephine for opening her gates and her arms in welcome to the sovereigns and dignitaries of the powers which had just crushed and humiliated both her husband and her country. But it was Napoleon himself who advised Josephine (according to Caulaincourt, who relayed the message from Fontainebleau to Navarre) to look to Alexander for help in the emergency, and said that the future of her children depended upon her returning to Malmaison. Josephine, furthermore, had reason to be-lieve that it was through Alexander's magnanimity that Napoleon had been spared imprisonment and had been assured sovereign status at Elba. (While, in Alexander's opinion, the conduct of the Beauharnais' toward Napoleon was "far superior to that of many others with far greater obligation to him.")

The stern and piercing eye of history has again fastened re-proachfully on Josephine for running up a bill of over six thousand francs with *couturier* Leroy that calamitous second week of April 1814. But if she felt better prepared to meet the vicissitudes of life in a new frock in the height of fashion, at least she met them squarely. Tearful, tremulous, flighty as she may have been, she was nonetheless a realist, if not an opportunist. It was by no accident, but rather by an ability to recognize and adapt to new conditions, new powers, new environments, that she had managed to survive revolution, terror, war, inflation, famine, coups d'état and a half-dozen political regimes. With the fall of the Bastille in 1789, the world in which she had been born had tumbled down about her head. Now the world of Napoleon, as she had known it for the past fourteen years, had come crashing down. She would struggle to secure her footing in this new world, to re-establish herself and her children by her old expedient, that of charming influential friends into assisting her. So her cultivation of Alexander and the other conquerors of France need not be interpreted as disloyalty or lack of sympathy for the vanquished.

Whether or not Josephine still loved Napoleon (granting that she had loved him once) is a question that fascinated and per-plexed her contemporaries as it has her biographers. Bourrienne is the only one to say that he heard her rail against the husband who had discarded her, and his testimony is contradicted by all the oth-ers who had opportunity to observe: by Baron de Méneval, Ma-dame de Rémusat, Mademoiselle Avrillon, palace prefect Count de Bausset, valet Constant and, here, Madame Junot: "The thought that Napoleon was alone on the rocks of the island of Elba, alone with his regrets and his memories, was a torment to Josephine."

And Georgette Ducrest quotes the Empress as saying, "It is, above all, at this moment when he has been generally abandoned that I would wish to help him bear his exile and to share his grief" (the moment being the one when she heard the news that Marie Louise had returned to Vienna, deaf to all Napoleon's pleas to keep the King of Rome out of the hands of his enemies and to join him with their child at Elba). "Even though I am no longer his lawful wife, I would go tomorrow to join him at Elba, did I not fear to cause him embarrassment with that companion whom he has chosen in preference to me. I have suffered since the very first day of the divorce, but never more than I do today." Dr. Horeau, Josephine's physician, heard her say much the same thing and later repeated it to Napoleon: "She said that had she still been Empress of France she would have driven straight through occupied Paris . . . to go to you at Fontainebleau, never again to be parted from you." ("And I believe she would have done it," was Napoleon's comment.)

Only one of Josephine's contemporaries had the temerity to ask her directly whether she still loved Napoleon: Madame de Staël, just back from the exile into which Napoleon had sent her for her brash and redoubtable tongue and pen. Paris was still buzzing over her most recently published anti-Bonaparte blast, her *Portrait d'Attila*, on the April day she accosted Josephine in the gallery at Malmaison and proceeded to analyze the ex-Empress's reactions to the drama of the century.

In one of her rare displays of pique and displeasure, Josephine cut off Germaine's questions, summarily dismissed her and returned to the salon "visibly agitated and unstrung." "Would you believe it?" she exclaimed to her guest Madame Oudinot. "Madame de Staël had the effrontery to ask me whether I still love the Emperor! As if I could feel less ardently for him today, in his misfortune—I who never ceased loving the Emperor in the days of his good fortune!"

Of course, it was a good question, the question any good reporter would have asked. But, even allowing for the bias of the witnesses who testified that Josephine still cared deeply for the Emperor, apparently she did. However limited her mental horizons, she knew—as her amazing struggle against divorce evidenced —that it was he who had raised her to the heights and sustained her there, that without him she must inevitably fall.

In April of 1814, the Bourbon monarch was denying that the Empire had ever existed, dating his edicts "this, the nineteenth year of our reign" (having "forgotten nothing and learned nothing during those many years of exile," as Talleyrand would admit). Louis XVIII had confirmed no title for either Hortense or Josephine, instructing the Paris newspapers to refer to "the former wife of General Bonaparte" as "the mother of Prince Eugène." Which clearly nettled her. "Whether the Bourbons care to admit it or not," she said indignantly to Louise Cochelet, "the fact remains that I have a name and that I sat on the throne of France, crowned and anointed empress by the hand of the Pope!"

She was indignant, too, at Madame de Rémusat, who came bearing the draft of a letter (which she had prepared in collaboration with Talleyrand), a humble petition for Louis XVIII's favor, to be signed by Josephine—the woman he had called "Angel of Mercy" for her benefactions to the royalist émigrés. Josephine seldom quibbled over expedients, but here she drew the line, and she allowed Claire de Rémusat to feel the full weight of her displeasure.

Eugène arrived in Paris on May 9, to be greeted by both the French and Russian monarchs with lavish compliments and still more lavish promises. The final decision on his status was to be left, however, to the Congress of Vienna, the meeting of the Coalition powers scheduled for the autumn. There, at last, Eugène would be granted the titles of duke of Leuchtenberg and prince of Eichstätt, with estates near Munich.

But Josephine would not live to know it.

4

She came home with a slight chill after a drive through Montmorency Forest in an open carriage on the afternoon of May 15, the second day of Alexander's two-day visit at Hortense's Château of St.-Leu.

Excusing herself, leaving her daughter and the Czar to wander together in the twilit gardens, Josephine retired to her apartments. There Louise Cochelet found her on her chaise longue, weak and shaky.

"I can't throw off this terrible melancholy, although I try to conceal it from the children," Josephine told Hortense's friend and secretary. "I'm beginning to lose hope. The Emperor Alexander's intentions are all of the best, but as yet nothing definite has been accomplished. He makes us glowing promises, but those here in Paris are unlikely to carry them out once he has departed. I have suffered enough already at the fate of the Emperor Napoleon, fallen so low, abandoned, relegated to an island far from France. Must I now see my children fortuneless wanderers?"

In fresh dismay, she warned Mademoiselle Cochelet not to let Hortense see that day's newspapers, which carried an announcement that the body of Hortense's first child, Napoléon-Charles, was to be removed from its burial place in Notre Dame Cathedral to a cemetery. "They are daring to violate the tombs again, as in the days of the Revolution. And to think that this insult comes to me by the hand of those who are under great obligation to me!"

The next day she was at Malmaison, greeting visitors in the gallery, her face flushed, her voice husky, her head and throat wrapped in a heavy cashmere scarf, and in the evening she appeared in full décolletage, answering Hortense's objections by the reminder that she never nursed a cold. Hortense was concerned, nevertheless, and told Louise Cochelet, "My mother is always courageous and in good spirits when she is in company, but once she is alone she gives way to despondency. I am afraid that she has been so deeply afflicted by our recent disasters that her health has been affected."

Josephine promised to rest "once my affairs and those of my children have been settled"—but not on the twenty-third, of course, when the King of Prussia and his party were expected at Malmaison for the evening.

On May 24, admitting to chills and fever, she allowed Hortense and Eugène to do the honors in the afternoon for the Russian imperial visitors, but that night, clad in one of Leroy's wispy organdies, she opened the ball with the Czar and then went recklessly from the heated confines of the dance floor into the chill night air to oblige Alexander, who was tempted to the gardens by the scent of lilac and lily of the valley. "She lived to please," says Masson, "and died of it"—in character to the end, dancing, entertaining and charming guests, ordering new gowns, adorning herself, and running up bills to do it.

On May 25, in defiance of doctor's orders, Josephine was on her feet again, receiving callers in the gallery.

On the twenty-sixth, Dr. Horeau found her chest congested and her throat inflamed, and he prescribed a variety of mustard plasters.

On the twenty-seventh, a Friday, Alexander was due again for dinner, but Hortense received him alone, telling her mother that the Czar had canceled the engagement. "Perhaps he is embarrassed at still having no progress to report to us concerning our affairs," was Josephine's comment to her daughter's white lie.

That same night Alexander sent his personal physician. In the morning two other eminent medical men were summoned into consultation from Paris and pronounced Josephine's condition critical.

The artist Redouté, sketching new blooms in the experimental garden, stopped in to greet his patroness, but she waved him away —as she had her grandsons—fearing her fever might be contagious.

And Claire de Rémusat (obviously forgiven, and back in Josephine's good graces) found her elegant even on her deathbed, "dressed in rose-colored satin and beribboned."

By afternoon the physicians had abandoned hope of saving their patient. Her pulse almost indiscernible, she was rapidly losing consciousness and could scarcely speak, although Hortense thought she made out the words "Bonaparte . . . Elba . . . King of Rome . . ."

On the morning of May 29 the Abbé Bertrand administered the last sacrament, and at noon Josephine "went as sweetly and gently to meet death as she had met life," in the words of her stricken son.

The cause of death was "a putrid fever, an angina," according to the autopsy report, which confirmed the doctors' diagnosis; the symptoms and conditions described are interpreted by modern medical practitioners as those of diphtheria.

Josephine's body lay in state for three days on a catafalque in the Malmaison entrance hall, which, its bright-winged birds banished and its walls draped in black, had been transformed from an aviary into a *chapelle ardente*. All the church bells of the parish tolled day and night in a dirge for the Empress—and perhaps for the Empire which she had survived by only a few brief weeks. Throngs flocked out from Paris to her in death as in life; twenty thousand came, most of them to pay their respects and to shed a tear at the bier of Notre Dame des Victoires, La Bonne Joséphine; others no doubt for a less sentimental reason—to get a glimpse behind the walls of Malmaison, at the famous star-shaped rose garden and the orangery, open to the public for the first time.

Hortense and Eugène, following imperial protocol which proscribed the appearance of direct heirs of sovereigns as public mourners, did not attend their mother's obsequies. Close to collapse, they had returned on May 29 to Hortense's Château of St.-Leu, where the Czar had come the next day to offer his condolences and to deliver that long-awaited patent of nobility, finally sealed and signed by Louis XVIII, creating Hortense the duchess de Saint Leu.

At noon on June 2, 1814, the funeral cortege moved from Malmaison to the little church at Rueil (an object of Josephine's benefactions), led by the Russian Imperial Guard and by local National Guardsmen. Ahead of the casket marched two pages in mourning garb, each bearing on a black velvet cushion a small vermeil box; one box contained the deceased's viscera, the other her heart—another curious tradition of royal funeral ritual. Beside the hearse, holding the four corners of the pall, walked the pallbearers, all members of Josephine's family: Grand Duke Charles Frederick of Baden, niece Stéphanie's husband; François, Marquis de Beauharnais, the brother of Josephine's first husband; his cousin Claude, Count de Beauharnais; and Josephine's cousin the Count de Tascher. The column of mourners was led by Hortense's two sons, Napoléon-Louis and Charles-Louis-Napoléon. Behind the children came General von der Osten-Sacken, representing the Emperor of Russia, side by side with Frederick Louis of Mecklenburg-Schwerin and the adjutant general of the King of Prussia; then the Empress's honor attendants; then a long line of French and foreign dignitaries, generals, ambassadors.

Archbishop de Barral of Tours, the Empress's first almoner, officiated at the High Mass, assisted by the bishops of Évreux and of Versailles. His funeral oration, a model of tact and diplomacy, contained only the vaguest reference to the man to whom the deceased had been married for thirteen years ("A man appeared on the world scene with such marks of genius and grandeur as led men to hope great things of him"; while Josephine herself was absolved by the archbishop of any presumptuousness in having briefly occupied the throne of the Bourbons ("She did not ascend it voluntarily, but was pushed onto it"). When she had been laid to rest in the crypt under the church floor, her grave was marked only by a simple slab innocent of any imperial cipher, crest or crown.*

No one had notified Napoleon of her death. He heard of it from a lackey who, dispatched on an errand from Elba to the Italian mainland, saw the story in a newspaper and sent it back to his master on the island. A valet named Marchand who had accompanied Napoleon into exile noted in his memoirs: "At the news of the Empress Josephine's death, the Emperor appeared grievously stricken, shutting himself up in his private apartments and seeing no one except his Grand Marshal."

5

Malmaison lay shuttered, silent, empty, a flowery solitude, until the spring of 1815 when Napoleon made good his escape from Elba and re-established himself triumphantly in Paris—a Paris ringing again with the old familiar shouts of "Vive l'Empereur!"— and one day asked Hortense to open Malmaison for a visit on the morrow. It cost her a painful effort, for she had not had the heart to return since her mother's death, but she did as he had asked.

He arrived early the next morning. His emotional state was clearly discernible as he walked with Hortense through the château

---

* The marble statue of the Empress which stands today in the small private chapel of the church was commissioned later by Hortense and Eugène and was completed in 1825.

and the gardens, and he said at every step, "Everywhere I look I seem to see her! I cannot believe she is no longer here."

Before leaving, he went alone to Josephine's room, the room in which she had died. And he stood there for a long time beside her gilded and canopied swan bed. When he and she had parted, he had been at the zenith of glory and power; in the five years since the divorce, everything had gone against him.

Two months afterward, in late June, after Waterloo and his second abdication, it was again for Malmaison he headed; it was in Josephine's house that he chose to spend five of his last few days of liberty, his last few days on French soil. And it was Josephine's daughter to whom he turned, in preference to his own family, for comfort and consolation.

Hortense was well aware that in going there with him she forever forfeited the favor of the returning Bourbons and of the Emperor Alexander, that the rest of her days would be spent in exile, a wanderer across the face of Europe. But, she says, "I would never have abandoned the man whom I had called my father. The hour of his misfortune was the one for me to manifest my gratitude to him. . . . He arrived at Malmaison the next morning [June 25] and I went with a heavy heart to receive him, remembering that this same Malmaison which had seen him at the height of his glory saw him now in his ultimate disaster; thinking sadly, too, that he would no longer find there his sweet companion, all tenderness and devotion. I, her daughter, could offer only my sympathy and solicitude. I could not take her place."

Walking in the gardens with her the day after his arrival—it was, says Hortense, the loveliest of days—he said, "That poor Josephine! I cannot accustom myself to this place without her. Every moment I expect to see her coming down one of the garden paths, gathering the flowers she loved so well. My poor Josephine! . . . You know, we had only one subject for quarrels, her debts, and I suppose I scolded her more than enough on that account! (As if to say, "If she was profligate, yet what exquisite taste she had—what beautiful things she collected and wrought in her extravagance.")

"She was the most alluring, most glamorous creature I have ever known," he went on. "A woman in the true sense of the word—

volatile, spirited, and with the kindest heart in the world. I wish you would have another portrait of her painted for me—one in a medallion."

Hortense promised to do it, and kept the promise: she sent him Josephine's portrait painted on the lid of a crystal box. But she could never be certain it had reached him in St. Helena. No letters from him came through to her in Augsburg, where Eugène managed finally to secure her a refuge in 1817, a respite from her wanderings. Napoleon preferred not to write at all rather than to submit his letters to the censorship exacted by the Allied commissioners.

But a portrait of Josephine did hang in his room at Longwood Plantation, as has been described by the many chroniclers of his exile. That portrait of her was in his line of vision as he lay dying. If he died with her name on his lips ("France . . . the army . . . at the head of the army . . . Josephine!"), General Montholon is the only one of the witnesses in the death chamber who heard or reported it, and some historians remind us that his account of Napoleon's captivity was written in the 1840s, at a time when Montholon had hitched his wagon to the rising star of Josephine's grandson Charles-Louis-Napoléon, who was soon to seize power as emperor in 1851.

It is certain, however, that in the years between Napoleon's arrival at St. Helena in 1815 and his death in 1821, he talked of Josephine long and often to the dwindling band of Frenchmen, the ever fewer faithful few, who had followed him into the South Atlantic: to Count de Las Cases, General Gourgaud, General Montholon, General Bertrand (his last "Grand Marshal of the Palace"), and Dr. O'Meara, the physician from the English ship *Bellerophon*, all of whom made note of his every word and later published their memoirs or journals as soon as they could escape from the rock of exile.

In the presence of Emmanuel de Las Cases, the first to return to Europe and into print, the Emperor drew a comparison between his first and second wives: "He said that his life had been taken up with two very different women, the first all art and graces, the second all innocence, an entirely natural creature, but that each had had her merit." Of course Napoleon spoke these words about

Marie Louise's innocence before he had learned of her flagrant liaison with Count von Neipperg, to whom she had borne a second child in 1819, two years before her husband's death.

"That marriage [to Marie Louise] was my downfall," Napoleon would say later, avoiding mention of her name.

Of this Caesar's two wives, neither could be said to be above suspicion, as he himself well knew. Referring to Josephine's early infidelities in a conversation with General Bertrand, he had said, "Her conduct was irregular." And to General Gourgaud: "I suppose it is true that she cuckolded me?" (To which Gourgaud replied, "So they say, Sire.")

Napoleon could still remember his very first meeting with Josephine: "Until then I had never been indulged by women although I was certainly not insensible to their charms. But my character made me naturally timid in their company, and Madame de Beauharnais was the first to give me any degree of confidence."

"A child by Josephine was what I needed," he concluded at St. Helena, "and what would have served me best—not merely from the point of view of political significance but from that of my own personal happiness, my private life."

And, again, to Dr. O'Meara: "Josephine was grace personified, . . . the most amiable and the best of women."

It was to General Bertrand, on March 14, 1821, less than two months before Napoleon's death, that he had his final say on Josephine: "I truly loved her, although I didn't respect her. She was a liar and an utter spendthrift, but she had a certain something that was irresistible. She was a woman to her very finger tips."

Malmaison After Josephine's Death

MALMAISON after 1814 fell, like France, upon evil days. Josephine, consistently insouciant as to legal and financial details, had died intestate, and the domain of Malmaison with its vast properties passed into the possession of her son, who found himself obliged to sell all but the château and a remnant two thousand acres of park to pay the three million francs' indebtedness outstanding. (Hortense, as an equal participant in the estate, inherited her mother's jewels, the greatest private collection in Europe.)

Prince Eugène, in Bavaria, exiled from France like the Bonapartes, could not maintain Malmaison, yet neither could he bring himself to a final disposition of his mother's treasures. A number of paintings were sold to the Emperor Alexander I of Russia and a portion of the Egyptian and Italian antiquities were reclaimed or acquired by the Musée du Louvre, but some six thousand *objets d'art* remained, overflowing the gallery and the Salle des Antiquités and all the salons, onto the terraces, into the gardens, the grottoes, the pavilions and the annexes. These, like the gilded swan bed in Josephine's shrouded death chamber and the numerous silks and satins and laces in the armoires of her wardrobe room (211 gowns were listed in the last official inventory), still were gathering dust in that dark and desolate château in 1824 when Eugène died.

Five years later the executors of the Prince's estate, acting for hi minor children, put up the Malmaison properties at public auction. Georgette Ducrest, making a final pilgrimage there in 1829, bemoaned, in the epilogue of her *Mémoires contemporaines,* "the blight that had fallen so swiftly" on her imperial patroness's "favorite haunt": "The gallery, that model of taste and elegance, had been stripped bare; all its renowned canvases were lost to France, and only discolorations on the parquet floors remained to mark where once the superb Canova marbles had stood. . . . The sole ornaments in all those empty, echoing spaces were Her Majesty's tattered velvet armchair and a stuffed black swan, gray with dust, shedding feathers at every air current. . . . Even the park was altered beyond recognition. The rare shrubs and plants had been uprooted and sold; a deep ditch, rank with weeds, was the only landmark of the famous rhododendron hedges; the stagnant, slimy green waters of the pools and streams exhaled a noxious odor."

Malmaison had become the property of a Swedish banker named Hagermann when Hortense in 1831 returned to France incognita, briefly and surreptitiously, with her sole surviving son, Charles-Louis-Napoléon; Napoléon-Louis had died only a few months earlier, during a revolutionary uprising in the Papal States.

At the gates of Malmaison, Josephine's daughter and grandson were turned away. "I could not prevail upon the guard to contravene the proprietor's injunction that no one was to be admitted without a written permit," as Hortense told the story of her visit. Her face pressed against the iron railings, she peered in, but Malmaison was scarcely recognizable. "How could this be Malmaison, the once enchanted garden whose gates had always opened so joyously at my approach—now cruelly barred against me?"

One of Charles-Louis-Napoléon's fondest dreams was to buy back Malmaison and restore it to its original beauty, as he remembered it from his grandmother's day. As Napoleon III, in 1861, he acquired the château from its most recent owner, ex-Queen María Cristina of Spain, who, during her twenty-year residence, had demolished the gallery to make way for a chapel. The Empress Eugénie in 1867 founded there the Museum of Souvenirs of the Consulate and Empire.

The Prussian conquerors of France in 1870 and 1871 were to prove greater vandals than the Cossacks in 1814 and 1815: Malmaison, the scene of bitter fighting during the siege of Paris, sustained further damage during the occupation. After the fall of the Second Empire it became national property, but it was broken up into lots and sold once again in 1877.

In 1904 the banker Daniel Osiris, the last of a long succession of proprietors, bestowed the château and its vestigial twenty-acre park upon the Third Republic, which, with a dawning awareness of Malmaison's historical significance, embarked upon a costly, extensive and meticulous program of restoration. This program, which continues felicitously under the Fifth Republic, has made Malmaison one of the foremost historical attractions of France.

Sources

The Memoirists

Laure Junot, Duchess d'Abrantès

LAURE JUNOT, "Duchesse d'Abracadabrantès" by Théophile Gautier's sobriquet, was one of the most complex and colorful of the memoir writers whose words have been quoted in these pages.

Neither her contemporaries nor more recent historians have been able to reach an agreement as to whether her name is to be included in the long list of Napoleon's paramours. If he heaped honors and rewards upon his military commanders, he outdid himself in the case of General Junot—and Junot's Laure. Her fellow courtiers of Empire days would suspect that Laure was not entirely honest in her account of her tactful rebuff of Napoleon's curious amorous advances at Malmaison in 1802;* certainly in her later career as one of *les grandes amoureuses romantiques* (in which category Reval included her in his book by that title in 1928), she showed herself less "*cruelle*" to other suitors than she would have us believe she had been to the First Consul. Her affair with Metternich in 1809 erupted in a public scandal when her flagrantly unfaithful husband, advised of her infidelity by his mistress Caroline Murat, was roused to violence against his wife. Laure recorded that scene—not in her official, published *Mémoires*, where she was as discreet about her private life as she was indiscreet about that of others, but in her lurid *journal intime* and her *cahier rouge* (red notebook); these, coming to light long after her death, and to publication *in extenso* in 1927 in Chantemesse's *Le Roman inconnu de la duchesse d'Abrantès*, have revealed the story of her romance with royalist Maurice de Balincourt and of the attempt at suicide for which Napoleon threatened to banish her in 1812.

* See p. 273.

411

Widowed, her four children orphaned, at Junot's death in 1813, and the Junot fortune gone up in smoke with the smoking ruins of the Empire in 1815, the Duchess d'Abrantès, dauntless and irrepressible, played a prominent role in Restoration society.

In the 1820s her liaison with a youthful Honoré de Balzac bore notable literary fruit. There can be small wonder that his *Comédie Humaine* was permeated with the Napoleonic legend; he had heard it from the lips of this eyewitness and born storyteller. For his part, Balzac encouraged her to write her memoirs, arranged for their publication in 1831 and helped her perhaps to develop her breezy narrative style and her talent for dialogue and vivid characterization.

But not even the royalties from fifty-odd best-selling volumes, fiction as well as nonfiction, could maintain the Duchess in the style to which she was accustomed, and she died destitute in 1838, at the age of fifty-two, owing her apothecary—among a host of importunate creditors—for the opium cigarettes to which she had become addicted in the final years of misery and illness. The governor of Paris refused a burial plot in Père Lachaise Cemetery for the body of the woman who had been the wife of the governor of Paris only twenty years earlier, but the immortelles were supplied by the literary set of which she had been the darling—by Chateaubriand and Dumas and Hugo, who marched in her funeral procession. Hugo saluted her in the poem that begins:

> *It is for us to provide the laurels for your name*
> . . . .
> *Your noble spirit soared on noble wings,*
> *Sometimes in an eagle's flight,*
> *Always on an angel's course.*

And Balzac, who dedicated his *La Femme abandonnée* to Laure, evoked her in both that romance and his *La Femme de trente ans* —as his "fallen angel lifting her noble brow to face the world."

Claire de Rémusat

It was history's loss, that March day in 1815, when Claire de Rémusat, in a panic at the news of Napoleon's escape from Elba, burned her journal, the secret record of every eventful day of the twelve eventful years she had spent as a lady of the palace to Josephine.

In view of the active roles she and her husband had played, in 1814, in Talleyrand's conspiracy for the restoration of the Bourbons, the Rémusats had cause for anxiety at the Emperor's return to power, and they must have been relieved at the moderation with which his displeasure was expressed: exile from the capital, but not from France. After Waterloo and the return of Louis XVIII to the Tuileries, the King appointed Monsieur de Rémusat as Prefect of the Haute-Garonne department at Toulouse, later as prefect at Lille, and it became obvious to the Rémusats that the rewards of the Bourbons were to be less handsome than those of the Bonapartes. The couple found further cause for disillusionment in the absolutism and reaction of the legitimist regime.

It was in her enforced leisure in the provinces in 1818 that Claire turned again to the writing of her memoirs, this time from memory. Her death in 1821, at the age of forty-two, found her still in the midst of that project. She had completed only the first three of the proposed five parts and had covered only the years 1802-1808, from her debut at court to the outbreak of the Peninsular War. Fortunately, *Les Lettres de Madame de Rémusat*, a collection of the letters she wrote to her husband and to her son between 1804 and 1814, which was published by her grandson, Paul de Rémusat, in 1881, supplemented the unfinished *Mémoires*, published in 1880. Out of consideration for the personages and immediate descendants of those involved in her account of the era, her son, Count Charles de Rémusat, had considered that publication should be delayed beyond their lifetime, and thus the editorial task had been bequeathed to his son.

If Madame de Rémusat's intimate association with Talleyrand was as platonic as she claimed, the instance was unique in that statesman's long life and long history of amours. Talleyrand himself maintained his customary discretion on the subject of his friendship with "Clari" de Rémusat: in his "word portrait" (a popular literary pastime of the period), he touched only lightly on her physical attractions—"her beautiful eyes, lips and teeth" (which compensated for "a perhaps overlong nose"), "the dimples which appeared with her smile to make it as piquant as it was gentle"—and dwelt instead on her intellectual charms: "Her wit was extremely versatile and extremely polishd," and he had known "no better conversationalist," although "it came as a sign of her confidence and friendship when she chose to manifest her erudition. Clari's husband has the intelligence to know that he possesses a treasure, and to revel in it."

Bourrienne

Louis-Antoine Fauvelet de Bourrienne was to claim in his memoirs that it was not peculation but speculation—investment in a firm dealing in military contracts, a practice as common in that regime as in most—which brought down Napoleon's wrath upon his head in 1802.

Napoleon, in a rare instance of procrastination, put off for months the dismissal of his confidential secretary and trusted friend, for Bourrienne, "with his prodigious memory and facility for languages and with his training in law and administration," was, in General Savary's appraisal, "an invaluable man to the First Consul"; furthermore, friendships dating back to his childhood and to his youth held tremendous significance to Napoleon. In 1805, three years after Bourrienne had been replaced as secretary by Méneval, the Emperor even appointed his former schoolmate as minister plenipotentiary to the duchies of Brunswick and Mecklenburg-Schwerin.

The total breach came when Napoleon recalled Bourrienne from Hamburg, but refused to grant him an audience and explain the reasons for the disgrace. He denied Bourrienne his presence ever after, although he offered no objection to his continued friendship with Josephine, over whom, in Laure Junot's opinion, Bourrienne exercised considerable influence. It was the Minister of Foreign Affairs who was delegated by the Emperor to relay to Bourrienne the message that he was expected to make a substantial "contribution to the building fund of the new Ministry of Foreign Affairs" in expiation of his "misappropriation of public funds at Hamburg." "Tell him he can go to the devil!" is the message Bourrienne claims to have sent back to Napoleon.

If he dared not give vent to his resentment at that point, an opportunity presented itself in 1814, after Napoleon's defeat by the Coalition armies: summoned by the victorious monarchs to serve as a member of the Council for the provisional government of France, Bourrienne cast his vote (along with Fouché's and Talleyrand's) for a Bourbon restoration and against both Napoleon's continued sovereignty and a regency for the young King of Rome. Serving Louis XVIII as minister of police, he fled the capital in March of 1815, along with his King, at the approach of the Emperor. Of the thirteen men in France excluded from Napoleon's general amnesty, Bourrienne's name (along with Talleyrand's and Marshal Marmont's) headed the list.

Bourrienne's confinement in an asylum during the latter years of his life cannot be considered to have invalidated the testimony of his memoirs, which had been written in the earlier years when he was apparently of sound mind. He himself points out his special significance as a biographer: "I do not think I have altered two words of those that Bonaparte spoke; so interesting was the subject matter that I made a practice of retaining his every word." Although Bourrienne's memory had occasionally faltered in the passage of a quarter of a century (his errors were so numerous as to have formed the subject of a book, *Bourrienne et ses erreurs, volontaires et involontaires*), he could generally fall back upon the voluminous records he had made, in that famous shorthand of his, of Napoleon's dicta and conversations during the long years of their close association, and he must be counted as one of the most important witnesses of Bonaparte's private and public life during the Italian campaign and the Consulate.

Bourrienne, in the compilation of the five volumes of his memoirs, enjoyed the services of a ghost writer, as did a host of amateur memoirists in the second decade of the nineteenth century—including lady's maid "Mademoiselle Avrillon" and valet Constant—who were eager to gratify the growing public curiosity about the private lives of the Bonapartes.

Georgette Ducrest

Flighty Georgette Ducrest—who attributed her dismissal from the Empress's honor household to malicious and unfounded gossip about her flirtation with the Empress's son—was to prove still another royalist doomed to disillusionment in the restoration of the Bourbons, who failed to restore her family's properties and pensions. Abandoned, with an infant, by a reprobate husband after a brief and injudicious marriage, she discovered that her only assets were her memories of her imperial patroness. Under the title of *Mémoires contemporaines sur l'impératrice Joséphine*, they found their way into print and into instant popularity in 1829, opening the floodgates to a stream of memoirists in the first great resurgence of interest in the Napoleonic epic.

The Letters of Napoleon and Josephine

SINCE the death of Napoleon, more than 250 authenticated letters that he had written to Josephine have been published. The world's first glimpse of the lyrical Honeymoon Letters came in 1824, in a most unexpected place—a two-volume work published in London and prosaically entitled *A Tour Through Parts of the Netherlands, Holland, Germany, Switzerland, Savoy and France, in the Year 1821 . . .* , by Charles Tennant, Esq.; an appendix to the second volume carried lithograph facsimiles of seven of Napoleon's impassioned letters from Italy. These, Mr. Tennant would later tell Prosper Mérimée, had come into his hands from a Polish gentleman, a former secret diplomatic agent of Napoleon's, who had "acquired the documents several days after the Empress's death from a trusted member of her household." If the Polish man of mystery set a high price on the holographs, they were worth it, for their authenticity was to be confirmed by experts.

Eight more of General Bonaparte's letters to his wife from Italy appeared in print in 1827, again entirely out of context—among the adventures of a woman who called herself Ida Saint-Elme, in a volume entitled *Mémoires d'une contemporaine*; these eight were originals or copies of originals purloined by a valet out of a desk drawer in Josephine's death chamber and sold to the Duchess of Courland (prominent in Paris society as a mistress of Talleyrand), who showed them to her friend Madame de Genlis; the latter, in turn, showed them to her editor and publisher, Ladvocat, who was also the publisher of *Mémoires d'une contemporaine* and who included them in that work.

Six years later, in 1833, Queen Hortense published her official collection of her mother's letters, *Lettres de Napoléon à Joséphine*. Significantly, none of the 228 letters from Napoleon in this collection* was written prior to Josephine's belated arrival in Italy. The omission of the group of fifteen letters published previously and unofficially was doubtlessly intended as a denial of their authenticity. Indeed, Hortense, presented with an opportunity to shape the Napoleonic legend, resorted to wholesale expurgation as well as omission. Not only was the heroine to be preserved from appearing, in the eyes of posterity, as a reluctant bride, but the hero was to be preserved from offending the sensibilities of an increasingly prudish nineteenth-century society; his "thousand and one kisses" might be allowed to stand in the text, but the designation of the portions of the anatomy to which the kisses were destined was deleted.

In 1854 Napoleon III, son of Hortense and nephew of Napoleon I, appointed a committee to assemble, annotate and publish his uncle's correspondence. One of the committee's members was Prosper Mérimée, who urged that the honeymoon letters be included, on the ground that their extraordinary quality and the extraordinary passion they expressed would add dimension to the figure of the extraordinary man who had written them. Mérimée was overruled by the other committee members, however, and the fruit of their efforts, the thirty-two volume *Correspondance de Napoléon I*er (Paris, 1858-1870) contains none of the letters written by General Bonaparte to Madame Bonaparte during the years 1796 and 1797; all of the ninety-three letters to Josephine that do appear there were written by Napoleon after he became emperor.

Napoleon III is accused of having destroyed some four hundred of his uncle's letters. Certainly he set the tone for the reverent editorial practice that persisted throughout the rest of the nineteenth century, of correcting the great man's orthographic and grammatical errors and resorting to the stratagem—suggested possibly by the Napoleonic scrawl itself—of substituting the notation "illegible word" for any term deemed indelicate. As a result, editors in the more realistic twentieth century have encountered tremen-

* The collection also included seventy letters from Josephine to Hortense and two of the four surviving letters from Josephine to Napoleon.

dous difficulties in their endeavor to render accurate transcripts of the hitherto abridged and doctored texts. Unfortunately, the opportunity to collate the previously published versions of a letter with the original presents itself to the researcher all too rarely—when, say, a holograph appears at a public auction, or when a private collector into whose hands such a holograph has drifted gives permission for it to be used or examined.

For almost a century, Hortense's bowdlerized *Lettres de Napoléon à Joséphine* remained the fullest available collection of Napoleon's letters to her mother. Not until 1929, when Léon Cerf's edition of the same title appeared, were the unexpurgated and, as far as possible, complete texts of the letters in Hortense's collection published; Cerf's edition includes also the fifteen letters from Italy that Hortense omitted from hers. In 1941 Jacques Bourgeat, with his *Napoléon: Lettres à Joséphine*, brought the total of authenticated letters up to 254 and provided further restoration of the original texts. Jean Savant's *Napoléon et Joséphine*, published in 1960, added eleven letters. The possibility that other letters of Napoleon's to Josephine will come to light from unexpected or unexplored sources diminishes with the passage of years, and the latter-day researcher's main hope lies in the Beauharnais-Bonaparte family archives. Jean Hanoteau, who edited *Mémoires de la reine Hortense* (Paris, 1927) under the sponsorship of Prince Napoleon, great-grandson of Jérôme Bonaparte and present head of the family, was afforded a glimpse of, but not the privilege of copying or reporting, a number of unpublished letters and portions of letters in the Prince's private collection. From the Leuchtenberg archives in Munich, however, Hanoteau was able to bring to publication some seventy-odd letters from Josephine to Eugène, in his *Les Beauharnais et l'empéreur* (Paris, 1936). The letters of Josephine to Hippolyte Charles which were discovered by Louis Hastier are in his *Le Grand Amour de Joséphine* (Paris, 1955).

Chronology

1763	June 23	Birth of Marie-Josèphe-Rose de Tascher de la Pagerie (Josephine).
1769	August 15	Birth of Napoleone Buonaparte.
1779	December 13	Marriage of Josephine and Alexandre de Beauharnais.
1781	September 3	Birth of Eugène de Beauharnais.
1783	April 10	Birth of Hortense de Beauharnais.
1789	July 14	Fall of the Bastille. French Revolution.
1792	June 20	First attack on the Tuileries.
	August 10	Second attack on the Tuileries; massacre of the Swiss Guards.
	September 2–6	September Massacres.
	September 21	Proclamation of French Republic (the First) by National Convention.
1793	January 21	Execution of Louis XVI.
	June 2	Beginning of Reign of Terror.
	October 16	Execution of Marie Antoinette.
1794	July 24	Execution of Alexandre de Beauharnais.
	July 27	(9th Thermidor) Fall of Robespierre; end of Reign of Terror.
1795	October 5	Coup d'état of 13th Vendémiaire; establishment of Directory.
1796	March 9	Marriage of Josephine and General Napoleon B(u)onaparte.
1796–97	March–February	Bonaparte's campaign in Italy.
1798–99		Bonaparte's Egyptian expedition.
1799	November 9	Coup d'état of 18th Brumaire; establishment of Consulate, with Bonaparte as one of three consuls.
	December 13	Bonaparte appointed First Consul.
1802	January 4	Marriage of Hortense de Beauharnais and Louis Bonaparte.

	August 2	Proclamation of Bonaparte as first consul for life.
	October 15	Birth of Napoléon-Charles, son of Hortense and Louis Bonaparte.
1804	March 21	Execution of Duke d'Enghien.
	May 18	Proclamation of Napoleon as emperor of the French.
	October 11	Birth of Napoléon-Louis, second son of Hortense and Louis Bonaparte.
	December 2	Coronation of Napoleon and Josephine as emperor and empress.
1805	May 26	Coronation of Napoleon as king of Italy, at Milan.
	September–December	War of Third Coalition (England, Austria, Russia, Sweden) against France.
	November 13	First French occupation of Vienna.
	December 2	French victory at Austerlitz.
	December 26	Peace at Pressburg.
1806	January 13–14	Marriage of Eugène de Beauharnais and Princess Amalia Augusta of Bavaria.
	July 12	Formation of Confederation of the Rhine.
1806–1807	October–July	War of Fourth Coalition (Prussia and Russia) against France.
1806	October 14	French victories at Jena and Auerstadt.
1807	February 7–8	Battle of Eylau.
	May 5	Death of Hortense's son Napoléon-Charles.
	June 14	French victory at Friedland.
	June 25	Meeting of Napoleon and Czar Alexander I at Tilsit.
	July 7–9	Treaties of Tilsit.
1808	February 2	French occupation of Rome.
1808–14		Peninsular War in Spain and Portugal.
1808	April 20	Birth of Charles-Louis-Napoléon (future Napoleon III), third son of Hortense and Louis.
	September 27	Congress of Erfurt (Napoleon and Alexander I).
1809	April–October	War of France against Austria.
	May 13	Second French occupation of Vienna.

	May 17	Annexation of Papal States by France.
	June 10	Excommunication of Napoleon by Pius VII.
	July 5	Arrest of Pius VII by Napoleon.
	July 5–6	French victory over Austrians at Wagram.
	October 14	Treaty of Schönbrunn.
	December 15	Divorce of Napoleon and Josephine.
1810	April 1–2	Marriage of Napoleon and Marie Louise of Austria.
1811	March 20	Birth of King of Rome.
1812	June	French invasion of Russia.
	September	Battle of Borodino.
	October–December	French retreat from Moscow.
	October 23	Malet conspiracy in Paris.
	November 26–28	Crossing of Berezina River.
	December 18	Arrival of Napoleon in Paris.
1813–14		War of Sixth Coalition against France.
1813	October 16–18	French defeat at Leipzig.
1814	March 30	Capitulation of Paris.
	April 1	Provisional government, headed by Talleyrand.
	April 6	Abdication of Napoleon. Restoration of Bourbon monarchy: Louis XVIII, former Count de Provence.
	April 11–13	Treaty of Fontainebleau; exiling of Napoleon to Elba.
	May 29	Death of Josephine.
1815	February 28	Escape of Napoleon from Elba.
	March 20–June 22	The Hundred Days.
	June 18	Defeat of Napoleon at Waterloo.
	June 22	Second abdication of Napoleon.
	July 8	Return of Louis XVIII.
	August	Exile of Napoleon to St. Helena.
1821	May 5	Death of Napoleon.
1824	February 21	Death of Eugène de Beauharnais.
	September 16	Accession of Charles X, former Count d'Artois, as king of France.
1830	August 2	Abdication of Charles X; accession of Louis Philippe, King of the French.

1831	March 17	Death of Napoléon-Louis, second son of Hortense.
1832	July 22	Death of King of Rome.
1837	October 5	Death of Hortense de Beauharnais.
1848	February 24	Abdication of Louis Philippe; Second Republic declared.
	December 10	Charles-Louis-Napoléon, third son of Hortense, elected president of France.
1851	December	Charles-Louis-Napoléon proclaimed Emperor Napoleon III.
1852–70		Second Empire.
1870		Third Republic declared.

Bibliography

MEMOIRS, JOURNALS AND OTHER CONTEMPORARY ACCOUNTS

Abrantès, Laure Permon Junot, Duchesse d': *Histoire des salons de Paris*. Paris, 1836-38.

———: *Mémoires*. Paris, 1831.

Arnault, A. V.: *Souvenirs d'un sexagénaire*. Paris, 1833.

Avrillon, Mademoiselle: *Mémoires de Mademoiselle Avrillion* [sic], *première femme de chambre de l'impératrice, sur la vie privée de Joséphine, sa famille et sa cour*. Paris, 1833.

Barras, Paul, Vicomte de: *Mémoires de Barras, membre du Directoire*. Paris, 1895-96.

Bausset, L. F. J. de: *Mémoires anecdotiques sur l'intérieur du palais*. Brussels, 1827-29.

Beauharnais, Prince Eugène de: *Mémoires et correspondances politiques et militaires*. Paris, 1858-60.

Bertrand, Henri-Gratien, Général: *Cahiers de Sainte-Hélène*, ed. Paul Fleuriot de Langle. Paris, 1949-59.

Beugnot, Claude, Comte: *Mémoires*. Paris, 1866.

Biographie universelle (also referred to as *Biographie Michaud*), 52 vols., 1811-28; rev. edition, 45 vols., 1853-66.

Bonaparte, Lucien: *Lucien Bonaparte et ses mémoires*, ed. Théodore Iung. Paris, 1882-83.

Bouillé, Louis-Amour de: *Mémoires*. Paris, 1906.

Bourrienne, Louis-Antoine Fauvelet de: *Mémoires*. Paris, 1830.

Campan, Madame: *Journal anecdotique*. Paris, 1824.

Caulaincourt, Louis, Marquis de, Duc de Vicence: *Mémoires*. Paris, 1933.

Champagny, Jean-Baptiste, Comte de: *Souvenirs*. Paris, 1846.

Chastenay, Victorine, Comtesse de: *Mémoires*. Paris, 1896.

Chateaubriand, François-René, Vicomte de: *Mémoires d'outretombe*. Paris, 1848-50.

Cochelet, Louise: *Mémoires sur la reine Hortense et la famille impériale*. Paris, 1836-38.

Constant (Louis-Constant Wairy): *Mémoires de Constant, premier valet de chambre de l'empereur, sur la vie privée de Napoléon*. Paris, 1830.

Denon, Dominique Vivant, Baron: *Voyages dans la Basse et la Haute Égypte pendant les campagnes de Bonaparte en 1798 et 1799*. London, 1807.

Ducrest, Georgette: *Mémoires contemporains sur l'impératrice Joséphine, ses contemporains, la cour de Navarre et de la Malmaison.* Paris, 1829.

Elliot, Grace Dalrymple: *Journal of My Life During the French Revolution.* London, 1859.

Favre, Louis: *Le Luxembourg, 1300-1882. Récits sur un vieux palais.* Paris, 1882.

Fouché, Joseph: *Mémoires.* Paris, 1945.

Georges, Mademoiselle (Marguerite-Joséphine Weimer): *Mémoires inédits de Mlle Georges.* Paris, 1908.

Girardin, L. S. C. X. de: *Discours et opinions, journal et souvenirs de S. Girardin.* Paris, 1828.

Gohier, Louis-Jérôme: *Mémoires de Louis-Jérôme Gohier, président du Directoire au 18 brumaire.* Paris, 1824.

Goldsmith, Lewis: *The Secret History of the Cabinet of Bonaparte.* London, 1810.

Gourgaud, Gaspard, Baron, Général: *Mémoires pour servir à l'histoire de France sous Napoléon, écrits à Sainte-Hélène par les généraux qui ont partagé sa captivité et publiés sur les manuscrits entièrement corrigés de Napoléon,* Tome Ier. Paris, 1823.

————: *Sainte-Hélène, Journal inédit de 1815 à 1818.* Paris, 1899.

Hamelin, A. R.: "Douze Ans de Ma Vie," *Revue de Paris,* Novembre 1926-Janvier, 1927.

Hortense, Queen of Holland: "Lettres à Alexandre Ier," *Revue de Paris,* Septembre-Octobre, 1907.

————: "Lettres de la reine Hortense à Eugène," *Revue des Deux Mondes,* Juillet-Aôut, 1933.

————: *Mémoires de la reine Hortense,* ed. Jean Hanoteau. Paris, 1927.

Larevellière-Lépaux, Louis-Marie: *Mémoires.* Paris, 1873.

Las Cases, Emmanuel, Comte de: *Mémorial de Sainte-Hélène.* Paris, 1823.

Lavallette, A. M. C., Comte de: *Mémoires et souvenirs.* Paris, 1831.

Malouet, Baron: *Mémoires.* Paris, 1874.

Marbot, Antoine, Général: *Mémoires.* Paris, 1892.

Marchand, L. J. N.: *Mémoires de Marchand, premier valet de chambre et exécuteur testamentaire de l'empereur.* Paris, 1955.

Marmont, A. F. L., Maréchal: *Mémoires.* Paris, 1857.

Méneval, Claude-François, Baron de: *Mémoires pour servir a l'histoire de Napoléon Ier.* Paris, 1894.

Mercier, Louis-Sébastien: *Almanach des gens de bien.* Paris, 1798.

————: *Paris pendant la Révolution (1789-1798), ou Le Nouveau Paris.* Paris, 1862.

Metternich, Prince: *Mémoires, documents et écrits divers.* Paris, 1880.

Miot de Mélito, André-François, Comte de: *Mémoires.* Paris, 1873.

Montgaillard, J. G., Comte de: *Souvenirs du comte de Montgaillard, agent de la diplomatie secrète pendant la Révolution, l'Empire, et la Restauration.* Corbeil, 1895.

Bibliography

Montholon, C. J. F. T., Comte de, Général: *Récits de la captivité de l'empereur Napoléon à Sainte-Hélène.* Paris, 1847.

Montigny-Turpin, Charles de, Général: *Grands épisodes inédits et causes secrètes de la politique et des guerres sous le Directoire exécutif, le Consulat et l'Empire.* Paris, 1852.

Mounier, C. P. E. (later, Comte d'Hérisson): *Souvenirs intimes et notes du baron Mounier, secrétaire intime de Napoléon Ier.* Paris, 1896.

O'Meara, Barry: *Napoleon in Exile; or, A Voice from St. Helena.* Philadelphia, 1822.

Oudinot, Eugénie de Coucy, Maréchale: *Récits de guerre et de foyer; le maréchal Oudinot, duc de Reggio, d'après les souvenirs inédits de la maréchale.* Paris, 1894.

Ouvrard, G. J.: *Mémoires.* Paris, 1826.

Pasquier, Étienne-Denis, Duc de: *Histoire de mon temps: Mémoires du chancelier Pasquier.* Paris, 1893-95.

Réal, P. F.: *Indiscrétions, souvenirs anecdotiques et politiques.* Paris, 1835.

Rémusat, Claire de Vergennes, Comtesse de: *Lettres de Mme de Rémusat* (1804-1814). Paris, 1881.

———: *Mémoires* (1802-1808). Paris, 1880.

Roederer, Pierre-Louis, Comte de: *Bonaparte me disait, conversations notées par le comte Roederer.* Paris, 1942.

———: *Mémoires de la Révolution, le Consulat et l'Empire.* Paris, 1942.

Sade, D. A. F., Marquis de: *Zoloé et ses deux acolythes, ou quelques décades de la vie de trois jolies femmes (par un contemporain).* Turin, An VIII.

Ségur, Philippe-Paul, Comte de: *Mémoires.* Paris, 1894-95.

Stendhal: *Mémoires sur Napoléon.* Paris, 1930.

———: *Les Temps héroïques de Napoléon.* Paris, s.d.

———: *Vie de Napoléon.* Paris, 1876.

Talleyrand-Périgord, Charles-Maurice de, Prince de Bénévent: *Mémoires.* Paris, 1891-92.

Thibaudeau, A. C.: *Mémoires, 1799-1815.* Paris, 1913.

Thiébault, D. A. P. F. C. H.: *Mémoires du général baron Thiébault (1792-1820).* Paris, 1962.

Later Works

Arjuzon, Caroline, Comtesse d': *Hortense de Beauharnais.* Paris, 1897.

———: *Joséphine contre Beauharnais.* Paris, 1906.

Arthur-Lévy: *L'Homme du devoir et l'amoureux.* Paris, 1927.

Aubénas, J.: *Histoire de l'impératrice Joséphine.* Paris, 1857.

Aubry, Octave: *Le Roi de Rome.* Paris, 1932.

———: *Le Roman de Napoléon Bonaparte et Joséphine.* Paris, 1927.

————: *Vie privée de Napoléon.* Paris, 1939.

Bernardy, Françoise de: *Charles de Flahaut.* Paris, 1954.

Bord, G.: *L'Hôtel de la rue Chantereine.* Paris, 1930.

Bulos, A.: *Bourrienne et ses erreurs, volontaires et involontaires.* Paris, 1830.

Castelnau, J.: *Madame Tallien.* Paris, 1937.

Castelot, André: *The King of Rome.* New York, 1960.

Chanlaine, Pierre: *Pauline Bonaparte.* Paris, 1959.

Faure, Élie: *Napoléon.* Paris, 1924.

Gastine, L.: *Reine du Directoire, La Belle Tallien.* Paris, s.d.

Gavoty, André: *Les Amoureux de impératrice Joséphine.* Paris, 1961.

Goncourt, Edmond et Jules de: *Histoire de la société française pendant le Directoire.* Paris, 1855.

Guérard, Albert: *Reflections on the Napoleonic Legend.* New York, 1924.

Hanoteau, Jean: *Joséphine avant Napoléon; Le Ménage Beauharnais.* Paris, 1935.

Hastier, Louis: *Le Grand Amour de Joséphine.* Paris, 1955.

Herold, J. C.: *Bonaparte in Egypt.* New York, 1962.

————: *Mistress to an Age: A Life of Madame de Staël.* New York, 1958.

Lacroix, Paul: *Directoire, Consulat et Empire.* Paris, 1884.

Langle, P. Fleuriot, Vicomte de: *Élisa, Soeur de Napoléon.* Paris, 1947.

————: *La Paolina,* Paris, 1944.

Lenotre, G.: *Paris Révolutionnaire.* Paris, 1894.

————: *Vieilles Maisons, vieux papiers.* Paris, 1900.

Lescure, Pierre de: *Le Château de Malmaison.* Paris, 1867.

Ludwig, Emil: *Napoleon.* New York, 1926.

Madelin, Louis: *Le Consulat et l'Empire.* Paris, 1948.

————: *The French Revolution.* New York, 1916.

Masson, Frédéric: "L'impératrice Joséphine et le Prince Eugène," *Revues des Deux Mondes,* Octobre-Novembre, 1916.

————: *Joséphine de Beauharnais.* Paris, 1899.

————: *Joséphine, impératrice et reine.* Paris, 1899.

————: *Joséphine répudiée.* Paris, s.d.

————: *La Journée de l'impératrice Joséphine.* Paris, 1933.

————: *Madame Bonaparte.* Paris, 1898.

————: *Napoléon chez lui.* Paris, s.d.

————: "Napoléon et Eugène de Beauharnais," *Revue de Paris,* Janvier, 1926.

————: *Napoléon et les femmes.* Paris, 1921.

————: *Napoléon et sa famille,* 13 vols. Paris, 1907.

————: *Quatre Conférences sur Joséphine.* Paris, 1924.

Maurois, André: *Les Trois Dumas.* Paris, 1957.

Nabonne, Bernard: *La Reine Hortense.* Paris, 1951.

Ornano, Comte d': *Marie Walewska, l'épouse polonaise de Napoléon.* Paris, 1938.

Pichevin, R.: *L'Impératrice Joséphine.* Paris, 1909.

Saint-Amand, Imbert de: *La Cour*

Bibliography

de l'impératrice Joséphine. Paris, 1889.
———: Les Dernières Années de l'impératrice Joséphine. Paris, 1924.
———: La Jeunesse de l'impératrice Joséphine. Tours, s.d.
Sainte Croix de la Roncière, Georges: Joséphine, impératrice des Français, reine d'Italie. Paris, 1934.
Savant, Jean: Les Amours de Napoléon. Paris, 1956.
———: Napoléon et Joséphine. Paris, 1960.
———: Napoleon in His Time. New York, 1958.
Stirling, Monica: A Pride of Lions:

A Portrait of Napoleon's Mother. London, 1961.
Turquan, Joseph: Le Générale Bonaparte. Paris, 1895-96.
———: La Générale Junot, Duchesse d'Abrantès. Paris, s.d.
———: L'Impératrice Joséphine. Paris, s.d.
———: La Reine Hortense. Paris, 1896.
———: Les Soeurs de Napoléon. Paris, 1954.
Welschinger, Henri: Le Duc de Reichstadt: Notes inédites du chevalier de Prokesch-Osten. Paris, 1907.
Wright, Constance: Daughter to Napoleon. New York, 1961.

Notes

44 Mme. de Vaudey's remark is quoted in the valet Constant's *Mémoires*.

45 The quotations attributed to her lawyers are from the Viscountess de Beauharnais's petition for separation *mensa et toro, submitted to the* Châtelet Court Dec. 11, 1783, by her counselor at law, Louis Joron. These legal papers were discovered in Joron's files by Caroline d'Arjuzon and first printed in her book *Joséphine contre Beauharnais.* Extracts likewise appear in Hanoteau's *Le Ménage Beauharnais,* as do Alexandre's letters. The originals of the letters and of the legal papers are to be found in the Archives Nationales, the Bibliothèque Nationale, and the Fonds Masson in the Bibliothèque Thiers.

48 Excerpts from Monsieur de Tascher's letter in criticism of his son-in-law's deportment are quoted by Jean Hanoteau in *Le Ménage Beauharnais* and by André Gavoty in *Les Amoureux de l'impératrice Joséphine.*

50 Letter from father of one of Josephine's attorneys is quoted by Jean Hanoteau in his *Le Ménage Beauharnais.*

51 The quotation from Alexander de Beauharnais', legal retraction in the settlement *à l'aimable* is likewise from *Le Ménage Beauharnais.*

66 The scandalized companion was Delphine de Custine, as quoted in Joseph Turquan, *La Générale Bonaparte.*

69, 77 The Mercier quotations are from his *Almanach des gens de bien.*

73 The opinions on Barras are quoted in Louis Madelin, *The French Revolution.*

97 The letter quoted here was written June 15, 1796, from Tortona.

98 The comment on Mme. Tallien's beauty was made by the Duchess d'Abrantès in her *Histoire des salons de Paris.*

132 Napoleon's statement, "Wurmser shall pay dearly for your tears," is quoted by Hortense in her *Mémoires.*

148 The chronicler quoted on the subject of Josephine's attitude toward the Bonapartes is General Gourgaud, in *Mémoires pour servir à l'histoire de France sous Napoléon,* Tome I.

PAGE

157 The description of Lyons' reception of Josephine is from Masson, *Madame Bonaparte* (excerpts from the city archives).

172 General Dumas's bedside interview with General and Madame Bonaparte is from André Maurois's *Les Trois Dumas.*

176 Constant's *Mémoires* contain a detailed description of Josephine's accident at Plombières. The medical data is from Martinet, *Journal physico-médical des eaux de Plombières.*

177 Lucien Bonaparte's *Mémoires* make note of Madame de Montesson's remark on the subject of General Bonaparte.

204 The unnamed source cited is the *Biographie universelle.*

209 The Duchess d'Abrantès describes Hippolyte Charles's appearance at court.

216 Napoleon's remark to Talleyrand was related by him to Madame de Rémusat and quoted by her in her *Mémoires.*

219 The Brumaire breakfast scene is described in Gohier's *Mémoires* and in Bourrienne's.

228 The sidelight on Josephine's discriminating choice of décor to enhance her costume comes from the Duchess d'Abrantès' *Histoire des salons de Paris.*

241 Napoleon's story of the statue proposal and his remark to Josephine is included in Las Cases' *Mémorial de Sainte-Hélène.*

243 The quotation on the subject of the Spanish Infanta is from Turquan, *La Générale Bonaparte.*

243 Elisa Bacciocchi is quoted in *Lucien Bonaparte et ses Mémoires.*

248 Hortense, in her *Mémoires,* tells of Louis's threat.

266 Étienne Pasquier, as well as Constant, describes the scene in the morning, after the Duke d'Enghien's execution.

268 Mme. de Rémusat's *Mémoires* include the scene between Louis and his brother.

281 The comment on Josephine's discretion in public is Madame de Rémusat's; Napoleon's injunction of silence is quoted by the Duchess d'Abrantès.

286 The valet Constant joins with Mlle. Avrillon in description of the return journey from Turin to Paris.

288 Frédéric Masson, in *Impératrice et reine,* quotes the legend of Josephine as "a fairy queen, glittering in pearls and diamonds."

295 Masson, in *Impératrice et reine,* tells the stories of Josephine's prognostications.

296 The quotations from Napoleon's bulletin from Prussia are from Emil Ludwig's *Napoleon.*

299 Countess Walewska's account of her romance with Napoleon is in *Marie Walewska, l'épouse polonaise de Napoléon,* by Count

PAGE

d'Ornano, her son by General Count Philippe-Antoine d'Ornano, to whom she was married after Count Walewski's death and Napoleon's exile to St. Helena. Her son (whose birth cost Marie her life at the age of thirty) compiled the book from her copious notes.

312 Ludwig is the source for Queen Louise's description of Napoleon.

313 Duchess d'Abrantès' Mémoires contain the quotation of Pauline's remark to Mme. de Barral.

315 It is Miot de Mélito who quotes Joseph Bonaparte's remark to Napoleon.

323 Napoleon's opinion of the Spanish Queen is quoted by Mlle. Avrillon.

323 Constant describes Charles IV's method of summoning his confessor; Mlle. Avrillon's is the reference to "the secret demon" that drove Josephine.

332 The description of Josephine waiting, "her heart in her throat," is Mlle. Ducrest's.

349 It was Gourgaud and Constant to whom Napoleon confided the story of the premature wedding night. To Gourgaud about the giggling—to Constant "Marry a German girl."

351 The "We will weep together" line is from Ducrest, Mémoires.

363 Josephine's plea for "just twenty-four hours at Malmaison" was made in a let-

ter to Hortense, October 1810.

367 Napoleon's words, "To whom shall I leave all this?" are quoted by Constant.

368 It was to Mlle. Ducrest that Josephine spoke of Napoleon as the "most irresistible, most winning man in all the world."

368 And Mlle. Ducrest again mentions "the informer" whom Josephine suspected the Emperor of having placed in the Navarre company.

373 Mme. de Montesquiou's account of her conversation with Napoleon and of the meeting at the Bagatelle is from André Castelot, King of Rome. The King of Rome's comment on Josephine is from the notes of Anton Prokesch von Osten as quoted in Henri Welschinger's Le Duc de Reichstadt.

375 It was Mlle. Ducrest who saw the Emperor and Empress sitting under the tulip tree.

375 Napoleon's words to Fouché about his dream of a United States of Europe are from Ludwig, Napoleon.

381 The "Grim Reaper" remark is quoted in Jean Savant, Napoléon et Joséphine.

388 Josephine, in a letter to Hortense dated March 28, 1814, from Malmaison, referred to her inadequate guard of disabled war veterans.

389 Chateaubriand, in his Mé-

Index

Rome, King of, *see* King of Rome
Rosetta Stone, 170
Roure-Brison, Captain Scipion du, 54-55
Rousselin, Alexandre, 152
Roustam (former slave), 194, 256
Ruccieri (chef), 380-81
Ruggieri, Maestro, 143, 291

Sade, Donatien, Marquis de, 73, 308
St.-Cloud, Palace of, reopened by Napoleon, 251
St. Sulpice, Cemetery of ("Bal des Zéphyrs"), 69
Savant, Jean, 419
Savary, Gen. René, 344, 414
Schérer, Barthélemy, 107, 163, 165n
Scott, Sir Walter, 139
Ségur, Gen. Philippe-Paul, Count de, on Josephine, 217
Sensible (ship), Josephine's return to France aboard, 54-55
September Massacres, 57
Staël, Germaine de, 159-60, 271, 396
Stendhal (Henri Beyle), 84; on Napoleon, 106, 120-21
Sulkowski, Brigadier, 135, 152

Talleyrand, Charles de, 119, 158, 195, 215, 294, 319, 320, 322, 329, 357, 389, 397, 415, 417; intrigue against Napoleon of, 325, 326, 387, 388; on Josephine, 247, 336; on Napoleon, 120; on Claire de Rémusat, 413-14

Tallien, Jean, 67, 69, 71, 93, 304
Tallien, Thérèse, 67, 69, 93, 107; affair with Ouvard of, 94, 223, 304; friendship with Josephine of, 73, 98, 101, 130, 304, 382-83
Talma, François Joseph, 254
Tascher, Baron de (Josephine's uncle), 38
Tascher, Catherine de, 39
Tascher, Joseph-Gaspard de, 36, 38, 48
Tascher, Marie-Françoise de, 39
Tascher, Marie-Josèphe-Rose de, *see* Josephine, Empress
Tennant, Charles, 417
Théâtre Français, 254
Thibaudeau, Antoine, 215, 250
Thiebaut, Gen. D. A., on Josephine, 72-73
Tortoni, Maestro, 143
Treaty of Campoformio, 151, 155
Treaty of Fontainebleau, 389, 394
Trois-Ilets, Les, Josephine's early life at, 37
Tuileries Palace, Napoleon and Josephine move to, 227-29
Turpin de Crissé, Count, 366

Variétés, Les (publication), 224
Vaudey, Madame de, on Josephine, 44
Vergennes, Claire de, *see* Rémusat, Claire de Vergennes de
Viconti, Signora, 143n
"Victims' Balls," 70
Viel-Castel, Count de, 366